IMAGES OF AGING

It is true to say that aging is about the body, yet in the study of aging we often lose sight of the lived body. Previous works have tended to concentrate on a gruesome cartography of aging infirmities, or on policy developments. The result of this has been to make gerontology and the study of aging data rich and theory poor. It is remarkable that there is almost a complete absence of study of culture and self-image of the middle aged and old. *Images of Aging* changes this. The editors have drawn together a team of international contributors who discuss the images of aging which have come to circulate in the advanced industrial societies of today. They address themes such as: body and self-image in everyday interaction; experience and identity in old age; advertising and consumer culture images of the elderly; images of aging used by governments in health education campaigns; the diversity of historical representations of the elderly; gender images of aging; images of senility and second childhood; images of health, illness and death.

Images of Aging will make refreshing reading for all those concerned with the culture and self-image of the middle-aged and old.

Contributors: Andrew Achenbaum; David Chaney; Norman Denzin; Christian Lalive d'Epinay; Mike Featherstone; Tamara Hareven; Jeff Hearn; Mike Hepworth; Jenny Hockey; Cornelia Hummel; Allison James; Stephen Katz; Jean-Charles Rey; Kimberly Sawchuk; John Tulloch; Bryan Turner; Schuichi Wada; Andrew Wernick and Kathleen Woodward.

Editors: **Mike Featherstone** is Professor of Sociology and Director of the Centre for the Study of Adult Life at the University of Teesside. **Andrew Wernick** is Professor of Cultural Studies and Director of the Graduate Program in Methodologies for the Study of Western History and Culture at Trent University, Canada.

IMAGES OF AGING

Cultural representations of later life

Edited by
Mike Featherstone and
Andrew Wernick

London and New York

First published 1995
by Routledge
11 New Fetter Lane, London EC4P 4EE

Simultaneously published in the USA and Canada
by Routledge
29 West 35th Street, New York, NY 10001

Typeset in Baskerville by
Ponting–Green Publishing Services, Chesham, Bucks
Printed and bound in Great Britain by
T.J. Press (Padstow) Ltd, Padstow, Cornwall

British Library Cataloguing in Publication Data
A catalogue record for this book is available from
the British Library.

Library of Congress Cataloguing in Publication Data
Images of aging: cultural representations of later life /
[edited by] Mike Featherstone and Andrew Wernick
        p.   cm.
Chiefly papers presented at a conference held at
Trent University, Peterborough, Ont., in May 1992.
Includes bibliographical references (p.   ) and index.
1. Aged in popular culture–Congresses.
2. Agism–Congresses.
I. Featherstone, Mike.   II. Wernick, Andrew.
III. Title: Images of aging.
HQ1061.I33   1995
305.26–dc20   94–49031
CIP

ISBN 0–415–11258–3 (hbk)
ISBN 0–415–11259–1 (pbk)

CONTENTS

List of Illustrations   vii
Contributors   viii
Preface   xi

1 INTRODUCTION   1
   Mike Featherstone and *Andrew Wernick*

Part I Historical and comparative perspectives

2 IMAGES OF OLD AGE IN AMERICA, 1790–1970: A VISION
   AND A RE-VISION   19
   Andrew Achenbaum

3 IMAGES OF POSITIVE AGING: A CASE STUDY OF
   RETIREMENT CHOICE MAGAZINE   29
   Mike Featherstone and *Mike Hepworth*

4 THE STATUS AND IMAGE OF THE ELDERLY IN
   JAPAN: UNDERSTANDING THE PATERNALISTIC
   IDEOLOGY   48
   Shuichi Wada

5 IMAGINING THE LIFE-SPAN: FROM PREMODERN
   MIRACLES TO POSTMODERN FANTASIES   61
   Steven Katz

Part II Gender and identity

6 TRIBUTE TO THE OLDER WOMAN: PSYCHOANALYSIS,
   FEMINISM, AND AGEISM   79
   Kathleen Woodward

7 IMAGING THE AGING OF MEN   97
   Jeff Hearn

Part III Relations between the generations

8 CHANGING IMAGES OF AGING AND THE SOCIAL
   CONSTRUCTION OF THE LIFE COURSE   119
   Tamara K. Hareven

9 BACK TO OUR FUTURES: IMAGING SECOND
   CHILDHOOD   135
   Jenny Hockey and *Allison James*

10 CHILDREN'S DRAWINGS OF GRANDPARENTS: A
    QUANTITATIVE ANALYSIS OF IMAGES   149
    *Cornelia Hummel, Jean-Charles Rey, and
    Christian J. Lalive d'Epinay*

Part IV Consumer culture

11 FROM GLOOM TO BOOM: AGE, IDENTITY AND TARGET
    MARKETING   173
    Kimberly Anne Sawchuk

12 *CHAN IS MISSING*: THE DEATH OF THE AGING
    ASIAN EYE   188
    Norman K. Denzin

13 CREATING MEMORIES: SOME IMAGES OF AGING IN
    MASS TOURISM   209
    David Chaney

Part V The body, aging and technology

14 POST-BODIES, AGING AND VIRTUAL REALITY   227
    Mike Featherstone

15 AGING AND IDENTITY: SOME REFLECTIONS ON THE
    SOMATIZATION OF THE SELF   245
    Bryan S. Turner

Part VI Death

16 FROM GRIM REAPER TO CHEERY CONDOM: IMAGES OF
    AGING AND DEATH IN AUSTRALIAN AIDS EDUCATION
    CAMPAIGNS   263
    John Tulloch

17 SELLING FUNERALS, IMAGING DEATH   280
    Andrew Wernick

ILLUSTRATIONS

3.1	First issue of *Retirement Choice*, October, 1972.	35
3.2	*Retirement Choice*, November, 1973.	36
3.3	*Pre Retirement Choice*, December, 1974	39
3.4	*Choice*, October, 1978	41
3.5	*Choice*, March, 1984	42
3.6	*Choice*, April, 1984	43
3.7	*Choice*, July, 1993	45
10.1	Grandmother by Swiss girl, aged 8	161
10.2	Grandfather by Swiss girl, aged 10	161
10.3	Couple by Dutch girl, aged 8	162
10.4	Grandmother by Bulgarian girl, aged 9	163
10.5	Grandfather by Bulgarian boy, aged 11	163
10.6	Grandmother by Czech girl, aged 12	164
10.7	Grandfather by Czech boy, aged 9	164
10.8	Couple by Indian girl, aged 12	164
10.9	Grandmother by Guatemalan boy, aged 11	165
10.10	Grandfather by Guatemalan girl, aged 11	165
10.11	Factor analysis of the grandmothers' activities	167
11.1	Life-cycle stage	174
11.2	Another view of product differentiation and market segmentation	176

CONTRIBUTORS

W. Andrew Achenbaum is Professor of History at the University of Michigan and Deputy Director of its Institute of Gerontology. With Vern Bengtson he edited *The Generational Contract* (Aldine, 1993); he co-edited *Aging and Social Structures: Historical Perspectives* (Springer, 1993) with K. Warner Schale. Achenbaum is just completing a manuscript on the history of gerontology in the US, *Crossing Frontiers* (Cambridge University Press, forthcoming).

David Chaney is Professor in Sociology at the University of Durham. His fields of interest include: the cultural history of popular culture; and theories of culture and collective identity in postmodern societies. Recent publications include (1994) *The Cultural Turn*; and (1993) *Fictions of Collective Life* (both London, Routledge).

Norman K. Denzin is Professor of Sociology, Communications and Humanities at the University of Illinois, Urbana-Champaign. He is the author of numerous books, including *Sociological Methods*; *The Research Act*; *Interpretive Interactionism*; *Images of Postmodern Society*; *The Recovering Alcoholic*; and *The Alcoholic Self*, which won the Cooley Award from the Society for the Study of Symbolic Interaction in 1988. He is the editor of *Studies in Symbolic Interaction: A Research Journal* and *The Sociological Quarterly*.

Christian J. Lalive d'Epinay, Professor of Sociology at the University of Geneva, is Director of the Centre for Interdisciplinary Gerontology (CIG). His research fields are socio-cultural changes and gerontology. His most recent books are *Les Suisses et le travail* (*The Swiss and Work*) and *Vieillir ou la vie à inventer* (*Ageing, or the Life We Have to Shape*).

Mike Featherstone is Professor of Sociology and Director of the Centre for the Study of Adult Life at the University of Teesside. He is editor of *Theory, Culture & Society* and co-editor of *Body & Society*. His publications include *Consumer Culture and Postmodernism, Undoing Culture, Surviving Middle Age* (with M. Hepworth) and edited books on *Global Culture, Cultural Theory and Cultural Change, The Body* (with M. Hepworth and B.S. Turner), *Global Modernities* (with S. Lash and R. Robertson).

Tamara K. Hareven is Unidel Professor of Family Studies and History at the University of Delaware, Adjunct Professor of Population Sciences and Member, Center for Population Studies, Harvard University, and founder and editor of the *Journal of Family History*. She is author of several books and numerous articles on the history of the family and work and the life course, and aging. Her best known books are *Family Time and Industrial Time* (Cambridge University Press, 1982, reprinted by University Press of America, 1993); *Amoskeag: Life and Work in an American Factory City* (Pantheon, 1978); *Transitions: The Family and the Life Course in Historical Perspective* (Academic Press, 1978, edit.); and *Aging and the Life Course in Interdisciplinary and Cross-Cultural Perspective* (Guilford Press, 1982, co-edit. with Kathleen Adams). She has completed a comparative study in Japan to be published in her book *The Silk Weavers of Kyoto: Family and Work in a Changing Traditional Industry* and is currently writing a book entitled *Generations in Historical Time* which is based on a cohort comparison of life transitions and generational relations in the later years of life, discussed in her article in this volume.

Jeff Hearn is Reader in Sociology and Critical Studies on Men at the University of Bradford. His publications include '*Sex*' at '*Work*' (co-author); *The Gender of Oppression* (both Wheatsheaf/St Martin's); *Men, Masculinities and Social Theory* (co-edited) (Unwin Hyman); *Men in the Public Eye* (Routledge). He is currently working on an authored book, *The Violences of Men* and a co-edited book *The Men of Management* (both Sage).

Mike Hepworth is Reader in Sociology at the University of Aberdeen. He is a member of Age Concern Scotland, the British Society of Gerontology, and a founder member of the Centre for the Study of Adult Life at the University of Teesside. His publications on the images of aging include 'Images of ageing' (with Mike Featherstone), second revised edition, 1993, in J. Bond, P. Coleman, and S. Peace (eds), *Ageing in Society* (London: Sage).

Jenny Hockey is a social anthropologist who lectures in health studies at the University of Hull. She has published *Experiences of Death: an anthropological account* (Edinburgh University Press, 1990) and, jointly with Allison James, *Growing Up and Growing Old: Ageing and Dependency in the Life Course* (Sage, 1993).

Cornelia Hummel graduated in sociology. She is an assistant in the Department of Sociology and researcher at the Centre for Inter-disciplinary Gerontology (CIG) at the University of Geneva. Her licence dissertation, 'Children's Drawings – Images of grandparents', won the Pro Senectute Switzerland Award.

Allison James is a social anthropologist who lectures in Applied Anthro-pology at the University of Hull. She has published *Childhood Identities: Self and Social Relationships in the Experience of the Child,* (Edinburgh University Press, 1993) and, jointly with Jenny Hockey, *Growing Up and Growing Old: Ageing and Dependency in the Life Course* (Sage, 1993). She has also co-edited, jointly with Alan Prout, *Constructing and Recon-structing Childhood* (Falmer Press, 1990).

Stephen Katz is Associate Professor of Sociology at Trent University, Peterborough, Canada. Research interests are in critical gerontology, history of the human sciences and sociology of the body. He has published articles in *Journal of Aging Studies, Political Studies,* and *Women's Studies International Forum,* and is currently writing a book on gerontological knowledge.

Jean-Charles Rey graduated in sociology and management. He is a researcher at the Centre for Interdisciplinary Gerontology (CIG) at the University of Geneva. He is co-author of the *Encyclopédie genevoise 1993.* His licence dissertation, 'The image of Valais in the press' won the Academic Society of Valais Award.

Kimberly Anne Sawchuk is Assistant Professor in Communication Studies, Concordia University. Her recent publications include, 'Sem-iotics, cybernetics and the ecstasy of marketing communications', '(Re)packaging difference: globalization and culture' and 'Le market-ing du corps: les couches jetable'. She is presently completing a co-edited anthology on North American conceptions of pain and pills entitled *When Pain Strikes.*

John Tulloch is Professor of Cultural Studies at Charles Sturt University, NSW, Australia. He is the author of ten books, including, recently, *Televison Drama: Agency, Audience and Myth* (London, Routledge, 1990), *Science Fiction Audiences* (London, Routledge) and *Televison, Sexuality and AIDS* (Sydney, Allen & Unwin, forthcoming).

Bryan S. Turner is Professor of Sociology and Dean of Arts, Deakin University, Geelong, Victoria, Australia. He is the founder of the Centre for the Study of the Body and Society at Deakin University. His principal

|publications in the sociology of the body have been *The Body and Society* (1984), *Medical Power and Social Knowledge* (1987) and *Regulating Bodies* (1992).

Shuichi Wada is Professor of Sociology in the Department of Sociology, Waseda University, Tokyo, Japan. His publications include *People's Adjustment to Life Changes in the Retirement Process* (edited with Kazuo Aoi in Japanese) and *Daily Life in Later Life* (edited by Karen Altergott).

Andrew Wernick is Professor of Cultural Studies and Director of the Graduate Program in Methodologies for the Study of Western History and Culture at Trent University, Canada. He is the author of *Promotional Culture* (Sage) and co-editor (with Philippa Berry) of *Shadow of Spirit: Religion and Postmodernism* (Routledge).

Kathleen Woodward is Professor of English at the University of Wisconsin-Milwaukee where she directs the Center for Twentieth Century Studies, a postdoctoral research institute in the critical humanities. The author of *Aging and Its Discontents: Freud and Other Fictions* (1990) and co-editor (with Murray Schwartz) of *Memory and Desire: Aging – literature – psychoanalysis* (1986). She is currently at work on a book on representation of older women.

PREFACE

A number of the papers in this volume were presented at the first Images of Aging conference held at Trent University, Peterborough in May 1992. The idea of a conference was an outgrowth of a long-standing project on images of aging carried out by the Centre for the Study of Adult Life at the University of Teesside and the work on images of popular culture carried out by the Trent Institute for the Study of Popular Culture. The conference, which was supported by the Canadian Social Sciences and Humanities Research Council, brought together humanities and social science research on images of aging. We would like to thank Eldean Wills at Trent and Barbara Cox at Teesside for their help with the organization.

A subsequent development has been the formation of a network on Images of Aging with a second conference, supported by the University of Geneva and the Swiss Gerontological Society, held at Sierre, Switzerland in June 1993. Further conferences are planned.

We would particularly like to acknowledge the help and support of Mike Hepworth who has worked jointly with Mike Featherstone on images of aging for over twenty years now and has helped to develop an Archive of Images of Ageing at the Centre for the Study of Adult Life. The subsequent emphasis upon images of aging at the two international conferences on The Future of Adult Life sponsored by CSAL, as well as the plea for a turn towards a more culturally and theoretically informed gerontology, and the subsequent network, has been an outcome of this work. We also acknowledge with gratitude the support of the various people we have discussed the images project with over the years including Ana Zahira Bassit, Guita Grin Debert, Norman Denzin, Christian Lalive d'Epinay, Katsu Harada, Tamara Hareven, Christopher King, Stephen Kline, Victor Marshall, Mica Nava, Gisela Taschner, Bryan S. Turner, Shuichi Wada and Kathleen Woodward.

1

INTRODUCTION

Mike Featherstone and *Andrew Wernick*

IMAGING THE AGING BODY

Human beings are embodied persons with a finite life-span. We are born, we live, we die. As Heidegger graphically remarked 'we are born dying'. Along the way in our journey through life, we usually become accredited persons who are accorded adult status. In later life there is the threat of the loss of this status through the bodily decline we usually, often confusingly, refer to as aging.

It is a truism to say that aging is about the body, yet in the study of aging we often lose sight of the lived body. In the recent upsurge of interest in the body in the social sciences and the humanities there has been a critique of the academic division of labour, the legacy of Cartesian dualism, which ceded the material body to the natural sciences, with the social sciences and humanities for the most part left to argue for the autonomy of the mind, culture and the social (Featherstone *et al.*, 1991; Featherstone and Turner, 1995; Turner, 1985; Turner in this volume). The study of aging human beings, as a consequence of this division of labour, has often been split into a number of areas. There are those whose concern has been to carry out gerontological research into the effects of the aging process on the body, largely focusing upon the symptoms of bodily decline in later life. This has become a powerful trend which has been referred to as 'the bio-medicalization of geronto-logy', (Estes and Binney, 1991; Moody, 1993). Sociology and social policy have in parallel manner often reduced the aging body to a set of indicators: the 'social bookkeeping' tradition has amassed a great deal of data about aspects of bodies (diet, height, weight, health, sickness, etc.) and living conditions. Both state agencies and their critics have demanded such empirical data in order to assess, and argue about, the distribution of resources to the frail, the sick and the infirm.

The result of this biomedical and policy impetus has often been to make gerontology and the sociology of aging 'data rich and theory poor', as Andrew Achenbaum reminds us in his chapter. Yet the blame cannot be completely laid at the door of gerontology for social and cultural theory has likewise often ignored aging (Kohli, 1988). Given the universality of the aging process and death, this is remarkable. Perhaps as Norbert Elias (1985) argues it has something to do with the fact that we resist the thought of bodily decline, deep old age and our eventual death, a theme which Bryan Turner discusses in his chapter in this volume. In addition, when one considers the aging of human beings in terms of the relationship between individual lifetime and the collective lifetime which makes up the unbroken chain of human generations which we call history, then we can see how this process could pose important and demanding theoretical problems for sociology and the social sciences. Yet such has been the power of the over-social image of social life and the abstraction we have learned to take for granted which we call 'society', that few have been willing to confront the problems of embodiment and its relation to social life and culture.

It is only from the limited amount of ethnographically sensitive research that we get glimpses of the actual practices and experiences of being old and the ways in which the aging body works, and doesn't work (see Hazan, 1980; Hockey, 1990; Stephens, 1976; Hockey and James, in this volume). Here we see the struggles with bodily betrayals, stigmatization and various modes of disempowerment. This focus on embodied persons relating to each other through the visible body, the body which sees and can be seen, gives us a much richer sense of the dark side of the aging process, and the notion that for some the outer body and face can become a rigid alien structure of imprisonment which can mask forever the possibilities of expressing the self within (Featherstone and Hepworth, 1991; forthcoming). It is this sense of the meaning of aging and old age that Simone de Beauvoir has characterized as 'an unrealizable'. It also has a dehumanizing aspect which can even lead us to consider the elderly to be a separate species (Gadow, 1986).

Given this problem of translating experience across the generations to human beings who are generally preoccupied with the view of the world from their particular juncture in the life course, we often have to resort to literary and artistic forms, to novels, poetry, films and other modes to get a sense of the meaning of old age. Here we think of the grim depictions of the aging body, the preoccupation with memory, the past and impending death, in Thomas Mann's *Death in Venice* or Patrick White's *The Eye of the Storm* (see discussion in Woodward, 1988–89; Berg, 1983). It is from the humanities, then, that we find attempts to grapple with the meaning of the aging process (Cole *et al.*, 1992; Cole *et al.*, 1993: Spicker *et al.*, 1978; Woodward, 1988–9, 1991). Such research points to the way in which the aging body is never just a body subjected to the imperatives of cellular and organic decline, for as it moves through life it is continuously being inscribed and reinscribed with cultural meanings.

To highlight the importance of the body for the study of aging, then, is not to raise the spectre of biologism, the reduction of culture to the biological, nor is it to vaunt a social constructionism in which the body is conceived as a blank slate on which culture can write at will. There are strong culturalist accounts of the religious compensations the elderly can enjoy, which emphasize the way people went happily to death confident in the certainties of a cosmology which made this ultimate life transition seem a mere step towards a better life (see Ariès, 1978). Yet it is hard to take such accounts of the happy death at the end of a fulfilled life as the complete story, given the existence of other accounts which focus more on the body politics of everyday life, on the power deficit and threat of violence experienced by those whose bodies weaken and do not work well (Stearns, 1978; Elias, 1985). The capacity to re-code the body itself is part of a historical process in which the religious capacity to give significance to aging, old age and death, is itself subject to change, not merely through shifts in modes of cultural classification, but also through the way a particular form of knowledge through biomedical and information technology has increasingly developed the capacity to alter not just the meaning, but the very material infrastructure of the body. Bodies can be reshaped, remade, fused with machines, empowered through technological devices and extensions. The current significance of the aging body has to be understood at a point in history at which there are strong claims that the capacity to crack the code of the human aging process is about to be achieved.

It is here we encounter the problem of the relationship between culture and the body. Because the body has material presence, its very tangibility and visibility as it moves through the everyday world of practical actions seem to suggest that we know what we see. Likewise with images of the body. They seem to possess a high degree of realism and indexicality: as if the body is something which has slipped under the guard of discourse and the process of representation to the extent that bodies are things which are self-evidently what they seem to be (Falk, 1993). There is then, the tendency to see the body as something which can easily be copied or represented – as in the case of a photograph which is often seen as an accurate record of the way a person looked at a particular moment in time. This aspect, the notion of copying and producing an accurate likeness of the original, is one of the meanings of the term image which can be traced back to the original Latin meaning of the term *imago* (Williams, 1976).

The term image has, however, a second aspect, referring to imagina-

emphasis is more on distortion and refashioning, on refraction as opposed to reflection. Anyone who has looked at a photograph of themselves has doubtless discovered this second aspect to making an image. For it is rare that we feel that the photographer has produced an adequate rendition of our selves – the assumption being that a good photographer is one who artfully arranges and waits for what they take to be a particular apt expression of ourselves, manifest in our face, appearance and posture, which lets the self somehow shine through. This second sense steers us away from the notion of documentary evidence, to one of the original sense of photography: painting with light. It suggests that the making of an image is an interpretative act in which the subject's body is clothed and adorned in particular ways and framed in a setting of other material objects, all of which carry a particular symbolic weight, emotional tone and resonance.

The image is, then, the result of an act of perception and construction which frames a world. Yet the artful construction of an image should not be taken to imply that its meaning is a self-evident product of its construction. The meaning of the image gains its resonance in the practices and ways in which it is viewed, in the discourses and ceremonial rituals which surround its use. As a photograph relates to a specific point in the lifetime of a person and their relations to other persons at that time, it carries a hidden significance and emotional charge which are themselves unstable, altering with the changing vicissitudes of their subsequent lives. It is the openness to the sense of loss of the substance of one's own body and face with all it might have been able to represent: the sense of discrepancy between one's self-image and the image we take others to see, and their subsequent dialectical interplay, which envelops photographs with poignancy and the potential for nostalgia, once we reach 'a certain age'.

AGEISM AND OTHER 'ISMS'

Living as we do in societies saturated with images of the human body we find that both aspects of images we have referred to have been subjected to analysis within the humanities and the social sciences in general and cultural studies and sociology in particular. Since the 1960s a number of critiques have been developed about the misrepresentations inherent in the images which portray minority groups. Critiques have been increasingly made of what are seen as demeaning images of women, gays, the elderly, ethnic groups and regional minorities. Here the assumption is that such groups suffer from the imposition of negative stereotypes: images which do not accurately represent their everyday realities and aspirations.

Such stereotypes are constructed from a complex blend of discourse and sensory images (largely visual). Here we can broaden our understanding of image to refer, not only to the body, but to a simplistic and emotionally-charged model which highlights one façade only of a group's activities and potentialities. Such images often are based on depictions of the outsider groups by established groups, which do not just work on articulated discourses, but are grounded on culturally-sedimented information about the body and senses. Hence the rationalizations for discrimination are often based on the assumption that minority groups have inherent bodily characteristics which make them different. They are not only less competent, but recognizably so: they look different, they speak differently, they even smell differently. The latter aspect has a particularly powerful emotional force, especially when the smells are associated with dirtiness and lack of control over the body, which connotes childhood dependence and even animality. Some negative stereotypes of the elderly and black people share this characteristic where the majority, or established group, emphasizes its authority as 'civilized' fully competent adults who are superior over those whose dependence is allegedly manifest through an inability to adequately control bodily functions held to be disgusting. Hence we have had racist stereotypes of 'the dirty nigger', and ageist stereotypes of 'the smelly old man'. Such notions must be understood in terms of a historically-formed 'disgust function', through the development of a heightened sensitivity about bodily demeanour and functions as part of civilizing processes, as well as through the dynamics of the power struggles between the established and outsiders (Elias, 1978, 1985, 1994)

In his discussion of the often over-simplistic and romantic images of old age in America which predominated in the past, Andrew Achenbaum makes some germane points in this context. He argues that many of the photographs of old Americans which he used in his book *Images of Old Age in America* (Achenbaum and Kusnerz, 1978) were of white people, despite his intention to get away from over-simple stereotypes. In reviewing this project in his contribution to this volume, he argues that a much more variegated set of images of later life is needed which accentuates class, gender, regional and ethnic differences. In the context of our discussion of ethnicity, one image he now feels he would like to have included and commented on, is a striking image of old black slaves in the US in the 1860s, who are photographed naked and in chains like animals.

The critique of this capacity to over-simplify, to construct an image where a part is represented as a whole, is central to the attempts to deconstruct and discredit negative stereotypes. Hence feminists have not only criticized sexist speech, but also sought to combat the display of women in narrowly-defined sexual ways: women as the 'bimbo' and pin-up, or the vulnerable and passive 'coy and winsome'. There are attempts to remove such images from public view and challenge their implications (see Root, 1984). In a similar manner we have critiques of racist stereotypes which not only focus on language, but also carefully document the ways in which racist visual representations have been a taken-for-granted element in the iconography of everyday life in advertisements, toys and food labels (Nederveen Pieterse, 1992). The assumption behind such critiques is that our identities are shaped by the recognition other people grant or do not grant us. In the case of sexism and racism it is the misrecognition of others which induces women and ethnic minorities to adopt a negative image of themselves based upon the internalization of images of their own inferiority (cf. Fanon's 1986 discussion in *Black Skins, White Masks*).

Those who militate against this process seek to discredit the demeaning public images and replace them with a more nuanced view of the category in question which admits to a range of differences. Their efforts can also be regarded as the latest phase in a long-term shift away from hierarchical social relationships in which people demand respect and treatment in terms of their specific identity and potential (Taylor and Gutman, 1992). This view draws upon two strands. First, the Enlightenment view that all human beings are equally worthy of respect and should enjoy universal access to citizenship rights. Second, the politics of difference which has developed since the 1960s with its emphasis upon the particularistic claims of minority groups, whose different cultural values should be fostered and preserved with the public educated to accept reverse discrimination.

In the case of aging, there have been a number of movements in the west (the most noted being the Gray Panthers, American Association of Retired Persons, Age Concern, Help the Aged) largely since the 1960s which have sought to combat age discrimination in labour markets, the reversal of the mandatory retirement age, as well as ageist language and negative stereotypes of the aged in general. The images of positive aging they seek to advance amount to a deconstruction of the image of old age as a necessary phase of bodily decline.

We will discuss the new images of positive aging shortly, but first it is important to note that such images are not new: as Stephen Katz outlines in his contribution there is a long history of concern with longevity and improving the quality of life in old age through diet and discipline. In the nineteenth century doubts about the claims of the marvellous and miraculous cures of the past were accompanied by a shift to a concern with clinical and biological evidence and the finite laws of development of cells and tissue. Tamara Hareven also notes this shift, remarking that popular images from the 1860s onwards change from the concern with attaining longevity to a discussion of the medical symptoms of senescence. In the late nineteenth century in the United States aging began to be seen as a period of decline, weakness and obsolescence. Investigations of the relationship between aging and efficiency drew negative comparisons between the young and the old: something which became incorporated into the early twentieth century scientific management movement which transformed the workplace.

Capitalist industrialization, with its continually revamped technologies of production also led to the transformation of domestic production and consumption. It idealized youth (including the eroticized youthful female body as the universal consumer image of desirability) while fundamentally weakening the value of accumulated life experience, both in itself and as a marker of social status. In his study of inter-war American advertising Stuart Ewen (1976) has shown how the cult of youth, tied to a wider valorization of the new, was integral to the orchestrated modernization of spending habits and attitudes which industrialists deemed was economically and politically necessary in the age of mass production. The work society with its loss of function and income which came with mandatory retirement became bolstered by a consumer culture with its images of youth, fitness and beauty lifestyles which produced a new set of exclusions for older people.

One powerful image of old age which causes concern is the notion that the elderly go into a second childhood. As Jenny Hockey and Allison James argue in their chapter, this long-standing image in our culture is still with us, bolstered by a range of representations such as the elderly wearing Donald Duck hats for tea-parties in old people's homes. This too has an embodied aspect, for the frail elderly, especially those in 'deep old age', the over-80-year-olds, are often dwarfed by the bodily presence of a young nurse or attendant. Ageism can therefore operate through the dominance of images of dependency which take away the adult status and personhood of the elderly. As Hockey and James remark, 'By linking old age with childhood the hegemony of adulthood remains unbroken'. The bodily betrayals of old age can therefore result in a stigmatizing process which has been referred to as the 'mask of ageing', pointing to the inability of the body to adequately represent the inner self (Featherstone and Hepworth, 1991, 1994, forthcoming; Goffman, 1968).

Nevertheless, the notion of a second childhood need not necessarily be a totally negative process. In Japan, for example, once past 60 one is assumed to have completed the first cycle of life and entered another in which childish and mischievous behaviour is not only expected but looked on with affection. We should also be cautious about attributing the same negative meaning to wrinkles and frailty across cultures, for in Japan the elderly can be seen as 'cute', and the source of affection from young people, as in the case of the centenarian twins Kin and Gin

7

who became media celebrities. Hence the wrinkles, greying hair, and slurring speech may under certain circumstances be ignored, and even perceived positively as signs that the elderly have attained a state of grace and are nearer to God and the next world. In his contribution, Shuichi Wada discusses these approaches through an examination of the positive images of the second childhood and the development of the dominant filial pietism and paternalism, which condition the treatment of the elderly in Japan.

So far we have considered the stigmatization of the elderly in terms of the similarities to other minority groups. But we must be careful about pushing the parallel between ageism and other 'isms' too far. While gender and race continue to be constituted as relatively unambiguous social categories which entail discrimination and power deficits for the outsider group, this division is by no means as clear cut with reference to the elderly and its relations to the young and middle-aged. Unlike the other social oppositions, youth and old age, and indeed all positions in the life course, are transitional statuses within a universal process. Unlike the other oppositions, provided we live long enough we will experience a movement into the opposite status. Without effort we will move from youth to old age and what was from the point of view of youth the distant 'unrealizability' of old age, becomes a haunting possibility for people in mid life once they have reached 'a certain age'. Of course there is the growing popularity of gender bending and cross-dressing, of wanting to experience the forms of embodiment of the opposite sex, yet this is largely a matter of choice and effort: with aging all we need to do is stick around, time will do the rest.

It is when we start to compound the 'isms' that we get interesting effects. For women ageism and sexism work in combination to provide, in Susan Sontag's (1978) words, 'a double standard of ageing', where women are required to match up to the adolescent ideal throughout their lives. Sontag also remarks on the centrality of bodily presentation for being a woman. It is therefore not surprising that many of our representations of women are constructed in terms of physical appearance and that images and self-images of the bodies of older women cause such problems.

When we move down from the high level of generality evident in the simple dichotomy 'women and men', and consider some of the nuances, we encounter some interesting complications. Jeff Hearn, for example, in his chapter argues that the category men necessarily points to age, as it implies a fundamental distinction within the male gender between men and boys. The category of men also collapses into a number of significant differences when we consider that middle-aged men often hold the reins of organizational power; yet for men youth signifies physical strength and sexual virility. To be an old man points to a loss of both these forms of empowerment and one image that remains is the old man as 'other', the return to the disruptive role of being one of the boys again, as captured in the BBC television series *The Last of the Summer Wine*. Hearn's chapter is also interesting in terms of his discussion of the diversification of the category 'older man'; we need to be aware of the challenge to heterosexual stereotypes which is provided by gay men's accounts of their experience of aging.

Kathleen Woodward also introduces complexities into some of the simple binary images of gender and aging. She points out that Freud had great difficulties incorporating the aging woman into his theory: the older woman past the age of reproduction was also deemed to be past sexuality and gender and could not therefore easily be fitted into the discourse. In addition, Woodward also makes some very interesting observations about generational conflict and the treatment of older women by members of the Women's Movement.

CONSUMER CULTURE

This tension between the pull towards over-simplifying stereotypes of youth and old age and the opposite pull towards the discovery of increasing complexity and differentiation is also found within the emergent consumer culture discourse and images of old age. It is evident that the extension and development of consumer culture in the twentieth century has depended upon the creation of new markets not least through the production of images and advice on lifestyles and practices (Ewen, 1976; Featherstone, 1991, 1995; Featherstone and Hepworth, 1982; Wernick, 1991).

Kimberley Sawchuk's contribution provides an analysis of the marketers' discourse on the potential of the rising 'age wave'. Seniors who were previously depicted as 'sexless, senile, crotchety, frail and unhappy', are now seen as a major new market segment. Given that the over-50 age segment already holds over 50 per cent of discretionary income in the United States, and that by 2006 they will make up 33 per cent of the population of Canada, it is no surprise that promoters of the newly-discovered golden age should come up with enthusiastic headlines such as 'Dipping into Granny's Wallet'. This new market is in part based upon the emergence of private pension and savings schemes which, within the middle classes in particular, has made an active consumer retirement lifestyle possible. In Britain the Pre-Retirement Association which was created in the early 1970s, produced a new magazine *Pre Retirement Choice* to develop this market. In their chapter Featherstone and Hepworth analyse the history of the magazine and the way in which it became turned into a typical glossy consumer culture magazine with advice on fashion, insurance, housing, fitness, cookery, holidays, along with lifestyle features on celebrities and stars. Through-out the magazine youthfulness and a positive attitude towards aging are extolled: qualities which it is assumed can be achieved through careful consumption and lifestyle planning.

David Chaney in his contribution provides a nuanced discussion of the new market for holidays for the elderly in Britain. Holiday bro-chures are concerned to show images which affirm identity through an invented tradition which emphasizes communalism and collective rituals. The brochures targeted at the lower end of the new elderly market present the holiday-makers themselves as participating in a dramatized performance and enacting populist forms of ceremonial-ization which could be called 'capitalist realism'.

Hence when gerontologists argue for the need for positive images of aging to combat the old models of decline and disengagement, perhaps they should look around themselves in the everyday life of consumer culture where, for the middle classes at least, positive aging is alive and well. Of course positive aging does not provide the solutions to the problems of deep old age and death: its message is essentially one of denial, keep smiling and carry on consuming. Yet as we shall see shortly, in the discussion of Andrew Wernick's paper, we should not presume a uniform response, rather the generation now approaching their fifties shows signs of developing a wide range of differentiated responses, including self-help consumer movements, to retirement, deep old age and death.

IMAGES, BODIES AND DEATH IN THE POSTMODERN LIFE COURSE

Within consumer culture one tendency often remarked upon is the fragmentation and differentiation of markets. In its most extreme formulation this is seen as entailing the end of the social and the consumption of an endless series of signs and images which do not cohere and cannot be used to formulate a structured lifestyle and set of tastes. While there may have been a tendency towards increasing disorder in the life course as fewer people hit the designated status passages and life transitions (work, marriage, grandparenthood, retire-ment, etc.) on schedule (see Featherstone and Hepworth, 1991 and Katz's paper in this volume), it would seem premature to announce the death of the social. At the same time for certain groups there do appear to be shifts away from the type of embodied collective memories which Bryan Turner speaks of in his chapter. The body may be a walking memory, but this does mean that significant others are required who can read the code written on to the body and affirm the other. If some cultural practices and rituals become more particularized and frag-

10

mented, then we may well be driven along the road towards postmodern de-conceptualization and the acceptance of pluralism in the sense that we become required to speak about bodies not the body, histories and not history, women and not woman. Of course the use of such terminology may well be a form of ritualized obeisance, an enactment of the respect we feel required to show to minority groups and cultures (something we discussed earlier in the introduction), which may not help us get a better theoretical purchase on the social world. Yet Norman Denzin in his chapter entitled 'Chan is Missing', may well persuade us otherwise and that we need to take postmodernism more seriously.

Charlie Chan, the central character in a series of Hollywood detective films for a number of years, represented the stereotype of the wise aging Asian patriarch. As Denzin argues, Chan 'enacts the cultural belief that wise Asian men are able to find the truth that escapes the investigative gaze of impulsive, childish Westerners'. Yet the film *Chan is Missing* moves in a completely different direction. Although it is full of Asian bodies it provides the message that there is no single American-Asian identity. Even Chan is many-sided and acts differently to different people. Clues lead everywhere and there is no final resolution, only uncertainty. Chan is not only missing, the legacy of Charlie Chan is dead as there is no space for his myth in contemporary American culture. For Denzin the shift in *Chan is Missing* to a polymorphous multi-vocal text points to the end of over-simple stereotypes of aging along with the postmodern shifts in an American culture which is discovering its ethnic and minority cultural complexity.

We have argued for the centrality of the body in the construction of images of aging and the sustenance of collective memory. In effect images of aging represent bodies which become increasingly fixed and inflexible as they move towards the end of the life course in terms of the range of cultural messages they are allowed to depict. Consumer culture does of course offer a wide range of images of positive aging reparative measures and strategies, ranging from fitness routines to cosmetic surgery in order to reinscribe the body in a more youthful manner. Yet, as we have argued, for those who are in deep old age, who are weak, frail or disabled, the body is not only a masking device which conceals and distorts the self which others interact with, in addition the lack of mobility and functioning capacity may make the body seem to be a prison. One potential avenue of escape is the new modes of disembodiment and re-embodiment which are becoming possible through developments in information technology. In virtual reality it is possible for disabled people to enter a simulated environment where through a full range of sensory input and output devices they can not only see and hear, but feel and touch simulated objects and beings. The simulation of their body that can move, fly, interact with other bodies need not be a replica of their actual body, but could be a version of the person when they were younger, or it could be that of another person or gender – hence the term 'computer cross-dressing'. Such virtual environments clearly have great potential for the elderly and disabled both as operative systems for their everyday work and home environment and as a play area offering mobility and a wide range of sensory experiences. Here the image culture is not merely the source of inflexible and demeaning stereotypes, but through the capacity 'to go into the image' it potentially offers new forms of creativity, freedom and mobility – something which is more in line with the second meaning of image identified by Raymond Williams which we discussed earlier.

One of the possibilities now on the horizon through technological developments is the medical capacity to crack the aging code. While not guaranteeing immortality, this would make it possible to slow down or even reverse an individual's biological clock. It hardly needs saying that the ability (for example) to reverse human cellular decline which, it is held, will be available for the next generation, would not be universally available for all. William Gibson's novels, especially *Neuromancer* (1985), give a glimpse of the dystopian possibilities. However, for those here and now death continues to be an ineluctable reality of the life course.

In modern industrial society, as Ariès and others have shown, death is feared all the more because it makes life seem meaningless. Contemporary culture continues to deal with this by various modes of denial, including through consumer goods which, cosmetically or through fashion, clothe the aging body in images of perpetual youth. In the popular media dying (as opposed to killing) is generally avoided, together with the shadow it casts over the happy selling medium advertisers seek. The cultural effects of death denial are also, perhaps especially, apparent in the rituals and symbols that in the twentieth century have come to surround death itself. To be sure, the falsely sugared 'American way of death' described by Jessica Mitford (1963) is giving way, through industry-wide mergers and trends to cremation and self-arrangement, to a less sentimentalized system, adapted to a greater range of funerary needs. Individuals are increasingly having a say in the management of their final arrangement, often bypassing the expensive and complicated memorial goods and services proferred by funeral homes. However, as Andrew Wernick argues in his chapter, 'Selling funerals, imaging death', such changes, felt in Europe as well as North America, are ambiguous. For if the decline of memorial rituals and monuments makes it possible to have a more personalized or culturally-sensitive funeral, it equally points to the continuing (if less disguised) exclusion, or bowdlerizing, of death in the public symbolism of advanced industrial culture.

'Positive' images of aging can contain their own form of death denial. In deflecting attention from the physical deterioration of deep old age, such images aim above all not to present the aged as signs of the terminal process they may be beginning to undergo. Correlatively, the AIDS epidemic, which in the west has been concentrated in younger men, provides a contemporary image of the dying quite disconnected from that of old age. Especially as refracted by media, death in our culture means premature death, whether by violence or disease. Even movies about people with cancer seem to focus on young or middle-aged victims (*Love Story, Hannah and her Sisters*). This to some degree anxiety-driven separation of aging and dying can lead to the paradoxical case examined by John Tulloch in his chapter on 'Images of aging and death in Australian AIDS education campaigns'. Here, in the benign figure of the sex-affirmative 'Grannie' musing about her own (continuing?) safe pleasures, the old becomes a sign for Life against Death, with the latter being associated with the carelessness of youth.

The same image serves to remind us, finally, that the contemporary cultural place of death, as of all the other aspects of the discourse and imagery surrounding aging, has a gender dimension to which more attention needs to be given. From the perspective of many feminists, the existential model of human consciousness as 'living unto death' is peculiarly male in its abstraction from human continuity through childbirth, the family, and the wider processes of social reproduction.

CONCLUDING NOTE

It is a distinctive feature of the human sciences, especially where the focus is on understanding some aspect of present-day society, that the subject of knowledge is never wholly outside the object it seeks to understand. This is clearly so here. The authors assembled in this anthology (including the editors) are almost all in their forties and fifties. Greying baby-boomers, they belong to a generation that has been at the forefront of cultural attention throughout their lives, if for no other reason than its size and importance as a market. The radical experience of the sixties, moreover, has made it into a generation in Mannheim's sense: self-consciously formed by a relatively unifying historical experience. At once socially critical, narcissistically self-absorbed, and self-defined as forever young, what could be more natural, then, than that those of this generation with a professional interest in culture and society should now begin to turn attention to the next – and last – life-course experience we are collectively beginning to undergo?

REFERENCES

Achenbaum, W.A. and Kusnerz, P.A. (1978) *Images of Old Age in America, 1790 to the Present*, Ann Arbor: Institute of Gerontology.

Ariès, P. (1978) *Death in Western Society*, Princeton, NJ: Princeton University Press.

Berg, M-A. (1983) 'Aspects of time, ageing and old age in the novels of Patrick White, 1939–1979', *Gothenburg Studies in English* 53.

Cole, T.R., van Tassel, D.D. and Kastenbaum, R. (eds) (1992) *Handbook of Humanities and Aging*, New York: Springer.

Cole, T.R., Achenbaum, W.A, Jakobi, P.L. and Kastenbaum, R. (eds) (1993) *Voices and Visions of Aging: Toward a Critical Gerontology*, New York: Springer.

Elias, N. (1978) *The Civilizing Process, Volume 1*, Oxford: Blackwell.

Elias, N. (1985) *The Loneliness of the Dying*, Oxford: Blackwell.

Elias, N. (1994) *The Established and the Outsiders*, London: Sage.

Estes, C. and Binney, E. (1991) ' The biomedicalization of aging', in M. Minkler and C. Estes (eds) *Critical Perspectives on Aging: the Political Economy of Growing Old*, New York: Baywood.

Ewen, S. (1976) *Captains of Consciousness*, New York: McGraw Hill.

Falk, P. (1993) 'The representation of presence: pornography', *Theory, Culture & Society* 10(2).

Fanon, F. (1986) *Black Skins, White Masks*, London: Pluto Press.

Featherstone, M. (1991) *Consumer Culture and Postmodernism*, London: Sage.

Featherstone, M. (1995) *Undoing Culture*, London: Sage.

Featherstone, M. and Hepworth, M. (1982) 'Ageing and inequality: consumer culture and the new middle age', in (ed.) D. Robins *et al. Rethinking Inequality*, Gower Press.

Featherstone, M. and Hepworth, M. (1991) 'The mask of ageing' in M. Featherstone, M. Hepworth and B.S. Turner (eds) *The Body*, London: Sage.

Featherstone, M. and Hepworth, M. (1994) 'Images of ageing', in J. Bond and P.G. Coleman (eds) *Ageing in Society: An Introduction to Social Gerontology*, 2nd edn, London: Sage.

Featherstone, M. and Hepworth, M. (forthcoming), *The Mask of Ageing*, London: Sage.

Featherstone, M., Hepworth, M. and B.S. Turner (eds) (1991) *The Body*, London: Sage.

Featherstone, M. and Turner, B.S. (1995) 'Introduction', *Body and Society* 1(1).

Gadow, S.A. (1986) 'Frailty and strength: the dialectic of Aging', in T.R. Cole and S.A. Gadow (eds) *What does it Mean to Grow Old? Reflections from the Humanities*. Durham, NC: Duke University Press.

Goffman, Erving (1968) *Stigma*. Harmondsworth: Penguin.

Hazan, H. (1980) *The Limbo People*, London: Routledge & Kegan Paul.

Hockey, J. (1990) *Experiences of Death. An Anthropological Account*, Edinburgh: Edinburgh University Press.

Kohli, M. (1988) 'Aging as a challenge for sociological theory', *Ageing and Society* 8: 367–94.

Mitford, J. (1963) *The American Way of Death*, New York: Simon and Schuster.

Moody, H.R. (1993) 'What is critical gerontology?', in T.R. Cole, W.A. Achenbaum, P.L. Jakobi and R. Kastenbaum (eds) (1993) *Voices and Visions of Aging: Toward a Critical Gerontology*, New York: Springer.

Nederveen Pieterse, J. (1992) *White on Black?* New Haven, Conn: Yale University Press.

Root, J. (1984) *Pictures of Women*, London: Pandora.

Sontag, S. (1978) 'The double standard of ageing', in V. Carver and P. Liddiard (eds) *An Ageing Population*, London: Hodder & Stoughton.

Spicker, S.F., Woodward, K. and van Tassel, D.D. (1978) *Ageing and the Elderly: Humanistic Perspectives on Gerontology*, Atlantic Highlands, NJ: Humanities Press.

Stearns, P. (1978) *Old Age in European Society*, London: Croom Helm.

Stephens, J. (1976) *Loners, Losers, and Lovers: Elderly Tenants in a Slum Hotel*, Seattle and London: University of Washington Press.

Taylor, C. and Gutman, A. (1992) *Multiculturalism and the Politics of Recognition*, Princeton, NJ: Princeton University Press.

Turner, B.S. (1985) *The Body and Society*, Oxford: Blackwell.

Wernick, A. (1991) *Promotional Culture*, London: Sage.

Williams, R. (1976) *Keywords*, London: Fontana.

Woodward, K. (1988–89) 'Youthfulness as masquerade', *Discourse* 11(1).

Woodward, K. (1991) *Aging and its Discontents*, Bloomington, Ind.: Indiana University Press.

Part I

HISTORICAL AND COMPARATIVE PERSPECTIVES

2

IMAGES OF OLD AGE IN AMERICA, 1790–1970

A Vision and a Re-Vision

Andrew Achenbaum

Whatever new object we see, we perceive to be only a new version
of our familiar experience, and we set about translating it at once
into our parallel facts. We have thereby our vocabulary.
(Ralph Waldo Emerson, 'Art and Criticism', 1859)

There are close connections, Ralph Waldo Emerson noted, among
images seen, imagined, and communicated. With our mind's eye, we
translate objects to conform to our sense of reality. Yet we cannot
possess images totally; they have as well a life of their own. Images are
deeply and historically rooted in 'parallel facts' that ultimately predate
and transcend our perceptions. That images have past and future
representations accentuates our present-day sense of their historical
qualities.

Definitions of 'image' have not changed much since the twelfth
century. The English word (as are its French, Italian, and Spanish
equivalents) is derived from the Latin *imago* and is related to the verb
imitari. An image is an 'artificial imitation', a 'likeness' or 'appearance'.
The term has long had a technical connotation: according to the *Oxford
English Dictionary*, physicists and opticians in 1315 referred to images
produced by reflection or refraction through a lens (Compact *OED*, I:
1376). Even though people have understood the word 'image' in similar
ways over the centuries, the importance of 'images' in western civilization has increased over time. Images, claims US cultural historian
Daniel Boorstin (1977: 185), have become pseudo-ideals – 'synthetic,
believable, passive, vivid, simplified, and ambiguous'. Advertising
images motivate men and women to buy things. Campaign managers
work hard to 'package' their candidates' reputations and messages in
appealing images. Collective memories are evoked through representations of the past in ways that presumably resonate with ideals that
various elements in society hope will be sustained in the future.

Because images are so ubiquitous in past and present societies and because they serve so many disparate purposes simultaneously, it is reasonable to hypothesize that images of aging are an integral component of empirical and qualitative gerontologic inquiry. Researchers in other disciplines, after all, use images (such as falling apples or biomorphologic patterns) to describe observable phenomena and to convey scientific principles. Some images, such as Da Vinci's renditions of the human anatomy, seem timeless. Schematics of the atom, on the other hand, must be reconstructed to remain credible in the face of unfolding developments in the physical sciences. Similarly, displaying the icons of a particular stage of life – the hourglass, the cane, gray hairs – differentiates the interests of geriatricians from those of pediatricians. The apparent absence of integrative ideas and symbols, or the misuse of age-specific images, conversely, appears to have the effect of impeding scientific advancement in multidisciplinary fields such as gerontology. 'We are in a phase of being data-rich and theory-poor', observes James E. Birren (1989), arguably North America's most esteemed researcher on aging. He adds that 'An investigator's first research on aging usually begins with a microtheory derived from a subpart of the discipline in which the investigator was trained. It is perhaps to be expected that the narrow view and the microtheory characterize our present phase'. Gerontology, Birren suggests metaphorically, is a 'land of many islands with few bridges between them'.

Emerson and Birren, of course, focused on different subjects and they wrote at different times for different audiences. Yet there are 'parallel facts' in their interpretations of the process of connecting independent domains. Images are integral to making bridges across conceptual islands. Here I wish to show that the integrative process itself is also subject to historical alterations. Images, once envisioned, become subject to collective and idiosyncratic reworking. Images of age may be transformed, even over a relatively short period of time, as circumstances change and their architects grow older. To illustrate this point, I shall refer to an earlier excursus of my own. In that sense, this re-vision serves to illuminate the initial vision.

On the surface, this is a simple story about crossing boundaries from the printed word to the visual image: in 1976 a historian (me) and an art librarian (Peg Kusnerz) were given six months to produce an exhibit of 'Images of Old Age in America, 1790 to the Present'. We were to explore how the cultural-historical factors in the US had shaped the meanings and experiences of old age. We agreed that two lithographs – 'The Life and Age of Man/Woman. Stages of a Man's/Woman's Life from the Cradle to the Grave', – which were published by James Baille in 1848 encapsulated many of the themes of human senescence that remained constant over time. We then divided the presentation into three parts. The first section (1790–1864)

20

accentuated the positive, the second (1865–1934) the negative, the third (1935–c. 1976) blended the first two (Achenbaum and Kusnerz, 1978: 2).

The Smithsonian Institution Traveling Exhibition Services took 'Images' to colleges, banks, zoos, art galleries. The exhibit hung at the 1981 White House Conference on Aging; the catalogue won several awards, suggesting an impact beyond our wildest expectations. Now, it seems appropriate to ask how well we *really* accomplished our objectives. Did we present images sufficiently rich in composition and content to show the diversity of earlier generations of older Americans? Are better resources available? Have our perceptions of historical realities greatly changed since 1976? Let us consider these issues in terms of content, method, and interpretation.

CONTENT

'Rather than attributing divergent conceptions of older people's worth to the March of Progress or the Loss of Virtue, we tried to indicate that they represent differences in kind rather than quality of values operating in society over time' (Achenbaum and Kusnerz, 1978: viii). We wanted to smash 'simplistic' and 'simple-minded' images of what old age was like in the past. As a corollary, we also thought it possible to create images that would facilitate our desire for 'older men and women – and ultimately ourselves – to play roles in society that ensure meaning and dignity to their lives' (ibid.).

We raised many questions about 'diversity': we were concerned that women, Afro-Americans, orientals, and native Americans, were sufficiently represented in the exhibit. We did not maintain a quota system, but some simple retrospective counts do reveal our biases. We used thirty-four images to cover the period between 1790 and 1864. Two-thirds came from the 1840s and 1850s. Women are in ten images, couples in two. Blacks are in two photographs; there is a pencil drawing of Pagh-Paght-sem-i-arn, a native American named 'Woman of Good Sense'. Six graphics stress intergenerational themes – although we discarded literally hundreds of sentimental renditions of the bonds between young and old. Six pictures portrayed American heroes (including Benjamin Franklin and Johnny Appleseed).

In retrospect, there are several interesting features to our choices. Canes are prominent icons in six graphics, yet we selected only three images executed between 1790 and 1864 that emphasized the risks of dependency or death in late-life. Were there simply none to choose? Or were we, then both in our twenties, loathe to confront the frailty and disability likely to confront us in later life? Furthermore, the faces of older Americans in the first section are remarkably ebullient, regardless of their social condition or economic status. Even the etching of the 'hermit who lived upwards of 200 years' looks none the worse for wear after spending most of his life in a dank cave.

The thirty graphics used in the second section convey a darker image. Nearly a third of the pictures accentuate unflattering features of living (too) long, although curiously, there are *no* pictures of the old-old in this part! This lacuna lends credence to the possibility that Kusnerz and I were (too) eager to accentuate the positive. Elderly people are shown among the other deserving poor in an almshouse, at the Freedman's Bureau, or claiming veterans' benefits. Only one famous person (Henry Wadsworth Longfellow) is represented here. Among the ordinary citizens portrayed are five couples, three older people in the company of younger people, six women, two Blacks, one native American, and one Oriental.

Thanks to the photographs taken for the Farm Security Agency in the latter part of the 1930s, we had no difficulty accentuating old-old diversity in the 'contemporary' section, with photographs of a Texas Mexican husband and wife, Mennonite farmers, an Hispanic woman, the wife of a migrant worker in California, a male ex-slave in Georgia, and a Spanish-American farmer. The very old once again seem slighted in this section, represented only by an ex-slave and Imogen Cunningham's picture of her father at 90. None the less, endorsing the 'new' social history then in vogue, there are many images of ordinary people shopping, dancing, learning and protesting.

Women constitute about a third of the images in all sections, but in the last part, by design, large numbers are shown together – sitting on benches with men conspicuously absent. We wanted to show the widening gender gap. But we seem to have conceptually differentiated ageist and sexist artifacts, never exploring how the two kinds of stereotypes reinforce one another. Despite our sensitivity to intergenerational issues, there is only one picture of a child walking with her grandfather. Did we take too literally the gerontologic notion, fashionable in the 1970s, that age cohorts were becoming increasingly segregated? Did we fail to detect images in which the elderly were scapegoated?

Were Peggy Ann Kusnerz and I to revise 'Images of Old Age in America', we would still want to stress the heterogeneity of elderly Americans accentuating the theme of 'diversity' even more forcibly in five ways:

(a) *The introductory section would be longer, so as to underscore the importance of perduring themes of old age in western civilization over the centuries.* Prototypes for the first two visuals can be traced back to fifteenth century Augsburg. Even though renditions of this motif of rise-and-decline over the human life course have persisted for nearly four centuries, viewers need to appreciate that there have always been many ways to conceptualize the stages of life in human aging. That there were at least *sixteen* different versions of the 'steps of the ages' popular in nineteenth century France alone (Achenbaum and Kusnerz, 1978: 71) substantiates this observation. Some were three-stage (youth, middle age, old age); one offered eleven steps divided by decades. Continuities might be shown in other ways. Patrick McKee and Heta Kauppinen selected 116 portraits of age from western art that 'express the challenges, satisfactions, sorrows, and joys in the human experience of growing old' (1987: 13). J.A. Burrow's *The Ages of Man* (1986) concentrates on contrarieties in medieval iconography. Mary Dove (1986) offers an alternative interpretation of the same material, stressing the ambiguity inherent in notions of *The Perfect Age of Man's Life*. By incorporating these works, it would be possible to begin, not end, with the notion that various artists at divergent stages of life have stressed different features at distinct stages of life. Artists of the same age, moreover, often have disagreed in their conceptions of the journey of life. The elderly themselves face life's finitude differently. Hence it might be useful to have referred to late works by Rembrandt, which inspired folk art imitations in the US. It is a fruitless distortion to invoke a single motif to capture the variegated images of late life.

(b) *The gender-specific themes identified in the two introductory graphics would be accentuated and then the theme carried out more systematically in the catalogue.* In my Afterword (Achenbaum and Kusnerz, 1982: ix), I noted some important gender-specific variations in the first two graphics. The officer in his prime at 50 still appeared vigorous twenty years later. In contrast, by the sixth decade, the burdens of caregiving appear to have drained the woman of her vitality. Then the pattern seems to reverse in later years: the gentleman 'retires' at 70 to increasing obsolescence; the woman is not depicted as a 'useless cumberer' until 90. Current research (Gilligan, 1982; Gutmann, 1987) supports several presuppositions embedded in these historical images. Carol Gilligan (1982) argues that men and women think and speak 'in a different voice'. I would invoke Nancy Cott's *Bonds of Womanhood* (1971) and Terri Premo's *Winter Friends* (1989) to underscore the point that women in the early years of the Republic developed ties with other women that sustained and nurtured them over the interconnected lives. Greater reference should be made to women's roles as caregivers and as widows.

In retrospect, I wish we had not been so hasty in passing over an eirenic photograph of Maggie Kuhn. Showing the feisty convener of the Gray Panthers as reflective and content might have underlined the complexity of sentiments about growing older within each of us as we age. It also might have underscored the fact that women more than men generally manage, and are expected, to learn to cope with increasing physical decrepitude.

(c) *The 'political' content of old age often affects how we see the elderly's assets, liabilities, contributions and circumstances.* 'Diversity' nowadays is a political term in politically correct circles, not merely a sociological construct. Accordingly, we should have acknowledged that norms and conventions often determine the ways in which the content in the images we selected was expressed. Perhaps overly influenced by de Tocqueville's image of equality in America, we paid too little attention to 'class' in the images of old age. *The Gallery of Illustrious Americans* by Mathew Brady (1850), for instance, offered a dozen daguerreotypes of 'representative' older men, including two mediocre presidents (Zachary Taylor and Millard Fillmore).

We also want to try to capture the degradation and horrors of slavery through a cache of photographs discovered recently. In 1850 Louis Agassiz, a distinguished Harvard professor of natural science, commissioned J.T. Zealy, a South Carolina daguerreotypist, to take pictures of the faces and bodies of black slaves. Rather than honour the hoary heads of 'illustrious', 'representative' citizens, the subjects of Zealy's photographs stand naked. They are specimens, 'types', exhibited for the advancement of science. 'The Zealy pictures reveal the social convention which ranks blacks as inferior beings, which violates civilized decorum, which strips men and women of the right to cover their genitalia' (Trachtenberg, 1989: 56). The sullen looks, the pain, the scars on older women's sagging breasts and aging men's sunken chests, are haunting. Such traits also characterize late nineteenth-century photographs of the elderly sick, which presumably also were taken for 'scientific' purposes. Such images attest to the extent to which objectivity dehumanizes.

(d) *More attention should have been paid to Hispanics and native Americans.* Most of the graphics in *Images of Old Age* dealt with subjects who live(d) east of the Mississippi. To be sure, a comparable eastern, northern, urban bias runs through most of the historical literature on old age in the United States. As a result, the extent of the diversity that has long existed among the people who settled in the plains and the American south-west is not fully evident here. Too bad that Peg and I did not know that child psychiatrist Robert Coles and photographer Alex Harris had published a book about *The Old Ones of New Mexico*. 'The people are strong, proud, vigorous, independent. They are of "Spanish" descent, yet can be called "oldline" Americans', Coles reports. 'Others from the Anglo world might consider them aloof, old-fashioned, superstitious, all too set in their ways. They look upon themselves quite differently;

they hold to certain values and assumptions, and, God willing, they will not forsake them' (Coles and Harris, 1973: xii–xiii). We also would want to include pictures and graphics about the native Americans and Mormons who interact(ed) with Spanish-speaking peoples in the southwest. For instance, a 1974 acrylic entitled 'Emergence' by Hopi artist Dawakema-Milland Lomakema might be used, not only to contrast the 'stages of life' graphics in the Introduction, but also to show a highly distinctive conception of time, one not linear but cumulative (Boyle and Morriss, 1987).

(e) *That time passes within the country of the old must be underlined.* Despite the attention paid in *Images of Old Age* to the old-old in the nineteenth century, with its daguerreotypes of centenarians, this exhibit does not stress that Americans now expect to live longer than ever before, that two-thirds of all gains in life expectancy in the world have been made since 1900. Nor did we indicate that with added years has come a greater incidence of chronicity, which puts strains on the country's health-care system. Those added years simply did not exist for most people even a century ago.

We might have emphasized some of the tragedies associated with the medicalization and bureaucratization of age – ranging from the prolongation of vegetable-like existence through heroic interventions to the impoverishment of middle-class citizens so that they qualify for Medicaid while in nursing homes.

METHOD

In her comments in the 1982 Afterword (p. x), Peg Kusnerz stated what friends and critics had already told us privately: 'I believe the weakest section of the book is part three (1935-present)'. Had Kusnerz and I embarked on this project a few years later, we would have been able to take advantage of the outpouring of monographs and basic reference works that deal with humanistic perspectives on aging (Polisar *et al.*, 1988). Relying exclusively on print media permitted consistency, but it precluded some of the best images produced in twentieth century America. 'Stills' from motion picture and television should have been included. Robert Yahnke's survey of films (1988) would be the starting point for analysing the incidence of older people in cinema, as well as how aging actors and actresses must adapt their *personae* in the latter stages of their careers. Tracing views of aging on television since the 1950s would have added much to what we know about images in postwar America. Older people are among the most important consumers of network programming, both in terms of numbers of hours per day they watch programs as well as in terms of the companionship they derive from 'friends' on the screen (Davis and Davis, 1985).

Even without additions from television or films, better selections from the print media might have broadened the range of imagery in the third part. Archibald MacLeish's *Land of the Free* (1938) is 'a book of photographs illustrated by a poem' (p. 89). Roughly an eighth of the photographs, mostly taken for the Resettlement Administration, feature elderly subjects – including a picture of a pair of beautiful wrinkled hands. Picture 22 in Walker Evans's *American Photographs*, 'An Alabama Tenant Family Singing Hymns' (1936), shows a couple in their 30s holding a dog-eared hymnal. Their daughter, mouth closed, looks off vacantly. One of the parent's mothers keeps her distance from the couple; eyes closed, she sings from memory. There is nothing dramatic here, but in Lincoln Kirstein's words, Evans so powerfully conveys 'the effect of circumstances on familiar specimens' (Evans, 1938: 197) that it makes manifest the strength as well as the attenuation in inter-generational bonds. (The photograph itself resembles advertisements from the 1930s showing middle-aged adults talking on the phone and listening to the radio while grandma revels (?) in memories.) Powerful photographs of well-known elderly people that appeared in *Life* merit consideration. So do advertisements representing ordinary people. Yet a systematic survey of the magazine suggests that, until recently, the elderly rarely appeared in the magazine's pages (Poit, 1990). Nor were the editors of *Life* alone in ignoring or stereotyping the old. It is remarkable that there is not one memorable picture of the aged in Robert Frank's *The Americans* (1958), arguably the best collection of photographs published during the decade. Much of the art of presenting images of old age becomes a matter of critical interpretation.

INTERPRETATION

On balance, *Images of Old Age in America* did succeed in indicating changes in values attributed to old age and in the ways that the elderly have lived during the past two centuries, but the tripartite division is too neat. The presentation would have been more compelling had more effort been made to portray aging over time as a dynamic, variegated process. Were Kusnerz and I to update *Images of Old Age*, we would want to underline our interpretation of 'time' as a central element (factually and metaphorically) of aging.

One way to underline themes in the pre-American Civil War (*ante bellum*) and contemporary periods of US history would be to compare the ways that a well-known artist from each era interpreted the human life course. The first section of *Images* now ends with a copy of Smillie's 1849 engraving of Thomas Cole's 'Old Age' (1849), which was one of four paintings Cole did to convey his sense of the 'Voyage of Life'. In a revised version of *Images of Old Age*, I would reproduce 'Childhood', 'Youth', and 'Middle Age', pointing out some of the obvious motifs. Bright light radiates the promise of youth; darkness, in contrast, shrouds old age except for that stream of light focusing the old mariner's attention to the eternal. The waters become progressively turbulent. The guardian angel who hovered over the innocent child is the one who shows the way in the last act. In the middle pictures, the angel is there, but ignored by the sailor who feels that he is in his prime. Cole's interpretation is meant to be inspirational; as befits his message, he paints on huge canvasses.

Jasper Johns's series on the voyage of life, 'The Seasons' (1986) would be an apt counterpoint. Cole's protagonist braves the elements; Johns also frames his message *in* nature. True to contemporary sensibilities, however, Johns offers a complex, fragmented, chaotic sense of aging. No longer God, but science, offers any promise of stability. Whereas shadows convey a sense of mystery in the nineteenth-century series, they underscore ambiguity in the later work. As symbolic in composition as Cole, Johns is more eclectic in his idiosyncratic blending of ancient icons and modern motifs. 'Where Cole's "Voyage" is about keeping one's faith and surviving life's trials, Johns's "Seasons" is about essential questions of identity, change and continuity in our perplexing and foundationless "post-modern" world', notes cultural historian Tom Cole (who is no relation to the *ante bellum* painter). 'The sense of vision presented by Johns involves the resurrection of the past, the necessity of traditional archetypes to help guide us into our uncertain future' (Cole, 1991; Rosenthal, 1988).

Johns's provocative 'vocabulary' brings us full circle back to Emerson's epigraph and Birren's plaint about the paucity of gerontologic theory-building. Johns borrows from tradition to give his viewers images from 'our familiar experience' so we can try to make sense of issues so profound, so elusive that we really do not know how to possess them, how to translate them 'into our present facts'. Johns does not present us with a neat picture: he deftly treats the contingent, uncertain manner in which people must wrestle with historically grounded and universal features of human aging. Jasper Johns's 'The Seasons' makes possible a continuing dialogue about aging. Conversations about age and aging must begin rather than end with an appreciation of the pluralism inherent in the human condition, which affirms various and divergent ways of growing older. The dialogue need not rely just on words, but on any form of communication that facilitates insights about aging. Sometimes silence is appropriate in the face of mysteries of human senescence dimly perceived. At other times it makes sense, as I have done here, to put aside immature, if not necessarily childish, notions of what it means to grow older. By capitalizing on their own self-knowledge as well as the growing expertise, gerontologists themselves gain the insights to make better connections between continuity and change over the life course.

REFERENCES

Achenbaum, W.A. and Kusnerz, P.A. (1978) *Images of Old Age in America, 1790 to the Present*, Ann Arbor: Institute of Gerontology.

Achenbaum, W.A. and Kusnerz, P.A. (1982) *Images of Old Age in America, 1790 to the Present*, rev. edn, Ann Arbor: Institute of Gerontology.

Birren, J.E. (1989) 'My perspective on research on aging', in V.L. Bengtson and K.W. Schaie (eds) *The Course of Late Life: Research and Reflections*, New York: Springer.

Boorstin, D. (1977) *The Images*, New York: Atheneum.

Boyle, J.M. and Morriss, J.E. (1987) *The Mirror of Time*, Westport, CT: Greenwood Press.

Burrow, J.A. (1986) *The Ages of Man*, Oxford: Clarendon Press.

Callihan, D. (1987) *Setting Limits*, New York: Simon and Schuster.

Cole, T.R. (1991) 'Aging, metaphor, and meaning', in J.E. Birren and G.M. Kenyon (eds) *Metaphors in Science and the Humanities*, New York: Springer.

Coles, R. and Harris, A. (1973) *The Old Ones of New Mexico*, Albuquerque, NM: University of New Mexico Press.

Compact Edition of the Oxford English Dictionary, (1971), 2 vols, Oxford: Oxford University Press.

Cott, N. (1971) *Bonds of Womanhood*, New Haven, CT: Yale University Press.

Davis, R.H. and Davis J.A. (1985) *TV's Image of the Elderly*, Lexington, MA: Lexington Books.

Dove, M. (1986) *The Perfect Age of Man's Life*, Cambridge: Cambridge University Press.

Emerson, R.W. (1859) 'Art and criticism', in *The Complete Works of Ralph Waldo Emerson*, vol. 12 (1904), Houghton Mifflin: Riverside Press.

Evans, W. (1938) *American Photographs*, New York: Museum of Modern Art.

Frank, R. (1958) *The Americans*, New York: Grove Press.

Gilligan, C. (1982) *In a Different Voice*, Cambridge, MA: Harvard University Press.

Gutmann, D. (1987) *Powers Reclaimed*, New York: Basic Books.

MacLeish, A. (1938) *Land of the Free*, New York: Harcourt, Brace, and Company.

McKee, P. and Kauppinen, H. (1987) *The Art of Aging*, New York: Human Sciences Press.

Poit, K. (1990) 'Images of the elderly through the eyes of *Life*', unpublished seminar paper, University of Michigan.

Premo, T. (1989) *Winter Friends*, Urbana, IL: University of Illinois Press.

Rosenthal, M. (1988) *Jasper Johns: Work since 1974*, Philadelphia: Philadelphia Museum of Art.

Trachtenberg, A. (1989) *Reading American Photographs*, New York: Hill and Wang.

3

IMAGES OF POSITIVE AGING

A case study of *Retirement Choice* magazine

Mike Featherstone and *Mike Hepworth*

THE EMERGENCE OF 'POSITIVE' AGING

Since the mid-1960s there has been a gradual increase in public interest in the processes of human aging and old age (Featherstone and Hepworth, 1993). One indication of the level of age-consciousness in contemporary society is the near-impossibility of avoiding images of aging and old age in the cinema, television, radio, novels, magazines and newspapers (Hepworth and Featherstone, 1982). At the same time every visual image of the human body is an image of a person who is aging, of someone who has been captured at a point in their movement through the life course, a process which necessarily entails changes in the visible surfaces of the body (Featherstone, 1987). While it can be argued that when we see a human body age is one of the first qualities we attribute to it, there are many situations in everyday life, especially the habitual routine interactions with significant others and people we are familiar with, in which a person's age, detected through their appearance, does not strike us as significant. In effect we often see and *don't* see. In contrast to this tendency in habitual interactions in everyday life to 'normalize' aging, it can be argued that within the vast array of images daily produced by consumer culture which we encounter in newspapers, magazines, advertisements in public transport systems, television and video, we are often encouraged to carefully scrutinize physical appearance and home in on the age characteristics of the human bodies presented. Many of the texts accompanying images of the human body identify and comment on, either directly or indirectly, the person's age. Younger people, especially women, are warned of the dangers in store and the need to engage in body work to maintain their appearance. Older people who have preserved their youthful beauty, fitness and energy are usually the subject of praise. Occasionally there are disturbing images of people who are seen to have failed – those whose bodies have betrayed them and, whether through neglect, illness, accident or fate, face a future in which they have been accorded the negative status of a dependent and premature old age.

29

When we examine these popular images it is noticeable that many of the themes and preoccupations dealt with here also figure in the world of academic and professional gerontology. In other words, the issues which become central preoccupations within gerontology cannot be understood to have been generated solely within an insulated scientific environment. Academics and the journalists and other cultural intermediaries who formulate the various agendas for the popular media often draw upon similar sources and common-sense assumptions. Both groups have necessarily to be sensitive to changes in public opinion, new policy initiatives, technological advances and shifts in cultural values. Hence while few gerontologists have directly studied images of aging and the various modes of dissemination and use in everyday life by the public, it is noticeable how closely some of the central issues and crusades which they have developed parallel the assumptions about aging which are found in the popular media and the discourse of marketing people who have identified a new market in selling the consumer goods, techniques and paraphernalia for active, positive old age (see the chapter by Sawchuk in this volume). This is all the more striking given the fact that for some gerontologists the solution to the current problems of coping with increasing numbers of old people involves the development of more positive images of aging, which it is assumed will encourage the elderly to achieve a better quality of life and persuade the rest of us to reduce our age discrimination.

The increasing preoccupation in social gerontology with positive aging, then, arises out of the critical belief that we live in an ageist society, one in which the predominant attitude towards older people is coloured by a negative mixture of, pity, fear, disgust, condescension, and neglect (Biggs, 1989; Scrutton, 1990). Ageism is not only seen as the source of a widespread discrimination against older people but also as a crucial factor in undermining their 'personal value and worth' (Scrutton, 1990: 13). In Britain, for example, the popular textbook by Anthea Tinker, *Elderly People in Modern Society*, endorses the appeal for 'positive thinking' about aging and old age in a context where, she argues, a great deal of the discussion of this subject is 'inappropriately negative, pessimistic and too often couched in crisis terms' (1992: 9).

One of the chief weapons in the battle against ageism is the conceptualization of aging and old age as social constructs. According to this perspective aging cannot be understood solely as a biological process (or more accurately a number of processes). Aging and old age 'are certainly real, but they do not exist in some natural realm, independently of the ideals, images and social practices that conceptualise and represent them' (Cole, 1992: xxii). Whilst the biological processes of aging, old age, and death cannot in the last resort be avoided, the meanings which we give to these processes and the evaluations we make of people as they grow physically older are social constructions which reflect the beliefs and values found in a specific culture at a particular period in history. If, therefore, the source of many of the disagreeable aspects of the experience of later life can be traced to a negative culture of aging (what has been described as 'societal ageism' (Coupland *et al.*, 1991: 13)) then it should be possible to reconstruct these attitudes and beliefs through the creation of a culture of positive aging and old age. From this perspective images have two functions: first they are a cultural resource we draw upon to give meaning to later life – in the everyday practical business of living they are an essential element in 'the appraisal of living' (Cole, 1992: xviii); and, second, for the sociologist concerned with the analysis of the social construction of aging they provide important evidence of the kinds of cultural resources a specific society draws upon to give meaning to later life. Images, then, can act as representations of the general ideals which shape the 'appraisal' of everyday social practices; as such their meanings are flexible and open to interpretation and reinterpretation in accordance with broader socio-historical change.

Following the theory of social constructionism, social gerontologists have advocated the radical deconstruction and displacement of negative images of aging and the elaboration of an alternative positive imagery. This requires no less than a concerted attempt to establish a new discourse of later life through the deconstruction of the long-held associations between old age and illness, disability, disengagement and decline. Two significant features of the construction of positive aging are evident in the literature: first, a critical attack on the belief that aging is essentially a disease. The central feature of the new positive image of normal aging is of a number of variable biological processes which need not necessarily result in serious mental or physical impairment. Consequently the problems of old age can be attributed either to clinical pathology, that is, a specific disease which is at least in theory medically curable, for example, Alzheimer's Disease (Gubrium, 1986) or, as we indicated above, to the effects of ageism which is remediable through programmes of social reconstruction and education. The second noteworthy feature of positive aging is the elaboration of new norms of age-related behaviour and associated rites of passage out of the more traditional and arguably static concept of an amorphous and undifferentiated old age (Cole, 1992; Kammen, 1980). One aspect of this process of social differentiation which is of particular relevance to our case study of images of positive aging in the retirement magazine, *Choice*, is what Dorothy Jerrome has described as the 'emerging interest in the lives of fit and active older people – those defined as 'young-old' in the literature . . .' (1992: 5).

It can therefore be argued that since the 1960s images of aging in

31

Britain have become, in line with the developments mentioned above, much more positive. Various processes of interchange and cross-fertilization have occurred between the images of aging in the gerontological literature and those circulating in popular culture and public life. A typical example of the latter can be found on the cover of the Spring 1993 issue of *050* (Association of Retired Persons, 1993a) where an exuberant middle-aged couple are displayed clinging lovingly together in a wild country garden. Superimposed over this glossy image of an idyllic rural environment are signposts to this month's selection from the stock-in-trade ingredients of the commercialized version of positive aging: 'healthy living' for the over 50s; 'cosmetic surgery – would you dare?'; 'seven ways to improve your memory'; osteoporosis and, inevitably, advice on ways of saving money. In passing, it is worth observing that in its more popular representations, and following a lingering tradition dating at least back to images of later life in Victorian painting, positive aging is intimately associated with the countryside. Rustic imagery is a pervasive characteristic of successful retirement as it is with pre-paid funeral plans such as 'Golden Charter', illustrated on the back cover of *050* with a photograph of an enchanting woodland scene where sunlight filters through autumnal leaves on to an older woman attending on a pram and a small child on a leaf-strewn pathway. In a similar typical vein, the front cover of Hill Samuel's *Financial Monitor* for Summer 1993 included a feature on 'Action Time For Pensions' highlighted against a five-bar gate leading to a pathway across a vista of summer fields stretching endlessly away to a cloudless blue horizon.

It is clear therefore that the construction of positive aging has spread far beyond the endeavours of social gerontologists and other professionals. Consequently it is necessary for sociologists of aging to investigate not only the professional discourses of aging and old age (Miller, 1987) but also to explore the ways in which discourses of aging have developed in other spheres and, in particular, have become a significant feature of popular and consumer culture especially during the course of the last two decades. An important force behind the emergence of popular images of positive aging, the 'ageing industry' as Thomas R. Cole (1992: 222) describes it, is a growing sensitivity on the part of merchandisers to the potential new markets in middle and later life (Featherstone and Hepworth, 1982; Hepworth and Featherstone, 1982). Indeed, it is now recognized that the '50 plus' age group is the only remaining group of people in the western world with a substantial and untapped disposable income (Ostroff, 1989; see also the discussion in the chapter by Sawchuk in this volume). Previously it was assumed that members of this social group (or more accurately in this context, market segment) survived into later life with minimal investment and expenditure. In short, they were both unable and unwilling to engage in the active construction of a consumer lifestyle. In contemporary society it is not only the young who are encouraged to develop an interest in fashion, presentation of self and the continuous construction and reconstruction of an individualistic self-expressive lifestyle through consumer goods (Featherstone, 1991), but the over-50s as well.

These developments are closely related to the institutionalization of retirement planning which has also gradually developed in Britain since the 1950s. In an area where central and local government provision for pre-retirement education remains a low priority and is therefore both scarce and inadequate in form and content (Coleman and Chiva, 1991; Phillipson and Strang, 1983), commercial concerns, especially since the late 1980s, have moved into the vacuum and exercised a notable influence on the positive reconstruction of the imagery of retirement. Recognition by commercial organizations of the need for planning for the later years has helped to change the face of later life. There is a rich ground here for the marketing of health products, leisure goods and services, retirement homes, private pensions and holidays which translates retirement planning into lifestyle planning. For us one of the most significant aspects of this change has been the consolidation of connections between retirement planning, positive aging and consumer culture (Featherstone and Hepworth, 1982). The necessary premise on which institutionalized retirement planning is promoted in a market economy is inevitably the development of retirement pensions and saving schemes which allow people to participate fully in the new consumer lifestyles. Regular features of the expanding commercially-produced retirement literature in Britain (*Choice; 050; Saga Magazine; Yours*) are housing, health, fitness, fashion, make-up, relaxation, and sexuality. These display numerous examples of what Jeff Ostroff (1989), an American expert in marketing to the over-50s, has described as the 'soft sell': the intermingling of recommendations for consumer goods and services with information, and advice about the enhancement and empowerment of later life. Although there is a sense in which the soft sell exploits the hopes and aspirations of older people – in particular – the 'dream' of an idyllic retirement which is a persistent legacy from our Victorian past – it is also the case that such commercialized images do promote an anti-ageist perspective and in this sense at least help to promote the cause of positive aging in a 'greying world'.

IMAGES OF POSITIVE AGING:
RETIREMENT CHOICE MAGAZINE

In Britain the first issue of the first magazine for retirement planning, now known as *Choice*, appeared in October 1972 under the title

Retirement Choice (Figure 3.1). Significantly, in the early years of the publication, the word 'Retirement' in the cover title was given the greater prominence with the word 'Choice' playing a much more subordinate role. At first, then, the magazine addressed itself to the traditional image of retirement as a phase of disengagement from active life and a period of well-deserved relaxation (Figure 3.2). During the intervening years *Choice* has passed through a number of changes, including becoming part of a European publishing network, and continues to reflect the complex of interweaving commercial, professional and lay interests we outlined above. For these reasons changes in the form and content of *Choice* magazine from 1972 to the present day can be seen as a case study of images of aging in Britain which has, because of the global transformations implicated in its development, relevance for the social construction of aging in the wider international sphere.

In this context the most important feature of *Retirement Choice* from day one was the explicit attack on the traditional ageist image of retirement in Britain. In the second issue (November 1972) Lord Raglan, the then president of the Pre-Retirement Association, adopted a constructionist stand: society, he said, 'arbitrarily imposes the rules of retirement, and, therefore, society should play its full part in providing pre-retirement education to help people adjust to a new way of life, at what after all is a time in life when change is proverbially difficult'. He added that 'in the interests of the community there must be a quite dramatic change in attitudes to the whole question of retirement' (*Retirement Choice*, November 1972: 2). For too long, retirement had been associated with a useless and passive old age and it was now the responsibility of society to transform retirement into an active stage of life. Given that retirement was at the time largely a male province, the section on women's fashion was particularly interesting because it adopted an especially militant stand towards the image of retirement as reflected in clothing. In 'Strictly Between Women – Yes, You Can Wear These Clothes', readers were told that they need no longer dress themselves in the 'dull uniform' of the retirement: 'Time was when, once you were forty or so, you could climb into a "uniform" of long black skirt, severe blouse and sensible shoes, sit back and officially enter old age for ever'. In contrast, the grandmothers of 1972 were praised for their modern outlook: gone were the days when they could skimp on make-up and wear something old and comfortable around the house, 'Now, when your husband is going to be home most of the time, is the moment to make him sit up and take notice of your elegant new image'. Perhaps as an added inducement, the photographic models demonstrating the new youth-related clothing were much younger women than the presumed readership (ibid.: 18–19).

Figure 3.1 First issue of *Retirement Choice*, October, 1972

Figure 3.2 Retirement Choice, November, 1973

Promotion of a reconstructed image of retirement continued to appear throughout the relatively brief lifetime of *Retirement Choice*. In December 1972 readers were invited to contribute to a new series, 'Then and Now', a photographic celebration of the influence of passage of time on age-related clothing (Polhemus and Proctor, 1978; Lurie, 1981) which also doubled as a convenient medium for the disengagement of the image of retirement from traditional associations with inactive old age now, of course, defined as negative and defeatist. Reproductions of old photographs showed how the pressure on men and women to dress in an elderly fashion in the 1880s had been reduced in the 1960s when liberation seemed for the first time to be at hand. The brief text accompanying the photographs was a constructionist plea to free men and women 'from their chronological bonds': to remove those external pressures which made people feel old. 'Generations of older people were expected to conform to a rigid age pattern, today we are trying to let in a healthy gust of air to blow these wretched cobwebs away' (*Retirement Choice*, December 1972: 8).

In February 1973 the editorial expressed a continuing sense of grievance over the association of old age with retirement, 'We no longer wear the kind of clothes which earlier generations of elderly folk donned simply to denote that they were "elderly"'. Yet at the same time older people still remained 'trapped within a fence of outworn stereos'. 'Isn't it about time the news got around that nowadays people stay younger and are not old in the same way that people were old in times of yore?' The processes of aging, concluded the editor, were 'inevitable enough without officialdom giving them a shove along with an outdated vocabulary' (*Retirement Choice*, February 1973: 3). To reinforce the argument Dr Wright, Chairman of the Pre-Retirement Association, told reporters and journalists attending a press conference organized to mark the first birthday of *Retirement Choice* that there was still widespread ignorance of the financial and philosophical problems of retirement and, with a keen sense of publicity values, an enormous gold pocket watch made from plastic, plaster and wire was ceremonially destroyed with a hammer (*Retirement Choice*, October 1973: 11). On the cover of the issue was a photograph describing the ceremony as 'breaking a golden spell'. It was also announced that for the first time the magazine, previously only available to members of the Pre-Retirement Association, was now on sale at newsagents and bookstalls throughout the country.

It was between October and November 1974 that the most dramatic changes took place in the format of the magazine. Having already gone commercial, the title was changed to *Pre Retirement Choice* with the emphasis in the title shifting to the word '*Choice*' and the original monochrome covers and contents (where only the occasional word had been highlighted in colour for emphasis) were abandoned in favour of glossy covers featuring for the first time close-ups of the faces of celebrities from politics, show business and the media – all of whom presented an anti-ageist image in the crucial areas of personal appearance and lifestyle. The publication of the journal was placed in the hands of a commercial organization and, as the new title suggested, the focus of the magazine was henceforth on *preparation* for retirement, leisure, and lifestyle choice. Examples of the cover-photographed celebrities endorsing the image of the youthfully extended middle age included figures as diverse as politician Margaret Thatcher (Figure 3.3); popular war-time singer Vera Lynn ('How Vera Lynn defeats middle-age') (January 1975); popular comedian Eric Morecambe ('Laughing off a heart attack') (February 1975); and trade unionist Tom Jackson (May 1975). The express rationale for this transformation was to create 'a magazine which will become essential for all caught up in *preparing for retirement*' (emphasis ours) (October 1974). The intention was to expand the concept of pre-retirement to include a younger audience: the middle-aged who were looking for a positive orientation towards the future: 'people looking ahead to retirement'. People 'who *know* that sooner or later they have to *fashion their lives afresh*' (October 1974).

In the first issue of *Pre Retirement Choice* the editorial presented a defence of the decision to go commercial which can be read as a significant index of the difficulties which continue to surround pre-retirement planning. It was pointed out that the Pre-Retirement Association had endured a 'long hard struggle for survival and solvency'. A government grant in 1973 and help from the Parkhill Trust had provided some relief and some of that money had gone into this 'brave and exciting attempt to produce and run an entirely new magazine'. Although the previous magazine had 'done reasonably well', it had, nevertheless, lost money and did require the strength of 'an overt publishing organisation' behind it. It still, however, retained its connections with the Pre-Retirement Association and its philosophy would be much the same as before (*Pre Retirement Choice*, November 1974: 5). To reinforce the new image an item on the back page announced that forthcoming attractions would further the cause of 'Putting real CHOICE into Pre-Retirement' and December's new improved issue was, to contain more 'informative and entertaining features' including 'down to earth advice on keeping your body trim in middle age' (November 1974).

Between May and June 1975 'choice', a word closely associated with consumer culture (Featherstone, 1991; Featherstone and Hepworth, 1982) was further highlighted when the word 'Pre Retirement' was

Figure 3.3 Pre Retirement Choice, December 1974

finally dropped from the front cover and the magazine renamed simply *Choice*, subtitled: 'The only magazine for retirement planning' (June 1975) (Figures 3.4 and 3.5). One important consequence of these developments is the inevitable dominance of the image of pre-retirement/retirement as a consumer lifestyle. The earlier attempts of *Retirement Choice* to create an active and more positive image for those entering retirement finds its expression through hobbies associated with the traditional image (associated with retreatist relaxation ideally in rural settings) such as gardening, painting, photography, watching sport, keeping pets and making and collecting model soldiers. In these traditional pastimes the self-conscious stylization of the body, presentation of a youthful appearance and the cultivation of an expressive lifestyle (an aspect of what Polhemus and Proctor, 1978: 12, have defined as 'anti-fashion') were given relatively low priority. But it must be stressed that the anti-fashion of retirement and its associations still tenaciously persist alongside the new positive imagery we have described. In continuing reflection of the dual imagery of retirement/ aging, and despite the avowed intention of refurbishing and updating the image of retirement, the illustrations in *Retirement Choice* and subsequent variations lapse on occasions and in certain contexts into the more traditional portrayal of retirement as a time of tranquil inactivity and disengagement from active life.

Nevertheless, consumer-oriented innovations marked a watershed in the imagery of positive aging in the magazine (Figure 3.6). Since that point it has become the vehicle for the promotion of the benefits of an active positive lifestyle where the consumption of goods and services has an integral role to play in the battle against ageism. The speedy changeover to the title *Choice*, with the words 'The magazine for leisure and retirement planning' printed as a less visible subtitle, reflected this trend. None of the celebrities whose photographs now appear on the cover of *Choice* have expressed any intention of retreating into passive retirement; indeed, several of those interviewed over the years have apparently no intention of retiring at all. In July 1975, for example, Lord George Brown, former Deputy Leader of the Labour Party, proudly stated that he had no outside interests 'apart from work, politics, and watching West Ham win the Cup occasionally'. He stressed the importance of continuing in employment to make sufficient money to live comfortably and expressed no intention of retiring from active involvement in his various business interests (*Choice*, July 1975: 25). In cases where celebrities featured in *Choice* have retired they have usually lost no opportunity to take up alternative employment thus in effect adding a further reinforcement to the reconstructed image of aging as a vigorous, lively and above all enjoyable pathway to self-realization.

Figure 3.4 Choice, October, 1978

Figure 3.5 Choice, March, 1984

Figure 3.6 Choice, April, 1984

THE PROBLEM OF THE MEANING OF OLD AGE

Our reference to the dual imagery of retirement/ageing – the persistence of a more traditional 'anti-fashion' imagery of later life alongside the new consumer-oriented positive imagery – inevitably raises the question of the relevance of the new imagery for the majority of the population in a society characterized by enormous inequalities in income and opportunity (Figure 3.7). In a society which still has to make revolutionary changes in pre-retirement and continuing education, retirement means enforced idleness and for many, the absence of an adequate income to pursue many of the consumer values central to our society. During the early days of the venture *Retirement Choice* was prompted to respond to two published letters from readers with the question: 'Are We "Middle-Class"?' One correspondent wrote that he had 'yet to read a letter or an article describing his plans for retirement and life after retirement from, say, an agricultural labourer, a builder's labourer, factory hand or one of the very large class who on retirement have for income the state pension'. The writer added, 'my finance will not permit me to indulge in some of the hobbies enjoyed by some of your correspondents'. The second correspondent expressed confusion about the aims of the magazine. He felt that people whose only source of income was the old age pension could not afford to buy the journal and added, 'My guess is that your readers are chiefly those who are getting or will get two pensions. I suggest that, therefore, your appeal should be to the middle-class and less often to the old age pensioners who may be eligible for supplementary benefit'. The editor replied that his task was to provide a service of information for readers before and after retirement who were living in all kinds of social circumstance. He was, he said, attempting to steer a course between 'a genteel, mild glossy publication slanted at the well-heeled' and 'a kind of old folks comic cuts, full of bingo and telly, deliberately keyed to the mass market' (*Retirement Choice*, January 1974: 14–15).

Over the intervening years, the number of magazines on retirement planning has increased with a consequent multiplication of the consumer-oriented images of retirement/aging. One significant feature is the emergence of a consensus amongst professional and lay image-makers about the benefits of positive aging and in particular consumer culture lifestyles. Magazines like *Choice* are targeted at the 'young old'; they rarely depict the 'old-old' associations between 'deep old age, terminal illness and death'. The dominant image of the body as a machine which can be serviced and repaired, and the array of products and techniques advertised, cultivate the hope that the period of active life can be extended and controlled into a future where ultimately even death can be mastered (Featherstone and Hepworth, 1982). The aging

44

Figure 3.7 Choice, July, 1993

process is thus represented as endlessly open to construction and reconstruction: it's only a matter of either advances in medicine and/ or social reconstruction.

It is not the purpose of this chapter to pour scorn upon the positive reconstruction of later life; on the contrary the battle against ageism and the encouragement of a fully active later life are essential in a 'greying world' into which politicians on the whole seem positively reluctant to intrude. But we do wish to argue that the dominant consumer-culture images of positive aging have serious shortcomings. As Thomas R. Cole forcibly reminds us, the attack on ageism and attempts to create 'new positive images of old age' have 'yet to confront the de-meaning of age rooted in modern culture's relentless hostility toward decay and dependency' (1992: xxvi). As a consequence there is a 'profound failure of meaning that currently surrounds the end of life' (Cole, 1986: 130) which leaves aging and the 'third age' (the 'young-old') as an extended plateau of active middle age typified in the imagery of positive aging as a period of youthfulness and active consumer lifestyles.

NOTE

This chapter is a substantially revised and updated version of material which was first published as M. Featherstone and M. Hepworth, 1984, 'Changing images of retirement. An analysis of representations of aging in the popular magazine *Retirement Choice*', in D. B. Bromley (ed.) *Gerontology: Social and Behavioural Perspectives*, London: Croom Helm.

REFERENCES

Association of Retired Persons (1993a) *050* Spring.
Association of Retired Persons (1993b) 'Dumping Grandma' *Reporter* 19 (Summer): 2.
Biggs, Simon (1989) *Confronting Ageing*, London: Central Council For Education and Training in Social Work.
Choice (1975) June.
Choice (1975) July.
Choice (1978) October.
Choice (1984) March.
Choice (1984) April.
Choice (1993) July.
Cole, Thomas R. (1986) 'The "enlightened" view of ageing: Victorian morality in a new key', in T. R. Cole and S. A. Gadow (eds) *What Does It Mean To Grow Old? Reflections From The Humanities*, Durham NC: Duke University Press, pp. 115–30.
Cole, Thomas R. (1992) *The Journey of Life: A Cultural History of Ageing in America*, Cambridge: Cambridge University Press.
Coleman, Allin and Chiva, Anthony (1991) *Coping With Change: Focus on Retirement*, London: Health Education Authority.

Coupland, Nikolas, Coupland, Justine and Giles, Howard (1991) *Language, Society and the Elderly: Discourse, Identity and Ageing*, Oxford, Blackwell.

Featherstone, M. (1987) 'Leisure, symbolic power and the life course', in S. Horne, D. Jary and A. Tomlinson (eds) *Sport, Leisure and Social Relations*, Sociological Review Monograph, London: Routledge & Kegan Paul.

Featherstone, Mike (1991) 'Lifestyle and consumer culture', in *Consumer Culture and Postmodernism*, London: Sage.

Featherstone, Mike and Hepworth, Mike (1982) 'Ageing and inequality: consumer culture and the new middle age', in D. Robbins, L. Caldwell, G. Day, K. Jones and H. Rose (eds) *Rethinking Social Inequality*, Aldershot: Gower, pp. 97–126.

Featherstone, Mike and Hepworth, Mike (1993) 'Images of ageing', in J. Bond and P. Coleman (eds) *Ageing in Society: An Introduction to Social Gerontology*, London: Sage, pp. 250–75.

Gubrium, Jaber F. (1986) *Oldtimers and Alzheimer's: The Descriptive Organisation of Senility*, Greenwich, Conn.: JAI Press.

Hepworth, Mike and Featherstone, Mike (1982) *Surviving Middle Age*, Oxford: Basil Blackwell.

Hill, Samuel (1993) *Financial Monitor* Summer.

Jerrome, Dorothy (1992) *Good Company: An Anthropological Study of Old People in Groups*, Edinburgh: Edinburgh University Press.

Kammen, M. (1980) 'Changing perceptions of the life cycle in American thought and culture', *Proceedings of the Massachusetts Historical Society* 91: 35–66.

Lurie, Alison (1981) *The Language of Clothes*, London: Heinemann.

Miller, Leo (1987) 'The professional construction of aging,' *Journal of Gerontological Social Work* 10 (3–4): 141–53.

Ostroff, Jeff (1989) *Successful Marketing To The 50+ Consumer: How To Capture One of The Biggest and Fastest Growing Markets in America*, Englewood Cliffs, NJ: Prentice Hall.

Phillipson, C. and Strang, L. (1983) *The Impact of Pre-Retirement Education*, University of Keele.

Polhemus, Ted and Proctor, Lynn (1978) *Fashion and Anti-Fashion: An Anthropology of Clothing and Adornment*, London: Thames & Hudson.

Pre Retirement Choice (1974) October.

Pre Retirement Choice (1974) November.

Pre Retirement Choice (1974) December.

Pre Retirement Choice (1975) January.

Pre Retirement Choice (1975) February.

Pre Retirement Choice (1975) May.

Retirement Choice (1972) October.

Retirement Choice (1972) November.

Retirement Choice (1972) December.

Retirement Choice (1973) February.

Retirement Choice (1973) October.

Retirement Choice (1973) November.

Retirement Choice (1974) January.

Scrutton, Steve (1990) *Age: The Unrecognised Discrimination*, London: Age Concern.

Tinker, Anthea (1992) *Elderly People in Modern Society*, 3rd edn, London and New York: Longman.

4

THE STATUS AND IMAGE
OF THE ELDERLY IN JAPAN
Understanding the paternalistic ideology
Shuichi Wada

One of the key assumptions of modernization theory with respect to aging is that 'the role and status of the aged varies systematically with the degree of modernization of society and that *modernization tends to decrease the relative status of the aged and to undermine their security within the social system*' (Cowgill, 1972: 13, my emphasis). This global tendency needs to be modified in a pluralistic direction to take into account each society's modernization trajectory, as Kiefer (1990) argues with reference to Japan.

Kiefer (1990) approaches Japanese aging through its cultural and historical contexts by identifying three aspects: age-grading, the Confucianism tradition, and corporate structures. A problem with her approach is that she misses, or does not grasp fully, the ideological changes which occurred in Japan along with its modernization. The focus on the Confucian tradition has proved to be a very popular point of departure in discussion of Japanese aging, but we need to be aware that practically no Japanese, save a few academics, are today at all familiar with Confucianism. The social position of Confucianism in Japan is very different from that of Christianity in the west. I will argue that the current paternalism in Japanese society, which is a legacy of the Confucian tradition, contributes to soften the effects of utilitarian ideology which is often prevalent in modernizing nations. The notion of a paternalism, I will argue, could therefore provide a useful analytical concept, one which is absent in studies such as Kiefer's (1990). Hence my assumption that the Japanese attitude toward aging and the old is a reflection of the paternalistic nature of the society, something which has to be understood with reference to the terms '*okina*' and '*kô*'.[1]

There is often the assumption that modernization has a negative impact on life because of the utilitarian emphasis on the work ethic and efficiency, ideologies which have dominated modernization (Cowgill, 1972; Achenbaum, 1985). The age consciousness which was nurtured

48

at the turn of the century due to the introduction of the modern system of education and welfare strengthened the sense of age stratification (Chudacoff, 1989), resulting in age segregation and 'ageism' (Butler, 1975). Japan's trajectory differs from this modernizing process in Western European and North American societies. Japanese modernization took place over a short period of time and was a centrally-planned change. The Meiji Restoration (1868) was a particularly salient point in the shift from a feudal to an industrial society, as was the enactment of the New Constitution and the legal and institutional reforms which occurred after World War Two.

IMAGES OF JAPANESE AGING

A characteristic and influential portrayal of the status of the elderly in Japan is that of Palmore (1975: 64) who argues that despite the high levels of industrialization and urbanization, 'the Japanese have maintained a high level of respect for their elders and a high level of integration of their elders in the family, work force, and community . . .' and old age is recognized as '. . . a source of prestige and honor'. A good many American gerontologists presented pictures of the Japanese elderly which are very similar to that of Palmore. Skord (1989: 131), for example, argues that 'Japanese attitudes toward aging are firmly rooted in principles of respect, reverence, and deference toward the aged'. Evidence for this tendency, she maintains, is found in the existence of 'Respect for the Aged Day' (*Keirô No Hi*), a national holiday honouring elderly citizens and the relative absence of nursing homes or retirement colonies due to a long-standing presumption that elderly parents will remain in the family home in the care of their adult offspring. The policy of 'Silver' seats, specially reserved for the elderly or infirm on all public transport is further evidence. As is the Japanese philosophy that posits that one is not a master of any art (including business management) until at least middle age (Skord, 1989: 131).

In the 1960s and early 1970s, when Japan attained its high post-war economic growth rate, Japan was seen by American gerontologists as a Utopian society for the elderly in the industrial societies, in which the elderly were still respected and revered and able to live a happy life. As Plath (1972: 133) writes,

> As one of our favored vehicles for wish projection, Japan also carries some of our visions of the golden pastures. We know that it is not Shangri-la, where time's arrow has been stopped, but we would like to believe that it is a land where (unlike our own) custom has equipped men to live their after years in dignity, not indignantly.

49

American scholars attributed this respected status of the Japanese elderly to the Confucian tradition inherited by the Japanese. Confucian philosophy stresses progress and meaningfulness at each stage of the life course:

> At forty I was free from doubts. At fifty I understood the laws of Heaven. At sixty my ear was docile. At seventy I could follow the desire of my heart without transgressing the right.
>
> ('Concerning Government' in *The Analects*).[2]

The assumption here is that identity development and maturation are capable of progressing until death. One of the basic moral codes in Confucianism is filial piety, and Confucianism also stresses that filial piety produces respect for the elderly, as, 'The philosopher Yu said: "He who lives a filial [to parents] and respectful [to the older] life, yet who is disposed to give offence to those above him is rare" (Confucius, 1910: 121, parenthesis added). A popular representation of the social position of the Japanese elderly is consequently, according to the American scholars, that the Confucian ideology has declined with economic growth.

Kiefer argues that even though the elderly in America lost prestige and power after the main social and economic changes of the industrial revolution, in Japan 'the prestige and power of the elderly were maintained at fairly high levels through the industrialization process. Material security, although less than optimum, was about as good as that of other age groups'. Recently, however, the elderly in Japan 'have not shared equally in the great improvement in power that economic affluence has brought to their society'. That is, 'they can be said to suffer from relative power deprivation' (Kiefer, 1990: 193). Plath (1972) mentioned two negative aspects of the life of elderly people in affluent Japan. The first is the high rate of suicide. While the high rate of suicide is not peculiar to the Japanese elderly, he insists, it is important to note that suicide runs contrary to Confucianism. This seems to indicate a weakening of the hold of Confucianism among the Japanese elderly (Plath, 1972: 135–7). The second aspect is *obasute* ('abandoning granny'). This term, which originates in a Japanese folk-tale, is now used to point to the increasing numbers of old people living alone, or in old age homes.

American scholars, then, have emphasized that Japan was formerly a Utopia for the old, but that this ideal state is now being lost in the face of economic growth. We can compare these images with those of a Japanese critic, Sugahara (1988: 66–7), who argues that when we investigate the actual condition of the elderly we find them to be: physically weak and senile; economically poor; of low educational background; dependent on younger generations; passive; living in rural areas; self-employed; tending to be retrospective in life; lonely; homogenous. If we look more closely it is clear that Sugahara's position involves a rejection of the older lifestyle or consciousness as 'premodern', and is based upon an idealization of the independent and active type of old age of American elderly people. It would, therefore, seem that the image of the old in Japan as revered and respected is an over-simplification, something which points to the importance of examining the social and cultural background in greater detail.

PATERNALISTIC NATURE OF JAPANESE SOCIETY

Japan's later entrance in the world capitalist economy forced Japan to trace a quite different modernizing trajectory from the west. A modified patriarchalism continued to be a dominant social idea until after World War Two. Japanese modernization has not given birth to an immanent individualism. Japan is still much more paternalistic compared to West Europe and North America.

That Japanese society has a paternalistic nature seems to be a fundamental assumption in Dore's (1958; 1987; 1990) approach to modern Japan. Dore emphasizes the acceptance of the legitimacy, competence and belief in the good intentions of the person in authority. A belief that stresses concern with the welfare of subordinates, something which he notes cuts less ice in Britain than in Japan because 'It smacks of paternalism which, in an egalitarian Britain, we do not like to be accused of practicing and feel demeaned to be the recipient of' (Dore, 1987: 107).

The paternalistic nature of Japan was also demonstrated by Bennett and Ishino (1972). They emphasize two main features of paternalistic economic organization. First, there is a degree of hierarchy in which the status difference between employer and employee is not purely a matter of instrumental necessity, but contains a cultural or ideological element which suggests that the employer is more than just an employer: he is a 'superior' person in control because of this superiority. Second, the employer is expected to be concerned with the lives of his employees which go beyond the work situation; he is assumed to be *responsible* for his workers and usually their families too (Bennett and Ishino, 1972: 225).

De Vos (1979) argues that the paternalistic structure is a legacy of traditional Japan, and is sustained through adaptions developed from the traditional apprenticeship system. The traditional apprentice training was defined in quasi-familial terms in which the master-apprentice relationship was modelled on the father-child relationship. Although this traditional type of apprenticeship, with its lengthy commitment to a hierarchical structure is now relatively rare, it should be seen

51

as the prototype of Japanese occupational employment and career development.

A further feature of Japanese paternalism is rank order based on seniority in accordance with chronological age. Ruth Benedict (1974: 43) argued that any attempt to understand the Japanese must begin with their version of what it means to 'take one's proper station' (*kakukaku sono tokoro o u*). For her 'Japan's confidence in hierarchy is basic in her whole notion of man's relation to his fellow man and of man's relation to the State' (Benedict, 1974: 43). Lebra (1976) discusses more fully this strong consciousness of hierarchical status and role by relating them to the Japanese traditional sense of hierarchical order, *bun*. This form of status orientation is now called *joretsu ishiki* in Japanese and means sensitivity to rank order. Most generally, when two persons talk without considering one another's rank order, like position in company, the rule of conversation governing usage of polite expression in the Japanese language (*keigo*) which has to be adopted is age difference: the younger is required to use more polite expressions. This is also evident when we examine the force of age in the specific case of promotion in a Japanese company.

Jones (1991), in a summary of her survey of British executives working in Japanese companies, mentions that age and length of service are the key factors in gaining promotion and recognition in Japan, especially in the most conservative companies, a policy which often equates status with age. Jones recorded the complaints by young British employees that they must be considerably older and more experienced to reach a high position in a Japanese company. According to European management practices, a highly-talented and successful person can be appointed to the main board of a group, particularly in the financial sector, at the age of about 35; and it would not be unusual for a director of a subsidiary board to be only in his late twenties or early thirties.

While it can be argued that seniority is one of the foundations supporting the hierarchical structure of organizations in any industrial society, in Japan seniority is excessively valued. Abegglen and Stalk remark that 'Japan remains, in important respects, an age-graded society, and the concept of compensation and position being determined by age is deemed appropriate' (Abegglen and Stalk, 1987: 203). When an employee is hired directly from school, as is very common in Japan, 'age and length of service become parallel, and seniority becomes an appropriate basis for reward' (ibid.). Promotion is also a function of age in the sense that promotion will rarely if ever take place until adequate seniority has been attained. It is undeniable that the Japanese consciousness of age-grading is related to the Japanese sense of authority.

How is this Japanese linkage of seniority with age legitimated? It is a basic assumption of sociological theory that a stable authority relation needs legitimization, as it is insufficient to assume that Japanese people are blindly obedient to authority or ideological power. The social apparatuses will be considered next, and cultural aspects in a later section. As has been indicated, Japan retains a strong paternalistic impulse, a style which was formed in the process of modernization through the powerful ideology of *kô*, or filial piety.

Kô IDEOLOGY AND THE JAPANESE HIERARCHY

If we consider the differences between the European and American type of modernization and Asian modernization, it is clear that Asian countries were more or less forced to modernize in an intensively planned way which involved drastic social changes (Pye, 1985). In the Japanese case European and American ideas, which flooded into Japan after the opening up of the society, were intermingled undigested in a unique way with the Japanese traditional notions. The Meiji bureaucrats constantly faced the possibility of social disorganization in the process of modernization soon after the Meiji Restoration in 1868, but the historical turning point was the institution of the Meiji Constitution in 1889 and the establishment of the legal and the parliamentary systems, after which the Meiji government maintained stable power as an absolutist government. At this time the government also began to institutionalize a system of moral training to educate the Japanese. The core of the moral ideology was family, the traditional *ie* system of the patriarchal samurai household.

The Meiji government was concerned with putting the Japanese family system under the moral and legislative control of the state for the purpose of controlling individual Japanese through the traditional family ideology. The traditional family system's boundary is rather diffuse because its nature is strongly associational, in the sense that the members' identification is primarily based on assuming roles. It was accordingly not difficult to generalize the ideologies of status distribution and role performance in the family to that in a community, or even in the country as a whole. The Meiji government declared through the Civil Codes that the patriarchal family system, a legacy from the feudal samurai culture, was the officially legitimized type of family, and it ideologically strengthened patriarchy by giving force of law to Confucian family ethics.

By using the feudalistic dogmas of *on* (a favour) and *ongaeshi* (redeeming the favour), and disseminating the patriarchal ideology, above all to students at primary schools, the Meiji government aimed to make people loyal to the absolutist power.[3] The Imperial Prescript on Education was significant here as the feudalistic patriarchal ideology embodied in the notion of *kô* (filial piety) and the family state ideology were strictly administered through textbooks on moral training whose content was censored by the Ministry of Education. These moral ideologies were also institutionalized in the laws, including the Meiji Civil Codes established in 1898, which determined 'the family institution' based on the strong power of household head (Kawashima, 1957: 4–5).

In his discussion of paternalism in Victorian England, Roberts (1979: 2) points out the four basic assumptions held by almost all Victorian paternalists about society: that society should be authoritarian, hierarchic, organic, and pluralistic. Authoritarianism derives from the father: fathers command and exact obedience. The typical paternalist never doubted the sacred nature of paternal authority. The paternalist never doubted that God had created a hierarchical society and that such a hierarchical society was necessary and beneficial, and at the heart of a paternalist's hierarchical outlook is a strong sense of the value of dependency, a sense that could not exist without those who are dependent having an unquestioned respect for their betters. Those who held a paternalistic outlook believed in the body politic, one in which every part had an appointed and harmonious place. They believed that each individual had his function, his place, his protectors, his duties, his reciprocal obligations, and his strong ties of dependency. According to Roberts, a pluralistic outlook distinguishes English paternalism from the Continental variety. In England, personal intercourse with one's dependents was believed to lead to the right management, and each authority which was derived from his property had his own ideas of paternalism (Roberts, 1979: 2–4).

While there are parallels between Victorian English paternalism and that developed in Japan with the *kô* ideology, the latter was in contrast to English paternalism, organized by the national government and enforced on the people in an absolutist top-down way. Japanese patriarchalism extolled the family ideology and the suppression of the individual self. The concept of *kô* (Chinese *hsiao*), the central idea in classic Confucianism meaning filial piety, was further expanded in the Japanese Confucianism to cover absolute loyalty to the emperor, political authority, business authority, landlord, teacher, and so forth.

If we examine the moral contents in the textbooks utilized for the ethical training at the primary school level in the late 1890s, it should be borne in mind that all textbooks for primary education were censored by the Ministry of Education. In the textbook, heading the list of basic moral codes is the axiom, 'Never forget *on*!', which shows how significant the code of *on* was. This philosophy of *on* is repeated again and again in other parts of the textbook. According to the *kô* ideology, a child is assumed to feel and accept absolutely the *on* of his parents, because his parents gave birth to him and raised him. This parents' *on* should be reciprocated by the child according to the *kô* ideology. First, a child should be respectful to parents and obey and revere parents. The position of father as a household head was assumed to be sacred and inviolable, and his sayings were accordingly unquestionable. Second, the child was obliged to move up in society to make the name of his family glorious and praiseworthy. Third, a child takes care of parents in every respect, especially after they have grown older. Fourth, a child is never allowed to terminate the family lineage, and he is thus obliged to give birth to his own child to keep the lineage alive and to keep worshipping his ancestors in the rituals.

This family ideology was extended to include absolute obedience to the Emperor and the Imperial government. This absolute loyalty to the state, legitimized by the *kô* ideology, is expressed in the Emperor's Prescript on Education (1890). As Hozumi (1914) argues, in Japan – and in East Asian societies which also followed the Confucian tradition – the reverence for the old is an ideological extension of '*kô-tei*' (filial piety and brotherly affection). The respect of father and affection to elder brother are also applied to the old. The attitude toward the old should be the same as toward the father and elder brother.

This family ideology was the underpinning of the social order in Imperialist Japan. This ideology, which was legitimized under the name of Emperor, was beyond criticism. Many institutions and organizations were established in accordance with this quasi-family ideology such as schools, business corporations, the armed forces, government organ-izations, etc. In this ideology the elderly were not only respected or revered according to the moral codes, but they were assigned an important social role in family, organization, and community: the key role of mentor. In the traditional apprenticeship system it was the masters who were elderly, who were the mentors. Thus, 'this attitude of mentorship on the part of older men toward younger workers continues even in industrial units' (de Vos, 1979: 214).

This patriarchal ideology and social order which were supported by the Imperialist legal system, the core of which was the Meiji Constitu-tion and the Old Civil Codes, was legally disestablished by the en-actment of the New Constitution and the New Civil Codes following the move towards formal democratization with the defeat of Japan in World War Two. According to Kleining (1984) patriarchalism was transformed into paternalism through the influence of liberal ideology. In contrast to the west, Japan has never developed its own ideology of liberalism, but the democratic changes introduced by the occupation bureaucrats contributed to modify the traditional patriarchalism towards the dir-ection of the west. The change was, however, so rapid and drastic, that far from being a gradual social reform, the traditional notions have remained embedded within the Japanese character structure.

The *on* and *kô* ideology is kept alive, in modified form in the concepts of benevolence or empathy (*onjo* or *omoiyari*) and dependency (*amae*). This ideology, which lacks the coercive power of the patriarchy, is based on the Japanese sense of rank order. As Lebra (1976: 51) remarks 'The "child"-role player can expect to depend upon the "parent"-role player for security and protection by appealing to the latter's *oyagokoro* ("parental sentiment"), which is characterized as warm, benevolent, and nurturing'. The image of the father, and thus the image of the old, was therefore deprived of its coercive aspect as the family head in patriarchy. This is the origin of the image of the Japanese old as loved and respected.

THE *OKINA* IMAGE AND JAPANESE BENEVOLENCE

Since aging usually entails bodily decline and illnesses such as senility which make people more weak and dependent, we need to consider this more negative image of aging. This sense of aversion is also found in the classic literature of Japan (Hozumi, 1914: 500). Yet alongside the image of frailty and weakness we have in many cultures positive images of aging in which the old were seen as 'the authoritative voice of God', as possessing wisdom, solemnity, serenity, experience, and so forth. A powerful image of the sacred is that of old people, in particular the old man.

While more than forty variants of the motif of the discarding of old people can be found in Japanese folk-tales (Dorson, 1975: 243), Yanagita interprets this type of the Japanese 'abandoning granny' folk-tale as a device to persuade children of the importance of an old man's wisdom (Yanagita, 1970). In a study of an earlier period in Japanese history, Miyata (1990: 48–9) remarks that the Japanese people pictured the old as 'playing with pleasure and having fun like children'. The popular saying which emphasized the 'second childhood' of the elderly was hence unlike that of the west, a positive image.

With regard to the old's wisdom and spiritual maturity, I think that the image of *okina* ('old man') has played an important and central function in sustaining this positive image of old age. This image emphasizes the process of maturation of the spirit and mental outlook towards the divine. *Okina*, which literally means old man, also has a further meaning:

> The usage of the word *okina* [old person] includes a variety of images of '*okina*' formed in the world of performing arts in earlier times. The *okina* in this usage is not merely an old man. It is the

concept which was derived by superimposing an image of *okina* on the image of the senior in artistic domains. The traditional meanings of *okina* and *omina* (old woman) indicate the elevation of older persons in to the highest position. . . . The traditional meaning of the words *okina* and *omina* were sustained by a seniority system and indicated an elevated position in social organization.

(Origuchi, 1975: 371–2, my translation)

Yamaori (1984: 124–86), reviewing documents written in the middle and early modern periods, identified a religious function of the image of *okina* which acted as a bridge between this secular world and the divine realm. This new image of *okina* which became influential during the ninth to the fourteenth centuries, emphasized that old people were able to mediate between gods and humans. Hence we can find two different descriptions of *okina*: a mythological description which classifies *okina* next to the gods, and an ethnographical description which recognized *okina* as human being. Yamaori observes that *okina*'s abilities to shift positions between the figures of the god and the old man, and the capacity to work miracles were associated with the concept of 'maturity through aging'. The image of *okina* presents an ideal image of the old which is assumed to exhibit a sort of divine maturity in a variety of realms: personality, mental outlook, skills, and so forth. It is this concept of maturity which adds legitimacy to the Japanese sense of seniority.

CONCLUSION

The images of the old in any society, either traditional or industrial, have both positive and negative aspects. We could hypothesize that while the negative aspect may derive from people's aesthetic sensibilities or utilitarian calculation, the positive aspect seems to have more to do with people's moral and/or religious cosmology, conscious or unconscious. I have tried to trace the elements of the moral cosmology, the image of *okina* in the Japanese religious folklore and the image of the old in the traditional *kô* ideology, the national ideology of the process of modernization, back to Japanese social and cultural history.

The religious image of *okina*, the symbol of an old person's wisdom and mental and spiritual maturity, lies deeply embedded in the Japanese unconsciousness, and may well exercise a similar function to the Jungian archetype of the 'wise old man'. This positive image of the Japanese old was inculcated by the post-1868 Japanese governments through moral training at primary school. The prototype of images of the old which emerged in the process is the image of parents, and it was generalized and expanded to be applicable to any realm in Japanese society.

Finally, I would like to point to the qualitative shift in this ideology after World War Two, a change which reduced the power of the patriarchal head of household and resulted in the birth of paternalism in Japan. The particular unique quality of Japanese paternalism cannot be understood without reference to the Japanese sense of seniority, and this Japanese sense of seniority is tightly bound up to Japanese images of aging and the elderly.

NOTES

This paper is based on Shuichi Wada's *Images of Aging in Japan: Paternalism and the Old* (A Report of a Study Supported by a Grant In Aid for Scientific Research of the Ministry of Education, Science and Culture in 1990–1992). It is acknowledged with gratitude that the study was made possible by a grant from the Japanese Ministry of Education, as well as the accumulated results of a series of studies supported by the Specific Subject Fund of Waseda University.

1 My identification of the image of *okina* with Jung's (1969) archetype draws a good deal on the discussion of Yamaori (1984: 188–229).
2 This citation is from William E. Soothill's translation (*The Analects of Confucius*, 1910: 149–50). This part of *The Analects* is so popular among the Japanese that almost every Japanese who had some high school education can recite all, or some, of it.
3 *On* is a relational concept combining a benefit or benevolence given with a debt or obligation thus incurred. What makes this word difficult for foreigners to comprehend is that it is not a discrete object but is imbedded in the social relationship between the donor and receiver of a benefit. From the donor's point of view, *on* refers to a social credit, while from the receiver's point of view, it means a social debt. An *on* relationship, once generated by giving and receiving a benefit, compels the receiver-debtor to repay *on* in order to restore balance. *Ongaeshi* means repayment of *on*, and *onjin* means benefactor, both of which are among the most commonly used Japanese vocabulary.

(Lebra, 1976: 91).

REFERENCES

Abegglen, James C. and Stalk, George, Jr (1987) [1985] *Kaisha: The Japanese Corporation*, Tokyo: Charles E. Tuttle (first published by Basic Books).
Achenbaum, W. Andrew (1985) 'Societal perceptions of aging and the aged', in Robert H. Binstock and Ethel Shanas (eds) *Handbook of Aging and the Social Science*: 2nd edn, New York: Van Nostrand Reinhold Co., pp. 129–70.
Benedict, Ruth (1974) [1946] *The Chrysanthemum and the Sword: Patterns of Japanese Culture*, New York: New American Library.
Bennett, John W. and Iwao Ishino (1972) [1963] *Paternalism in the Japanese Economy: Anthropological Studies of Oybun-Kobun Patterns*, Westport, Connecticut: Greenwood Press (first published by the University of Minnesota Press).

Butler, Robert N. (1975) *Why Survive?: Being Old in America*, New York: Harper & Row.

Chudacoff, Howard P. (1989) *How Old Are You?: Age Consciousness in American Culture*, Princeton, NJ: Princeton University Press.

Confucius (1910) *The Analects of Confucius* (translated by William E. Soothill), published by the author.

Cowgill, Donald (1972) 'A theory of aging in cross-cultural perspective', in Donald Cowgill and Lowell D. Holmes (eds) *Aging and Modernization*, New York: Appleton-Century-Crofts.

de Vos, George A. (1979) [1975] 'Apprenticeship and paternalism', in Ezra F. Vogel (ed.) *Modern Japanese Organization and Decision-Making*, Tokyo: Charles Tuttle, pp. 210–27. (First published by University of California Press).

Dore, Ronald (1958) *City Life in Japan: A Study of a Tokyo Ward*, London: Routledge & Kegan Paul.

Dore, Ronald (1987) *Taking Japan Seriously: A Confucian Perspective on Leading Economic Issues*, London: The Athlone Press.

Dore, Ronald (1990) [1973] *British Factory–Japanese Factory: The Origins of National Diversity in Industrial Relations*, Berkeley and Los Angeles: University of California Press.

Dorson, Richard M. (1975) *Folktales: Told Around the World*, Chicago and London: University of Chicago Press.

Hozumi, Nobushige (1914) *Inkyo-Ron (A Study of Retirement)*, Tokyo: Yûhikaku.

Jones, Stephanie (1991) *Working For the Japanese*, London: Macmillan.

Jung, C. G. (1969) 'Archetypes of the collective unconscious' in *The Collected Works of C. G. Jung*, 2nd edn, volume 9, part I, Princeton, NJ: Princeton University Press.

Kawashima, Takeyoshi (1957) *Ideorogî toshiteno Kazoku-seido (The Family Ideology and Institution)*, Tokyo: Iwanamishoten.

Kiefer, Christie W. (1990) 'The elderly in modern Japan: elite, victims, or plural players?', in Jay Sokolovsky (ed.) *The Cultural Context of Aging: World Wide Perspective*, New York: Bergin & Gavey.

Kleining, John (1984) *Paternalism*, Totowa, New Jersey: Rowman & Allanheld.

Lebra, Takie Sugiyama (1976) *Japanese Patterns of Behavior*, Honolulu: University of Hawaii Press.

Miyata, Noboru (1990) 'Bunkaron-teki ni Miru Rôjin no Yôjika' ('A cultural discussion on recurrence of the old to the infantile') *Itto (It)* 30: 48–51.

Origuchi, Shinobu (1975) 'Okina no Hassei' ('Birth of a traditional image of old people'), in *Origuchi Shinobu Zenshu*, Dai-2 kan (*Collected Papers of Origuchi Shinobu*, vol.2) Tokyo: Chûôkôronsha: 371–415.

Palmore, Erdman (1975) 'What can the USA learn from Japan about aging?', *The Gerontologist* 15: 64–7.

Plath, David (1972) 'Japan: the after years', in Donald O. Cowgill and Lowell D. Holmes (eds) *Aging and Modernization*, New York: Appleton–Century–Crofts, pp. 133–55.

Pye, Lucian W. (1985) *Asian Power and Politics: The Cultural Dimensions of Authority*, Cambridge, Mass.: The Belkan Press of Harvard University Press.

Roberts, David (1979) *Paternalism in Early Victorian England*, New Brunswick, NJ: Rutgers University Press.

Skord, Virginia (1989) 'Withered blossoms', in Prisca von Dorotka Bagnell and Patricia Spencer Soper (eds) *Perceptions of Aging in Literature: A Cross-Cultural Study*, New York: Greenwood Press, pp. 131–44.

Sugahara, Mariko (1988) 'Jiritsushi, Rentaishi, Tasukeaeru Nyû Shirubâ',

('Toward a new type of the old who has an independent life through coordination and mutual help'), *Itto* (*It*) 28: 66–70.

Yamaori, Tetsuo (1984) *Kami Kara Okina E* (*A Folklore of God and Okina*), Tokyo: Seidosha.

Yanagita Kunio (1945) *Mura to Gakudô* (*Village and Pupil*), Tokyo: Asahi-Shinbûnsha, cited in *Collected Papers of Yanagita Kunio*, (1970) Tokyo: Chikumashobo.

5

IMAGINING THE LIFE-SPAN
From premodern miracles to postmodern fantasies

Stephen Katz

As I write this paper, Dr Deepak Chopra's *Ageless Body, Timeless Mind: The Quantum Alternative to Growing Old* (1993) is the hottest selling commodity in advice literature (*Globe and Mail*, Toronto, 17 August 1993). Blending bits of historical wisdom on keeping old age at bay with postmodern self-discipline on keeping the body 'ageless', this book, like so many published today on living the long life, appeals to our cultural preoccupation with challenging the limits of the human life-span. The human life-span, whatever duration it assumes, is a peculiar kind of fact because it represents a possibility that is rarely achieved. Unlike life expectancy, which is a statistical figure based on the average person's length of life, the life-span is 'the extreme limit of human longevity', that is, the longevity of the longest living individuals (Gruman, 1966: 7). Hence, the life-span embodies the boundaries of human existence, and, in our culture, these boundaries are set by the scientific community at 110 years. However, if one considers the life-span to be more than an indisputable biological fact, and examines it as a discursive or imagined production, symbolic of a culture's beliefs about living and aging, then one can also glimpse something of the larger social and ideological orders from which such beliefs derive their significance. In other words, the life-span provides an intellectual key to how general discourses of existence are organized, whether such discourses are conceived in biological, philosophical, political, theological or consumerist terms.

In this paper, I am interested in the human life-span, as it has been historically imagined in medical-hygiene literature and culturally constituted in postmodern culture. Historical literature is a valuable source of insight for understanding not only the discursive dimensions of the past, but also the postmodern life course today, where the idealization of long life has become such a lucrative component of consumer culture. In their exhaustive research studies, notable gerontological historians, such as W. Andrew Achenbaum, Thomas Cole, Carole Haber and David Troyansky, have transformed the dusty passages of historical treatises into a vibrant and critical dimension of contemporary gerontological scholarship.[1] Their work has focused on aging and old age in their time, as relational, socially-constructed phenomena that mediate the cultural production of knowledges, images and bodies. This paper contributes to this growing body of research by also considering how images of timelessness in the human life-span reflect cultural priorities around bodily life. Since the Renaissance, the possibility of a timeless living was pursued with scientific rigour and popular fascination. In the nineteenth century, medical, demographic and insurantial investigations proved the life-span to be fixed, thus disbanding premodern images of excessive longevity as fanciful.

In postmodern culture, the prospect of an endless life has been revived through consumer images of perpetual youth and a blurring of traditional life course boundaries (Featherstone and Hepworth, 1991). Bauman (1992) says of the 'postmodern strategy of survival', compared to 'traditional ways of dabbling with timelessness', that,

> instead of trying (in vain) to colonize the future, it dissolves it in the present. It does not allow the finality of time to worry the living . . . by slicing time (all of it, exhaustively, without residue) into short-lived, evanescent episodes. It rehearses mortality, so to speak, by practicing it day by day.
>
> (Bauman, 1992: 29)

LONGEVITY AS SCIENTIFIC INQUIRY: PREMODERN TO MODERN FORMULATIONS

Popular literature on the history of the body and old age is often laced with romantic and positivist tendencies that diminish the historical complexity and contingency of the past. Thus premodern historical writings on the life-span are cast as pre-scientific and pre-gerontological, mired in the superstition, magic and ignorance which the laboratory 'breakthroughs' of modern science eventually overcame. However, if we consider 'facts' in a different way, one less judged from the presentistic viewpoints of twentieth-century science, then, as Lorraine Daston comments, there is a strong relationship between 'facts', 'evidence' *and* 'miracles' (1991). She claims that during the Enlightenment, preternatural phenomena, such as monstrous births or prodigies, lost their status as religious signs and became increasingly naturalized. Furthermore, she says of these phenomena:

> Long marginal to scholastic natural philosophy, and now stripped of their religious significance, they had become the first scientific

facts. The very traits that had previously unfitted them for use in natural philosophy, and which had then disqualified them from use in theology, made this new role possible.

(Daston, 1991: 109)

In other words, the science of the Enlightenment challenged the traditional division of the natural and preternatural, assuming that the latter should be investigated as extensions of the former. Rather than separating the marvels, anomalies and oddities from scientific inquiry, scientists from Francis Bacon to Charles Darwin would insist that by studying them more directly one could truly learn about nature. Similarly, premodern writers on aging imagined that the lives of centenarians and cases of excessive longevity, however marvellous, were facts that illustrated the rationality of human existence, and the contours of the human life-span. This partially explains the 'bizarre' coupling in the same texts of scientific observations with fantastical beliefs in the longevity of life (Troyansky, 1989: 113).

How then, during and after the Renaissance, did individual cases of excessive longevity become interpreted as 'facts' by writers on medicine and hygiene? In turn, how did these facts reflect the historical construction of a humanist, rational outlook on human nature? By excessive longevity I am referring to persons who supposedly lived between 100 and 200 years. The works of Luigi Cornaro (supposedly 1484–1566) and Francis Bacon (1561–1626) are cited in the historical literature as exemplary cases of late Renaissance reformulations of the human life-span.[2] Cornaro, a sixteenth-century Venetian nobleman, first published his treatise, *How to Live One Hundred Years and Avoid Disease* (one of its many translated titles), in Padua in 1558. He went on to write revised editions as he supposedly progressed past the centenarian mark, and remained healthy until his death in 1588 at the presumed age of 102 years, although other reports claim that he only lived to be 96 years (Minois, 1989: 271). It is more likely that Cornaro falsified his date of birth in order to claim to be a centenarian (Lind, 1988: 5). However, his actual age is not as relevant as his imagined one, which became a fact, and a foundational aspect of the literature in the following centuries. Cornaro became ill between the ages of 35 and 40. Physicians told him that unless he lived 'a sober and orderly' life, he would soon die (Cornaro, 1935: 33). He simplified and reduced his diet, exercised and slept regularly and made sure to enjoy his gardens and artistic activities. At the age of 83 he wrote,

the life which I live at this age, is not a dead, dumpish, and sowre life; but cheerful, lively and pleasant. . . . Yet I am sure, that my end is farre from me: for I know (setting casualities aside) I shall

63

not die but by a pure resolution: because that by the regularitie of my life I have shut out death all other ways.

(Cornaro, 1935: 50)

Cornaro's text was widely translated, distributed and quoted through-out Europe (Gruman, 1966: 71; Troyansky, 1989: 79,111) and America (Cole, 1992: 147). In England it went through fifty editions (Gruman, 1966: 71). His treatise was not unique in that its focus on the means for prolonging life typified a general preoccupation of Renaissance writers. However, Cornaro's popularity in medical literature was a consequence of his combining a fabulously detailed confessional on self-discipline with a practical demonstration of Galen's principles of moderation and balance of the body's humours.[3] Indeed, Cornaro can be considered one of the earliest proponents of an Enlightenment approach to aging because he focused on the miraculous lives of centenarians, his own life in this case, as *evidence* for a scientific approach to old age. While Freeman may exaggerate that 'Luigi Cornaro, exemplary of his age, wrote a little book and changed his world' (1965: 16), Cornaro did inaugurate a literary tradition that inspired writers up until the early twentieth century to create similarly optimistic longevity models of their own.

Francis Bacon's treatise, *The Historie of Life and Death* (1977) [1638],[4] is one of the most recognized attempts at bringing a scientific emphasis to the human life-span and life expectancy. Bacon, while opposing the traditional theory of the humours (Minois, 1989: 274), stressed the related Galenic idea that dryness is a primary characteristic of aging:[5]

Age is a great but slow dryer; for all naturall bodies not rotting or putrefying, are dryed by Age, being the measure of time, and the effect of the in-bred spirit of bodies, sucking out bodies moysture there by decaying, and of the outward ayre, multiplying above the inward spirits, and moysture of the body, and so destroying them.

(Bacon, 1977 [1638]: 27–8)

As for life expectancy, Bacon explains that people lived longer in Biblical times and, since the flood of Noah, life-spans have contracted to an outside limit of one hundred years (ibid.: 74). Bacon recommends the use of life-prolonging medicines such as betel-nut, poppy-juice, tobacco and other stimulants that thicken the blood and strengthen the spirit. 'Venery' or sex is also useful for stirring up the spirits and causing 'heat'. Finally, advantageous emotional states are joy, sorrow, grief and compassion since fear, anger and envy shorten life. Perhaps Bacon offers very little beyond traditional ideas about health and old age. However, the importance of his work is that it repositioned longevity as evidence of the systematicity of human nature. Furthermore, Bacon's prestige as a scientist added legitimacy to the growing literature on prolonging the life-span (Gruman, 1966: 81; Boyle and Morriss, 1987: 99).

In the spirit of Cornaro and Bacon, writers from the seventeenth to the early nineteenth centuries continued to explore the mysteries of longevity. Their narratives on the human life-span combined neo-Galenic practicalities and Enlightenment optimism with a widening focus on evidence. For example, Dr John Smith, in his *The Portrait of Old Age* (1752) [1666], follows tradition and makes reference to the Galenic processes of coldness and dryness that characterize life in old age, along with fear, which is 'the most notorious trouble of the mind' (ibid.: 135). However, this text attempts to integrate traditional notions of aging with those of medicine, itself recently inspired by William Harvey's discovery of the circulation of blood. In fact Smith provides an allegorical interpretation of the twelfth chapter of Ecclesiastes in terms of its foretelling the circulation of blood (Livesley, 1975: 15). In so doing, he states that while 'the lives of the Patriarchs before the flood were extended to almost a thousand years', after the flood 'God abbreviates the course of man's life, and seems precisely to set it at one hundred and twenty years' (Smith, 1752 [1666]: 5). And, even at this 'precise' old age, Smith asks 'Is there not something in man . . . altogether independent of the body? and perfectly free from the frailties of age?' (ibid.: 25). In other words, is there not a natural state of grace beyond corporeality where 'man' may flourish in old age?

For Smith as with Bacon, the assertion that the human life-span was at least one hundred years was an important element in their theoretical models. Further evidence was to come by way of a series of miraculous cases, the most popular of which was the Englishman Thomas Parr. Parr died at the reputed age of 152 in 1635. Apparently he married twice; at the age of 80 and again at the age of 120 (Gould and Pyle, 1898: 373). His autopsy was performed and given scientific credibility by William Harvey (Haber, 1983: 54), who claimed of Parr that his death was the result of an overly rich life in his latter days at Court in London. Parr's case, like Cornaro's, was important enough to warrant mention in medical books for almost three centuries. There were many other popular reports as well. Dr James Keill of Northampton, England, reported in 1706 that John Boyles, a button-maker, was believed to have died at the age of 130 years (ibid.: 59). James Easton, in *Human Longevity* (1799), collected the names of 1,712 centenarians that lived from AD 66 to 1799, offering little in the way of substantiation. These were the kinds of marvellous facts that bolstered the Enlightenment's optimistic claim that the capabilities of the human body revealed the munificence of the natural order and the mysteries of the life force.[6]

In the early nineteenth century, two texts of importance cited in the literature are, *The Code of Health and Longevity* (1807) by Sir John Sinclair, and *An Essay on the Disorders of Old Age* (1817) by Sir Anthony Carlisle. The investigations of Sinclair and Carlisle follow the same discursive track laid out in the texts on old age in the previous century; the familiar list of remarkable cases of human longevity, focusing on Thomas Parr along with detailed proposals for dietary, exercise and behavioural regimes that would ensure long life. However, a marked difference is their insistence on more medical intervention in the study of aging. Sinclair complains of a lack of post-mortem evidence, 'to ground any positive opinion regarding the effects of old age, and the causes of death of old men'. (Sinclair, 1807: 62). He admits that some of his information has been researched from hospital and workhouse reports (ibid.: 39). Surgeon and anatomist Carlisle, writing his treatise for the Royal College of Surgeons in London, also advocates a more important role for medicine:

> The age of Sixty may, in general, be fixed upon as the commencement of senility. About that period it commonly happens, that some signs of bodily infirmity begin to appear, and the skilful [sic] medical observer may then be frequently able to detect the first serious aberrations from health.
>
> (Carlisle, 1817: 13)

The texts of Carlisle and Sinclair signal a growing trend in the nineteenth century which was to construct old age as a clinical problem, one for which the centuries' old tales of Parr and others would play a dwindling role as evidence.[7]

By the mid-nineteenth century, the study of old age and the aging process had become increasingly distinct from traditional ideas about the life-span. Modern medicine had reconstructed the body in terms of pathological anatomy, displacing degenerative processes to micro-levels of tissues and cells, and gradually separating old age as a special part of the life course, one marked by systematic signs of senescence (Cole, 1992: Ch.9; Haber, 1983, 1986; Kirk, 1992). Von Kondratowitz reports in his study of the medicalization of old age (1991) that as the nineteenth century progressed there were fewer references in mortality statistics to death 'due to old age' and more references to death due to specific illnesses in old age (ibid.: 154). The concept of death from old age as the obstacle to be overcome was essential to Enlightenment longevity arguments. Death as a consequence of specific diseases in and of old age signals very different kinds of epistemological inquiries, therapeutic systems and concepts of the aged subject.

Thus, while longevity literature was still popular in the nineteenth and early twentieth centuries, there were important differences in approach. For example, Thomas Bailey's *Records of Longevity* (1857) introduces a skepticism about the marvellous 'facts' of the past. His work consists of a fabulous list of over 300 pages which rank in alphabetical order cases of persons in England and Wales who lived to be between 100 and 185 years, with obituary-like descriptions of each case. However, departing from the earlier literature Bailey admits that, 'It is true, that many of these alleged facts are deficient in that strict verification which would enable a man to speak positively as to the truth of the statements '(ibid.: 4). The Austrian doctor Arnold Lorand's *Old Age Deferred* (1912) represents another departure. While he too quotes the cases of Thomas Parr (ibid.: 60) and Henry Jenkins (ibid.: 81), who apparently lived to be 169, Lorand's concern is with heredity and environment, ideas relatively foreign to the Enlightenment's principle of the life-span as a symbolic marker of the laws of nature. Elie Metchnikoff, who coined the term 'gerontology', writes in his *The Prolongation of Life: Optimistic Studies* (1907), that 'Centenarians are really not rare' (ibid.: 86). He concludes that, 'human beings may reach the age of 150, but such cases are certainly extremely rare, and are not known from the records of the last two centuries' (ibid.: 88). Again, the secret to longevity is heredity, a modern scientific issue. Just as the glands were Lorand's key to long life, for Metchnikoff it was the intestines.

The most salient expression of the modern perspective on longevity is William J. Thoms's book, *Human Longevity: Its Facts and Its Fictions* (1873).[8] Thoms was the deputy librarian for the House of Lords. His investigation questions the sensationalizing of and lack of evidence for excessive cases of longevity.

> The duration of human life has hitherto been treated almost exclusively by Naturalists and Physiologists – men eminently qualified by their professional attainments to do full justice to the subject, so far as relates to the scientific conclusions to be deduced from the facts before them. They have, however, taken as facts what are really, in the majority of cases, mere assertions, and, by arguing from false premises, have arrived at very erroneous and unjustifiable conclusions.
>
> (Thoms, 1873: vii)

Thoms settles accounts with the past by delineating the common sources of evidence – baptismal certificates, tombstone inscriptions and personal recollections – and describes the inaccuracies that can taint them. He says, 'it is surely no unreasonable law to lay down that certificates of baptism, unsupported by corroborative testimony, cannot be received as evidence of longevity' (ibid.: 37). Sometimes more than one child can have the same name, or the father and son can have the same name. An inquirer needs to check the evidence more thoroughly, such as dates of public or armed forces registrations, employment records, place and time of marriage and numbers of children (ibid.: 40).

In the remainder of the book, Thoms takes on a variety of cases of extreme longevity to prove his points about misleading evidence. In the end, he disproves most of the famous cases including those of Thomas Parr and Henry Jenkins. The evidence, or the new concept of evidence, simply doesn't support the apocryphal stories of their lives. Of Parr's story Thoms concludes,

> In the absence of a single scrap of information in support of any one of the minute particulars recorded of the 'old, old man', it seems impossible to arrive at any other conclusion than the particulars in question have no other foundation than idle gossip.
>
> (Thoms, 1873: 92)

After refuting Jenkins's case, Thoms advises that, 'I hope the time is not far distant when the reputed age of Henry Jenkins will no longer interfere with scientific inquiry into the average duration of Human Life' (ibid: 84).

Thoms's work was not met everywhere with sympathy, especially since Jenkins had been honoured with a monument in Yorkshire and Parr had been interred in Westminster Abbey (Gruman, 1966: 74). Nevertheless, his investigations destroyed the idea that an individual could conserve vital powers and extend life beyond the normal range of statistical and medical probabilities. In so doing, Thoms contributed to a medical fixing of the human life-span that would be supported in other bureaucratic domains such as life insurance[9] and pension and retirement structures. Previous assumptions had been that a person could live to about 200 years given the right physical, moral and environmental conditions. One can hardly question that a life-span of eighty or ninety years, implied by Thoms, is obviously more realistic than one of 200 years. However, Thoms's work had a more important impact: it signalled the shift in concept from the human life-span as a philosophical-medical fact, with miraculous possibilities, to a clinical-biological certainty. As such, the modern concept of the life-span conferred to the aged body a fixed period of time. This fixing corresponded to the growing cultural and governmental differentiation of old age in the late nineteenth and early twentieth centuries.

The modern period produced a dual concept of the life-span. On the one hand, excessive longevity was still possible according to popular hygiene literature, which became gradually separate from the medical framework.[10] On the other hand, the life-span was a scientific, demographic fact that operated within prescribed statistical limits. This fact was primarily established by Belgian statistician, Adolphe Quetelet, in

A Treatise on Man and the Development of his Faculties (1968) [1842]. Quetelet's statistical calculations on the norms, curves and variations of the 'average man' numerically verified that the 'biblical count of threescore and ten closely reflected the maximum length of human existence' (Haber 1983: 42).[11]

POSTMODERN TIMELESSNESS

This paper has supported the view that the medical and hygiene writers on longevity from the late Renaissance to the early nineteenth century imagined the life-span to be substantiating of the knowable and miraculous laws of nature. Non-presentistic evaluations of the popularity of excessive longevity cases, such as that of Thomas Parr, show them to reflect the optimistic rationalism of the Enlightenment and its neo-Galenic medical regimes. From the mid-nineteenth century onwards, changing administrative and medical perspectives on old age radically altered the image of the life-span by reclassifying the aged body in terms of temporal finitude. The vitality of living was no longer dependent upon personal discipline, moderation and diet, but upon laws of development within the body's cells and tissues. Where the Enlightenment's medicine, science and philosophies constructed old age as a special but integral part of life, modernity's forms of calculation, division and hierarchy separated it as a distinct, developmental stage. The scope of this paper prevents me from elaborating this final point, but other authors have rigorously and insightfully done so.[12] Instead we return to the question of the postmodern present, where the life-span has been infused with rich cultural imagery based on the commodification, rather than the scientificity, of timelessness.

Western culture is still curious about reports of longevity. Texts, such as David Davies's *The Centenarians of the Andes* (1975) and G. Z. Pitskhelauri's *The Prolongevity of Soviet Georgia* (1982), and numerous documentaries on 'exceptional' long-living peoples from 'remote' habitats, reanimate the traditional interest in exceeding commonplace life-span limits. In addition, with increasing demographic evidence that life expectancy is drawing closer to life-span potential, westerners ideally anticipate long, active, healthy lives. However, the features of postmodern aging also derive from cultural industries that distribute pleasure and leisure across an unrestricted range of objects, identities, styles and expectations. In so doing, such industries recast the life-span in fantastical ways, in particular, the masking of age and the fantasy of timelessness.

With different emphases Bauman (1992), Cole (1992: 227–51), Conrad (1992), Featherstone and Hepworth (1991), Moody (1988, 1993) and Woodward (1991) note that the postmodern life course is characterized by a number of overlapping, often disparate conditions associated with the blurring of traditional chronological boundaries and the integration of formerly segregated periods of life. Fixed definitions of childhood, middle age and old age are eroding under pressure from two cultural directions that have accompanied the profound shifts in the political economy of labour, retirement and social inequality. First, since the 1960s gerontological writers, in their critique of negative 'ageist' stereotypes and practices, have produced more accurate and positive images that bespeak the vitality, creativity, empowerment and resourcefulness attainable in old age. In some instances the positivity of the discourse has repressed important issues in old age.[13] Second, elderhood has been reconstructed as a marketable lifestyle that connects the commodified values of youth with bodycare techniques for masking the appearance of age.[14] This development is aligned to the stratifying tactics of late capitalism whereby lifestyle hierarchies intersect with the complex of differences based on class, ethnicity, nationality and gender (see Featherstone and Hepworth, 1986). For older persons it means that the significance of age, positive and negative, dissolves in the fast-paced economy of images dominated by exercise, diet, cosmetic management and leisure activities. The chances of experiencing the aging of the body in a meaningfully temporal, open and unalienated way are slim. Thus the postmodern life course engenders a simulated life-span, one that promises to enhance living by stretching middle age into a timelessness hitherto associated only with the likes of Luigi Cornaro and Thomas Parr.

Harry Moody flags the film *Cocoon* as a 'postmodern fable' (1993: xxxiii). In it, as in postmodern culture itself, 'freedom is actually a massive form of denial and an escape from history' (ibid.: xxxviii). However, I also envision that the postmodern fantasy of living outside of time will provide the impetus for older individuals to resist western society's dominant obligations. Ethnographic research has already documented this process in local situations. For example, Haim Hazan, in his case study of a London Day Centre for older persons (1986), records that a beauty class was poorly attended (ibid.: 320), as were fitness classes, 'because members preferred to be engaged in activities where competition and testing out of achievements were not required' (ibid.: 317). From the cultural history of the past, as well as the present, we might also hope to learn that even the most universal of images, such as the life-span, opens a discursive window on to that which passes for the timeless truths about living, aging and dying.

NOTES

1 As the references and citations in this paper demonstrate, I am indebted to the many excellent secondary sources available on the history of old age.

Some of the leading publications in this area are the following: *Medieval history*: Burrow (1986); Goodich (1989); Sears (1986); Sheehan (1990); *History of death and dying*: Ariès (1981); Elias (1985); *American history*: Achenbaum (1978, 1983); Chudacoff (1989); Fischer (1978); Graebner (1980); Gratton (1986); Haber (1983); Quadagno (1982); van Tassel and Stearns (1986); *European history*: Kohli (1986b); Laslett (1989); Minois (1989); Pelling and Smith (1991); Stearns (1982); Troyansky (1989). *Literary and cultural history*: Achenbaum (forthcoming); Freeman (1979); Cole (1992); Covey (1991); *History of women and aging*: Premo (1990); Jalland and Hooper (1986).

2 Livesley contends that the detailed attention paid to the aging process by Cornaro and Bacon was due, in part, to their hypochondria (1975: 12). Freeman also mentions that Bacon 'was a bit of a hypochondriac who stuffed himself with varieties of evil tasting drugs' (1965: 17).

3 Cornaro's manual frames the body in the traditional Galenic mould, as dependent 'on the harmonie of humours and elements' (Cornaro 1935: 41). However, Cole (1992: 96) and Gruman (1966: 68) point out that Cornaro also challenged the reign of Galenic hygiene because of his individual optimism and desire for long life. I tend to disagree with Turner's rather rigid assessment that Cornaro conceived of his dietary regime 'within an exclusively religious framework as a defence against the temptations of the flesh' (Turner, 1991: 161–2). While Cornaro's text is narrated with theological reference points, his concern is less with spiritual afterlife than with the earthly pleasures of good health.

4 Bacon's work, originally in Latin, was *Historia Vitae et Mortis*, the third part of a longer text called *Instauratio Magna*, published in 1623. The full title of the English translation of 1638 is, *The Historie of Life and Death, with Observations Naturall and Experimentall for the Prolonging of Life* (Lind, 1988: 4).

5 Unfortunately, Bacon died in 1626 at the age of 65, after getting ill on a freezing winter day while stuffing a chicken with snow in order to prove that cold can preserve flesh. Faithful to his convictions, he chose to recover in a damp, rather than dry bed, which led to his death from bronchitis. So much for the scientific method.

6 Examples of eighteenth-century medical texts which express these sentiments are George Cheyne, *An Essay on Health and Long Life* (1725), John Floyer, *Medicina Gerocomica: Or the Galenic Art of Preserving Old Men's Habits* (1724), Benjamin Rush, *Medical Inquiries and Observations* (1797) and Christopher Hufeland, *The Art of Prolonging Life* (1797).

7 A characteristic of the life-span in all historical periods is that it is a male construction. Then, as now, it seems that women's lives were marginal to the medical understanding of the human life course, except in discussions of reproduction. As Carlisle admits, 'I pass over the diseases of women, because it would be improper to introduce them in a work, which is addressed to general readers' (1817: 89).

8 I am thankful to Carole Haber (1983: 42–3) and Gerald Gruman (1966: 74) for signalling the historical importance of Thoms's work.

9 Lorraine Daston mentions that while life insurance has a long history, it had little to do with people's age or mortality tables until the nineteenth century (Daston 1988: 168). (See also Haber (1983: 42–6) for discussion of the social scientific limiting of the life-span and the degradation of old age.) For excellent theoretical discussions that link insurance technologies, to the governing of risk, see the chapters by Ewald, Defert and Castel in *The Foucault Effect: Studies in Governmentality* (1991), edited by Burchell *et al.*

10 Cole (1992) describes how health reform, religion, medicine and quackery in America intersected in ways that kept alive the discourse of prolongevity.

11 Quetelet's influence in aging studies is acknowledged in gerontology. (See Birren and Clayton, 1975; Boyle and Morriss, 1987: 190; Haber, 1983: 41–2; and Kirk, 1992: 489.) One of the more interesting treatments of Quetelet is Bookstein and Achenbaum (1993). They argue that Quetelet's 'social physics', once introduced into gerontology, produced unfortunate consequences because, 'both the controversy over Quetelet and the existence of alternative models of statistical reasoning seem to have been ignored or overlooked by the founders of modern gerontology' (ibid.: 25). While Quetelet's work had already been criticized in the field of biometrics, gerontologists in the pursuit of methodological rigour and professional credibility embraced his erroneous calculation techniques.

12 In addition to authors cited in note 1, see Held (1986), Kohli (1986a), Mayer and Schoepflin (1989) and Modell (1989).

13 See Cole (1986), Harper and Thane (1989) and Moody (1988). Moody complains that

> Late life is hailed as a time to keep busy, to remain involved with others, engaged in activities. But vigorous activity and sustained meaning are not the same thing. In fact, frenzy of activity can simply mask an emptiness of shared meaning.
>
> (Moody, 1988: 238)

Cole more philosophically says that,

> The currently fashionable positive mythology of old age shows no more tolerance or respect for the intractable vicissitudes of aging than the old negative mythology. While health and self-control were seen previously as virtues reserved for the young and middle-aged, they are now demanded of the old as well. Unable to infuse decay, dependency, and death with moral and spiritual significance, our culture dreams of abolishing biological aging.
>
> (Cole, 1986: 129)

14 A representative text is Jeff Ostroff's *Successful Marketing to the 50+ Consumer* (1989). Of course there is no end to media examples that target the 50-, 60-, and 70-'somethings'. A striking term in this discourse is 'down-aging', which means, 'making it fashionable to be 50, look 40 and act 30' ('The New Middle Age', *The Globe and Mail Report on Business*, Toronto, May 1993: 47). For a critical account of 'Gold in Gray', see Minkler (1991).

REFERENCES

Achenbaum, W. Andrew (1978) *Old-Age in the New Land: The American Experience since 1790*, Baltimore: The Johns Hopkins University Press.

Achenbaum, W. Andrew (1983) *Shades of Gray: Old Age, American Values, and Federal Policies Since 1920*, Boston: Little, Brown.

Achenbaum, W. Andrew (forthcoming) *Crossing Frontiers: Gerontology Emerges as a Science*, New York: Cambridge University Press.

Ariès, Philippe (1981) *The Hour of Our Death*, trans. Helen Weaver, New York: Alfred A. Knopf.

Bacon, Sir Francis (1977) [1638] *The Historie of Life and Death with Observations Naturall and Experimentall for the Prolonging of Life*, New York: Arno Press.

Bailey, Thomas (1857) *Records of Longevity*, London: Darton.

Bauman, Zygmunt (1992) 'Survival as a social construct', *Theory, Culture & Society* 9 (1): 1–36.

Birren, James E. and Clayton, Vivian (1975) 'History of gerontology', in Diana S. Wooduff and James E. Birren (eds) *Aging: Scientific Perspectives and Social Issues*, New York: Van Nostrand.

Bookstein, Fred L. and Achenbaum, W. Andrew (1993) 'Aging as explanation: how scientific measurement can advance critical gerontology'. In Thomas R. Cole, W. Andrew Achenbaum, Patricia L. Jakobi and Robert Kastenbaum (eds) *Voices and Visions of Aging: Toward a Critical Gerontology*, New York: Springer.

Boyle, Joan M. and Morriss, James E. (1987) *The Mirror of Time: Images of Aging and Dying*, Westport: Greenwood Press.

Burchell, Graham, Gordon, Colin, and Miller, Peter (eds) (1991) *The Foucault Effect: Studies in Governmentality*, Chicago: University of Chicago Press.

Burrow, J. A. (1986) *The Ages of Man: A Study in Medieval Writing and Thought*, Oxford: Clarendon Press.

Carlisle, Sir Anthony (1817) *An Essay on the Disorders of Old Age*, London: Longman, Hurst, Rees, Orme & Brown.

Chopra, Deepak (1993) *Ageless Body, Timeless Mind: The Quantum Alternative to Growing Old*, Toronto: Harmony Books.

Chudacoff, Howard P. (1989) *How Old Are You? Age Consciousness in American Culture*, Princeton NJ: Princeton University Press.

Cole, Thomas R. (1986) 'The "enlightened" view of aging: Victorian morality in a new key', in Thomas R. Cole and Sally A. Gadow (eds) *What Does it Mean to Grow Old? Reflections from the Humanities*, Durham, NC: Duke University Press.

Cole, Thomas (1992) *The Journey of Life: A Cultural History of Aging in America*, Cambridge: Cambridge University Press.

Conrad, Christoph (1992) 'Old age in the modern and postmodern western world', in Thomas R. Cole, David D. van Tassel and Robert Kastenbaum (eds) *Handbook of the Humanities and Aging*, New York: Springer.

Cornaro, Luigi (1935) *How to Live For a Hundred Years and Avoid Disease*, trans. George Herbert, Oxford: The Alden Press.

Covey, Herbert C. (1991) *Images of Older People in Western Art and Society*, New York: Praeger.

Daston, Lorraine (1988) *Classical Probability in the Enlightenment*, Princeton, NJ: Princeton University Press.

Daston, Lorraine (1991) 'Marvelous facts and miraculous evidence in early modern Europe', *Critical Inquiry* 18(1): 93–124.

Davies, David (1975) *The Centenarians of the Andes*, London: Barrie and Jenkins.

Easton, James (1799) *Human Longevity*, London: John White.

Elias, Norbert (1985) *The Loneliness of the Dying*, trans. Edmund Jephcott, Oxford: Basil Blackwell.

Featherstone, Mike and Hepworth, Mike (1986) 'New lifestyles in old age', in Chris Phillipson, Miriam Bernard and Patricia Strang (eds) *Dependency and Interdependency in Old Age: Theoretical Perspectives and Alternatives*, Beckenham: Croom Helm.

Featherstone, Mike and Hepworth, Mike (1991) 'The mask of ageing and the postmodern life course', in Mike Featherstone, Mike Hepworth and Bryan S. Turner (eds) *The Body: Social Process and Cultural Theory*, London: Sage.

Fischer, David Hackett (1978) *Growing Old In America*, New York: Oxford University Press.

Freeman, Joseph (1965) 'Medical perspectives in aging (12th–19th Century)', *The Gerontologist* 5(1): 1–24.

Freeman, Joseph (1979) *Aging: Its History and Literature*, New York: Human Sciences Press.

Goodich, Michael E. (1989) *From Birth to Old Age: The Human Life Cycle in Medieval Thought, 1250–1350*, Lanham: University Press of America.

Gould, George M. and Pyle, Walter, L. (1898) *Anomalies and Curiosities of Medicine*, Philadelphia: W.B. Saunders.

Graebner, William (1980) *A History of Retirement: The Meaning and Function of an American Institution: 1885–1978*, New Haven and London: Yale University Press.

Gratton, Brian (1986) *Urban Elders: Family, Work, and Welfare among Boston's Aged, 1890–1950*, Philadelphia: Temple University Press.

Gruman, Gerald J. (1966) 'A history of ideas about the prolongation of life: the evolution of prolongevity hypotheses to 1800', *Transactions of the American Philosophical Society* 56(9), Philadelphia: American Philosophical Society.

Haber, Carole (1983) *Beyond Sixty-Five: The Dilemma of Old Age in America's Past*, Cambridge: Cambridge University Press.

Haber, Carole (1986) 'Geriatrics: a specialty in search of specialists', in David van Tassel and Peter N. Stearns (eds) *Old Age in Bureaucratic Society: The Elderly, the Experts, and the State in American History*, Westport: Greenwood Press.

Harper, Sarah and Thane, Pat (1989) 'The consolidation of "old age" as a phase of life, 1945–1965', in Margot Jefferys (ed.) *Growing Old in the Twentieth Century*, London: Routledge.

Hazan, Haim (1986) 'Body image and temporality among the aged: a case study of an ambivalent symbol', *Studies in Symbolic Interaction* 7(1): 305–29.

Held, Thomas (1986) 'Institutionalization and deinstitutionalization of the life course', *Human Development* 29(3): 157–62.

Jalland, Patricia and Hooper, John (eds) (1986) *Women From Birth to Death: The Female Life Cycle in Britain 1830–1914*, Atlantic Highlands NJ: Humanities Press.

Kirk, Henning (1992) 'Geriatric medicine and the categorisation of old age – the historical linkage', *Ageing and Society* 12(4): 483–97.

Kohli, Martin (1986a) 'Social organization and subjective construction of the life course', in Aage B. Sorensen, Franz E. Weinert and Lonnie R. Sherrod (eds) *Human Development and the Life Course: Multidisciplinary Perspectives*, Hillsdale, NJ: Lawrence Erlbaum.

Kohli, Martin (1986b) 'The world we forgot: a historical review of the life course', in Victor W. Marshall (ed.) *Later Life: The Social Psychology of Aging*, Beverly Hills: Sage.

Kondratowitz, Hans-Joachim von (1991) 'The medicalization of old age: continuity and change in Germany from the late eighteenth to the early twentieth century', in Margaret Pelling and Richard M. Smith (eds) *Life, Death and the Elderly: Historical Perspectives*, London: Routledge.

Laslett, Peter (1989) *A Fresh Map of Life: The Emergence of the Third Age*, London: Weidenfeld & Nicolson.

Lind, L. R. (1988) 'Introduction', in Gabriele Zerbi *Gerontocomia: On the Case of the Aged and Maximianus, Elegies on Old Age and Love*, Philadelphia: American Philosophical Society.

Livesley, Brian (1975) 'Galen, George III and geriatrics', *The Lecture of 1975*, London: Society of Apothecaries.

Lorand, Arnold (1912) *Old Age Deferred*, Philadelphia: F.A. Davis Company.

Mayer, Karl Ulrich and Schoepflin, Urs (1989) 'The state and the life course', *Annual Review of Sociology* 15: 187–209.

Metchnikoff, Elie (1907) *The Prolongation of Life: Optimistic Studies*, London: Heinemann.

Minkler, Meredith (1991) 'Gold in gray: reflections on business discovery of the elderly market', in Meredith Minkler and Carroll L. Estes (eds) *Critical Perspectives on Aging: The Political and Moral Economy of Growing Old*, Amityville: Baywood.

Minois, Georges (1989) *History of Old Age*, trans. Sarah Hanbury Tenison, Cambridge: Polity Press.

Modell, John (1989) *Into One's Own: From Youth to Adulthood in The United States, 1920–1975*, Berkeley: University of California Press.

Moody, Harry R. (1988) 'Toward a critical gerontology: the contribution of the humanities to theories of aging', in James E. Birren and Vern L. Bengtson (eds) *Emergent Theories of Aging*, New York: Springer.

Moody, Harry R. (1993) 'Overview: what is critical gerontology and why is it important?', in Thomas R. Cole, W. Andrew Achenbaum, Patricia L. Jakobi and Robert Kastenbaum (eds) *Voices and Visions of Aging: Toward a Critical Gerontology*, New York: Springer.

Ostroff, Jeff (1989) *Successful Marketing to the 50+ Consumer: How to Capture One of the Biggest and Fastest-growing Markets in America*, Englewood Cliffs: Prentice Hall.

Pelling, Margaret and Smith, Richard M. (eds) (1991) *Life, Death and the Elderly: Historical Perspectives*, London: Routledge.

Pitskhelauri, G. Z. (1982) *The Prolongevity of Soviet Georgia*, New York: Human Sciences Press.

Premo, Terri L. (1990) *Winter Friends: Women Growing Old in the New Republic, 1785–1835*, Urbana: University of Illinois Press.

Quadagno, Jill (1982) *Aging in Early Industrial Society: Work, Family and Social Policy in Nineteenth Century England*, New York: Academic Press.

Quetelet, Adolphe (1968) [1842] *A Treatise on Man and the Development of his Faculties*, New York: B. Franklin.

Sears, Elizabeth (1986) *The Ages of Man: Medieval Interpretations of the Life Cycle*, Princeton NJ: Princeton University Press.

Sheehan, Michael M. (ed.) (1990) *Aging and the Aged in Medieval Europe*, Toronto Pontifical Institute of Medieval Studies.

Sinclair, Sir John (1807) *The Code of Health and Longevity, vol. 1*, Edinburgh: Archibald Constable.

Smith, John (1752) [1666] *The Portrait of Old Age*, London: E. Whithers.

Stearns, Peter N. (ed.) (1982) *Old Age in Preindustrial Society*, New York: Holmes & Meier.

Tassel, David van and Stearns, Peter N. (1986) *Old Age in Bureaucratic Society: The Elderly, the Experts, and the State in American History*, Westport: Greenwood Press.

Thoms, William J. (1873) *Human Longevity: Its Facts and Its Fictions*, London: John Murray.

Troyansky, David G. (1989) *Old Age in the Old Regime: Image and Experience in Eighteenth Century France*, Ithaca: Cornell University Press.

Turner, Bryan S. (1991) 'The discourse of diet', in Mike Featherstone, Mike Hepworth and Bryan S. Turner (eds) *The Body: Social Process and Cultural Theory*, London: Sage.

Woodward, Kathleen (1991) *Aging and Its Discontents: Freud and Other Fictions*, Bloomington and Indianapolis: Indiana University Press.

Part II

GENDER AND IDENTITY

6

TRIBUTE TO THE OLDER WOMAN

Psychoanalysis, feminism, and ageism

Kathleen Woodward

I begin with a scene drawn out of memory from my childhood, remembered as I was reading psychoanalysis and feminism in preparation to write this essay about aging. I like to think that this memory of a long afternoon surfaced in response to thought and theory, and that in its way it corroborates the affective tone and theoretical trajectory my words take in the following pages.

I was 10 and on vacation with my father's parents. My grandfather stayed behind (he always did) while my grandmother and I went down to the beach. It was too cold to swim, it was our first day, and so we walked along the water's edge to the rocks at the far end of the shore. I remember climbing those rocks for hours. What we had forgotten, of course, was the deceptive coolness of the sun. We returned to the hotel, our skin painfully, desperately burned. We could put nothing against our bodies. Not a single sheet. We lay still and naked on the twin beds, complaining, laughing, talking. Two twinned, different, sunburned bodies – the body of a 10-year old girl and the body of a 62-year-old woman.

To my mind's retrospective eye it is crucial that this scene is not a story of the mother and the daughter, a story whose psychoanalytic plot revolves around identification and separation, intimacy and distance, and engages what I call the strong emotions of psychoanalysis (whether in the writing of Freud, Klein, or Lacan); I am thinking of the potentially explosive emotions of envy, fear, hostility, desire, guilt, and jealousy. Instead it is a story of an older woman (surely a missing person in psychoanalysis) and a young girl who are separated by some fifty years. Yet I do not want to say that the two of them are *divided* by generations. Rather, they are somehow *connected* by them. What would I say of the affect associated with this memory? I will return to this question, but first I want to take a brief detour to insist on the subject of affect.

In *Le Discours Vivant* (1973), an excellent if unfortunately little known book on the emotions and psychoanalysis, André Green shows how Freud moved from an emphasis on the role of *representation* in psychic life in his earlier work (notably in *The Interpretation of Dreams* (1900)) to an emphasis on *affect* itself in his later work ('Mourning and melancholia' (1917) and *Inhibitions, Symptoms and Anxiety* (1926) are two prime examples). This shift in emphasis parallels Freud's concern with castration and the figure of the father in his earlier work and with separation anxiety and the figure of the mother in his later work. The later work of Freud prefigures object relations theory and attachment theory, which inform my thinking here. In particular I welcome the later Freud's explicit analysis of the emotions, which all too often are implicitly associated with the feminine and thus denigrated.[1]

I turn first to a short text by Freud written late in his life, which does privilege the analysis of affect but which none the less returns us to the figure of the father and Oedipal anxiety. When he was 80 years old Freud mulled over the complex of negative feelings associated with a vacation he had taken to Greece with his brother a little over thirty years before (a coincidence of seaside vacations that has only now occurred to me). I am referring to his letter to Romain Rolland, published under the title of 'A disturbance of memory on the Acropolis' (1936). Freud tells us that what prompted him to write this text was the recurrence in recent years of a similar 'disturbance of memory' and, we are given to assume, a disturbance of similar feelings. These he describes as depression and gloom, as discontent and irresolution, as in short – and in a wonderful if morose phrase – 'the expression of a pessimism' (1953–74: 22: 242). What does it mean for feelings to cause a disturbance? I take it Freud means that they interrupted a false composure, or broke an illusion of peace, or interfered with a *mood* (I will come back to this in a moment). In the final analysis Freud attributes these disturbing feelings to filial guilt. An ambitious man, he concluded he had gone further than had his father (both literally in terms of travel some thirty years before and symbolically in terms of intellectual accomplishment over his long life) and that he was to be punished for it. His feelings of foreboding, his 'pessimism', are *themselves* that punishment, exacted by the superego. I have commented elsewhere on the place of this text in the context of Freud's work and the discontents of the aging body (Woodward, 1991). Here I want only to remark that in 'Disturbance of memory' we find ourselves thick in the Freudian world of two generations with the 80-year-old son still bound tragically after all these years to his long dead father by the cord of the Oedipus complex, with its dynamic of desire and prohibition, guilt and punishment. Thus this version of the Oedipus drama is not played out between two people but in the solitary *mise-en-scène* of the psyche.

What interests me also in Freud's 'Disturbance of memory' is the notion of the repetition not of an event but of a complex of emotions, particular emotions that Freud took as his task to analyse and that had long been central to the structuring narrative of the Oedipus complex. And yet earlier Freud had remarked that 'every affect . . . is only a reminiscence of an event' (1909, quoted in 1953–74: 20: 84). I take him here in his materialist sense. But actually I would insist that it is never the event itself that is ultimately important to us – it is the emotion (or complex of emotions) associated with it. Moreover, in the case of Freud's disturbance of affect, his feelings of foreboding are not in fact a reminiscence of an event but rather an *expectation* of one, foreboding that arises out of fantasy, the specifically Freudian fear of castration or punishment.

How would I understand the complex of emotions associated with my childhood memory of my grandmother and myself at the beach, of our two sunburned bodies? Not as a disturbance in Freud's sense, not as a foreboding 'expression of a pessimism', but as an expression of re-assurance. Yet not as *jouissance*, as an expression of woman's libidinal economy, which Hélène Cixous has described in 'Sorties' this way:

> Unleashed and raging, she belongs to the race of the waves. She arises, she approaches, she lifts up, she reaches, covers over, washes ashore, flows embracing the cliff's least undulation, already she is another, arising again, throwing the fringed vastness of her body up high, follows herself, and covers over.
>
> (1981: 91)

I break off here, unwilling to follow Cixous's fluvial prose any longer along this sinuous beach into its realm of intoxication, vertigo, mystery, and effervescence. Instead, I understand the affect associated with my memory of a seaside scene, which is drawn from everyday life, as nothing more perhaps but certainly nothing less than a palpable *sociality*, a convivial ease. My affective memory (Stanislwski), now over thirty-five years old, is a reminiscence of an event, not a fantasy that takes place in the private *mise-en-scène* of the psyche (Freud), not a textual feminist Utopia of rhapsodic proportions (Cixous).

John Bowlby (1973) would describe this scene in terms of attachment, Jessica Benjamin (1988) in terms of emotional attunement. Indeed, for me the emotional precipitate that is the reminiscence of this event I understand to be based on what Benjamin calls mutual recognition.[2] But we lack a variegated and rich theoretical vocabulary to describe such emotions. Given the discourse of psychoanalysis with its attention to the 'stormy passions', as Freud has put it (1953–74: 11: 75),[3] we should not be at all surprised by this: psychoanalysis has devoted little attention to the elaboration of what for want of a better term we might call the positive emotions (we certainly *do* need a better word than this) or what I have elsewhere called the 'quiet' emotions (Woodward 1990–91) and Sartre the 'subtle' emotions (1948: 22). Furthermore, within the classical parameters of psychoanalysis, it might be more accurate to refer to what I have described as a *mood.*

Here I want to draw on the excellent distinction made by Lawrence Grossberg between desire and mood, or more precisely, between what he identifies as libidinal economies of desire and affective economies of mood. The two economies represent different ways of organizing psychic energy, which Grossberg describes in the following way:

> If desire is always focused (as the notion of cathexis suggests), mood is always dispersed. While both may be experienced in terms of needs, only libidinal needs can be, however incompletely, satisfied. Moods are never satisfied, only realized. If desire assumes an economy of depth (e.g., the notion of repression), mood is always on the surface (which is not to be equated with con-sciousness). It is the coloration or passion within which one's investments in, and commitments to the world are possible.
>
> (Grossberg, 1988: 285)[4]

Desire is focused on an object and is goal-oriented; mood arises out of a situation and gives to it a certain tone.

Significantly, Grossberg implicitly (although not exclusively) associ-ates an affective economy of mood with a psychoanalysis of object relations; this is how he can understand the affective economy of mood to yield the possibility of difference. Affective needs, he writes, are 'never satisfied by particular relationships but only by a more general attitude or mood within which any particular relationship has its effects' (ibid.). Grossberg's theorization of the affective economy of mood (in its 'positive' manifestation) resonates with Benjamin's theorization of emotional attunement in an intersubjective space. How would I describe, then, the mood of my memory of that summer afternoon some thirty-five years ago? It was one of fluent companionship that, import-antly for what I turn to now, stretched across the continuity established by three generations.

Psychoanalysis is a discourse obsessed with the making of triangles out of the elements of two generations. Its developmental politics is twofold. First, the constitution of male and female sexuality is under-stood to be achieved simultaneously with the rigid separation of generations, and second, both the sexes and the generations are ever after to remain unequal in power. This geometry of the nuclear family is established only through force, which enlists the emotions of fear and anxiety. Thus classically the father (or the Name of the Father) is cast as the third term that intervenes in the mother-child dyad.

How might we rethink this triangulation? In 'Places names' and

'Motherhood according to Giovanni Bellini', Julia Kristeva introduces into the equation another term altogether: the mother's mother. As we shall see in a moment, however, for Kristeva it is not the mother's mother who is the third term. In the event of giving birth, Kristeva writes, a woman 'replays in reverse the encounter with her own mother' (1980b: 279), she 'enters into contact with her own mother' (1980a: 239).[5] Kristeva reads this alternative triangle as mother-mother-child, with the child serving as third term, as a kind of go-between who brings a woman into psychic continuity with mother. The woman, her mother: the two are, Kristeva writes in 'Motherhood', 'the same continuity differentiating itself' (ibid.). Kristeva is, however, ambivalent about this identification – and well she should be, given the mystical aura with which she endows it. Thus she also presents the child as the third term, which also breaks this imaginary and revelatory bond between the woman and her mother. As she puts it brilliantly in 'Place names', the child is also an *analyser* (ibid.: 279), who releases the woman, now a mother, from what Kristeva provocatively calls 'the homosexual facet of motherhood' (1980a: 239), and more clinically, 'the daughter-mother symbiosis' and 'the undifferentiated community of women' (1980b: 279).

I must leave behind many complexities here, but before I do I want to insist on three fundamental features of Kristeva's rewriting of this basic figure of psychoanalytic geometry. It is at the very least two-thirds female. It touches three generations. And the child plays an active if contradictory role.

Who is this child and what is the child playing with? By asking *who* I mean of course to introduce the question of gender. In his lecture on 'Femininity' (1933), Freud rehearses the process by which a woman 'comes into being . . . out of a child with a bisexual disposition' (1953–74: 22: 116). That is, he theorizes the constitution of a specifically female sexual identity where before, he assumes, there was none. In this late text Freud admits that the pre-Oedipal attachment of the little girl to the mother is much more powerful and richer than he had before believed. He comes to this conclusion in part by calling attention to the little girl's practice of playing with dolls. How does he explain her play? It can't be an expression of her 'femininity', for that has not yet been established. So he finds himself forced to conclude that it is an expression of her 'identification with her mother', with the phallic mother (she is 'phallic' because the little girl does not yet recognize her mother as 'castrated'). It is, in Freud's eyes, an 'affectionate' attachment, although he expresses it in ambiguous terms: the little girl 'was playing the part of her mother and the doll was herself: now she could do with the baby everything that her mother used to do with her' (1953–74: 22: 128). In the opening pages of his essay Freud cautions his readers not to think of masculinity and femininity – the polarity that dominates sexual life, as he puts it – in terms of activity and passivity. But in fact he can find no other way of describing (or theorizing) the little girl's behaviour: the little girl, identifying with her mother, substitutes 'activity for passivity' (ibid.). Notwithstanding many of Freud's disclaimers, then, the conventional connotations of sexual difference cling to the words 'active' and 'passive' like a phallic slip, reinscribing themselves retrospectively in the pre-Oedipal period. Similarly, by describing the pre-Oedipal mother as 'phallic', Freud continues to read the scene of a little girl's play in terms of a *sexual economy*.[6] Indeed, Freudian psychoanalysis can admit no other economy than a sexual economy. Just as importantly for my purposes, Freud can only imagine two generations in this scene: the mother and the child.

I want to read this scene differently: for the child, the doll represents not her self (as Freud would have it), nor the Other, but simply and profoundly, an other, a baby. This baby, however, is not a sibling, that is to say, a member of the same generation (in such a case we might predict jealousy of a conventional triangular sort).[7] Rather this 'baby' belongs to the next generation. She is a child to whom the little girl transfers, as Luce Irigaray has put it, 'quasi-maternal affects' (1989: 132).[8] We thus have a model of three generations, similar to but different from that sketched by Kristeva, where the third term, the child, does not separate the mother from the child but is added to the two of them (in fact, we again find several mothers here). We have, in other words, not a *triangle* but the further elaboration of a *line*, a plumb line – one that has specific gravity and weight to it. Furthermore, it is not sexual difference that distinguishes this economy, but generational linkage, or generational continuity.

In 'Femininity' Freud is concerned with sexuality and its structuring binary of masculinity and femininity. Within this framework he was bound to conclude the following: 'When you meet a human being, the first distinction you make is "male or female?"' (1953–74: 22: 113). Sexuality is the content, we can say, of Freudian psychoanalysis,[9] which is itself an instance of the seemingly endless production of the discourse of sexuality in western culture, a phenomenon to which Foucault has so persuasively drawn attention (1980). Thus Freud insists that sexual difference (although he does not use this term) is the most distinctive feature of a person. But we are not obliged to agree. What of race, for example? And what of the category of age? For indeed, when we meet someone, one of the first distinctions we make, as self-consciously or subliminally as distinctions of sexual or racial difference, is that of *age*, and more generally, of generation.

Lending support to my hypothetical model of generational continuity is the fascinating research of Ernest A. Abelin (1980) on pre-Oedipal triangulation during the *rapprochement* subphase (identified by Margaret Mahler as occurring at around 18 months). Abelin finds not one triangle but two. Both triangles are gender specific – one is for little girls, one for little boys. Significantly, however, only one of them is based on *sexual difference*. The triangle for the little boy is familiarly Freudian to us: it consists of father, mother, and self, and establishes gender identity for the little boy based on his perception of sexual difference. For the little girl, by contrast, the triangle is composed of mother, self, and baby, and establishes gender identity based on her perception of *generational continuity*. Abelin explains the difference between the two triangles this way:

> Generational identity establishes the self 'between' two objects, along one linear dimension. 'I am smaller than mother, but bigger than baby,' or, rather, in terms of wishes: 'I wish to be taken care of by mother and I wish to take care of baby.' By contrast, gender identity classifies the self in relation to the dichotomy male/ female.
>
> (Abelin, 1980: 158)[10]

For the little girl, then, core gender identity is not based on sexual difference but on generational linkage.

Abelin's research provides a critical vantage point from which we can see again just how saturated classical psychoanalysis is with the discourse of sexuality and sexual difference. The provocative conclusion of his research is that there is another gender-specific content to identity – that of generation – which has not been elaborated by psychoanalysis. Why? In part because in Freud's male hands the two founding figures of psychoanalysis – the hysterical Dora and the felonious Oedipus – present an impediment, if not a dead end, to thinking a third generation. The children of Oedipus were born out of incest and thus outside the law (and we know what happened to them). And the generational economy of the hysteric cannot count to three: the sterile hysteric will produce no children.[11]

But Abelin's geometry is complicit with Freudian analysis and is faulty. Where he sees a pre-Oedipal *triangle* for little girls based on generational identity, he should instead see a line. As Abelin himself says, generational identity is established along a 'linear' axis.

I have up to now used the word 'identity' without being precise about exactly what I mean by it. 'Identity' is often used in the sense of 'wholeness', and I do not wish it to carry that meaning here. 'Identity' is also often opposed to 'difference', and I do not want it to be construed in this sense either. Recent debates have placed a terrible strain on the notions of 'identity' and 'difference'. It will suffice, I hope, to say that in the context of this essay 'identity' does not preclude difference. Generational identity entails a difference based on *similarity* that finds its temporal expression in *continuity*.

To summarize, we have, then, this theoretical scene: a mother whose little girl, playing, invents the younger generation. The child is the third term, a term which signifies continuity and not intervention. The tragic binary of Freudian psychoanalysis of two generations can be written in this way.

But in doing so I find that I have reproduced the paradigm of the mother and the infant daughter, and I contend that we have had enough in recent feminist psychoanalytic criticism and theory of this very couple. A child, in my judgement, should not be asked to bear so much meaning. It would be appropriate, however, to ask an older woman to do so. Thus I propose we look at this plumb line, or lineage, from a different point of view, from the perspective of the older woman. Kaja Silverman has insisted that for the choric fantasy of women's unity to function effectively it must point forward as well as backward (1988: 153).[12] Turning our attention to the figure of the other woman, the older woman, as the third term is precisely one way of moving forward, of thinking prospectively rather than retrospectively (although it will involve this also). And to up the ante, I suggest that we imagine her as a figure of knowledge who represents the difference that history, or time, makes, a difference that she in fact literally embodies.

I have already remarked that the older woman is a missing person in Freudian psychoanalysis. The cultural historian Lois Banner has concluded that if Freud had difficulty in general in dealing with women in his writing, he had particular difficulty with aging women (1992). It is therefore not surprising to me that in the one place, to my knowledge, where Freud does discuss a cultural representation of three generations, only two generations are in effect present. The older woman is absent; she has been painted over. I am referring to Freud's analysis of Leonardo da Vinci's painting of St Anne with her daughter Mary and the baby Jesus (1910). Freud comments upon this painting in his study of Leonardo, which focuses on one of Leonardo's memories from childhood (naturally Freud interprets it in sexual terms) (1953–74: 11: 57–137).[13] Startlingly, Leonardo, with whom Freud clearly identifies, has painted the older woman (the grand-mother) as a member of the same generation as her daughter. St Anne is described by Freud as 'a young woman of unfaded beauty', indeed 'a woman of radiant beauty' (ibid.: 113). Why are there two mothers of the same generation for the Christ child instead of one? Why is the older woman not represented as such? Why is her older body recon-structed in the masquerade of youth?

Freud offers the following analysis based on the peculiarities of

Leonardo's birth and upbringing. The illegitimate Leonardo was raised exclusively by his birth mother until he was 5 and thereafter by his stepmother in his father's home. Thus Leonardo, so strongly attached to mother figures (and not to the father, who was missing from his first five years), has, in Freud's words, 'given the boy' – that is, himself – 'two mothers' (ibid.). But I would argue that Freud's own fascination with this painting tells us more than this: Freudian psychoanalysis could only figure a child's relation to a woman positively in terms of the paradigm of the younger mother and infant. The relationship portrayed in this scene – it is a doubled-over pieta – is maternally idyllic. The celebrated Leonardo smile is the familiar, almost banal 'blissful smile of the joy of motherhood' (ibid.). The affect here is Freudian Utopian sublime, one that can only be associated with the pieta of the young mother and infant in the 'prehistory' of man.

Although Freud asserts that he dismissed the notion, held by some of Leonardo's biographers, that Leonardo 'could not bring himself to paint old age, lines and wrinkles' (ibid.), Freud relegates St Anne – an older woman but not necessarily *old* – to the outcast territory of old age. In Freudian psychoanalysis a woman beyond child-bearing age is old, dysfunctional in sexual (reproductive) terms, a dysfunction which is written on her body in folds and wrinkles for everyone to see. Such a woman, we might say, cannot even be represented within the discourse of classical psychoanalysis. Within the parameters of psychoanalysis we can imagine a point when increasing age (it is ticking away) intersects with female sexuality at the biological time bomb of menopause – when female sexuality vanishes, leaving only gender behind. The dilemma, however, is this: Freudian psychoanalysis cannot contain the concept of gender as distinct from sexuality. Thus: the older woman cannot exist! If in Freudian terms a female child prior to the Oedipus complex is consigned to a *prehistorical* state, a postmenopausal woman, an older woman, is dismissed from the world as *posthistorical*, finding herself outside of the discourse of history yet again.

In old age women are subject to a double marginality at the very least, one that feminist critiques of psychoanalysis can help explain. To summarize: first, the male fear of woman as the all-engulfing mother is exacerbated when women grow old; moreover, in psychoanalysis the attraction to the mother is understood as taboo, and the older woman necessarily occupies the position of the mother or, worse, the grandmother. Thus the connection between sexuality and identity needs to be thought through in terms of the place of the postmenopausal woman in psychoanalysis. Simone de Beauvoir (1970) offers this analysis, which may itself be symptomatic of gerontophobia:

as men see it, a woman's purpose in life is to be an erotic object, when she grows old and ugly she loses the place allotted to her in society: she becomes a *monstrum* that excites revulsion and even dread.

(Beauvoir, 1978: 184)

Second, and perhaps most importantly, the consequences of the dread of aging for feminism itself need to be addressed. For feminism itself has been profoundly ageist.

In feminist criticism and psychoanalysis the older woman – the woman of the third generation (and she – or we – may be older than this) – has not found a place.[14] In much recent feminist psychoanalytic criticism in the United States a woman is implicitly theorized or represented as a mother to young children.[15] To be sure she may appear in the guise of a woman juggling work of her own with the demands and pleasures of motherhood, but at her oldest she tends to be cast as on the young side of middle age (I think here of the surprised, almost shocked tone with which I have heard some of my only slightly younger colleagues refer to an older woman as – of all the impossible things! – a *grandmother*). Or if age is explicitly analysed, what we find is the Freudian plot of a struggle for power between two close but emotionally distant 'generations': the mother and the daughter have gotten older but they don't seem to have learned much – or they have learned too well how to jockey for power. Thus literary critic Marianne Hirsch, writing candidly in her book *The Mother/Daughter Plot* (1989) of her experience as a fellow at the Bunting Institute, notes the

> painful set of divisions which emerged between the discourse of mothers and that of daughters; the sympathy we could muster for ourselves and each other *as mothers*, we could not quite transfer to our own mothers. This inability, this tragic asymmetry between our own two voices, was so pervasive as to be extremely difficult to discuss. It revealed the depth and the extent of the 'matrophobia' that exists not only in the culture at large but also within feminism, and within women who are mothers.
>
> (Hirsch, 1989: 26)

And thus, Alice Jardine in a recent essay (1989) describes the relationship between the two successive post-1968 groups of feminists in the American academy as thoroughly Oedipal. She does not want, she says, to 'succumb' to this paradigm, but in fact she does – and for good reasons: the Oedipal paradigm does describe accurately the struggle between two adjacent generations, a struggle that I suspect we have all witnessed and in which we have all probably consciously or unconsciously played at least one part and possibly two. As Jardine expresses it:

I would like to avoid the mother/daughter paradigm here (so as not to succumb simply to miming the traditional father/son, master/disciple model), but it is difficult to avoid being positioned by the institution as mothers and daughters. Structures of debt/gift (mothers and increasingly daughters control a lot of money and prestige in the university), structures of our new institutional power over each other, desires and demands for recognition and love – all of these are falling into place in rather familiar Freudian ways.

(Jardine, 1989: 77)

Yes, I agree. But I would argue that it is not just the patriarchal structure of the institution that places us in Oedipal struggle but also our way of analysing that relation between generations, limited as it is to two. For it is unmistakably clear that there are more than two generations of women in the academy.

Thus, one of the ways to construct a 'theoretical genealogy' of women[16] is to stretch our attention to include another generation. We must do so not in order to figure a new notion of a *horizontal* relation between women, such as Irigaray advises – indeed that is part of the problem. As the activist lesbian Barbara MacDonald has argued in *Look Me in the Eye: Old Women, Aging and Ageism* (1983), the emphasis on sisterhood in the women's movement reinforces and produces mistrust and divisions between younger and older women; 'youth is bonded with patriarchy in the enslavement of the older woman. There would, in fact, be no youth culture without the powerless older woman' (ibid.: 39). Instead we need to give a new meaning to the notion of *vertical*, which is conceived in classical psychoanalysis in terms of hierarchy and authority in terms of two generations only. Baba Copper, in *Over the Hill: Reflections on Ageism Between Women* (1988), insists that the traditional pattern of the nuclear family – with the mother caring for others and no one caring for the mother (that is to say, no patterns of reciprocity being established), itself generates ageism – and that we see this reflected in the women's movement. She is virulent about the traditional role of the grandmother, calling it one of the 'horrors' of old age, railing against 'the humiliation and self-sacrifice built into the role of the grandmother' (ibid.: 6). (I should note, however, that she too limits her analysis to two generations of feminists.) Nancy Chodorow does give a new and positive meaning to the notion of a vertical relation between women in a recent essay in which she reports on a series of interviews she had in the early 1980s with women psychoanalysts who had trained in the 1920s, 1930s, and 1940s (1989). I greatly admire this essay. In it Chodorow seeks to understand across time, history, age, and several generations why these older women were not feminists in

89

Chodorow's own sense of the word. The title of her essay – 'Seventies questions for thirties women: gender and generation in a study of early women psychoanalysts' – suggests the answer to her question. It is a simple lesson, one we too often forget: we must remember to respect the differences rooted in history. We have no right to expect to hear the answers we would give to the questions we ask of generational others. It is a vain and immature enterprise to wish either to be mirrored at our age (what is it? how old are you? *tell*), or to enter automatically into struggle.

What Chodorow conveys is precisely a sense of mutual recognition (Benjamin, 1988) between two generations widely separated by time and other generations but brought together in part by the very wish for understanding – that is, connection. But not symbiosis. We do not find, *pace* Kristeva, an 'undifferentiated community of women' (1980b: 279). Exactly not.

Chodorow had thought these older women, whom she esteemed in so many other ways, were – of all things – gender-blind. Through time and conversation she came to conclude that they had a different form of gender-consciousness, or gender identity. She came to see, she writes, that 'differences in women's interpretations of a situation may be understood not only in terms of structural categories like class and race but also historically, culturally, and generationally' (1989: 200). She came to recognize that 'hyper-gender-sensitivity' characterizes women of her – and I will say with Chodorow *our* – generation (ibid.: 218). One of the rare achievements of Chodorow's essay, which I hasten to add is not in any way eloquent (it does not move us emotionally to understanding), is its sense or tone of deep respect. This is achieved in part, I think, through its rhetoric of candour which disarms the hierarchy associated with positions of truth, a position that Chodorow has given up.

It is the time for many of us to invent ourselves consciously and critically as older women, making the place we want for ourselves to the best of our abilities. If the older woman has been a missing person in psychoanalysis and in feminist criticism in general, this is fortunately not the case in contemporary culture. Older women are making it, if we only know where to look. Women – and not all of them older – are contributing to the representation of older women. I am thinking, for example, of Yvonne Rainer's recent films, of the work of the perform-ance artists Suzanne Lacey and Rachel Rosenthal, of Margaret Drabble's novel *A Natural Curiosity*, of Annie Dillard's *An American Childhood*, of Amy Tan's *The Joy Luck Club*, of so much of Marguerite Duras's writing, of Alice Noggle's photographs of old women, of Cecelia Condit's videotape *Not a Jealous Bone*. There is much more: rich and varied work for us to investigate and to live into the future with, for identifications do not cease with childhood nor is fantasy bound only to infancy. As Teresa Brennan suggests, we make not just formative identifications but also identifications that permit different ways of thinking – and, I would add, of living (1989: 10). And the phantasmatic, as Laplanche and Pontalis emphasize, is constantly drawing in new materials (1973: 317).

Informing my paper is a fantasy of a particular kind of older woman, one I confess is narcissistic, although it is a very general one (one you could not guess from my opening anecdote). Chodorow, drawing on the work of Judith Kestenberg, concludes that for women analysts of the 1930s whom she interviewed, three faces of femininity presented themselves: motherhood, sexuality, and intellectual work (1989: 210). In my essay I have been implicitly privileging the latter aspect of the older woman – intellectual work, characterizing a woman who as a teacher and writer is bound through her work to many generations. When I was young this is how I perceived many older women, including my grandmother. I am not alone in this, of course. I do not think we should dismiss what our experience in everyday life has so often told us. It is common knowledge that struggle can 'skip' a generation, that many of us have formative relationships with women a generation, if not more, older than our mothers. I also think we should attend to Simone de Beauvoir's second great book, an analysis as sweeping and trenchant as *The Second Sex*. I am referring of course to *La Vieillesse*, published under the title *The Coming of Age* in the US, a book which has been virtually ignored by feminists.

In closing, then, I want to echo my opening anecdote with words drawn not out of my memory but from my recent reading. They are taken from a collection of essays by bell hooks, a black American who teaches at Yale (1990). 'bell hooks' (also known as Gloria Watkins) is in fact the name of her great-grandmother which Watkins took as her own, a name signifying 'talking back' (1986–7). bell hooks (who is she then?). She writes about going to school in the rural south and the women there. She tells us in her essay 'The Chitlin circuit',

> It was a world of single older black women school teachers, they had taught your mama, her sisters, and her friends. They knew your people in ways that you never would and shared their insight, keeping us in touch with generations. It was a world where we had history.

> (bell hooks, 1990: 33)

To her grandmother Sarah Hooks Oldham, a woman with a 'renegade nature' who instructed bell in the ways of establishing 'kinship and connection', a woman who could not read or write, a long-lived woman who had taught her so much, to her bell hooks dedicates an essay in this collection. It is a portrait of her grandmother as a maker of quilts, of 'history worked by hand' (ibid.: 115). Entitled 'Aesthetic inheritances', this essay is a tribute to an older woman, as in a way also is mine. Here the Freudian stormy emotions of two-generational same-sex Oedipal violence are nowhere in evidence, much less privileged. Not at all.

It may be wondered if in my emphasis on the subtle emotions (I will use Sartre's word), on a quiet and companionable geniality in my case, on a boisterous conviviality in the case of bell hooks, I have not strayed too close to that emotion – or better, mood – held most in contempt in contemporary cultural studies. I am, of course, referring to nostalgia. Nostalgia is generally associated with a regressive and weak, wistful longing for the past – with, in short, a retrograde politics.[17] But neither hooks – if I may speak for her – nor I have a desire to return to the past.

Nor am I arguing that certain emotions are specifically, essentially female, and others male. What I have been concerned to do is to see where the analysis of an affect – the mood of convivial ease – would lead me, and it took me to the figure of the older woman, who was in fact present in my past all along, and who will be – 'she' will be 'I' – present in my future, time willing.

NOTES

1 See, for example, Morwenna Griffiths, 'Feminism, feelings and philosophy' (1988).
2 Benjamin writes: 'What I call *mutual recognition* includes a number of experiences commonly described in the research on mother-infant inter-action: emotional attunement, mutual influence, affective mutuality, shar-ing states of mind' (1988: 16). For Benjamin the analogue in adult life to mother-infant interaction is erotic union. I would disagree and argue that a reciprocal sociality, in its many modes, is a more appropriate model. I would further disagree with Benjamin's insistence that we can share feeling states with other people; I do not think we can ever know that.
3 The complete sentence reads: 'The stormy passions of a nature that inspires and consumes, passions in which other men have their richest experience, appear not to have touched him' (Freud 1953–74: 11: 75).
4 Grossberg's distinction between libidinal economies of desire and affective economies of mood resonates with Winnicott's distinction between doing and being (Winnicott associates the former with masculinity, the latter with femininity). See Winnicott, 'Creativity and its origins' (1971).
5 I am indebted to Kaja Silverman's reading of these essays (see n.12). I am also grateful to Tim Murray for his helpful comments. Elizabeth Grosz calls this identification of the birth mother with her own mother 'vertiginous' (1989: 80), which, I would argue, it certainly need not be.
6 Luce Irigaray also makes this point (1985).
7 It is of the utmost importance that we specify *which* generation. Both Freud and Lacan have commented on the explosive emotions of sibling rivalry. Lacan, for example, is fond of quoting St Augustine on this point: 'I have seen with my own eyes and know very well an infant in the grip of jealousy: he could not yet speak, and already he observed his foster-brother, pale and

with an envenomed stare' (1977: 20). Freud links the drive to knowledge, or epistemophilia, to the arrival of a new baby, which stimulates the child's sexual curiosity. The question to be asked is: where do babies come from? Freud develops this idea in *Three Essays on the Theory of Sexuality* (1905) 1953–74: 7: 194–5. See also his 'Notes upon a case of obsessional neurosis' (1909) 1953–74: 10: 237–49.

For recent work on epistemophilia from a feminist point of view, see Toril Moi, 'Patriarchal thought and the drive for knowledge' (1989). Moi concludes, 'If reason is always already shot through with the energy of the drives, the body, and desire, to be intellectual can no longer be theorized simply as the "opposite" of being emotional or passionate' (ibid.: 203). See also the brilliant essay by Gloria-Jean Masciarotte, 'The Madonna with Child, and another child, and still another child . . .: sensationalism and the dysfunction of emotions' (1991–92). Masciarotte observes that in a later edition of *Three Essays* Freud 'notes that girls never question a new baby. This', she concludes, 'suggests a different relation to knowledge, a different ordering of curiosity and expectations based on gender' (ibid.: 124, n.8).

8 In her 1989 essay Irigaray comments on the difference between the play of little boys and little girls in the absence of the mother. Irigaray contrasts the famous Freudian paradigm of play for little boys (Freud's grandson Ernst and the spool, the solitary game of *fort-da*), which she reads as play with an *object* (the mother is 'reduced' to an object), with the little girl's play with a doll, which she regards as a 'quasi-object', because the 'mother's identity as a subject is the same as hers' (ibid.: 132). This is convincing enough, although I would argue that the doll could be either a boy doll or a girl doll; it does not matter, as we shall see. More important, it is not at all necessary to hypothesize the *mother's absence*. The daughter's play can – and often does – go on in the presence of the mother. My point is that these two models of play, based on gender, are *not* symmetrical. Finally, Irigaray concludes (not on the basis of this paradigm alone, of course) that the 'mother always remains too familiar and too close' (ibid.: 133); this also need not necessarily be the case. I should add that Freud himself saw the little girl's relation to her doll in terms of subject and object. As he puts it in 'Female sexuality' (1931), the child 'actually makes its mother into the object and behaves as the active subject towards her' (1953–74: 21: 236).

9 It is not surprising that many feminists, critiquing Freudian psychoanalysis (and its patriarchal followers), have chosen to do so precisely in terms of sexuality itself, and in terms of same-sex or lesbian practices. For excellent recent work in this vein, see Parveen Adams, 'Of female bondage' (1989), and Teresa de Lauretis, 'Film and the primal fantasy – one more time: On Sheila McLaughlin's *She Must Be Seeing Things*' (1990–91).

10 I discuss gender and generational identity with reference to Eva Figes's novel *Waking* in *Aging and Its Discontents* (Woodward, 1991: 92–108).

11 With regard to the hysteric, Freud explains in his letter 52 of 6 December 1896 to Wilhelm Fliess, the internal exchange between the two generations this way: 'an exchange occurs between the generations: first generation: Perversion, second generation: Hysteria, and consequent, sterility' (Freud, 1954: 180).

12 The word 'choric' is, of course, a reference to Kristeva. For a thoughtful discussion of several of the texts by Kristeva and Freud to which I have referred here, see Silverman (1988: 101–86). Silverman argues that the little girl's attachment to the mother in the pre-Oedipal period is one of both identification and object-choice (sexuality enters her analysis here in a way that it

does not enter mine); and at one point she suggests, albeit tentatively, that 'although there *is* a third term, and it is – as usual – the father', she 'cannot help but wonder whether there is not another, more important third term here, one that plays a far more central place within the daughter's early libidinal economy than does the father. I refer, of course, to the child' (ibid.: 153). Thus Silverman reads Robert Altman's 1977 film *Three Women* in terms of three generations of women. But she does not pursue this analysis.

13 Interestingly enough, Freud identifies one of the conflicts central to Leonardo's character as that between knowledge (reason) and emotion, concluding that Leonardo sublimated passion into the search for knowledge. Could one not say the same of Freud himself?

14 We might note, for example, that Teresa de Lauretis prefaces her essay 'The violence of rhetoric' with an epigraph from Nietzsche. It is a quotation from *The Gay Science* that begins: 'Older women are more skeptical in their heart of hearts than any man'. De Lauretis, however, generalizes from 'older women' to 'woman': the opening line of her essay reads: 'Woman's skepticism, Nietzsche suggests, comes from her disregard for truth' (de Lauretis, 1987: 31). Mary Ann Doane, on the other hand, comments pointedly on the recurrent image of the older woman in Nietzsche (see her 'Veiling over desire: close-ups of the woman' (1989)).

15 The bibliography is too lengthy to be rehearsed here. One of the most influential books, of course, is Nancy Chodorow, *The Reproduction of Mothering: Psychoanalysis and the Sociology of Gender* (1978). See also, for example, *The (M)Other Tongue: Essays in Feminist Psychoanalytic Interpretation*, edited by Shirley Nelson Garner, Claire Kahane, and Madelon Sprengnether (1985) and Luce Irigaray, *Le Corps-à-corps avec la mère* (1981).

16 I am here echoing Rosi Bradotti (who is referring, of course, to Irigaray), 'The politics of ontological difference' (1989: 96). Yet even as Bradotti subscribes to the project of constructing a new female symbolic and reads Irigaray's work as a strategic intervention in patriarchal culture, she nevertheless seems to subscribe to what psychoanalysis has had to say about generational politics. Bradotti:

> The psychoanalytic situation brings about, among other things, the fundamental dissymmetry between self and other, that is constitutive of the subject; this is related to the non-interchangeability of positions between analyst and patient, to the irrevocable anteriority of the former, that is to say, ultimately to time. Time, the great master, calling upon each individual to take his/her place in the game of generations, is the inevitable, the inescapable horizon. One of the ethical aims of the psychoanalytic situation is to lead the subject to accept this inscription into time, the passing of generations and the dissymmetries it entails, so as to accept the radical otherness of the self.
>
> (Bradotti, 1989: 98)

Thus Bradotti can speak elsewhere in the same essay of that old bugaboo – generation gaps.

17 See, for example, Renato Rosaldo, 'Imperialist nostalgia' (1989).

REFERENCES

Abelin, Ernest A. (1980) 'Triangulation, the role of the father and the origins of core gender identity during the rapprochement subphase', in Ruth F. Lax,

Sheldon Bach, and J. Alexis Burland (eds) *Rapprochement: The Critical Subphase of Separation-Individuation*, New York: Jason Aronson.

Adams, Parveen (1989) 'Of female bondage', in T. Brennan (ed.) *Between Feminism and Psychoanalysis*, London: Routledge.

Banner, Lois (1992) *In Full Flower: Aging Women, Power, and Sexuality*, New York: Alfred A. Knopf.

Beauvoir, Simone de (1978) [1970] *The Coming of Age, [La Vieillesse]* trans. Patrick O'Brian, New York: Warner.

Benjamin, Jessica (1988) *The Bonds of Love: Psychoanalysis, Feminism, and the Problem of Domination*, New York: Pantheon.

Bowlby, John (1973) *Separation: Anxiety and Anger*, London: Hogarth Press.

Bradotti, Rosi (1989) 'The politics of ontological difference', in T. Brennan (ed.) *Between Feminism and Psychoanalysis*, London: Routledge.

Brennan, Teresa (ed.) (1989) *Between Feminism and Psychoanalysis*, London: Routledge.

Chodorow, Nancy (1978) *The Reproduction of Mothering: Psychoanalysis and the Sociology of Gender*, Berkeley: University of California Press.

Chodorow, Nancy (1989) 'Seventies questions for thirties women: gender and generation in a study of early women psychoanalysts', in N. Chodorow (ed.) *Feminism and Psychoanalytic Theory*, New Haven: Yale University Press.

Cixous, Hélène (1981) 'Sorties', in Hélène Cixous and Catherine Clément (eds) *The Newly Born Woman*, trans. Betsy Wing, Minneapolis: University of Minnesota Press.

Copper, Baba (1988) *Over the Hill: Reflections on Ageism Between Women*, Freedom, CA: Crossing Press.

Doane, Mary Ann (1989) 'Veiling over desire: close-ups of the woman', in Richard Feldstein and Judith Roof (eds) *Feminism and Psychoanalysis*, Ithaca: Cornell University Press.

Foucault, Michel (1980) *The History of Sexuality*, in vol. 1, *An Introduction*, trans. Robert Hurley, New York: Vintage.

Freud, Sigmund (1953–74) *The Standard Edition of the Complete Psychological Works of Sigmund Freud*, edited and translated by James Strachey, 24 vols, London: Hogarth Press.

Freud, Sigmund (1900) *The Interpretation of Dreams*, vols 4, 5.

Freud, Sigmund (1905) *Three Essays on the Theory of Sexuality*, vol. 7.

Freud, Sigmund (1909) 'Notes upon a case of obsessional neurosis', vol. 10.

Freud, Sigmund (1910) *Leonardo da Vinci and a memory of his childhood*, vol. 11.

Freud, Sigmund (1917) 'Mourning and melancholia', vol. 14.

Freud, Sigmund (1926) *Inhibitions, Symptoms and Anxiety*, vol. 20.

Freud, Sigmund (1931) 'Female sexuality', vol. 21.

Freud, Sigmund (1933) 'Femininity', vol. 22.

Freud, Sigmund (1936) 'A disturbance of memory on the Acropolis' vol. 22.

Freud, Sigmund (1954) *The Origins of Psycho-Analysis: Letters to Wilhelm Fliess, Drafts and Notes: 1887–1902*, ed. Marie Bonaparte, Anna Freud and Ernst Kris, tr. Eric Mosbacher and James Strachey, London: Imago, p. 180.

Garner, Shirley Nelson, Kahane, Claire, and Sprengnether, Madelon (eds) (1985) *The (M)other Tongue: Essays in Feminist Psychoanalytic Interpretation*, Ithaca: Cornell University Press.

Green, André (1973) *Le Discours Vivant*, Paris: Presses Universitaires de France.

Griffiths, Morwenna (1988) 'Feminism, feelings and philosophy', in Morwenna Griffiths and Margaret Whitford (eds) *Feminist Perspectives in Philosophy*, Bloomington: Indiana University Press.

Grossberg, Lawrence (1988) 'Postmodernity and affect: all dressed up with no place to go', *Communication* 10: 271–93.

Grosz, Elizabeth (1989) *Sexual Subversions: Three French Feminists*, Boston: Allen & Unwin.

Hirsh, Marianne (1989) *The Mother/Daughter Plot: Narrative, Psychoanalysis, Feminism*, Bloomington: Indiana University Press.

hooks, bell (1986–7) 'Talking back', *Discourse* 8 (Fall-Winter): 123–8.

hooks, bell (1990) *Yearning: Race, Gender, and Cultural Politics*, Boston: South End Press.

Irigaray, Luce (1981) *Le Corps-à-corps avec la mère*, Montreal: Editions de la Pleine Lune.

Irigaray, Luce (1985) *Speculum of the Other Woman*, trans. Gillian G. Gill, Ithaca: Cornell University Press.

Irigaray, Luce (1989) 'The gesture in psychoanalysis', in T. Brennan (ed.) *Between Feminism and Psychoanalysis*, London: Routledge, trans. Elizabeth Guild.

Jardine, Alice (1989) 'Notes for analysis', in T. Brennan (ed.) *Between Feminism and Psychoanalysis*, London: Routledge.

Kristeva, Julia (1980a) 'Motherhood according to Giovanni Bellini', in *Desire in Language: A Semiotic Approach to Literature and Art*, trans. Thomas Gora, Alice Jardine, and Leon S. Roudiez, New York: Columbia University Press.

Kristeva, Julia (1980b) 'Place names', in *Desire in Language: A Semiotic Approach to Literature and Art*, trans. Thomas Gora, Alice Jardine, and Leon S. Roudiez, New York: Columbia University Press.

Lacan, Jacques (1977) 'Aggressivity in psychoanalysis', in *Ecrits*, trans. Alan Sheridan, New York: W.W. Norton.

Laplanche, Jean, and Pontalis, J.-B. (1973) *The Language of Psychoanalysis*, trans. Donald Nicholson-Smith, New York: W.W. Norton.

de Lauretis, Teresa (1987) 'The violence of rhetoric', in *Technologies of Gender: Essays on Theory, Film, and Fiction*, Bloomington: Indiana University Press.

de Lauretis, Teresa (1990–91) 'Film and the primal fantasy – one more time: on Sheila McLaughlin's *She Must Be Seeing Things*', Center for Twentieth Century Studies, Working Paper 7, University of Wisconsin, Milwaukee.

MacDonald, Barbara (1983) *Look Me in the Eye: Old Women, Aging and Ageism*, San Francisco: Spinsters, Ink.

Masciarotte, Gloria-Jean (1991–92) 'The Madonna with child, and another child, and still another child . . .: sensationalism and the dysfunction of emotions', *Discourse* 14 (1): 88–125.

Moi, Toril (1989) 'Patriarchal thought and the drive for knowledge', in T. Brennan (ed.) *Between Feminism and Psychoanalysis*, London: Routledge.

Rosaldo, Renato (1989) 'Imperialist nostalgia', in *Culture and Truth: The Remaking of Social Analysis*, Boston: Beacon.

Sartre, Jean-Paul (1948) *The Emotions: Outline of a Theory*, trans. Bernard Frechtman, New York: Philosophical Library.

Silverman, Kaja (1988) *The Acoustic Mirror: The Female Voice in Psychoanalysis and Cinema*, Bloomington: Indiana University Press.

Winnicott, Donald W. (1971) 'Creativity and its origins', in *Playing and Reality*, London: Tavistock.

Woodward, Kathleen (1990–91) 'Introduction to special issue on the emotions', *Discourse* 13 (1): 3–11.

Woodward, Kathleen (1991) *Aging and Its Discontents: Freud and Other Fictions*, Bloomington: Indiana University Press.

7

IMAGING THE AGING
OF MEN

Jeff Hearn

Bury me in mauve Reeboks
With my neatly fitting tracksuit
my Walkman
blaring 'I will survive'
As I'm lowered into the ground
Not yet frozen.

INTRODUCTION

This chapter focuses explicitly on the social category of 'men', and the changing significance of aging in the contemporary imaging of men, and of men for imaging age and aging. This necessitates an engagement with the three-way relationship between imaging, aging and men. This focus is partly in terms of the cultural construction of men in later life, of 'older men', but also, and in some ways more importantly, in the complex constructions between 'men' and 'age'/'aging'/'agedness'. Thus in writing of 'the aging of men', I do not specifically mean the chronological process by which men are assumed to become older; rather I am referring to the ways in which 'men' are constructed as meanings through and by reference to 'age'. This is both a matter of the social construction of the category 'men' and of particular men; it is also a question of the construction of men's experience through the lens of age.

The issue of older people is of growing political importance. Contemporary concerns come partly from governmental interest about the aging population – and their cost. The Organization for Economic Co-operation and Development (OECD) forecasts published in 1988 indicated that whilst 15.1 per cent of Britain's population would be over 65 in 1990, the figure was likely to rise to over 20 per cent by 2040. The comparable figures for Germany were 15.9 per cent and 29.6 per cent. State pensions are the biggest item of social security expenditure in the UK and similar societies.

In the 1980s and 1990s the changing age structure of the population has attracted increased interest especially in relation to employment, as the major determinant of post-retirement incomes. The situation is summarized by Itzin and Phillipson.

> Older workers in Britain have experienced conflicting pressures in the 1980s and early 1990s. In the early and middle part of the 1980s they were being urged to leave the workforce as soon as possible, as a way of coping with high unemployment and large numbers of school leavers (Laczko and Phillipson, 1991). By the early 1990s, however, concern about the ageing of the workforce shifted the debate towards how to stem the flow of older workers out of employment, and remove age barriers in areas such as recruitment and retention (Naylor, 1990; Taylor and Walker, 1992; Trinder, Hulme and McCarthy, 1992).
>
> (Itzin and Phillipson, 1993: 1)

Concerns about older people have, however, frequently remained ungendered. When gender has been 'brought in', it has often been in terms of the growing numbers of older women. Less often has there been an explicit focus on the category of 'older men'. This applies in policy debate, and in popular discussion, and indeed in sociological and other social science literature. In the case of sociological work, analyses of aging have not usually had an explicit and critical focus on older men. This means that existing literature and theorizing on aging needs to be applied to both women and men, and needs to be subject to critique on the grounds of gender. The sociology of aging, accordingly, should be fully, not partially, gendered. Interesting exceptions to this general rule include Blakemore and Boneham's (1994) review of 'older black and Asian people' and Fennell, Phillipson and Evers's (1988) sociology of old age. There is a wide range of sociological theories of aging, which may be relevant in the analysis of older men. These include theories of life stages, social activity, disengagement, individuation, existential construction, economic power and redundancy within capitalism, gendered power within patriarchy, embodiment, media construction, and textual deconstruction. In each case, and indeed with other theories, it is useful to ask – what do these theories say or imply about older men?

The aging of men cannot be separated from the question of political context and ideology. A focus on older men needs to be considered in the context of change of and about men and has been occurring in the full range of social awareness, from the global to the societal, local, domestic, and personal, as well as in cultural, media and academic sites and forums. In particular a focus on older men may problematize dominant forms of men and masculinities, including hegemonic masculinities.

IMAGING MEN

Men are talked of, pictured, imaged. To do so invokes age and agedness. Men and masculinities, whether in image, text, social practice, or social structure, are necessarily about aging, sometimes explicitly so, often implicitly. There is a recurring inseparability of 'men' and age/aging. Age is implicated in the social construction of men – both in the distinction of men from young men and boys, and in the construction of particular types of men.

In developing this critique of imaging men, I take issue with notions of 'images of', whether images of men or images of aging. Rather than speak of specific images *of* men, I understand imaging and men as mutually inclusive of each other. Images and imaging involve references to culturally assigned meanings of looking, showing, being looked at, being shown. The very notion of image rests upon such cultural processes of looking and showing, which themselves rest upon dominant forms of men, which themselves look upon images. Thus I am as much concerned with the gendering of imaging as with the imaging of gender. Moreover, these processes of representation and signification are not limited to the formal media and institutional forms of communication; they exist in all forms and instances of social practice. They apply not only in imaging gender; they are themselves gendered. For what is important is not what images are, but who produces them, how they are produced, and by whom and how they are consumed. Images are produced in their consumption, so that looking and imaging are inseparable and reciprocally gendered.

In this chapter I am concerned with three kinds of imaging: in historical constructions of the category of older men, in more self-conscious biographical and autobiographical accounts of older men, in the mass media portrayal of older men. I am also necessarily concerned with the interaction of history, biography and representation. These three foci are the concern of the following three sections. In each case, imaging aging and imaging older men is not some absolute process, but is culturally and historically specific, with its own sets of references and frames of meaning. And in each case there are contrasting processes: of consolidation and fragmentation in the historical category of older men; of identification and fracturing in the experience and accounts of older men; and of dominant and occasionally subversive representation in the mass media of older men (cf. Hearn, 1992). Throughout issues of power, difference and ageism are important in understanding the category, experience and portrayal of older men (see Butler, 1963; Biggs, 1993).

IMAGING AGING MEN AND MEN'S POWER IN HISTORY

Age, that is increasing and greater age, has been a major source of power for men in this and many other societies. In some, and particularly pre-industrial, societies, it has been the major determinant of the social power of different men. Furthermore, 'maleness' and 'age(dness)' were usually mutually reinforcing and reaffirming as means to power. The age of men is often related to both the generalized power of men, and men's power over descendants and dependants. Let us then consider some of the ways in which this changing relation of age and power is imaged, and how for older men that power is both consolidated and fragmented.

In industrialized societies this relationship has become much more complex, especially through the valorization of employed labour and organizational statuses within capitalism (Phillipson, 1982) and public patriarchies (Hearn, 1992). Labour-power has been transformed from generational ownership to ownership of the body on the 'free market'. First, beyond a certain point, the older the man, the weaker he becomes not just physically and bodily, but also socially. While life expectancy was low this shift was not very significant as the decline was relatively rapid and the 'age of weakness' was shortlived. However, increased life expectancy has meant that there is now a longer period of physical and social decline, indeed of 'old age' itself. This may be constructed in terms of 'disengagement' (Cummings and Henry, 1961), the continuation of 'activity' (Havinghurst, 1963), or some combination of both.

Second, the focus of labour and labour-power has been transformed from the body to the mind/technology, with the expansion of tertiary (service), quaternary (information), office, state and professional work. This means that aging does not necessarily reduce the value of labour, and may indeed in some cases increase it until death or close to death.

Third, the cessation or reduction of employment after retirement and creation of state pensions has formed a 'subclass' of older men. Although there was a series of governmental investigations into the question of pensions and the aged poor in the nineteenth century (1885–7, 1895, 1896 and 1899), state pensions were not introduced until 1908 for those over 70 (Thane, 1982). Interestingly, exceptions were made for the 'undeserving', such as those who had been imprisoned in the previous ten years. Age is from there on defined through retirement, and thus in contrast to employment. Retirements have very different significances for women and men, not least because women never retire from what is for many their prime work – their unpaid work at home (Fennell *et al.*, 1988).

Older people in the UK and in most of the world are predominantly women, and older women are disproportionately represented among poor older people (Brown, 1990). Retired men fare better financially than women, partly through their greater access to occupational pension schemes following full-time employment. Increasingly there is a dual system of welfare for older people with state provided subsistence on the one hand and occupational funding on the other (Midwinter, 1991). While this division is to some extent gendered, it is also important to fully acknowledge the power of older men. This has long been exacerbated by lower take-up of supplementary benefits of only two-thirds (Hansard, 1986) and the de-indexation of pension from earnings by the Conservative Government in 1980 (Barrett, 1993).

In recent years the occupational structuring of 'retired' older men has been greatly complicated by 'early retirement', 'voluntary severance', 'retirement at 50', and 'no jobs for life'. In middle-class and professional sectors, there has been a creation of a new younger 'retired' group, who in turn have been a significant consumer grouping in the organizing of pensions, insurances and purchasing. The construction of men as 'retired' has in turn produced a wealth of literature, including that on retirement planning, retirement courses, the University of the Third Age, and so on (for example, Kemp and Buttle, 1979). This also addresses men in marriage, and the possible problems of the man spending more time at home, and even in the kitchen. Men are constructed here as newcomers to the home. On the other hand, there appear to be far more older men taking caring responsibilities than previously imagined (Arber and Gilbert, 1990). Specialist organizations have also developed, for example, REACH (Retired Executives Action Clearing-House), giving advice on how executives might manage the transition to retirement through further work, often in the voluntary and charity sector (Kirby, 1984).

Fourth, the production of older men as a 'subclass' has also occurred through generational, social and geographical segregation, and the modernization of death. Geographical and social mobility have created separable social age-sets and generational-sets. In particular older people have become separated off from those who are younger and closer to child-rearing age. Continuing this theme, older men are also defined by virtue of their earlier death than women. Older men are constructed as pre-death. They are relatively redundant, even invisible, not just in terms of paid work and family responsibilities, but more importantly in terms of life itself.

101

An interesting example of this is the relative 'invisibility' of grand-fatherhood. What is perhaps most interesting about grandfatherhood is the fact that it is not talked about very much (*Nurturing News*, 1985), and indeed appears to be often constructed implicitly, and through allusion, joking, and even absence, rather than any more direct narrat-ives. Cunningham-Burley (1984) has written specifically on the complex connections between the construction of gender and the gendered construction of grandfatherhood. The topic is becoming more ex-plicitly addressed, not least because grandfatherhood is now more problematic. This is not only because of the 'new social contract' (Kornhaber, 1985; Kornhaber and Woodward, 1985) whereby the generations settle for a mutual remoteness, but also because men now tend to live longer and so have adult grandchildren (Baranowski, 1985). Thus grandfathers are now being defined more fully by adults than by their own adult power over young grandchildren.

Fifth, generational power and the power of the father has been to some extent superseded by the power of the state and state law, and the men that control them. Thus, the older men become, the more they become dependants not just on the state, but on other younger, more powerful men there. This applies especially around retirement and beyond.

Sixth, a much more complex set of changes surround the links between consumerism and older men, whether it is the figuring of fit, healthy men (patients and doctors) in BUPA adverts or the spread of youth fashion (trainers, tracksuits, toiletries) into the older men's market. Old men can now die with their Reeboks on!

In all of these ways the association of age and power has become more complex for men. The political economy of aging and of older men can no longer be reduced to a simple reference to retirement. While the category of 'older men' has been produced through the historical processes described, the relationship of men's age and men's power has also become more diversified. Older age may signify power not just through the historical carry over of generational and patriarchal power, but through mental labour-power and the accumulation of resources. 'Middle age' may signify power for men through formal, organizational statuses as well as through physical labour-power and indeed patriarchal power. Youth may signify power for men through physical strength, body shape, cultural image, and sexual virility. Thus men's power can be understood in a number of 'aged' ways. This may help to explain why age has such a contradictory significance for men. It may imply power at a common-sense, even emotional, level, even though this is only part of the picture. The important issue is that age is construed as a maker of power, or as a reference point of power, even when power is lacking.

IMAGING OLDER MEN'S EXPERIENCE

Despite the wealth of connections between 'age' and 'maleness', there has been relatively little concern with the relationship of aging and the social construction of older men and masculinities. This applies to most of the literature on both aging and the construction of old age, and the literature on the social construction of men. Additionally, as already noted, aging, and in particular the cultural construction of later life, has sometimes been understood as primarily about women, not least because of the greater life expectancy and greater number of older women than older men. When men have been focused on, it has often been primarily in terms of retirement and redundancy.

In contrast, there is now much more focused interest in the critical debate on men and masculinities. Accordingly, in deconstructing imaging men, I am writing in a critical relationship to recent practical and theoretical problematizations of men and masculinities. Much of the impetus for this has come from feminist theory and practice; it has also come in a different way from gay liberation and scholarship; and from the more limited and more ambiguous development of anti-sexist theory and practice by men. Interestingly in much of this literature, critique has been directed towards younger adult men, including the critique of certain patterns and styles of young men and youth masculinities. These masculinities are presented as dominant and hegemonic, though they may be in practice modelled primarily on the actions of young white able-bodied heterosexual men.

Similarly, much of the recent critical literature has given priority to the experiences of men as fathers, or in relation to childcare or in relation to sexuality. The upsurge in interest in the social and political problematization of 'men' came very largely from the 1960s – from the Women's Liberation Movement, the Gay Liberation Movement, and some men's responses to feminism. Initial concerns from women were very much around male violence, men's control of employment and discrimination against women, and men's intrusions in personal life. From men interest was focused much more on sexuality, personal relationships, children, identity. Little concern was expressed for issues around older men, aging, intergenerational relationships, disability, illness, care, and death. Much of this literature has been produced by those, both women and men, strongly influenced by the Second Wave Feminism of the 1960s and 1970s in their own youth or young adulthood. This is probably partly a question of the prime concerns amongst women within Second Wave Feminism (see, for example, Hanmer, 1990), and partly a question of the changing priorities in people's own personal lives.

More recently, interest has shifted to older men's critical reflection on older men's lives. This can be made sense of in a variety of ways. It is itself partly a reflection of a greater awareness of the complexities of both later life and men's lives. The lives of older men contradict both the usual characteristics of men in terms of men's power; and the usual characteristics of older people in terms of lack of power. And older men are re-forming themselves by reflecting on themselves and each other 'as older men', in a personally and sometimes politically self-conscious way. This movement can be located as part of the broad development of identity politics and of identifications with given, yet changing, social categories.

One way in which interest in the lives of older men has developed is through men's own changing priorities as men age. As noted, these include concern with changing family relationships, physical/bodily change, illness, caring, disability, death. This applies to the impact of personal experience in autobiographical writing, and (auto)biographical reflection more generally. An example of the changing place of mutual care in men's experience is the growth of the 'buddy' system for gay men who are HIV positive.

Men's reflection on themselves as older men might also be seen as an example of the continuing and conscious search for both identity and intimacy, a sign of the assumption of modernity in the times of postmodernity and the destruction of intimacy and identity. Thus the statement of identity paradoxically became established with the passing of identity. Men became self-recognized as older men with the passing of that identity. This applies to identification of 'old(er) men', as well as 'older gay men', 'black male elders', 'grandfathers', as well as men facing the prospect of death.

Whereas academic studies of older people have emphasized changing roles, life stages and crises, disengagement, social exchange, and the meaning of new social activities, older men's personal experience has often hinged around a different set of concepts and images. For example, there is a growing interest in the sexuality of older men, both gay and heterosexual. This parallels the growing concern with issues of sexuality for people with disabilities, people in residential institutions, and others who have been marginalized. There is now a considerable literature on the experiences of older gay men, partly a reflection of the aging of men who were young during the days of the early Gay Liberation Movement. Such men have organized to a limited extent, and have written and been written about as researchers, campaigners and interviewees. These writings can also be located within the growing interest in oral history, reminiscence work, and life review. Examples of this gay biographical/autobiographical genre are *Between the Acts* (Porter and Weeks, 1991), *Walking After Midnight* (Hall Carpenter

Archives, 1989), the *Daring Hearts* collection (Brighton Ourstory Project, 1992), and *Quiet Fire* (Vacha, 1985).

Between the Acts is a book of accounts of gay men gathered from interviews conducted in 1978–9 about their experiences 'between the acts' – the Labouchère Amendment of the Criminal Law Amendment Act of 1885, which criminalized male homosexuality, and the Sexual Offences Act of 1967, which partially decriminalized male homosexual activities 'in private'. The oldest man interviewed was born in 1892 and spoke of a lifetime of being homosexual but often without the sex, especially in his later years. The next described how he had led a covert homosexual life, and how after his wife died, and approaching his eighties, he had attended the local gay liberation group and become its 'mascot' (Porter and Weeks, 1991: 12). The third had been a loner much of his life and in his retirement home had fallen in love with a fellow resident, a heterosexual man of 85. The fourth born in 1897 had had two quite separate lives: a private homosexual life and a public respectable life.

These stories are of interest for many reasons. They are largely retrospective; they describe the diverse ways of mediating 'illegality' in individual men's lives; they present a body of work that affirms 'being older gay men'. As such, they both challenge dominant stereotypes of older (heterosexual) men, and of (younger) gay men. They show identities; they provide material for the formation and re-formation of the identities of others, as readers and talkers; and they also speak of the fracturings of experience and accounts of experience.

Walking After Midnight is a more finely crafted book; the interviews are presented in a more reworked, less direct way. It also adds further elements of interest, including the attention to ethnic and cultural diversity amongst older gay men. It also addresses the issue of aging and death between gay men, in terms of both personal bereavement and financial hardship, because of the general structuring of pensions and ownership (Hall Carpenter Archives, 1989: 38).

A different kind of reflection is found in David Jackson's (1990) critical autobiography, *Unmasking Masculinity*. Written in his early fifties, the question of aging is central throughout the text. The key moment is probably his recent physical and emotional collapse, and subsequent heart surgery:

> My bodily crack-up provoked me to take on a critical reassessment of my traditional bodily relations and masculine identity. My body reasserted its claims for a fuller representation in my existence by disrupting the illusion of my coherent, unified, rational intellect and shredding it into small fragments.
> This shocking invasion blew up the fantasy dream of 'He-Man',

masculine power in my body. It forced the actual state of my damaged body into critical visibility. And without creating another fantasy of total, harmonious reintegration between my mind and my body, it showed me why it was necessary, while living within the fragments, to bring my bodily experience and my emotions into a closer creative contact with my intellect. That process is still continuing, bumpily and unevenly.

Physical breakdown is a terrifying experience for many men because it connects the masculine body with weakness, dependency and passivity – all the supposedly 'feminine' qualities they have spent a lifetime defining and defending themselves against. Often for the first time in some men's lives it opens up fearful cracks in the 'hard case' front of heterosexual masculinity. Breakdown, illness and injury can also be a strategy for renegotiating dominant, heterosexual, masculine identities that have become imprisoning for some men, like me, who have never felt completely at home within those kinds of conventional investments. In another way, falling apart helped me to negotiate the conflict between wanting to give up traditional power without losing face. It offered my partner and myself a safe place within which both of us could revert to temporary, secure identities, without giving up the combined struggle to change gendered inequalities. Very occasionally we could resort, as a temporary breather, to much more rigidly dichotomized identities. For example, I could enjoy my official permission to take to my bed and admit my dependency on my partner, at the same time as my partner might take fleeting pleasure in looking after me and getting closer, if it didn't go on for too long.

Falling apart turned out to be a way of refusing more thrusting, driving and pushing. And it also helped me to choose to make more confident investments in my other, transitional selves. With official legitimacy, I could turn my back on more patriarchal pressure, and start to put energy, in a different collaborative way, into 'changing men' issues at both a personal and social level. I have begun to set myself new physical limits, and have started to restructure and repace my life: with difficulty, it has to be admitted, but I am moving in that general direction.

(Jackson, 1990: 68–9)

He sees this as a turning point forcing him to re-evaluate his previous life 'as a man' and change his life in the present. His reflection is based on the link between aging, masculinity, and bodily change. These themes are central to his autobiography; they are not grafted on to other 'achievements' in the manner of the traditional heroic biography of men. Aging and the aging body constitute this older man, and possibly older men more generally, in a way that less self-conscious identifications of older men ignore. Thus in some ways *Unmasking Masculinity* is a paradigm or archetypical text, in that it interrogates, albeit in poststructuralist fashion, the subjectivity of 'the older man'.

Such biographical and autobiographical reflections can thus be made sense of in several ways. They can be understood as the personal products of large-scale political economic change. They can also be seen as the outcome of political organizing, the creation of voices that are not often heard, even though they come from within the dominant category of men. They can be an aspect of identity politics that allows older men to speak 'as older men', and simultaneously speak (of) the fracturing of experience. Alternatively, these personal reflections can be part of the process of individuation in the second half of life (Jung, 1933), or even the confronting of the crisis of integrity and despair before death (Erikson, 1982). Perhaps it is more satisfactory to consider all these and indeed other representations as relevant, all providing a part of the picture.

IMAGING OLDER MEN IN THE MEDIA

Having considered first, some matters of historical change, in the production and diversification of older men and, second, some examples of how these have been paralleled in the movement towards autobiographical reflection as 'older men', I now want to consider contemporary imaging of older men in the media. In particular I want to explore the relationship of power and difference in the changing cultural representation of men in later life. This concerns a number of paradoxical relationships. First there is the relationship between the separation of and identification as 'older men', and the breaking down of that category, including the blurring of those separations (from younger men) and identifications. Second, there is the relationship between the perpetuation of men's power in representations of older men, and the subversion of men's power. This includes the use of the category to develop new forms of power base for men, for example, 'grey power', pensions campaign organizations. Third, there is the relationship of the establishment of the category of older men and the diversification of older men. Diverse kinds of older men may contradict, even subvert, dominant stereotypes of men, older men, and relevant groups of younger men. Let us now turn to some examples of these paradoxes.

Imaging older men in the press and the mass media is through a number of genres. First and foremost are the formally successful men, that is, men who occupy formal positions of power and authority in organizations. These include 'world leaders', politicians, businessmen, experts, administrators, judges. These account for much of the more frequent portrayal of older men as against older women in the media. Lambert *et al.*'s (1984) study of UK television over a two week period found 50 per cent of programmes included people over the age of 60, and that the greater part of this could be accounted for by the portrayal of world leaders. Broadcasting men, especially introducers, commentators, hosts, 'link men', 'anchor men', and 'quiz masters' often appear at first rather ageless. Just as men may be presented as asexual in contrast to women's sexuality and sexualities, so too may men be presented a-aged. In discussing the significance that is given to the age of women broadcasters (such as Kate Adie), Suzanne Moore (1993) asks:

> Do John Simpson or Jon Snow or Peter Sissons worry about their lines, their paunches, their greying hair? Do their editors feel these old boys should not be inflicted on the rest of us any longer? Do we worry about the emptiness of their private lives, as we seem to do with Adie?

These successful men defy being simply 'older men'; as such they reproduce men's taken-for-granted asexual, agendered, a-aged power and authority.

BBC Radio 4 is a positive hive of such taken-for-granted older men – comedians, quiz show contestants, experts, commentators, and in particular Radio 4 panellists. The atmosphere on *Gardeners' Question Time, Does the Team Think?, Just a Minute* and many more is usually 'clubby'. The combination is white, aging, and funny, but not necessarily heterosexual. What we are dealing with here is another manifestation of the overwhelming implicitness of older men. Just as grandfathers are formed implicitly and reactively so are many male public figures. That does nothing to decrease their power and possible oppressiveness – again whether we are talking of the abusive grandfather or the dominating broadcaster.

Less common, but perhaps more interesting, are men also portrayed because of their imminent or recent 'moving on'. This can be men who have retired or are about to be retired, or who face the prospect of change in occupational status. The archetypes for this are to be found in sport – either amongst the senior players (Ian Botham, Viv Richards), who are about to move from the full-time professional ranks, or amongst sports managers and administrators (Ted Dexter, Graham Taylor, or the football league club manager).

These waves of succession are also frequently 'played out' on radio and television, and through the 'personalities' that operate there. Two examples of this from radio are the interest in the ages of the predominantly male group of disc jockeys on Radio 1. While its 'target audience' is 15 to 35, a good number of its DJs have been much older, and accordingly have been criticized for being 'out of touch'. Heading the list is Alan Freeman, aged 65, a founder father of Radio 1 and 'a passionate supporter of heavy rock'. John Peel, 53, is placed at the 'cutting edge of music', having been the first to play punk and rap on national radio. These facts of age take on a particular iconic significance as Radio 1 appears to be moving to 'a lighter approach and a younger audience' (Choudhary, 1993).

Here we have the theme of the 'aging king' replayed – men's structural power is refuelled by the loss of power of the individual powerful – a theme found in Greek and Shakespearian tragedy, and in many cultural traditions. The theme has recently figured in a number of films which speak of the sadness/status of the aging respectable man: *Shadowlands* (academic), *Remains of the Day* (butler), *The Browning Version* (schoolteacher). It is sometimes repeated by inversion through the son as with the rise of Michael Douglas, invoking the absence of father Kirk. This theme had taken a new turn in the era of AIDS and the double demise of Rock Hudson, both his latterly coming out as gay, and his death following his HIV positive diagnosis (Dyer, 1993).

All of these images are 'played out' in the broad context of the appeal of the youth and young men in America, film and Hollywood, such that men = youth = sex (see Hearn and Melechi, 1992). Indeed press reports that Eric Clapton (Cream) is a fly fisherman, and Roger Daltry (The Who) and Steve Winwood (Traffic) both fish and shoot, reaffirm their paradoxical relation with youth.

Further paradoxes are literally seen in the representation of older men in film, video and television. Indeed visual media give the opportunity of engaging in ambiguities between social meaning and the physical/aging body. This brings us to the complex question of stereotyping in the media, and particularly in television, entertainment and other non-current affairs broadcasting. Recent research has been conveniently summarized by Simon Biggs (1993: 44–5):

A 'perpetual middle-age' seems to populate UK soap-operas, according to Mullen and Von Zwanenberg (1988), where older people are almost universally omitted. Sit-coms (Marshall, 1990: 31) on the other hand promote the ends of the stereotypical spectrum. Older people are either '. . . enfeebled, vague and forgetful, or at the other extreme cantankerous old battle-axes'. Kubey (1980) found evidence of 'reverse-stereotypes', whereby the older person is portrayed as unrealistically 'exceptions to the rule'. More recently, the mass media has consciously promoted an active image of ageing (Nussbaum *et al.*, 1989), the athletic extended middle-ager, which corresponds to an increased awareness of the 'young-old' as relatively affluent consumers. However, these authors note a corresponding lack of concern for the problems of older age and ageing. . . . Enduring problems are unlikely to be newsworthy as they '. . . take place over time, with no easy examples or quick fixes' (Nussbaum *et al.*, 1989: 45). . . . Rodwell *et al.* (1992: 7) conclude their study of British television by saying:

> There was no dominant emphasis on passivity or dependency. If anything, there was a tendency to present a selective view of old age that played down the possible connections between old age, disability, ill health and death. The more frequent and dominant images tended to have strong positive elements . . . The most common negative characteristics often involved some combination of complaining, interfering, being miserable, bad tempered, gossiping and being a kill-joy.

These studies would suggest that whilst a positive, active image is portrayed, concerns are stigmatized or ignored.

A few films, notably Mark Rydell's box office record breaker *On Golden Pond* (1981), have directly featured old men in central roles, and through them have engaged with issues of aging, redundancy, illness and death. In that particular film this was given added poignancy through the casting of Jane Fonda and Henry Fonda as daughter and father. Thus the audience are given the enticing ambiguity of knowing this is, and is not, 'the real thing'. The 'seriousness' of its themes is illustrated by the comments of Pauline Kael in The New Yorker on the film: 'The kind of uplifting twaddle that traffics heavily in rather basic symbols: the gold light on the pond stands for the sunset of life, and so on'.

More usually older men figure as complements to the main characters, as exceptions to the general flow of the film narrative, as objects of fun, interest, and curiosity. Steven Spielberg's *Batteries Not Included* (1987) is an unusual example, with Hume Cronyn and Jessica Tandy playing an elderly couple in fear of ruthless violent developers saved by the magic of alien spaceships, and as such acting as both central and comical, eccentric characters.

Such 'portrayals' of older men as either central characters or characters of interest are relatively rare. More usual is the invoking of age in the portrayal of the aging male star. An archetypal example is Clark Gable as Gay Landland (as 49 years old), in John Houston's *The Misfits* (1961). This was Gable's last performance, and possibly his best according to Fisher (1993: 49), and the first time he played a man who was supposed to be 'old'.

Perhaps the apotheosis of this contemporary self-consciousness of age is found in the recently published magazine, *The Oldie,* its very jokey title mocking and reaffirming itself. *The Oldie* was begun in February 1992 and was being produced fortnightly until August 1994, and monthly from September that year. It is a cross between *Punch* and *Private Eye,* and edited by Richard Ingrams, former editor of the latter. It is full of gentle-ish humour, nostalgia and articles on aging, country-side, the arts. It oozes knowing satire, so characteristic of the male comic (cf. Hearn, 1994). The first issue included articles on satanic abuse, winter in the Languedoc, Lord Deedes (former editor of the *Daily Telegraph*), Kelmscott Manor, and 'What is Heavy Metal?'. In Issue 37 (July 1993) we find Tim Rice's 'pin-ups': Barbara Stanwyck, the Everly Brothers, Elaine Paige, Nigel Molesworth, Maria Seles and Frank Rich. The following issue gives us Richard Wilson (Victor Meldrew of *One Foot in the Grave*), who has become an institution of the 'old disgusted man' on television. Like 'Victor Meldrew' (Victorious Humdrum), *The Oldie* is set in the discourse of angry/mellow, easy-going/crochety older men.

It is thus through a mixture of older men's redundancy, 'crocheti-ness', quaint nostalgia, and yet activity that they are often available as figures of fun. This is often through the amusement of older men entering their second childhood, whether in *Last of the Summer Wine* or their occasional participation in *Blind Date.* In both cases older men are still frequently presented as amusing objects, in a dialectic with their power to the viewer, female or male.

CONCLUSIONS – OR THE WAY BACK

The central themes of this chapter have been imaging older men and imaging aging men. These have been considered in three ways – as historical construction, personal reflection, and contemporary imaging in the mass media. In each case the imagings that are found are complex, contradictory, even paradoxical.

I have charted some of the ways of imaging historical changes that have produced both a transformation of the association of age and men's power, and a category of older men. At the same time, there are powerful forces that are working towards the blurring of the categories of older men and younger men. Then there are the various ways in which specific groups of older men have been identified: black elders, older gay men, grandfathers, older sportsmen, and so on. These specific identifications often contradict dominant stereotypes of both older men and the younger men of that group (black men, gay men, male relatives, sportsmen). Thus through these paradoxes and blurrings, we are in the world of differentiation and de-differentiation – between older and younger men, men's power and powerlessness, multiple oppressions and social divisions, as well as multiple interpretations more generally. Much of the historical imaging of older men is informed by modernization narratives. These may emphasize the movement of such men from their place in the family. A good example of this is the debate, particularly the United States but also in the UK and elsewhere, around the new social contract of grandparents and grandfathers. This debate can easily carry with it notions of disruption of 'natural' family relations. The notion of disruption is an important one in the representation of older men. It is the more general disruption of 'men' that is assumed to disrupt older men, through the disruption of intergenerational relations. In this construction older men are gradually diverted from the centre of youth and the heterosexual family; they become the *other* of this centre, as they approach death. This is in effect a gendered version of the ideology of disengagement. The loss of grandparental links leads in turn to campaigns to rectify and reassess them.

Yet 'disruption' is not a novel phenomenon: it is endemic to capitalist and imperialist change – whether this is the nineteenth century migration to the European cities, the huge upheavals of the turn of the century, the world wars, the Depression, twentieth century migration of labour to Third World cities. Furthermore, these changes have often affected men in different ways according to racialization and ethnic organization. In particular, poor, black, ethnic minority and many other men have had to engage with the familiar movement from family so that, for example, many Afro-Caribbean people in the UK may have relatives in the Caribbean, in the United States, and elsewhere.

Men's experience 'as older men' is complex. It has been dominated by images of disengagement, changing roles, redundancy, retirement. It has been made 'other', despite some lingering associations with power. Increasingly particular groups of older men, such as older gay men, are identifying their experience as specific and significant. In doing so, they are challenging that otherness; they are also challenging dominant stereotypes of both older men and (younger) gay men. Resort to experience may affirm being 'older men' and challenge that categorization and separation. Imaging older men in the media is more complex still. It is frequently paradoxical – in its reference to succession, even youth. A different kind of otherness may be portrayed here – men as mellow, or crochety, themselves representing a further 'essential' maleness.

In all these cases we are concerned with the interrogation of genealogies – of the category of 'older men', of individual older men's 'experience', of the older men 'in the media'. In the last case, the imaging aging and imaging older men are made easily available for nostalgia/otherness through their reproduction in the specific medium itself, and its own removal/loss from the reader/viewer.

In all these ways the category of 'older men' is fundamentally a contradictory one. It makes gender explicit in a way that is often not done in talking of 'old(er) people'. It connects oldness to gender, to men, and to men's social power. On the other hand, while older men may enjoy certain benefits compared with older women, in most parts of the world men's life expectancy remains appreciably lower than women's. 'Older men' also contradict or may contradict dominant constructions of men and masculinities. Older men are often different or seen as different to 'other' men. Older men are, despite their social power as men also subject to ageism, both structural and interpersonal. Indeed it is the very hegemonic power of certain men that undermines older men (and in a different way younger men) through ageism – the power and oppression of age. Accordingly, older men despite and because of their contradictory social power may subvert dominant constructions of men and masculinities.

REFERENCES

Arber, Sara and Gilbert, Nigel (1990) 'Men: the forgotten carers', *Sociology* 23 (1): 111–18.

Baranowski, Marc D. (1985) 'Grandfatherhood: new perspectives', *Nurturing News* 7 (2): 2, 11–13.

Barrett, David (1993) 'Poor older women: how poverty pervades their lives in the early 1990s', paper at Social Policy Association Conference, University of Liverpool, mimeo, Inner London Institute of Higher Education.

Biggs, Simon (1993) *Understanding Ageism: Images, Attitudes and Professional Practice*, Milton Keynes: Open University Press.

Blakemore, Ken and Boneham, Margaret (1994) *Age, Race and Ethnicity: A Comparative Approach*, Milton Keynes: Open University Press.

Brighton Ourstory Project (1992) *Daring Hearts: Lesbian and Gay Lives in the 50s and 60s*, Brighton: Queer Spark Books.

Butler, R.N. (1963) 'The life review: an interpretation of reminiscence in the aged', *Psychiatry* 26 (1): 895–900.

Choudhary, Vivik (1993) 'Radio 1 reckons age shall not weary Britain's youth', *The Guardian*, 13 August: 4.

Cummings, E. and Henry, W.E. (1961) *Growing Old*, New York: Basic Books.

Cunningham-Burley, Sarah (1984) 'We don't talk about it . . . Issues of gender and method in the portrayal of grandfatherhood', *Sociology* 18 (3): 325–38.

Dyer, Richard (1993) 'Rock – the last guy you'd have figured', in Pat Kirkham and Janet Thumim (eds) *You Tarzan: Masculinity, Movies and Men*, London: Lawrence & Wishart: pp. 27–34.

Erikson, E.H. (1982) *The Life Cycle Completed*, New York: Norton.

Fennell, Graham, Phillipson, Chris and Evers, Helen (1988) *The Sociology of Old Age*, Milton Keynes: Open University Press.

Fisher, Joe (1993) 'Clarke (sic.) Gable's balls: real men never lose their teeth', in Pat Kirkham and Janet Thumim (eds) *You Tarzan: Masculinity, Movies and Men*, London: Lawrence and Wishart, pp. 35–51.

Hall Carpenter Archives/Gay Men's Oral History Group (1989) *Walking After Midnight: Gay Men's Stories*, London/New York: Routledge.

Hansard (1986) 231, 30 October.

Havinghurst, R. (1963) 'Successful aging', in R.H. Williams, C. Tibbits, and W. Donahue, (eds) *Processes of Aging, vol. 1*, Chicago: University of Chicago Press, pp. 311–15.

Hearn, Jeff (1992) *Men in the Public Eye: The Construction and Deconstruction of Public Men and Public Patriarchies*, London/New York: Routledge.

Hearn, Jeff (1994) 'Viz. the naming of the pose', *Journal of Gender Studies* 3 (1): 69–75

Hearn, Jeff and Melechi, Antonio (1992) 'The transatlantic gaze: masculinities, youth and the American imaginary', in Steve Craig, (ed.) *Men, Masculinity and the Media*, Newbury Park, Ca.: Sage, pp. 215–32.

Itzin, Catherine and Phillipson, Chris (1993) *Age Barriers at Work: Maximising the Potential of Mature and Older People*, Solihull: Metropolitan Authorities Recruitment Agency.

Jackson, David (1990) *Unmasking Masculinity: A Critical Autobiography*, London and Boston: Unwin Hyman.

Kemp, Frank and Buttle, Bernard (1979) *Focus on Retirement*, London: Kogan Page.

Kirby, Judy (1984) *Work after Work*, London: Quiller.

Kornhaber, Arthur (1985) 'Grandparenthood and the "new social contract"', in Vern L. Bengtson and Joan F. Robertson, (eds) *Grandparenthood*, Beverly Hills, Ca.: Sage, pp. 159–71.

Kornhaber, Arthur and Woodward, Kenneth L. (1985) *Grandparents and Grandchildren: The Vital Connection*, New Brunswick, NJ/Oxford: Transaction.

Kubey, R. (1980) 'TV and ageing', *The Gerontologist* 20: 16–35.

Laczko, F. and Phillipson, C. (1991) *Changing Work and Retirement*, Milton Keynes: Open University Press.

Lambert, J., Laslett, P. and Clay, H. (1984) *The Image of the Elderly on TV*, Cambridge: University of the Third Age.

Marshall, Mary (1990) *Age: The Unrecognized Discrimination*, London: Age Concern.

Mullen, C. and von Zwanenberg, E. (1988) *Study of Television Viewing*, London: BBC Books.

Midwinter, Eric (1991) 'The pension system – a hideous dichotomy', *Community Care* 16 May: 24.

Moore, Suzanne (1993) 'A certain ageism', *Guardian* 2, 13 August: 11.

Naylor, P. (1990) *Age No Barrier*, Solihull: Metropolitan Authorities Recruitment Agency.

Nurturing News (1985) vol. 7 (2), Special Issues: Grandfathers.

Nussbaum, J.F., Thompson, T. and Robinson, J. D. (1989) *Communication and Ageing* 11: 149–65.

The Oldie, various issues.

Phillipson, Chris (1982) *Capitalism and the Construction of Old Age*, London: Macmillan.

Porter, Kevin and Weeks, Jeffrey (eds) (1991) *Between the Acts: Lives of Homosexual Men 1885–1967*, London/New York: Routledge.

Rodwell, G., Davis, S., Dennison, T. *et al.* (1992) 'Images of old age on "British television"' *Generation Review* 2 (3): 6–8.

Taylor, P. and Walker, A. (1992) 'What are the employers doing to "defuse the demographic time bomb?"' *Skill and Enterprise Briefing* 21 August.

Thane, Pat (1982) *The Foundations of the Welfare State,* London/New York: Longman.

Trinder, C., Hulme, G. and McCarthy, W. (1992) *Employment: The Role of Work in the Third Age,* London: Public Finance Foundation.

Vacha, Keith (1985) *Quiet Fire: Memoirs of Older Gay Men,* Boston: Crossings Press.

Part III

RELATIONS BETWEEN THE GENERATIONS

8

CHANGING IMAGES OF AGING AND THE SOCIAL CONSTRUCTION OF THE LIFE COURSE

Tamara K. Hareven

INTRODUCTION

Concern with old age in our time has tended to focus attention on this stage of life in isolation from the entire life course. Without denying the unique problems of this period of life, it is important to interpret it in a life course and historical context. The recognition of old age as a unique stage of life in the twentieth century is part of a larger historical process involving the emergence of new stages of life and their societal recognition. It is also part of a continuing trend toward age segregation in the family and in the larger society (Hareven, 1976). A historical perspective is useful, therefore, because it sheds some light on long-term developments affecting 'middle' and 'old' age.

The first part of this article discusses the emergence of 'old age' as a new stage of life in the context of the discovery of other stages of life; the second part addresses the emergence of discontinuities in the life course; and the last part discusses the contribution of historical changes in the family and the life course to age segregation.

It was probably no coincidence that G. Stanley Hall, who had formulated the concept of 'adolescence' in the 1880s, offered a synthesis of 'senescence' as his last creative opus in 1920, when he himself was 80 years old: '*TO LEARN THAT ONE IS OLD* is a long, complex, and painful experience. Each decade the circle of the Great Fatigue narrows around us, restricting the intensity and endurance of our activities'. While his contemporaries focused on the deterioration characteristic of old age, or sought the secrets of longevity, Hall emphasized the unique psychological processes connected with aging and their societal significance. Rather than viewing old age as a period of decline and decay, he saw it as a stage of development in which the passions of youth and the efforts of a life career had reached fruition and consolidation: 'There is a certain maturity of judgement about men, things, causes and life generally, that nothing in the world but years can bring, a real wisdom that only age can teach' (Hall, 1922: 366).

The interest in the meaning of aging in the early part of the twentieth century had not sprung merely from idle curiosity. It was related to questions about the limits of usefulness and efficiency on the job that had arisen with industrialization and to the movement for providing social insurance for the aged. In 1874, psychologist George Beard had already begun to ask questions about the limitations of old age: 'What is the average effect of old age on the mental faculties?'; 'to what extent is the average responsibility of men impaired by the change that the mental faculties undergo in old age?' Analysing the record of 'human achievements', he tried to determine at what age the 'best work of the world' had been done. He found that 70 per cent of creative works had been achieved by the age of 45 and 80 per cent by the age of 50. Within this range, he identified 30 to 45, as the optimal period of life. Although he was emphatic about the need for setting a retirement age for judges, he did not recommend an automatic retirement age for labourers (Beard, 1874). Beard's investigation represented the first attempt at a scientific inquiry into the relationship between aging and efficiency, and it set the stage for the concept of the 'superannuated man' that was to come.

In the late nineteenth century, American society passed from an acceptance of aging as a natural process to a view of it as a distinct period of life characterized by decline, weakness, and obsolescence. Advanced old age, which had earlier been regarded as a manifestation of the survival of the fittest, was now denigrated as a condition of dependence and deterioration: 'We are marked by time's defacing fingers with the ugliness of age' ('Apology from age to youth', 1893: 170). Writers began to identify advancing years with physical decline and mental deterioration. Beginning in the 1860s, the popular magazines shifted their emphasis from attaining longevity to discussing the medical symptoms of senescence. By the beginning of the twentieth century geriatrics emerged as a branch of medicine. In 1910, I. L. Nascher, a New York physician, became the first to formulate the biological characteristics and medical needs of senescence as a life-cycle process. He drew on the work of his predecessors to conceptualize its medical treatment and thus laid the foundation for geriatrics (Nascher, 1914).

The gerontological literature approaches the problems of aging from several directions: the developmental perspective has focused on biological and psychological changes connected with aging; the institutional approach has stressed the socio-economic status and the roles of old people; and the cultural perspective has concentrated on stereotypes and perceptions of the elderly. Some of these approaches have also led to the confusion of the 'aged' as an age group, or as a social class with aging as a process. Little effort has been made to integrate these views or interpret them as interrelated processes over the life course.

The emergence of 'old age' as a social, cultural, and biological phenomenon can best be understood in the context of other stages of life. The social conditions of children and adolescents in a given society are related to the way in which adulthood is perceived in that society. Conversely, the role and position of adults and the aged are related to the treatment of children and youths. The formidable task of investigating the synchronization of individual development with social change requires an approach that would take into account the entire life course and various historical and cultural conditions, rather than simply concentrating on a specific age group. As Erik Erikson put it:

> As we come to the last stage [old age], we become aware of the fact that our civilization really does not harbor a concept of the whole of life. . . . Any span of the cycle lived without vigorous meaning, at the beginning, in the middle, or at the end, endangers the sense of life and the meaning of death in all those whose life stages are intertwined.
>
> (Erikson, 1964: 132–3)

THE DISCOVERY OF STAGES OF LIFE

Age and aging are related to biological phenomena, but their meanings are socially and culturally determined. 'Social age' is a relative concept and varies in different cultural contexts. In trying to understand the societal conditions affecting adulthood and old age, it is important to realize that the definitions of aging, as well as the social conditions and functions of every age group, have not only changed significantly over time but have also varied among different cultures. In western society, we are accustomed to referring to stages of life such as childhood and adolescence, as socially recognized stages of development encompassing specific age groups, which are also accompanied by certain cultural characteristics. The 'discovery' of a new stage of life is itself a complex process. First, individuals become aware of the specific characteristics of a given stage of life as a distinct condition among certain social classes or groups. This discovery is then made public and popularized on a societal level. Professionals and reformers define and formulate the unique conditions of such a stage of life, and then it is publicized in the popular culture. Finally, if the conditions peculiar to this stage seem to be associated with a major social problem, it attracts the attention of public agencies, and it becomes institutionalized: its needs and problems are dealt with in legislation and in the establishment of institutions aimed directly to meet its needs. Such public activities, in turn, affect the experience of individuals going through such a stage. They clearly influence the timing of life transitions in and out of such a stage by providing public supports and, at times, constraints that affect the timing of transitions.

In American society, childhood emerged as a distinct stage first in the private lives of middle-class urban families in the early part of the nineteenth century. The new definition of the meaning of childhood and of the role of children was related to the retreat of the family into domesticity, the segregation of the workplace from the home, the redefinition of the mother's role as the major custodian of the domestic sphere, and the emphasis on sentimental rather than instrumental relations at the very base of family life. As Philippe Ariès explained, the new child-centredness of urban domestic families in Western Europe in the late eighteenth and early nineteenth centuries was characterized by its focus on the couple and the children, rather than on a kinship group or a lineage. It was also a response to two major demographic changes: the decline in infant and child mortality and the increase in the conscious practice of family limitation (Ariès, 1962). Having emerged first in the life of middle-class families and having become an integral part of their lifestyle, childhood as a distinct stage of development became the subject of the voluminous body of child-rearing and family advice literature. These advice books and magazine articles popularized the concept of childhood and the needs of children, prescribed the means to allow them to develop as children, and called for the regulation of child labour.

The discovery of adolescence in the latter part of the nineteenth century followed a similar pattern to that of the emergence of child-hood. While puberty in itself is a universal biological process, the psychosocial phenomena of adolescence were only gradually identified and defined, most notably by G. Stanley Hall in the latter part of the nineteenth century (Hall, 1922). There is evidence that the experience of adolescence, particularly some of the problems and tensions associated with it, was noticed in the private lives of individuals reaching puberty during the second half of the nineteenth century (Demos and Demos, 1969). Educators and urban reformers began to observe the congregation of young people in peer groups and identify styles of behaviour that might be characterized as a 'culture of adolescence' from the middle of the nineteenth century on. Anxiety over such conduct increased, particularly in large cities, where reformers warned against the potential threat of youth gangs.

By the beginning of the twentieth century, Hall and his colleagues articulated adolescence as a new stage of life. This new stage of life was also widely popularized in the literature. The extension of school age through high school in the second part of the nineteenth century, the further extension of the age limits for child labour, and the establishment of juvenile reformatories and vocational schools were all part of the public recognition of the needs and problems of adolescence (Bremner *et al.*, 1970, 1971).

The boundaries between childhood and adolescence on the one hand and between adolescence and adulthood on the other became more clearly demarcated over the course of the twentieth century. The experience of childhood and adolescence became more pervasive among larger groups of the American population, as immigrant and working-class families made their entry into the middle class. Keniston has suggested that in the twentieth century the extension of a moratorium from adult responsibilities beyond adolescence has resulted in the emergence of yet another stage of life – that of youth (Keniston, 1971).

Despite the growing awareness of these pre-adult stages, no clear boundaries for adulthood in America emerged until much later, when 'old age' became prominent as a new stage of life, and with it, the need to differentiate the social and psychological problems of 'middle age' from those of 'old age'. There are many indications that a new consciousness of 'old age', along with institutional definitions and societal recognition, emerged in the latter part of the nineteenth and early part of the twentieth century. The convergence of an increasing volume of gerontological literature, the proliferation of negative stereotypes about old age, and the establishment of mandatory retirement represent the first moves in the direction of a public and institutional formulation of 'old age' as a distinct stage of life (Fischer, 1977).

The articulation of new stages of life and their recognition in American society in the past generally came as a response to external pressures and to a fear of the potential disorganization that might otherwise ensue from societal neglect of a particular age group. In the nineteenth century this apprehension was particularly dramatic as it was manifested in attitudes toward treatment of children and adolescents, where undisciplined and unsocialized young people were regarded as the 'dangerous classes'.

The elderly received comparatively little attention because they were not considered dangerous to the social order. The argument against the neglect of children was that they would grow up into dangerous, socially destructive adults. No parallel argument applied to the aged. In a society which had lost its fear of the afterlife, and in which awareness and contact with death was not integrated into everyday life (for death no longer held a mythical power over the living), there was no reason to fear any potential revenge from old people. Consequently, the first demonstration of organized political power on the part of the aged was not manifested until the Townshend movement in the 1930s, which succeeded in pressing the Federal Government into instituting social security.

As early as the late eighteenth century, however, American society had gradually begun, at least, to acknowledge the existence of various stages of life and to develop a corresponding series of institutions to deal with them. As we have seen, childhood was 'discovered' in the first half of the nineteenth century and adolescence was 'invented' toward the end of the century. Both stages of life emerged into public consciousness as a result of the social crises associated with those age groups in a manner similar to the emergence of old age later on. However, despite the growing awareness of childhood, adolescence, and youth as pre-adult stages, no clear boundaries for adulthood in American society emerged until much later, when interest in the 'middle years' as a distinct segment of adult life arose out of the need to differentiate the social and psychological problems of 'middle' from 'old' age. The social and cultural conditions of the past half century have since contributed to the sharpening of the boundaries between those two stages. More recently, even old age has been divided into stages such as the 'young old' and the 'old old' (Neugarten and Daton, 1973).

It is clear, however, that in American society 'old age' is now recognized as a specific period of adulthood. At least until recently it had a formal beginning – age 65 as far as an individual's working life is concerned. It was institutionalized by a rite of passage – retirement and the commencement of social security. Since so much of adult life has been contingent on work, especially for men, retirement also often involves migration and changes in living arrangements. More recently mandatory retirement has been revised following new legislation regulating retirement, and the policies of a 'golden handshake' adopted by various corporations.

In the beginning of the twentieth century, public concern for, and interest in old age converged from various directions. In addition to physicians, psychologists, and popular writers, efficiency experts and social reformers were instrumental in attracting public attention to old age as a social problem. A variety of medical and psychological studies by industrial-efficiency experts focused on the physical and mental limitations of old age. At the same time, social reformers began to expose the poverty and dependency suffered by many old people, as part of a general investigation of poverty, and to agitate for social security and social insurance (Douglas, 1936; Epstein, 1922).

Government recognition of old age evolved more gradually and emerged at the state level first. By 1920 only ten states had instituted some form of old-age legislation; all programmes were limited in scope, and most of them were declared unconstitutional by the Supreme

Court. Nevertheless, agitation for old-age security continued and finally culminated in the Social Security Act of 1935. It was not until the 1940s, however, that gerontology was recognized as a new field and even more recently that social scientists identified old age as constituting a new and pressing problem for western society. Social definitions of age limits and public treatment through institutional reform, retirement legislation, and welfare measures represent the most recent societal recognition of this stage of life (Tibbitts, 1960; Philibert, 1965).

The popular and social-science literature has recently devoted a great deal of attention to the social and economic plight of older people and to their isolation. The major developments that have been cited as explanations for these problems are: the overall impact of urbanization and industrialization, demographic changes arising from increases in life expectancy in childhood and early adulthood and from prolongation of life in old age due to advances in medical technology; the increasing proportion of older people in the population resulting from the decline in fertility and increase in life expectancy; the decrease in productive roles that older people are allowed to play as the result of the shift from a rural to an industrial economy; the technological revolution; and, finally, the denigration of old age, which has been explained by the 'cult of youth'.

Without denying the importance of these explanations, stereotypes of aging and the problems of old age and aging in American society can be more fully understood in the context of changes in the social and cultural construction of other stages of life and in fundamental historical discontinuities in the life course in relation to the emergence of age segregation in work life and in the family orientation and functions.

Because age boundaries and criteria for adulthood vary significantly across cultures, classes, and historical periods, the meaning of adulthood cannot be defined merely in terms of a specific stage in the life course. Unlike adolescence, which represents a person's passage through puberty, adulthood cannot be clearly defined in biological terms. Even within the same age group, the social meaning of adulthood and the functions associated with it vary among cultures and according to psychological conditions. For these reasons, it is important to determine to what extent and in what ways individuals in the past have perceived their entry into adulthood and transitions to old age under varying historical conditions.

THE EMERGENCE OF DISCONTINUITIES IN THE LIFE COURSE

The social experience of each cohort is influenced not only by the historical conditions it encounters currently, but also by the cumulative impact of past historical events over the life course of its members. Consequently, the position of the elderly in modern American society has been shaped in part by social and economic conditions which have combined to isolate their family and productive life when they enter their sixties or seventies, and in part by their previous cumulative experience along their life course. For example, individuals who reached the age of sixty in the 1890s and were still working had commenced work at an earlier age and continued to work until the end of life, or so long as they were able to. Having grown up in periods when life transitions were less rigidly marked or institutionalized, they would have found imposed retirement at a set age far more traumatic than a cohort which had come of age in the early twentieth century, when both entry into and exit from the labour force were more clearly timed according to age. The response of an older cohort to changing social and economic conditions is therefore significantly different from that of a younger one, because it is based on very different individual and social experiences (Hareven, 1986; Riley, 1978). In trying to understand those differences, it is necessary to view both the contemporary social milieu in which members of a cohort reach that age and their cumulative experience over their entire lives.

In pre-industrial society, demographic, social, and cultural factors combined to produce only a minimal differentiation in the stages of life. Childhood and adolescence were not regarded as distinct stages; children were considered miniature adults, gradually assuming adult roles in their early teens and entering adult life without a moratorium from adult responsibilities. Adulthood flowed into old age without institutionalized disruptions. The two major adult roles – parenthood and work – generally stretched over an entire lifetime without an 'empty nest' and compulsory retirement (Chudacoff and Hareven, 1979). In rural communities, the insistence of older people on self-sufficiency and their continued control over family estates delayed the assumption of economic independence by adult children and afforded aging parents a bargaining position for support in old age (Greven, 1970; Smith, 1973).

The integration of economic activities with family life also provided continuity in the usefulness of older people, particularly for widows, even when their capacity to work was waning. One should not, however, idealize the condition of the elderly in pre-industrial society. John Demos has pointed out that publicly they were venerated, but they were insecure in private life. Some of the symptoms of insecurity and uncertainty are reflected, for example, in wills where support for a widowed mother was made a condition for the inheritance of family estates (Demos, 1969, 1979). Nevertheless, old people experienced economic and social segregation far less frequently than they do today, and they retained their familial and economic positions until the end of their lives (Smith, 1973). If they became 'dependent' because of illness or poverty, they were supported by their children or other kin or were placed by the town authorities in the households of neighbours, or even non-relatives. They were placed in institutions only as a last resort (Greven, 1970).

DISCONTINUITIES IN THE LIFE COURSE

Under the impact of industrialization and the demographic changes of the nineteenth century, however, a gradual differentiation in age groups and a greater specialization in age-related functions began to emerge, although it was by no means complete by the end of the century. Discontinuities in the individual life course were still not marked, and age groups were still not completely segregated in accordance with their functions. Even in the family, age configurations were considerably different than today: the decline in mortality since the 1870s along with the decline in fertility has also affected family size and the age configurations within the family. One of the major historical changes in this respect has been a transition from a large family size to a smaller one, and from a broad age spectrum of children within the family to the compressed, closely spaced 2.3-child family in contemporary American society (Uhlenberg, 1978). Prior to the 1870s a larger number of children in the family of orientation meant not only the presence of a larger number of siblings but also a diversity in their ages.

In families containing larger numbers of children, age configurations were considerably different than in a two to three child family. For example, in families where children were spaced two or three years apart, and where the family had five or six children, the oldest child would be ready to leave home or get married, when the youngest child was still be in primary school. As Peter Uhlenberg notes:

Consider, for example, children in a family in which eight or nine children are born, compared with those in a two-child family. In the larger family, the first born enters a family with 3 members, but as he ages it keeps expanding up to a maximum of 10. The youngest child in the family enters a very large unit, which then contracts in size as he ages until finally he or she is the only remaining child. Furthermore, the ages of parents and ages and numbers of siblings present at different childhood stages will vary considerably for the various children in the large family, depending upon their birth order. In the small family, in contrast, the two

127

siblings may be born a few years apart, and throughout their childhood no additional changes occur.

(Uhlenberg, 1978: 77)

In families with a wider age spread among children, the youngest children had greater contact with the older siblings than with their own parents. Given the later age at marriage, parents would have already been in middle age when their youngest child was growing up. Under such circumstances, older siblings (especially sisters) often functioned as caretakers for their younger siblings. When one or both parents were dead, older siblings acted as surrogate parents. Such varied age configurations among siblings had significant implications for their relationships to one another, and especially for their interaction over their life course. Children growing up in families with age diversity were exposed to a variety of roles and responsibilities among their own siblings. Child care by older siblings enabled mothers to work outside the home. In working-class immigrant families young teenagers took care of their infant siblings (Hareven, 1978, 1982).

Prior to the turn of this century parenthood was not segregated to certain periods in the life course. While today parents generally complete their child-rearing functions with one third of their lives still ahead, nineteenth-century parenthood was a lifelong career. The combination of relatively late marriage, short life expectancy, and high fertility rarely allowed for an 'empty nest' stage. In addition, marriage was frequently broken by the death of a spouse before the end of the child-rearing period. Because they married earlier and lived longer than men, this pattern was more common among women. Widowed or not, however, the extension of motherhood over most of the life course continued to engage women in active familial roles into old age (Uhlenberg, 1978).

Under conditions in which the life course was compressed into a shorter and more homogeneous span, major transitions into adulthood, such as leaving school, entering the labour force, leaving home, establishing a separate household, marrying, and having children were not so clearly structured as they are today. Except for marriage and the formation of households, these transitions did not even necessarily represent moves toward independent adulthood. The order in which they occurred varied significantly, rather than following a customary sequence. Children and youth shuttled back and forth from school to work, depending on the seasons, the availability of jobs, and the economic needs of the family. Departure from school did not mark a definite turning point, nor, at a time when child labour was an established practice, did entry into the labour force necessarily imply the onset of adulthood. Leaving home, a phenomenon typically associated with the commencement of adulthood today, did not have such significance in the pre-industrial and early industrial period (Modell, Furstenberg, and Hershberg, 1976).

In nineteenth-century rural and urban working-class families, sons and daughters often continued to live at home until well into their twenties and to contribute their income to the common family budget. Some children left home in their early teens to become servants or apprentices, while others continued to live on the family farm and to postpone marriage and the assumption of adult responsibilities until much later. Irish immigrant families in Massachusetts, for example, customarily kept the youngest son at home through his late twenties. Among other immigrant industrial workers in New England, the last remaining daughter at home was expected to postpone or give up marriage and continue living in the family household to care for her parents as long as they lived. When unmarried children did leave home, they often spent transitional periods as boarders or lodgers with the families of strangers, rather than setting up their own households (Modell and Hareven, 1973; Hareven 1975; Hareven, 1981).

Even marriage, which is usually regarded as an 'adult' act in twentieth-century society, much less often marked the transition to autonomous adult life in the nineteenth. In urban communities, where immigration produced both scarcity in housing and unemployment, it was difficult to set up an independent household, so newlyweds often brought their spouses to live in their parents' households for a transitional period. Even when they lived separately, it was usually nearby, often in the same neighbourhood. In the early years of marriage and especially after the birth of the first child, young couples were willing to sacrifice privacy for the luxury of parental assistance and support, a willingness that increased during periods of economic crisis and depression or during family crises brought on by unemployment, sickness, or death (Chudacoff, 1978).

The most significant historical change in the timing of life transitions since the beginning of this century has been the emergence of greater uniformity in the pace at which a cohort accomplishes a given transition. This is particularly evident in the transitions to adulthood (leaving home, marriage, and the establishment of a separate household). Over the past century, life transitions have become more clearly marked, more rapidly timed, and more compressed in their timing. In contrast to our times, in the late nineteenth century, transitions from the parental home to marriage, to household headship, were more gradual and less rigid in their timing. The time range necessary for a cohort to accomplish such transitions was wider, and the sequence in which transitions followed one another was flexible. In the twentieth century, transitions to adulthood have become more uniform for the age cohort undergoing them, more orderly in sequence, and more rigidly defined (Modell, Furstenberg and Hershberg, 1976). The consciousness of embarking on a new stage of life and the implications of movement from one stage to the next have become more firmly established.

The historical changes over the past century, particularly the increasing rapidity in the timing of transitions and the introduction of publicly regulated and institutionalized transitions, have converged to isolate and segregate age groups in the larger society. At the same time, these examples have generated new pressures on timing within the family as well as outside its confines. The major historical change over the past century has been from a timing that is more closely articulated to collective family needs to a more individualized timing. Timing has become more regulated according to specific age norms rather than in relation to the family's collective needs.

CHANGES IN THE FAMILY

In earlier time periods, the absence of dramatic transitions to adult life allowed a more intensive interaction among different age groups within the family and the community, thus providing a greater sense of continuity and interdependence among people at various stages of life. But, as greater differentiation in stages of life began to develop, social and economic functions became more closely related to age, and ages of family members became more streamlined, a greater segregation between age groups emerged.

The major changes that have led to the isolation of older people in society today were rooted not so much in changes in family structure or residential arrangements, as has generally been argued, as in the transformation and redefinition of family functions and values. Among these changes, the erosion of an instrumental view of family relationships – and the resulting shift to sentimentality and intimacy as the major cohesive forces in the family have led to the weakening of independence between members of the nuclear family and extended kin. Affective relationships have gradually replaced instrumental ones.

This shift first occurred in the middle class, around the middle of the nineteenth century, but it soon affected the working class and various ethnic groups, as increasing conformity introduced middle-class values into working-class lives. Since then, the emphasis on domesticity and child-rearing as the major preoccupations of the middle-class family – and especially on the role of women as custodians of the domestic retreat – has tended to insulate middle-class urban families from the influence and participation of aging parents and other relatives. From the 1830s on, such families became avid consumers of popular child-

130

rearing advice literature, not because older relatives were not present to offer such advice, but because guidance based on personal experience and tradition was gradually rejected in favour of 'packaged' semi-professional information. This transition added to the loss of power and influence of the old people in the family.

The ideology of domesticity that emerged during the first half of the nineteenth century also enshrined privacy as a major value in family life. The home was glorified as a retreat from the world and, at the same time, as a specialized child-nurturing centre. Philippe Ariès succinctly summarized these changes for West European society:

> The modern family . . . cuts itself off from the world and opposes to society the isolated groups of parents and children. All the energy of the group is expended in helping the children to rise in the world, individually and without any collective ambition: The children rather than the family.
>
> (Ariès, 1962)

Under the impact of industrialization, the family surrendered many of the functions previously concentrated within the household to other social institutions. The retreat and growing privatism of the modern middle-class family led to the drawing of sharper boundaries between family and community and intensified the segregation of different age groups within the family, leading to the elimination of older people from viable family roles. The transfer of social-welfare functions, once concentrated in the family, to institutions in the larger society further contributed to the segregation of older people. The care of dependent, sick, delinquent, and elderly members of the community, which had been considered part of the family's obligation in the pre-industrial period, was gradually transferred to specialized institutions such as asylums and reformatories. The family ceased to be the only available source of support for its dependent members, and the community ceased to rely on the family as the major agency of welfare and social control (Bremner, 1956; Rothman, 1971).

CONCLUSION

The characterization of the aged as 'useless', 'inefficient', 'unattractive', 'temperamental', and 'senile' accompanied the gradual ousting of people from the labour force at age 65, since the beginning of the twentieth century. The development of what Erving Goffman has called the 'spoiled identity' or what others have referred to as the 'mystique of the aged', had already begun to appear in popular literature in the United States during the later part of the nineteenth century. The emergence of such negative stereotypes should not be misconstrued as causing an immediate decline in the status of older people, but it did reflect the beginnings of an increasing tendency to denigrate the aged in society.

Some people have attributed the emergence of a negative image of old age to a 'cult of youth' in American society, but while there is undeniably a connection, one cannot be construed as an explanation of the other. The glorification of youth and the denigration of old age are both aspects of far more complicated processes. They are results of the increasing segregation of different stages of life – and of their corresponding age groups – in modern American society.

The socio-economic and cultural changes of the past century have gradually led to a segregation of work from other aspects of life and to a shift from the predominance of familial values to an emphasis on individualism and privacy. Child-labour laws and compulsory education to age 14 (or 16) tended to segregate the young, increasingly so from around the middle of the nineteenth century (Bremner *et al.*, vol. 2, 1971). Similarly, the gradual ousting of older people from the labour force at the beginning of the twentieth century and the decline in their parental functions in the later years of life tended to disengage them from their offspring. One of the most important changes affecting the elderly, therefore, was the increasing association of functions with age and formation of segregated, age-based peer groups. This segregation by age occurred first among the middle class, and was only later extended into the rest of society.

These changes have affected each stage of life: they have resulted in the segmentation of the life course into more formal stages, in more uniform and rigid transitions from one stage to the next, and in the separation of the various age groups from one another. The problems of older people in American society are in some respects unique to this age group, but in others they reflect in its most acute form problems experienced by other age groups and other stages of life as well.

REFERENCES

'Apology from age to youth' (1893) *Living Age* CXCIII.
Ariès, Philippe (1962) *Centuries of Childhood: A Social History of Family Life*, trans. Robert Baldick, New York: Vintage.
Beard, George (1874) *Legal Responsibility in Old Age, Based on Researches into the Relationship of Age to Work*, New York: Russells.
Bremner, Robert H. (1956) *From the Depths: The Discovery of Poverty in the United States*, New York: New York University Press.
Bremner, Robert H. *et al.* (1970) *Children and Youths in America: A Documentary History, vol. 1 (1600–1865)*, Cambridge, MA: Harvard University Press.
Bremner, Robert H. *et al.* (1971) *Children and Youths in America: A Documentary History, vol. 2 (1866–1932)*, Cambridge MA: Harvard University Press.

Chudacoff, Howard P. (1978) 'Newly weds and familial extensions: first stages of the family cycle in Providence, R.I., 1864–1880', in Tamara K. Hareven and Maris Vinovskis (eds) *Demographic Processes and Family Organization in Nineteenth-Century American Society*, Princeton, NJ: Princeton University Press.

Chudacoff, Howard P., and Hareven, Tamara K. (1979) 'From the empty nest to family dissolution: life course transitions into old age', *Journal of Family History* 41: 69–83.

Demos, John (1969) *A Little Commonwealth: Family Life in Colonial Plymouth*, New York: Oxford University Press.

Demos, John (1979) 'Old age in New England', in David van Tassel (ed.) *Aging, Death and the Completion of Being*, Cleveland, Ohio: Case Western University Press.

Demos, John and Demos, Virginia (1969) 'Adolescence in historical perspective', *Journal of Marriage and the Family* 31(4): 632–8.

Douglas, Paul H. (1936) *Social Security in the United States*, New York.

Epstein, Abraham (1922) *Facing Old Age: A Study of Old Age Dependency in the United States and Old Age Pensions*, New York.

Erikson, Erik (1964) *Insight and Responsibility*, New York.

Fischer, David H. (1977) *Growing Old in America*, New York: Oxford University Press.

Greven, Philip, Jr (1970) *Four Generations of Population, Land and Family in Colonial Andover, Mass.*, Ithaca, NY: Cornell University Press.

Hall, G. Stanley (1922) *Senescence: The Last Half of Life*, New York: Appleton.

Hareven, T. K. (1976) 'The last stage: historical adulthood and old age', *Daedalus: American Civilization: New Perspective* 105(4): 13–27.

Hareven, T. K. (1978) 'Historical changes in the life course and the family', in J. M. Yinger and S. J. Cutler (eds) *Major Social Issues: A Multidisciplinary View*, pp. 338–45.

Hareven, T. K. (1981) 'Historical changes in the timing of family transitions: their impact on generational relations', in Robert Fogel, Sarah B. Kiesler, Elaine Hatfield and Ethel Shanas (eds) *Aging: Stability and Change in the Family*, New York: Academic Press.

Hareven, T. K. (1982) *Family Time and Industrial Time: The Relationship Between the Family and Work in a New England Industrial Community*, New York: Cambridge University Press, reprinted, University Press of America, 1993.

Hareven, T. K. (1986) 'Historical changes in the social construction of the life course', *Human Development* 29(3): 171–80.

Keniston, Kenneth (1971) 'Psychological development and historical change', *Journal of Interdisciplinary History* 2(2): 329–45.

Modell, John and Hareven, Tamara K. (1973) 'Urbanization and the malleable household: an examination of boarding and lodging in American families', *Journal of Marriage and the Family* 35 (3): 467–79.

Modell, John, Furstenberg, Frank and Hershberg, Theodore (1976) 'Social change and transitions to adulthood in historical perspective', *Journal of Family History* 1(1): 7–32.

Nascher, I. L. (1914) *Geriatrics*, Philadelphia.

Neugarten, Bernice L. and Daton, Nancy (1973) 'Sociological perspectives on the life cycle', in Paul B. Baltes and K. Warner Schaie (eds) *Life Span Development Psychology: Personality and Socialization*, New York: Academic Press.

Philibert, Michel A. J. (1965) 'The emergence of social gerontology', *Journal of Social Issues* XXI (4): 4–12.

Riley, M. W. (1978) 'Aging, social change and the power of ideas', *Daedalus: Generations*.

Rothman, David (1971) *The Discovery of the Asylum*, Boston: Little, Brown.

Smith, Daniel Scott (1973) 'Parental power and marriage patterns: an analysis of historical trends in Hingham, Massachusetts', *Journal of Marriage and the Family* 35 (3): 419–29.

Tibbitts, Clark (1960) 'Origin, scope and fields of social gerontology', in Clark Tibbitts (ed.) *Handbook of Social Gerontology*, Chicago.

Uhlenberg, P. (1978) 'Changing configurations of the life course', in Tamara K. Hareven (ed.) *Transitions: The Family and the Life Course in Historical Perspective*, New York: Academic Press.

9

BACK TO OUR FUTURES
Imaging second childhood
Jenny Hockey and *Allison James*

Very elderly people are patently not children. None the less, within contemporary western society old age is often popularly associated with childhood through both verbal and visual images. This chapter explores the significance and impact of this particular process of image-making. First it asks how the tendering of the image of the child occurs, given the quite evidently unchildlike nature of old age. Second, it explores the potential implications of this process for the quality of elderly people's experience.

The association between old age and childhood is variously constructed. First there is the remarking of parallels between childhood and old age, noted by Aristophanes in the fourth century, and contemporarily by Dylan Thomas:

First voice   All over the town, babies and old men are cleaned and put into their broken prams and wheeled on to the sunlit cockled cobbles or out into the backyards under the dancing underclothes, and left.
A baby cries.
Old man   I want my pipe and he wants his bottle.
(Dylan Thomas, *Under Milk Wood*, 1954:36)

Within this image the two social categories, positioned at either end of the life course, share the experience of dependency.

This image recurs in Carver and Liddiard's (1978) book on aging, *An Ageing Population*. An old man and a young child are photographed together at a garden gate. In safe companionship, old and young are engaged in hands-in-pockets scrutiny of an outside world from which they are excluded. And Frank Sutcliffe's sepia photograph *Morning and Evening*, taken in Whitby in 1884, similarly combines childhood with old age. An old man smokes a clay pipe, his arm encircling a child's shoulder, his hand enclosing the boy's small bare feet, drawing him into a shared intimacy. And through its title, the image conflates the beginning and end of the daily temporal cycle and the early and later

135

years of the life course. It grants a cyclical nature to the linear passage of the time of a life, rendering old age the turning point rather than end point of the life course.

This imaging of old age and childhood as not only parallel social categories but also parallel categories of experience is one way in which these two very different phases in the life course are brought into association. A second, more active and intentional imaging of old age as 'second childhood' enlists the transformatory power of metaphor in lived experiences (Lakoff and Johnson, 1980; Fernandez, 1970). Old age is no longer simply set alongside childhood; it becomes childhood. As adults we become metaphoric parents to those aging 'babies' who have 'gone gaga'. This transformation may be purely figurative, as in press reports such as:

> Twin sisters . . . celebrated their 90th birthday. The birthday girls celebrated on Tuesday with sherry and birthday cake.
>
> (*Post Midweek*, 7 October, 1982)

But it may also be literal. Well meaning acts – the comforting pat on the arm, the birthday treat, the helping hand – may be symptomatic of a more damaging and embedded set of practices known as infantilization, documented in Hazan's (1980) account of a London day centre for elderly Jewish people:

> the first suggestion to boost activities amongst the participants made by a new administrator introduced to the Centre was to arrange documentary and Walt Disney film shows 'like they used to do in my old school'. The bingo organized by outside volunteers was opened by the well-known phrase used to children 'Are you sitting comfortably? Then we'll begin.' On another occasion – a Sunday tea arranged by outsiders – small gifts in birthday-like packets were distributed amongst those attending.
>
> (Hazan, 1980: 31)

Dawson's (1991) account of a club for elderly people in Northumberland illustrates a similar practice. Two younger volunteer helpers approached the elderly people as follows:

> They planned to 'ease the strain' and 'inject a bit of life into the place'. They also explained, quoting from an Age Concern leaflet, that they hoped to make the participants aware of their potential value to the community. . . . The following week they returned, armed with scissors, glue, old greetings cards, cotton wool and used toilet rolls . . . the elderly participants were going to make some pretty collages to decorate the hall in time for the visit of the local school children.
>
> (Dawson, 1991: 10–11)

In these examples, therefore, the image of the child is connoted in such a way that the adult status, or personhood, of elderly people becomes obscured. The elderly people have been transformed into metaphoric children. The powerful impact of this process for elderly people themselves emerges out of Dawson's material: a spirited discontent developed amongst the elderly people, culminating in the eventual removal of the younger helpers from the club.

In exploring the imaging of 'second childhood' through infantilizing practices we are therefore describing an interactive social process in which elderly people may themselves engage or, in turn, resist. Given the considerable tension between the images of the child and the elderly person, to impose the former in such a way that it becomes an authentic representation of the latter is a complex, subtle process, ever at risk of collapse through contestation (Thompson, 1984). This makes the ideological aspect of the imaging of second childhood central, operating as it does in the interests of one group, adults, at the cost of others, children and elderly people. Thus, in the struggles and negotiations associated with the imaging of second childhood during deep old age, we find ample evidence of Gramsci's observation that ideological control is neither given nor static (Hall *et al.*,1976: 16).

SECOND CHILDHOOD

Given the extensive variation in the lives of elderly people in western societies, due to differences of class, gender, health and ethnicity, how is it that one culturally and historically specific image – old age as second childhood – dominates the representation of deep old age? Wherein lies the persuasiveness of an image which makes very elderly people's affinity with dependent children seem self-evident, their child-like qualities undeniable? These are central questions: as instanced above, so powerful are these images that echoes of their logic can resonate within and give literal shape to adult/elderly interactions everywhere, even in the absence of dependency (Hockey and James, 1993).

To make sense of this, therefore, the cognitive structures through which the idea of dependency is managed within western societies must be explored. Deriving from particularized conceptions of children and childhood, these work to sustain a whole range of cultural stereotypes of aging as 'second childhood'. Images of physical decline and social marginality are invoked and, whilst rarely having 'validity as accounts of how people see themselves', none the less act as powerful symbolic markers of identity which are used to attribute characteristics to others (Cohen, 1986: 13). Thus, as discussed below, the apparent 'limitations' of childhood are mapped on to a parallel series of 'inadequacies' believed to characterize old age. Within stereotypical images of old age as 'childlike' are embedded, therefore, the metaphoric strategies which create social distances between the worlds of adulthood and old age. By linking old age with childhood, the hegemony of adulthood remains unchallenged.

The historical emergence of individualism is central to this process (MacFarlane, 1978; Hockey and James, 1993). For example, in late nineteenth century Britain the introduction of compulsory education, the process of industrialization, and later the welfare state, combined to exclude children, elderly people and women from the workplace. At home, women became carers for new categories of dependent people (Wright, 1987) and in the 'work society', labour force participation became central to the attribution of personhood (Kohli, 1988). Denied their personhood, elderly people resumed the child's status as 'dependent', previously relinquished on becoming adult. However, the question remains as to why 'dependent childhood' has now come to image all forms of dependency. If the power of a metaphor to shape social experience lies in its cultural fitness or 'felt aptness' (Sontag, 1990: 6), why has the image of 'the child' come to speak so evocatively about other social experiences such as old age and disability?

Turner's (1974) discussion of root metaphors provides a useful starting place. Defined as a 'systematic repertoire of ideas by means of which a given thinker describes, by analogical extension, some domain to which those ideas do not immediately and literally apply' (Black, quoted in Turner, 1974: 26), root metaphors can powerfully shape everyday perceptions and experiences by bringing two previously unconnected thoughts together in a single word or phrase. This dynamic process goes beyond substitution or comparison. Indeed, in the historical antecedents of root metaphors may lie a full panoply of currently masked meaning (Turner, 1974). Here we ask, what meanings lie concealed within the metaphoric use of childhood for old age?

The term 'childhood' itself refers to a socially constructed phase in the life course which varies both historically and cross-culturally (James and Prout, 1990). From accounts of the emergence of contemporary western childhood (Pinchbeck and Hewitt, 1969, 1973; Demos, 1971; Ariès, 1979 [1962]; Wilson, 1980; Walvin, 1982; Pollock, 1983) it can be seen that conceptions of 'childhood' have increasingly stressed the differences, rather than similarities, between children and adults, as children's social, political and economic dependency and marginalization have become progressively compounded. Four characteristics of 'the child' can be distilled through these histories: (1) the child is spatially and temporally set apart as different, as 'other'; (2) the child is said to have a special nature, and to be associated with nature; (3) the child is innocent and therefore (4) vulnerability dependent (Hockey and James, 1993). Whilst not always explicit, these characteristics nevertheless help explain why childhood has become a culturally legitimated 'root metaphor' for dependency.

What must be established, however, is the nature of the processes through which the imaging of old age as childlike occurs. MacDonald, citing Barthes, argues that imagery, like myth, is 'intricate', operating on a 'less easily articulated level' so that rational argument often stumbles in the face of the more subtle power of the image (MacDonald, 1987: 3). Here we are describing an imaging process which renders the culturally variable experiences of childhood and old age as not only 'natural' but also 'naturally' comparable and compatible.

IMAGES OF 'THE CHILD'

What expectations and assumptions surround childhood in contemporary western cultures? Firestone (1971) argues that the images of 'the child' which have gained maximum currency are primarily nostalgic or sentimental. For Holt, the western 'child' is idealized as a 'mixture of expensive nuisance, fragile treasure, slave and super-pet' (Holt, 1975: 22). The mythical creature he describes is locked into the social institution of childhood, 'a kind of walled garden in which children, being small and weak, are protected from the harshness of the world outside until they become strong and clever enough to cope with it' (ibid.).

For Ennew two main characteristics define childhood in contemporary western societies. The first is 'a rigid age hierarchy which permeates the whole of society and creates a separating distance between adults and children' (1986: 17). This is exemplified in the multitude of specialist products for children in western cultures: clothes, films, toys, books, food, play spaces, schools and, more recently, telephone lines for counselling abused children.

The second characteristic identified by Ennew is 'the myth of childhood as a golden age' whereby children are 'obliged to be happy' (1986: 18). In this the theme of innocence predominates, personified by A. A. Milne in Christopher Robin, a curly-haired little boy in wellingtons, who whiles away his childhood 'in complete isolation from adults in the Hundred Acre Wood, accompanied by sexless woolly animals' (Ennew, 1986: 11). In sum, Ennew argues, western childhood is imaged as 'a period of lack of responsibility, with rights to protection and training but not to autonomy' (ibid.: 21).

Another set of images, whilst presenting a stark contrast, nevertheless stem from the same root and, precisely through their opposition, sustain these themes of innocence and dependence. Drawn largely from the Third World, images of victimized children are splashed across the newspapers of the First World, representations of 'incorrect childhood'

for which correction must be sought. The largely uncritical incorporation of a western ideal of childhood on to the agenda of international
children's agencies means that 'an association is constantly made
between white children who have a correct childhood and black
children who have none' (Ennew, 1986: 22). Recent controversies about
child sexual abuse in Britain have also sustained this concept of
childhood in society: 'the discourses of childhood innocence, passivity
and innate vulnerability' which permeate contemporary visions of what
'the child' is effectively socialize abused children into 'victimhood' and
oppression (Kitzinger, 1990: 158).

In summary, then, childhood should not be seen as the inevitable by-
product of biological infancy but a particular version of it. It is a
time of positively perceived culturally legitimated dependency which,
through contemporary western imagery, has created a boundary between the worlds of adulthood and childhood, a partitioning process
which 'naturalizes' children's dependency through the 'scientific' discourses of developmental psychology (James and Prout, 1990). Thus,
in literally embodying dependency in contemporary western cultures,
'the child' provides an organizing image which may be extended in its
use by adult carers to encompass and structure the lives of elderly
people, who are perceived to be illegitimately dependent. The conceptual dissonance of physical dependency and 'independent' adulthood is problematic: invoking 'the child' thus effects some kind of
resolution or ideological 'suture' (Eagleton, 1991). Further, within
a social world where individualism creates powerful links between
personal autonomy, paid work and personhood, retired people who
become economically dependent may be denied full personhood by the
working adult world. This stigma is also softened through imaging old
age as a form of second childhood. Indeed, it may be held at bay for
adult carers, such is the symbolic power of 'the child' to recast
stigmatizing dependency as a positively perceived social status.

However, for many elderly people themselves this kind of metaphoric
transformation may merely confirm a negative self identity, a confirma-
tion which at times is fiercely resisted. To exemplify the power of images
of 'second childhood' in delimiting the boundaries of elderly people's
personhood in western society we now focus on the social construction
of the body.[1] This is just one critical pathway along which the figurative
association of dependent elderly people with 'the child' is made literal
through infantilizing practices in society.

THE BODY AS A SIGNIFIER

A wealth of anthropological material reveals the body being used in
many societies to make statements about social status (Polhemus, 1978).

140

In western cultures forms of bodily alteration predominate – from breast enlargement through to dieting. As Featherstone (1982) argues, the body is taking on increasing social significance. Through the conjoining of the inner and outer body, appearance has now come to signify the self, with the result that 'the penalties of bodily neglect are a lowering of one's acceptability as a person'(ibid.: 26). With a 'self-preservationist conception of the body', imaged in the youthful bodies of contemporary western popular culture, the social consequences of this shift in emphasis are considerable (ibid.: 18). An old, fat or disfigured body implies an undesirable self and a correspondingly reduced social status. Thus, in western cultures, advertisers rarely depict people in the 50-plus age group (Grant, 1991). This contrasts with the traditional Chinese veneration of old age:

> In direct contradiction to the American custom, advertisers in Hong Kong who wish to promote such luxury products as expensive brandy or watches often depict the birthday party of an elder as the appropriate occasion for such a gift. Ancient laws allocated special meat rations to those who had attained advanced ages. These allotments were similar to the status markers denoting the nobility.
>
> (Sankar, 1984: 271)

The signifying and stigmatizing role of the aging body in the West is underlined in ethnographic accounts. Hockey (1990), for example, describes how the needs of the physical body are used by carers to define the social body of the elderly person. Thus, the frail residents of a residential home – seen as impaired in body and mind – were socially distinguished from fitter residents through different kinds of naming practices:

> Those who become incontinent, unable to walk without support, or perceptibly 'confused in their minds' will find themselves moved downstairs to what staff refer to as the 'frail' corridor. . . . in the dining room 'frail' residents are moved forwards close to the hatchway into the kitchen. Referred to as 'the little people' – who receive smaller meals – it is this group who will be addressed by Christian names only and will tend to be given nicknames.
>
> (Hockey, 1990: 100)

Their bodily condition provided the literal grounding for their social identity. Lost physical abilities meant lost adult social status as Mr or Mrs (see also Hazan, 1980; Martin, 1979).

However, while perceptions of the body play an important ideological role in the allocation of category-specific social identities, the metaphoric transformation of old age is based upon a very selective reading of the bodies of both adults and children. Their bodies are in fact very different. We now ask why the child's body provides a literal grounding for the metaphoric use of childhood in imaging old age and what the implications of this infantilization are.

A CHILDISH BODY

Contemporarily, the symbolic marking out of an ideology of childhood through the imaging of the physical body occurs in two ways. First through representations of the child's body as lacking the competencies of the adult. Second, through sentimentalizing the specific abilities and qualities which the child is seen to possess.

Tucker (1977), for instance, reaches for a universal definition of 'the child' through highlighting the primacy of the physical body. However, his account of childhood highlights the absence of adult bodily skills. The child is described as having 'intermittent concentration and intellectual limitations' (ibid.: 28); being 'prone to misconceptions' (ibid.: 29), 'innate fear and credulity' (ibid.: 29); with an 'immature physique' (ibid.: 42) the child is characterized by 'non-fertility' (ibid.: 45), by being 'small in a world where those in authority over him will be tall'(ibid.: 46) and by lacking 'differentiation between the self and the outside world' (ibid.: 77).

While childhood may have such a biological base what is significant, at the ideological level, are the exclusively negative connotations which such accounts of 'the child' have. They stress the child's disabilities, rather than its different abilities. In western societies the adult body and intellect provide the dominant yardstick by which other bodies and minds are to be judged. Yet 'growing up', in fact, involves the loss of children's abilities – to run, jump, fall, whirl, squeeze into small and secret spaces. However, the ideologically powerful and positive image of upward growth precludes this perception (Lakoff and Johnson, 1980). Thus, while some adults may remain capable of these activities, they have access to them only when formalized as sports, and confined to the time and space known as adult leisure. Outside these specified contexts adults who indulge in such activities may be condemned as 'childish', if not insane. As Holt observed:

> we tend to think that children are most cute when they are openly displaying their ignorance and incompetence. We value their dependency and helplessness. They are help objects as well as love objects. Children acting really competently and intelligently do not usually strike us as cute. They are as likely to puzzle and threaten us.
>
> (Holt, 1975: 91)

142

Contemporary attitudes towards 'gifted' children also illustrate this point (Freeman, 1979). Careful account and explanation of their talents must be provided, for through their exceptional capacities they have overreached their status as children. They are 'out of time' with the pace of a child's 'normal' development (James and Prout, 1990). In western cultures, then, an emphasis upon physical incompetency underscores children's historically constituted dependency and their 'need' for protection (Hendrick, 1990), an embodied imaging mirrored in the ideological framing of their emotional and intellectual development. Childhood is prized as a necessary period of cocooning, with happiness being its key (Ennew, 1986: 18), a state of bliss best achieved through 'ignorance', rather than knowledge.

Other societies' models of the child's body, however, highlight the different abilities of children. For example, among the Papagoin of Arizona, Benedict observed that no adult rushed to help a 3-year-old girl to shut a heavy door:

> it was assumed that the task would not be asked of her unless she could perform it, and having been asked, the responsibility was hers alone just as if she were a grown woman.
>
> (Benedict, 1955: 23)

Similarly, recalling childhood in Bali in the 1930s, Mead suggested that 'there is little acceptance of any task as being difficult or inappropriate for a child' (Mead, 1955: 40). More recently, Schildkrout (1978) describes urban Kano children of 7 or 8 looking after younger children and performing other 'adult' tasks in Hausa society.

In summary, therefore, a selective and culturally specific reading of the body and mind of the child forms the basis for the western conception of childhood as a period of culturally legitimated dependency which, in turn, provides the grounding for the parallels perceived between their bodies and those of elderly people. Through metaphoric recourse to the positively perceived 'limitations' of the child's body adults shield themselves from the approaching vision of illegitimate social dependency in old age. In doing so, however, the basis for the denial of elderly personhood is formed. At its most extreme this can lead to the social death of those who are merely growing old.

Some examples will image this process for us. In British culture, the complexity of the interplay between the literal and figuratively old and young often finds expression in everyday verbal imagery: old heads sit on young shoulders, little old ladies remain young at heart but old in body. Selective use is made of the body as a referential source through establishing metonymic relationships. Thus, the adjective 'wrinkly' can become a noun used to refer to elderly people, as in the following headline to a story about a bank-raider in his late 60s:

143

'Wrinkly in an old-up' (*The Sun*, 4 July 1990).

Here a metonymical part-to-whole relationship is established between the old surface of the body and the social identity of the person: through a highly selective reading of the body, a single part of the person – their wrinkled skin – is substituted for the whole. This relationship is, however, neither fixed nor consistent – babies' skin is also wrinkled but, in this instance, we highlight its smoothness, rather than its rippled texture; in this way babies' skin is positioned as pleasurable, admirable and desirable.

Infantilization is therefore underpinned by a creative metonymic relationship whereby certain physical features – incontinence, incoherent speech, immobility – are taken as defining criteria for the whole person. Thus, she who lacks bladder control becomes an 'incontinent'; he who has Alzheimer's disease is one of the 'dementing'. This metonymic relationship then serves to both justify, and is itself justified by, the metaphorical assertions of their childlike qualities made literal through infantilizing practices. Elderly applicants for residential care may therefore be assessed in terms of the capabilities of their physical bodies, rather than their personal qualities or social needs:

> The factors considered relevant are: Physical: mobility, dressing, feeding, continence, sleep; Mental: orientation, communication, co-operation, restlessness and mood.
>
> (Hazan, 1980: 31)

In this way elderly people are denied personhood through effectively 'obliterating their life history and social identity, and reducing them to their physical and mental disabilities' (ibid.: 30).

Imaging physical dependency as 'childlike' is however culturally specific. McCormack (1985) describes the aging process among the Sherbro people of Sierra Leone, where incoherent speech signifies close communication between the old person and the ancestors, the ultimate source of social blessings and misfortune. Here old people are cared for reverently as they grow into sacredness, a physical care which endorses, rather than diminishes, their status as an elderly person. Similarly, among the Venda speaking people of Southern Africa bodily indications of 'old age' – the birth of a grandchild or greying hair – are recognized as welcome signs of approaching contact with the 'real' world of the spirits (Blacking, 1990).

Under the Confucian tradition of gerontocracy, although both childhood and old age are phases in the life course 'characterized by having insufficient yang and by a soul that is not firmly attached to the body' this is not thought of as belittling (Sankar, 1984: 250):

The affection and respect accorded the elderly still remain, especially in rural areas. There the parents still maintain considerable control over the social and economic lives of their adult children. With social space allotted to them, the importance of the sick role to legitimise dependence is in effect negligible for the elderly. In fact, the opposite attitude very much obtains. Elderly people whose children are successful enough to care for them take great pride in the fact they they are able to rely on their children.

(Sankar, 1984: 273)

These examples contrast with the feelings of humiliation and degradation engendered by the infantilizing of elderly people in the west.

In encounters involving bodily intimacy the most explicit parallels may be drawn with children. Carers' and professionals' approach to the naked bodies of those in their care and the denial of the sexuality of elderly people leads to their metaphoric neutering. Arguably, too, the centrality of sexual relationships to notions of independent adulthood is threatened by their appearance among dependent people as newspaper headlines reveal:

'Able Mabel, 84, elopes to wed' (The Sun, 12 July, 1990).

A cartoon in the *Daily Mirror* (20 July 1990) depicts an old couple at Sunset Old Folks Home. The man, sporting a buttonhole and carrying a wine glass, is being berated by a woman: 'Go away! Its unlucky to see the bride without her teeth in'.

These images invite laughter at the very idea that sexuality and age could go together. And through laughter the danger is averted.

But the sexuality of elderly people is not only laughed at; it is also romanticized. Thus, when a Fuji film advertisement depicted 'geriatric eroticism' – a passionate kiss in a launderette between two elderly people – its designers refuted the charge of breaking the 'final taboo' – that older people have sex – by describing it as a picture 'that is about love'. Similarly, through populist images we are encouraged to admire the enduring love and romance of long-lived couples. Garvey describes the sexual fulfilment experienced by one such couple, noting that while this is not unusual, the couple are 'exceptional in admitting to it' (*Guardian*, 5 June 1991). A consultant geriatrician is reported as saying that

many old people feel that sex is something they should have grown out of; they feel guilty it's still going on, and although they may have physical problems such as lack of lubrication or arthritic limbs, many elderly people are reluctant to ask for help or advice for fear of ridicule or, worse, disgust. They don't want to be dubbed a Dirty Old Man or Not Quite a Lady.

(Garvey, 1991)

145

RESISTANCE AND REGENERATION

Tracing the ideological role of the body as a marker of social identity has shown how the image of 'second childhood', emanating from the adult world, can proscribe full personhood for those in old age. The culturally acceptable bodily limitations ascribed to childhood provide the literal grounding for the figurative images through which otherwise threatening bodily conditions associated with deep old age are framed. Little wonder that members of the dominant category 'adult' resist any diminution of their capacity for self reliance and physical attractiveness. Hence the expenditure by British women of £113.2 million on skin-care preparations in 1986, and the £42.4 million on toiletries and hair preparations spent by British men (*Independent*, 22 October 1988).

However, elderly people themselves also resist the power which 'second childhood' wields – with varying degrees of efficacy. For those who, as adults, had considerable social power – captains of industry, members of parliament and judges – the threat of 'second childhood' is mitigated by continuing careers and economic independence. And those adults already on society's margins – artists, writers, actors – may find themselves absorbed, rather than excluded from society in old age, as their work achieves retrospective status.

To those who are dependent upon care in deep old age, there remain none the less some forms of resistance. The power of the weak, of those who have little left to lose, may be used by very elderly people to regenerate aspects of their personhood denied by infantilizing practices (Martin, 1979). As outsiders, elderly people living in residential care may use the eccentricities of 'second childhood' as a deliberate subversive strategy. Hockey (1990) describes how female residents assumed tiny girlish voices to persuade staff that they might be unwell and others resorted freely to verbal violence in conflicts with other residents. As an alternative strategy residents made direct reference to their own mortality and refused the masking of bodily decay and eventual death upon which infantilizing practices are predicated:

> I won't live much longer. I'm 84. All my friends are dead.

> You can be struck down at any moment.

> If I live till next December I'll be 95.

In these throwaway lines the logic of adult cognitive structures is implicitly challenged. At issue are the boundaries of adulthood as currently imaged within western societies. Thus, in subverting their metaphoric status as children and in asserting their closeness to death, and its attendant frailties and dependencies, elderly people are actively regenerating their personhood as individuals who are not only vulnerable but also adult.

146

NOTE

1 Work and leisure are other contexts in which parallels between the experiences of elderly people and children are to be found. For a discussion of these see Hockey and James (1993).

REFERENCES

Ariès, P. (1979) [1962] *Centuries of Childhood*, Harmondsworth: Penguin.

Barthes, R. (1973) [1957] *Mythologies*, London: Granada.

Benedict, R. (1955) 'Continuities and discontinuities in cultural conditioning', in M. Mead and M. Wolfenstein (eds) *Childhood in Contemporary Cultures*, Chicago: University of Chicago Press.

Black, M. (1962) *Models and Metaphors: Studies in Language and Philosophy*, Ithaca, NY: Cornell University Press.

Blacking, J. (1990) 'Growing old gracefully: physical, social and spiritual transformations in Venda society, 1956–66', in P. Spencer (ed.) *Anthropology and the Riddle of the Sphinx*, London: Routledge.

Carver, V. and Liddiard, P. (1978) *An Ageing Population*, Milton Keynes: Open University Press.

Cohen, A. P. (1986) (ed.) *Symbolising Boundaries*, Manchester: Manchester University Press.

Dawson, A. (1991) '"Ageing Well": the construction of perceptions and responses to physiological ageing in clubs for the elderly', paper presented to the British Sociological Association Conference, Health and Society, Manchester.

Demos, J. (1971) 'Developmental perspectives on the history of childhood', in T. K. Rabb and R. Rutberg (eds) *The Family in History*, London: Harper Row.

Eagleton, T. (1991) *Ideology*, London: Verso.

Ennew, J. (1986) *The Sexual Exploitation of Children*, Cambridge: Polity Press.

Featherstone, M. (1982) 'The body in consumer culture', *Theory, Culture and Society* 1: 18–33.

Fernandez, J. W. (1970) 'Persuasions and performances: of the beast in every body . . . and the metaphors of everyman', in C. Geertz (ed.) *Myth, Symbol and Culture*, London: Hutchinson.

Firestone, S. (1971) *The Dialectics of Sex*, London: Paladin.

Freeman, J. (1979) *Gifted Children*, Lancaster: MTP Press.

Garvey, A. (1991) 'Will you still love me tomorrow?', *Guardian*, 5 June.

Grant, L. (1991) 'The Shock of the Old Hits Adland', *The Independent*, 30 June.

Hall, S., Clarke, J., Jefferson, T. and Roberts, B. (eds) (1976) *Resistance through Rituals*, London: Hutchinson.

Hazan, H. (1980) *The Limbo People*, London: Routledge & Kegan Paul.

Hendrick, H. (1990) 'Constructions and reconstructions of British childhood: an interpretive survey, 1800 to the present', in A. James and A. Prout (eds) *Constructing and Reconstructing Childhood*, Basingstoke: Falmer Press.

Hockey, J. (1990) *Experiences of Death. An Anthropological Account*, Edinburgh: Edinburgh University Press.

Hockey, J. and James, A. (1993) *Growing Up and Growing Old: Ageing and Dependency in the Life Course*, London: Sage.

Holt, J. (1975) *Escape From Childhood*, Harmondsworth: Penguin

James, A. and Prout, A. (1990) *Constructing and Reconstructing Childhood*, Basingstoke: Falmer Press.

Kitzinger, J. (1990) 'Who are you kidding? Children, power and the struggle against sexual abuse', in A. James and A. Prout (eds) *Constructing and Reconstructing Childhood*, Basingstoke: Falmer Press.

Kohli, M. (1988) 'Ageing as a challenge for sociological theory', *Ageing and Society* 8: 367–94.

Lakoff, G. and Johnson, M. (1980) *Metaphors We Live By*, Chicago: University of Chicago Press.

MacCormack, C. (1985) 'Dying as transformation to ancestorhood: the Sherbro coast of Sierra Leone', *Curare, Sonderband* 4: 117–26.

MacDonald, S. (1987) 'Drawing the lines – gender, peace and war: an introduction', in S. MacDonald, P. Holden, and S. Ardener (eds) *Images of Women in Peace and War*, London: Macmillan.

MacFarlane, A. (1978) *The Origins of English Individualism*, Oxford: Basil Blackwell.

Martin, P. (1979) *I Shall Wear Purple*, Occasional Paper 7, Mitcham: Age Concern England.

de Mause, L. (ed.) (1976) *The History of Childhood*, London: Souvenir Press.

Mead, M. (1955) 'Children and ritual in Bali', in M. Mead and M. Wolfenstein (eds) *Childhood in Contemporary Cultures*, Chicago: University of Chicago Press.

Pinchbeck, I. and Hewitt, M. (1969) *Children in English Society, vol. I*, London: Routledge & Kegan Paul.

Pinchbeck, I. and Hewitt, M. (1973) *Children in English Society, vol. II*, London: Routledge & Kegan Paul.

Polhemus, T. (ed.) (1978) *Social Aspects of the Human Body*, Harmondsworth: Penguin.

Pollock, L. (1983) *Forgotten Children: Parent-Child Relations 1500–1900*, Cambridge: Cambridge University Press.

Sankar, A. (1984) '"It's Just Old Age." Old age as a diagnosis in American and Chinese medicine', in D. I. Kertzer and J. Keith (eds) *Age and Anthropological Theory*, Ithaca, NY: Cornell University Press.

Schildkrout, E. (1978) 'Roles of children in urban Kano', in J. La Fontaine (ed.) *Sex and Age as Principles of Social Differentiation*, London: Academic Press.

Sontag, S. (1990) *AIDS and its Metaphors*, London: Penguin.

Thomas, D. (1954) *Under Milk Wood*, London: Dent.

Thompson, J. B. (1984) *Studies in the Theory of Ideology*, Cambridge: Polity Press.

Tucker, N. (1977) *What is a Child?* London: Fontana.

Turner, V. (1974) *Dramas, Fields and Metaphors. Symbolic Action in Human Society*, Ithaca, NY: Cornell University Press.

Walvin, J. (1982) *A Child's World. A Social History of English Childhood, 1800–1914*, Harmondsworth: Penguin.

Wilson, A. (1980) 'The infancy of the history of childhood: an appraisal of Phillipe Ariès', *History and Theory* 19(2): 132–54.

Wright, P. (1987) 'The social construction of babyhood: the definition of infant care as a medical problem', in A. Bryman, B. Bytheway, P. Allatt and T. Keil (eds) *Rethinking the Life Cycle*, London: Macmillan.

10

CHILDREN'S DRAWINGS OF GRANDPARENTS

A quantitative analysis of images

Cornelia Hummel, Jean-Charles Rey and
Christian J. Lalive d'Epinay

INTRODUCTION

Children's drawings have been studied by psychologists for more than a century and Luquet's work in the 1920s is still in use as a reference. Sociologists have only become interested in this field of research since the 1960s (Dennis, 1966). Even if today it is acceptable to see drawings as representations which convey the socio-cultural origins of the child, questions about the kind of sociological information we can expect to obtain from children's drawings have yet to find clear and definite answers. There is a further practical problem which we can add to these epistemological and conceptual questions: the analysis of images, compared to textual analysis, is more problematic and difficult to operationalize. Here we face the same problem semiology has tried to solve: how should we proceed to 'read' images properly?

In 1990 we came across an international collection of more than 13,000 children's drawings representing grandparents. Our first goal has been to analyse the richness of information by studying children's drawings as social representations. The second goal has been to evolve instruments which permit: (a) the objectivation and coding of the information in the children's drawings, and (b) an efficient analysis of this material. To do this we have taken the unusual step of choosing quantitative methods to study what can be regarded as highly qualitative 'material' – children's drawings. In this paper we will review briefly the first exploratory stage of the study.

THE STUDY OF CHILDREN'S DRAWINGS

The psychological influence

As early as 1880 children's drawings attracted the attention of several scientists working in the field of psychology. The development of the study of children's drawings can be closely related to the growth of psychology, still a 'young' science at the end of the nineteenth century. Researchers such as E. Cooke (1885), G. S. Hall (1882), M. B. Perez (1888) and C. Ricci (1887) published their studies on children's drawings between 1882 and 1888 and can therefore be considered as pioneers. At the beginning of the twentieth century there was a considerable increase in the number of publications, and studies based on large samples were undertaken. Although questions of cognitive development underlie much of this research, the studies are mostly descriptive and try to answer the following question: 'what do children like to draw ?'

By the second decade of the century children's drawings were considered to be an integral part of the intellectual development of the child. The drawing can be approached through two different points of view: the first is dynamic and understands drawing as a practice lying within the general process of motor and intellectual development; the second is static and understands drawing as a sign of the cognitive development of the child at a given period.

For almost eighty years, psychology has been the only science which considered children's drawings as a suitable source of knowledge and research topic. Since 1920 experimental attempts were made to use children's drawings as an intelligence test, and subsequently as a personality test ('Draw-a-Man Test' by Goodenough, 1926; 'New Draw-a-Man' by Harris, 1963; 'Human Figure Drawing – H.F.D.' by Machover, 1949). Cognitive psychology and psychoanalysis have fought over the interpretation of drawings, examining, for example, the amount of detail, or the symbolic value of colours ('House Test' by Minkowska, 1948; 'House Tree Person– H.T.P. Test' by Buck, 1949; 'Tree Test' by Koch, 1949; 'The Family Test' by Porot, 1952).

Drawing within child development

One of the main figures in the history of research on children's drawings is the French researcher Georges-Henri Luquet (1927), who offered the first systematic analysis of the different stages marking out the graphic activity of the child. Working on his daughter's drawings, Luquet developed a theory of the five successive stages of child development.

1 Scribbling (*le gribouillage*), until 2 years of age. The first 'drawings' arise from the casual encounter of a child's gesture and a surface. The child enjoys the process without understanding it and draws for the sake of drawing.
2 Casual realism (*le réalisme fortuit*), 2–3 years of age. The child makes

a fundamental discovery: the possible analogy between his drawings and real objects. This discovery leads him to intentionality.

3 Missed realism (*le réalisme manqué*), 3–4 years of age. The child wants his drawings to be realistic but comes up against two difficulties: physical nature (motor aptitudes), and psychical nature (lack of concentration, mental imagery that is too fragile).

4 Intellectual realism (*le réalisme intellectuel*), 4–8 years of age. The child draws objects with all their characteristics, the visible and the non-visible ones. In this stage, the child uses procedures like 'the transparency' (for example, a mother drawn with a baby in her womb, transparent house with people in it), 'the folding' (*le rabattement:* the objects are unfolded, for example, a cube, in order to show all faces), and 'the multiplication of points of view'. This stage is considered as the 'golden age' of children's drawing.

5 Visual realism (*le réalisme visuel*), from 8–9 years on. The child submits to the rules of linear perspective. Luquet defines this stage as marking 'the end of children's drawing'. Even if opinions differ on the ages defining the stages, this definition of the evolution of children's drawings is still with us. Graphical characteristics are typical of each stage and Luquet's work allows us to identify certain graphical elements as being exclusively related to the child's development and not to cultural influences.

In 1985 E. Tholome published a study of 2,700 drawings made by children and adults on the topic 'the family meal'. The purpose was to distinguish the genetic aspects (what is common to the graphics of all children) and the cultural or individual aspects of the drawing. He therefore proceeded to analyse his material with the help of stages and to compare his results with Luquet's work. The two authors agree on the first three stages and on the general evolution of the graphics, but Tholome notices that the milestones are not as clear between the third, fourth and fifth stage. Procedures used in the stage of intellectual realism last for over nine years and there is no definite appearance of visual realism. In fact, Tholome shows that from 9 years on, children begin to pay considerable attention to other's judgement: the drawing has to be lifelike and beautiful. Realism and aestheticism are the main criteria determining the drawing and children find all kinds of solutions to bypass the problem of perspective representation. This tendency increases as the children get older and is accompanied by a growing disinterest for drawing as an activity. Even if 12 year old children still use 'transparency' and 'folding', they try very hard to avoid the representation of volume as they increasingly conform to adult's graphic conventions. Tholome concludes that 'the child thus draws things not the way he sees them or the way he lived them, but the way

151

he knows how to represent them' (Tholome, 1985: 251; our translation). This conclusion changes the definition of realism: the child does not solve the problems of realism but circumvents them through various skilful or clever strategies.

Luquet's and Tholome's work indicate that it is very important to consider the factor 'age' in the analysis of children's drawings. Age is not only involved in the improvements in graphic skill, but also with changes in the way of 'representing' the world. Therefore, we will have to try to 'neutralize' this factor in order to compare properly the different drawings.

In addition to his analysis of the evolution of children's drawing in terms of stages, Luquet developed an explanation pattern ('*modèle explicatif*') introducing the notion of '*modèle interne*' (internal model). He argues that the drawing is not a simple copy of the object to be drawn, but the result of a 'mediation' provided by the internal model. The latter is defined as 'a refraction of the object to be drawn through the child's mind, an original reconstruction resulting from an elaboration which is very complicated despite its spontaneity. The term "internal model" is meant to distinguish clearly the actual object or model from the mental representation the drawing renders' (Luquet, 1927: 64). Proof of the internal model's existence are the drawings made 'from memory': the child must have remembered the constituent elements of the drawn objects, at the time of observations or previous drawings.

The construction of the 'internal model' implies the original activity of the mind, an unconscious elaboration of materials coming from experience (visual or tactile impressions provided by the real object, motif or model) and retained in memory. The elaboration appears under the form of a selection, a choice between different constituent elements of the object and the child's mind which institutes a true hierarchy among the essential and the secondary elements.

The notion of 'internal model' has been widely discussed since Luquet. A certain number of studies show that the 'internal model' does not necessarily reflect faithfully the child's knowledge of the drawn object (Kosslyn, Heldmeyer and Locklear, 1977; Lurçat, 1985). Freeman suggests that we alter the phrase 'the child draws what he knows' (associated in particular with intellectual realism) to 'the child knows more than what he draws' (Freeman, 1980).

We agree with the above authors in their differentiation between the 'internal model' and the graphical representation. But we have to remind ourselves that our purpose is not to approach the child's representations from the psychological perspective, and even less so to consider this representation as an entity. In other words, we are not seeking to argue about the question of individual representation versus the 'internal model', but are trying to bring out the social characteristics lying within the representation. In this sense, we are not working on representation, but on 'social representation' (Moscovici, 1976). Relying on the concept of 'internal model', we believe that an analysis based on a number of drawings can enable us to find the main cultural specificities. Thus, the opportunity to conceive the drawing as evidence, however incomplete, of the child's representations, is, in our view, sufficient to serve as a beginning for our work.

Many authors point to the influence of the child's particular environment, and more broadly his or her culture, upon the drawing. Perfecting her 'House Test' in 1948, Françoise Minkowska observes that the drawing of the house definitely reflects the socio-cultural origins of the child. Nevertheless, a sociological perspective on the study of children's drawings was only introduced in 1966 by W. Dennis. In his 'Group values through children's drawing', he examines how drawings show differences in cultural patterns and values. From this point on, a number of researchers have used drawings in order to study the perception children have of various sociological aspects or groups.

The sociological perspective

One of the important questions in the study of children's drawings concerns data collection. A German researcher, Martin Krampen (1991), has developed a study of children's drawings of buildings. His goal is to detect the cultural influence on very 'simple' drawings (apartment buildings, office buildings, churches, factories) and to this end he collected drawings made by German and Turkish children. The analysis is not made of the drawing considered as an entity. Krampen 'deconstructs' the drawings into elements like roof, windows, doors, walls, floors which are considered as independent variables. Characteristics like size, height, width, number, form, are used as dependent variables showing the cultural influence. The computer analysis of these basic elements gives Krampen the opportunity to 'reconstruct' very stylized drawings which are used as 'ideal types'.

The methodology developed in Krampen's study shows clearly that drawings can be handled like any other sociological data and analysed through the use of quantitative methods. This then supports our initial hypothesis that cultural influence can be detected in children's drawings.

Relying on W. Dennis's work, R. Nuttall (in Vasquez-Nuttall *et al.*, 1988) uses children's drawings to bring to the fore the representation of the family in different cultures. In the study 202 children (106 Chinese and 96 American) were asked to draw their family engaged in everyday activities. The subsequent data collected enabled the researchers to note great differences in the way families were represented

153

(number of persons, status of the persons) and in the type of activities depicted. The Chinese drawings, for example, show many people, members of the nuclear as well as the extended family. In contrast, American children never drew any member of the extended family and fewer members of the nuclear family. Studying, doing homework and watching television are the activities most frequently presented in Chinese drawings. In the American drawings, the static lined-up family appears most frequently with the family at play in second position. Nuttall suggests that the tendency of Chinese children to include the members of the extended family could be explained by the fact that they consider themselves to be members of both nuclear and extended families. In contrast American children seem to express strong feelings of individualism and independence towards the family. The research then led the author to conclude that the drawings do actually reflect the social and cultural values of each group.

The study made by Nuttall focuses on human figures which are more difficult to analyse than objects. A complex drawing showing several characters in a setting cannot be so easily 'broken down' into fundamental elements and tested with independent variables. Still, Nuttall shows that with an analysis based on only two axes like 'characters' and 'activity' it is possible to produce convincing results. These instruments used by Krampen and Nuttall will be used as a methodological basis for our research.

AIMS AND PROCEDURES OF THE RESEARCH

Objectives

On the basis of the results of the above-mentioned researches, the theoretical postulate of the study is that children's drawings are re-flections of the inter-generational structuration of the society where their authors live. These drawings aren't an absolutely accurate image of the grandparent's situation but they can give a lot of information about the role attributed to the elderly in the society concerned, more precisely the drawings give important information about the way the children perceive and imagine the elderly.

Our main objective is to bring to the fore the different representa-tions of grandmothers and grandfathers as found in the different drawings. We will try to identify which components of the representa-tion are related to the culture the drawings come from.

The variables

In this kind of study, the characteristics of the children who made the drawings are the independent variables. As we want to detect the cultural influence on drawings, our main independent variable is the country of origin of the drawings. This country of origin is a very 'crude' approximation of the children's culture, but it's the only one given by the corpus. In fact the corpus gives very little information about these children, only name, place of residence and age.

As previously mentioned, the age variable is difficult to handle, and this is especially so when different cultural areas are compared. The borders between the stages defined by Luquet, that is the age marking the transition from one stage to another, are not always easy to identify and vary from one country to another (Czechoslovakian children appear to be more precocious in their drawing than other European children). As the intention of the study is to focus on the sociological information given by the children's drawings, we decided to consider only the drawings which can be associated with the stages of 'intellectual realism' or 'visual realism'. Moreover, the influence of age was tested (and neutralized when necessary) for each dependent variable. By examining the forename we could identify the children's gender. Information about the place of residence helped us determine not only the country but the type of area (rural or urban).

In our research, the dependent variables are clearly the characteristics of the drawings. Each drawing can be broken down into an infinity of basic elements but each element does not have the same pertinence with regard to the problematic in question. As in any other analysis of images, we have to solve the tricky problem of the selection of pertinent elements. In order to minimize the risk here, we decide to use an iterative method proceeding by elaborating the complexities of the model.

The method

The main aim of our method is to reduce the complexity of each drawing by breaking it up into its component parts. Each one of these 'minimal elements', that are graphical elements identifiable without any ambiguity, is tested. If it introduces a discrimination of the corpus relevant for the given problematic, the element is introduced in an explicative model.

Our method is divided into four stages:

– **'Taming'** (*l'apprivoisement*) of the drawings: This stage is necessary to become familiar with the specific material. Paralleling the theoretical basis and the corpus allows us to elaborate the first hypothesis about the relevant 'minimal elements'. An observation grid is then constructed in order to identify the chosen elements in the different drawings.

– **Decomposition**: All drawings are sorted through the observation grid. The coded graphical 'minimal elements' are worked out through data processing and statistical analysis in order to test if they are really relevant for the considered problematic.

– **Reconstruction**: The non-relevant elements are left out. The relevant ones are structured in order to form 'ideal-types' or typologies. The quality of these explicative models is tested on all drawings. This procedure also helps to identify eventual new pertinent elements which have to be tested. In fact, the reconstruction is very often a 'taming' stage for a second analysis. With each new step in the analysis, that is with each iteration, the models become more complex. Process continues until the researcher thinks he has brought to the fore the most relevant elements.

– **Interpretation**: Explicative hypotheses are elaborated by comparing the results of the study with other researches conducted in the field of gerontology and sociology of the family.

THE CORPUS

The collection

Our graphic corpus consists of 13,839 children's drawings representing grandmothers and grandfathers. This collection is the result of an international competition entitled 'Draw your grandma' which took place between September 1989 and May 1990.[1] The participants were aged 6 to 14 years and came from thirty-three different countries.

There are three groups of countries in the corpus:

– the first group includes Switzerland, Czechoslovakia and Bulgaria. The number of drawings coming from these countries is large: 7,810 altogether (4,644 Swiss, 1,552 Czech, 1,614 Bulgarian). Moreover these drawings come from numerous different places in each country. So we can expect that the results obtained are representative for these countries.

– for the second group including the Netherlands, India and Guatemala, we have 1,796 drawings (521 Dutch, 730 Indian, 545 Guatemalan). This number is large enough to expect statistically significant results but their representativeness is less convincing because they do not come from as many different places as needed.

– for the twenty-seven other countries the number of drawings is too small (average 50) to allow meaningful observations about the representation of the grandparents.

For a number of drawings the country identification could not be made with certitude.

The task

The only constraint given to the children was to produce a drawing which had to be characteristic of their own grandmother. The handbook explaining the instructions specified that all types of representations were permitted and explicitly mentioned three examples: (a) a drawing of the grandparent in his/her everyday life, (b) a drawing of an event involving her/him, (c) depicting a situation in which the main character and her/his grandson/daughter are involved. The children were strongly encouraged to draw one of their grandmothers, but the instructions did not completely close the possibility of drawing one of their grandfathers. As the competition handbook was very carefully translated into fifteen languages, we can assume that each child received the same instructions. However, we do not know the precise conditions in which the drawings were produced, and therefore we cannot evaluate the disruptive influence of teachers or parents encouraging the children to work in a particular way. This will probably not affect our results because of the large number of drawings analysed.

As far as we know, the great majority of drawings were made in classrooms and the phenomenon of copying seems to have been a frequent occurrence. The diversity of the places of origin of the drawings should help to minimize this influence. Our material was produced by children knowing they participated in a competition in which very attractive prizes were offered. That probably influenced a certain number of children to draw a rather 'competitive' grandmother (the one they felt more suited to win the competition), rather than their real ancestor.

THE EXPLORATORY ANALYSIS: A COMPARATIVE APPROACH FOR SIX COUNTRIES

The 'taming'

This first stage of the research is not based on a clearly-formulated hypothesis. Our work is based on the assumption that the integration of grandparents differs according to the cultural origins. By integration, we mean the place given to the elderly in social and family life. This notion can therefore be approached by two axes of analysis:

1 The drawn characters (who is drawn: the grandfather, the grandmother, both grandparents? Are they alone or with other people?).
2 The activity (what is/are the grandfather/grandmother doing?).

The huge number of drawings to be analysed (more than 13,000) constrains us to elaborate a quite simple observation grid so that the 'minimal elements' would be very easy to identify and code.

The analysis

The drawn characters

The results show that the majority of the characters, grandfather or grandmother, are represented separately. Very few children draw their grandparents as a couple (less than 10 per cent); nevertheless, it is interesting to mention that drawings coming from India and the Netherlands show significantly more grandparents together than all other countries (22.8 per cent for the Netherlands, 26 per cent for India).

After having identified the main character (grandmother, grandfather or both), we looked at the other characters found in the drawing (children, other adults/elderly). This analysis splits the countries into three groups. A first one includes Switzerland, Czechoslovakia and the Netherlands, where the elder is represented alone in almost 90 per cent of the drawings. The second group consists of Bulgaria and Guatemala, countries where the elder is drawn alone in between 75 and 80 per cent of the cases. India, where the majority of the drawings show the elder represented accompanied (75 per cent), seems to be an exception. This country is also the only one where the percentage of drawings representing adults is significantly different from zero. These results are valid for all cases (either the main character is the grandmother, grandfather, or both grandmother and grandfather drawn as couple).

The analysis of the drawn characters shows two opposed representations of the grandmother/grandfather in the body of the material: the 'lone' grandparent (drawn neither with the spouse nor with any grandchildren or adults) and the 'surrounded' grandparent. The key countries for the 'lone' representation are Switzerland and Czechoslovakia; the emblematic country for the 'surrounded' representation is India.

Broadly speaking, it is surprising that, apart from India, very few children draw themselves with their grandparent. This absence could mean that the children don't consider themselves to be a part of their grandparents' environment. The adults (who could be the parents or members of the extended family) are also practically non-existent in the drawings. The children seem to completely separate the grandparent from the rest of the family and the social environment.

The activity

The first point we can make concerns the number of grandparents represented carrying out an activity. Most grandmothers are drawn being active; in the drawings coming from Guatemala, Switzerland and the Netherlands about 50 per cent of the grandmothers are active, for Bulgaria and Czechoslovakia the rate is around 60 per cent and it rises to 70 per cent for India.

The grandfathers are represented as much less active: less than 5 per cent are represented engaged in an activity. In this aspect the drawings of the different countries are very similar. The number of 'active' grandfathers is small, so the results concerning their activities have to be treated with caution.

The corpus shows 135 different activities. The five most represented activities for each country are listed in Table 10.1.

Inter-cultural similarities

Despite the fact that the six considered countries have very different cultures, standards of living and political and educational systems, important similarities can be observed in the grandparents' representation drawn by the children.

The six countries show a strong gender differentiation:

– The activities attributed to the grandmother tend to be associated with the home, and particularly to the household. Most of these activities are based on relationship to others: cooking appears in all countries, knitting in five, walking and taking care of children in four countries. The representation of the grandmother seems to show an important inter-cultural homogeneity.
– The grandfather is more frequently represented outside the house. When he is inside, his activities are more passive than those of the grandmother and generally they are focused on his own satisfaction rather than on the family. The image of the grandfather is strongly culturally differentiated as the only activities appearing in more than three countries are reading the newspaper and taking a walk.

Cultural specificities

In the case of Switzerland we have a strong gender differentiated image. The grandmother is represented as a wife totally devoted to the household. In contrast the grandfather is drawn as a retired person, rather passive, with completely self-centred activities.

The super-grans and grandpas are in marked contrast to these dominant and rather realistic images. These grandparents are drawn with the most severe physical signs of aging, but their clothes and activities are typically those of teenagers (for example, an old woman with one remaining black tooth and a hooked nose wears a pink mini-skirt and is roller-skating). Moreover, these kinds of drawings differ

159

Table 10.1: The five most frequent activities in the six countries

Switzerland		Netherlands	
Grandmother	*Grandfather*	*Grandmother*	*Grandfather*
to knit	to smoke	to cook	to give/receive affection
to have a walk	to have a walk	to knit	to watch TV
to cook	'super grandpa'	to have a walk	to have a walk
'super gran'	to read the newspaper	to take care of children	to give presents to children
to do housework	to watch TV	to take care of a pet	to hunt, to fish
(51%)	(47%)	(53%)	(61%)

Bulgaria		Czechoslovakia	
Grandmother	*Grandfather*	*Grandmother*	*Grandfather*
to knit	to breed animals	to knit	to smoke
to cook	to farm	to breed animals	to drink alcohol
to breed animals	to hunt, to fish	to cook	to read the newspaper
to have a walk	to read the newspaper	to read newspaper	to read a book
to take care of children	to read a book	to read a book	to breed animals
(57%)	(68%)	(57%)	(45%)

India		Guatemala	
Grandmother	*Grandfather*	*Grandmother*	*Grandfather*
to have a walk	to have a walk	to garden	to do sport
to cook	to play games	to knit	to read a book
to take care of children	to garden	to cook	to read the newspaper
to give/receive affection	to do sport	to take care of children	to pray
to pick flowers	to take care of children	to read a book	to have a walk
(55%)	(68%)	(53%)	(61%)

Figure 10.1 Grandmother by Swiss
girl, aged 8

Figure 10.2 Grandfather by Swiss
girl, aged 10

clearly from the other drawings, as their graphics are deliberately caricatural. Such figures are almost totally absent in the other countries (Figures 10.1 and 10.2).

Given that the **Netherlands** is a country similar to Switzerland by its standard of living and its political system we expected that the Dutch representation of the grandparents would be very close to the Swiss one. In fact we found significant differences. Even if the Dutch grandmother, like the Swiss one, is generally seen as a housewife, she is more often represented with children. The Dutch grandfather is more active and his activities are often conducted with his wife or grandson/ daughter (Figure 10.3).

The **Bulgarian** drawings refer to a rural society. The grandparents are mainly drawn as active farmers following the classical gender divisions of country life: the children and the household are the domain of the wife, and outside work is reserved to the man, the hen-house and the cowshed constituted a shared space (Figures 10.4 and 10.5).

The **Czechoslovakian** drawings present a marked contrast: on one side a busy grandmother working hard at home and in the cowshed and on the other side an idle alcoholic grandfather. The grandmother is more homely than the Bulgarian one and the grandfather is more passive than the Swiss one. A more detailed analysis shows that the

161

Figure 10.3 Couple by Dutch girl, aged 8

Czechoslovakian grandparents can be split into two groups: the first one is made up of 'rural' grandparents who are very close to the Bulgarian ones, and the second consists of 'urban' grandparents who are very similar to the Swiss. In Czechoslovakia two main models of grandparents seem to coexist. The association between grandfathers and alcohol occurs only in Czechoslovakia (Figures 10.6 and 10.7).

The **Indian** drawings depict a kind of paradise. The grandparents do not seem to have any hard work to do. Again the activities here are very gender differentiated. The grandmother is mainly in the house or in the garden, sharing her time between the children and leisure activities. The grandfather is generally represented outside, engaged in play or leisure activities. These representations reflect a privileged position in a very hierarchical society. The origin of the Indian drawings would suggest that we have a strong caste effect (Figure 10.8).

The **Guatemalan** drawings also show grandparents in a favourable situation. The grandmother enjoys a peaceful existence at home or in the garden. The grandfather spends most of his time in leisure activities. Here too we have a bias due to the class origins of the children. The great majority of them seem to be Hispanic children frequenting missionary schools. The odd drawing from the Amerindian community presents a very different image. Their number is unfortunately far too small to allow us to make any observations about the Amerindian representation of the grandparents (Figures 10.9 and 10.10).

Figure 10.4 Grandmother by Bulgarian girl, aged 9

Figure 10.5 Grandfather by Bulgarian boy, aged 11

Figure 10.6 Grandmother by Czech
girl, aged 12

Figure 10.7 Grandfather by Czech
boy, aged 9

Figure 10.8 Couple by Indian girl, aged 12

Figure 10.9 Grandmother by Guatemalan boy, aged 11

Figure 10.10 Grandfather by
Guatemalan girl, aged 11

The main type of activities associated with the grandparents:
a factor analysis

The statistical procedure of factor analysis, a formal method to ascertain the eventual underlying factor structure, was used to detect the main types of activities associated with each country.

For this purpose the 135 different activities have been classified into five groups:

- professional activities (working in a factory or office, breeding animals, farming, etc.)
- household activities (knitting, cooking, cleaning, etc.)
- leisure activities (going for a walk, taking part in sports, playing games, painting, etc.)
- self-care activities (washing, make-up, etc.)
- 'gift' activities (activities oriented towards the satisfaction of someone else's needs, for example, to take care of children, to give presents, etc.)

Given the important gender differentiation in the activities attributed to the elderly, the factor analysis has been carried out separately for the grandmother and grandfather. We are only able to present a factor analysis of the grandmother, as there were insufficient numbers of drawings representing grandfathers.

The results show once again the cultural specificity of the representations of grandmothers (Figure 10.11). In the Indian drawings the grandmother is strongly associated with 'gift' activities. However, the Czechoslovakians seem to associate their grandmother mainly with professional activities. In contrast to these countries where children strongly associate the grandmother to one specific type of activity, the situation of Switzerland and Bulgaria is less clear. The Bulgarian grandmothers are linked to domestic rather than professional activities, whereas the Swiss grandmothers seem to be linked to leisure activities and to a lesser extent to household activities.

Summary of the analysis

The two 'minimal elements' (characters, activity) are therefore clearly relevant in the analysis of our corpus. The six countries are differentiated by the number and the status of characters found in the drawings. They also differ a great deal in terms of the type of activity attributed to the grandmother and the grandfather. We can, therefore, retain these two elements for our model and can elaborate a first typology.

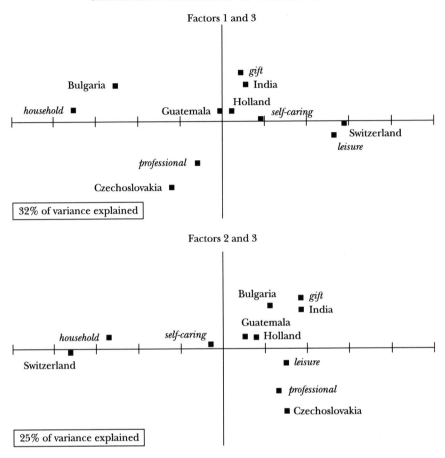

Figure 10.11 Factor analysis of the grandmothers' activities

A typology

If we pull together the analyses presented above, three main models of grandparents can be suggested:

- The first one presents the grandparents as people living alone, on the fringe of society. They are depicted spending their time in leisure and self-care activities, as if they no longer have any social role. This model, which fits the Swiss case, seems to be associated with most European industrialized countries. The Dutch model is most probably a different variant of the same model.

- The second model, which appears in the Bulgarian drawings, still describes grandparents as being isolated but having the same role as

167

any other adult. They fit into the classical model of gender division of labour ('the wife in the kitchen, and the man at work'). This model is probably associated with countries where agriculture still plays an important role.

• The third model, the Indian one, presents the grandparents as strongly integrated into society, but almost exclusively in the role of caregivers. We have to underline again that this model probably reflects the very privileged position of the upper class in a very hierarchic society.

The highly contrasting socio-economic structure of Czechoslovakia could help to explain that this country does not fit exclusively into one of the three models but manifests elements from two models: industrial and agricultural.

Beginning of the second iteration: 'taming' again

At this stage of the analysis, the explicative model based on the two minimal elements (characters-activities) has a weak predictive value. The model has to be improved and made more complex through the introduction of new variables. To enable this to take place, new 'minimal elements' need to be considered in the observation grid. The classification of the drawings based on this new model should help us to identify new 'minimal elements' which seem to be related to our cultural problematic. This new 'taming' would lead to the construction of a new observation grid. In this new grid, we will consider elements like the setting, the clothing and physical appearance of the characters. These elements, which can be related to the ones already used in the first grid, will strengthen the predictive value of the model. But the pertinence of the new elements is still to be tested.

CONCLUSION

The exploratory research carried out so far has shown that the use of a quantitative method is relevant for the analysis of images. The construction of an observation grid enables us to make a more object-ive presentation of the graphic information through the use of statist-ical analysis. Even a simple frame of analysis as the one used here in the first stage of the research has facilitated the detection of important differences in the representation of grandparents in the various coun-tries considered. The next stage of the analysis, again based on the iterative method, looks promising and will certainly help refine the model presented in this paper. Finally, we would like to join authors like Krampen and Nuttall in their conclusion that drawings can well be used as complex, but reliable, instruments in the field of sociological investigation.

NOTES

1 It should be borne in mind that the competition took place prior to the fall of the Berlin wall.
2 Several models of grandparents can be found in each of the six considered countries. But except for Czechoslovakia where two main models coexist, there is one dominant model in each country, the one which is described in this paper.

REFERENCES

Cain, J. and Gomilla, J. (1953) 'Le dessin de la famille chez l'enfant: critères de classification', *Annales Médico-Psychologiques* 4: 181–5.

Cocula, B. and Peyroutet, C. (1986) *Sémantique de l'Image*, Paris: Librairie Delagrave.

Cooke, E. (1885) 'Art teaching and child nature', *London Journal of Education* 465.

Dennis, W. (1966) *Group Values through Children's Drawings*, New York: Wiley.

Doise, W. and Palmonari, A. (1982) *L'étude des représentations sociales*, Neuchâtel: Delachaux & Niestlé.

Falchikov, N. (1990) 'Youthful ideas about old age: an analysis of children's drawings', *Aging and Human Development* 31 (2): 79–99.

Freeman, N. H. (1980) *Strategies of Representation in Young Children: analyses of spatial skill and drawing processes*, New York: Academic Press.

Gardner, H. (1979) *Gribouillages et Dessins d'Enfants*, Bruxelles: Pierre Mardaga.

Hall, G. S. (1882) 'Notes on children's drawings, literature and notes', *Pedagogical Seminary* 1: 445–7.

Hummel, C. (1992) *Dessine-moi ta Grand-mère*, Genève: mémoire de licence en sociologie sous la direction du Prof. Chr. Lalive d'Epinay, Université de Genève.

Jerrome, D. (1990) 'Intimate relationships', in J. Bond and P. Coleman (eds) *Ageing in Society: an introduction to social gerontology*, London: Sage.

Jodelet, D. (1989) *Les représentations sociales*, Paris: Presses Universitaires de France.

Kornhaber, A. and Woodward, K. (1985) *Grandparents-Grandchildren: the vital connection*, New Brunswick, NJ: Transaction books.

Kosslyn, S. M., Heldmeyer, K. H. and Locklear, E. L. (1977) 'Children's drawings as data about internal representation', *Journal of Experimental Child Psychology*, 23: 191–211.

Krampen, M. (1991) *Children's Drawings, Iconic Coding of the Environment*, New York: Plenum Press.

Lalive d'Epinay, Chr., Christe, E., Coenen-Huther, Jo., Hagmann, H-M., Jeanneret, O., Junod, J-P., Kellerhals, J., Raymond, L., Schellhorn, J-P. and de Wurstemberger, B. (1983) *Vieillesses*, Lausanne: Georgi.

Laslett, P. (1983) *Family Forms in Historic Europe*, Cambridge: Cambridge University Press.

Luquet, G-H. (1927) *Le Dessin enfantin*, Neuchâtel: Delachaux et Niestlé.

Lurçat, L. (1985) 'Réalisme et modèle interne: a propos du dessin de l'enfant', *Bulletin de Psychologie* 369 (XXXVIII): 231–41.

Marcoen, A. (1979) 'Children's perception of aged persons and grandparents', *International Journal of Behavioral Development* 2: 87–105.

Martin, M. (1982) *Sémiologie de l'image et pédagogie*, Paris: Presses Universitaires de France.

Moscovici, S. (1976) *La psychanalyse, son image et son public*, Paris: Presses Universitaires de France, 2nd edn.

Nanpon, H. (1986) 'Les parents et les grands-parents dans le dessin de la famille', *Enfance* 39 (4): 367–77.

Perez, M-B. (1888) *L'art et la poésie chez l'enfant*, Paris: Alcan.

Perraudin, J. Y. (1988) *Images de la Personne Âgée dans la Bande Dessinée* (ecole franco-belge), Dijon: doctoral thesis, unpublished.

Ricci, C. (1887) *L'Arte dei Bambini*, Bologna: Zanichelli.

Roberto, K. (1990) 'Grandparent and grandchild relationships', in T.H. Brubaker (ed.) *Family Relationships in Later Life*, London: Sage.

Seefeldt, C., Jantz, R. K., Galper, S. and Serock, K. (1977) 'Using pictures to explore children's attitudes toward the elderly', *The Gerontologist*, 17 (6): 506–12.

Seefeldt, C. (1982) 'Paraguay and United States: a cross cultural study of children's attitude toward the elderly', *International Journal of Comparative Sociology* XXIII (3–4): 236–41.

Tholome, E. (1985) 'Les aspects génétiques et culturels de l'expression graphique-étude de 2700 dessins d'enfants et d'adultes sur le thème "le repas familial"', *Bulletin de Psychologie* 369 (XXXVIII): 243–54.

Vasquez-Nuttall, E., Nuttall, R. L., and Chieh L. (1988) 'Views of the family by Chinese and US children: a comparative study of kinetic family drawing', *Journal of School Psychology* 26: 191–6.

Wallon, P., Cambier, A., and Engelhart, D. (1990) *Le dessin de l'enfant*, Paris: Presses Universitaires de France.

Widloecher, D. (1965) *L'interpretation des dessins d'enfants*, Bruxelles: Dessart.

Part IV

CONSUMER CULTURE

11

FROM GLOOM TO BOOM
Age, identity and target marketing

Kimberly Anne Sawchuk

For several years – that is, since my job as a coder in a marketing research firm – I have realized that my perambulations within the sphere of North American commodity culture are under surveillance. Like you, I am a contemporary moving target leaving behind a trail of information about my habits, preferences, locations and desires every time I use a credit card, coupon, subscribe to a magazine or journal, or answer a questionnaire, which I rarely do now. Every act of consumption is a potential source of information for the smart marketer.

In response, I am engaged in an academic pursuit that I ironically consider counter capitalist espionage. I have assigned myself the task of monitoring the marketing world, reading marketing textbooks, manuals, and articles in trade journals to keep myself informed of how capitalism secures my consumer identity. These practical how-to-be-a-business-person manuals have assisted me in understanding how our present economic and ideological system maintains its hegemony, and how my own chronic condition of addictive consumption is incorporated and effectively sustained.

A study of marketing discourses must examine this incorporation of texts *and* bodies, or textured bodies. As Foucault says, histories of bodies investigate 'how what is most material and vital in them has been invested'.[1] Investment is an apt word in the context of marketing to those who are now being described tactfully and respectfully as 'mature' adults. As Jeff Ostroff writes in *Successful Marketing to the 50+ Consumer*:

> The aging of America will spawn some of Wall Street's most glamorous and profitable stocks. Those who buy them over the next five to ten years will realize the greatest potential return on their investment.[2]

These investment strategies – connected to bodies, functions, physiological processes, and sensations – work in an inextricable circuit that binds the biological and the historical '. . . in an extremely complex fashion in accordance with the development of modern technologies

173

of power that take life as their objective'.[3] For example, marketing texts set up a homologous relationship between the consumer's body and the product: both have a life expectancy from infancy to old age to 'obsolescence' (Figure 11.1). Marketing research documents this life cycle in an extraordinarily detailed way. This documentation is revealing what marketers consider 'startling new discoveries'.[4]

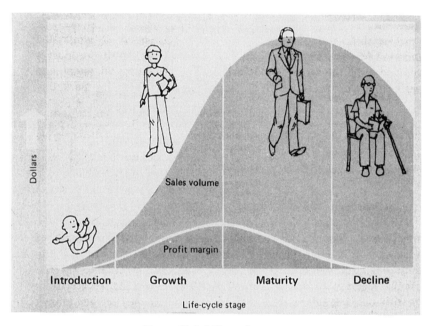

Figure 11.1 Life-cycle stage

What previously was assumed obsolete and without value is turning into gold.[5] Trade magazines blazon headlines like these: 'New products for the young at heart'; 'The nifty fifties of the 1990's'; 'Marketing's golden age is dawning'; 'Age Wave: the challenge and opportunities in an aging America'; 'The golden revolution'; 'Over fifties form a rare Canadian growth market'; and perhaps the most forthright of them all, 'Dipping into granny's wallet'.[6] The over-fifties, the mature market, *le bel age*, seniors, the Third Age, prime lifers: all are euphemisms for a growing baby boom generation and a growth sector to be targeted with a multiplicity of new consumer goods, or old items, such as aspirin, adapted to the aging body. The alchemical trope – grey turning to gold – constitutes one of the major discursive regularities in contemporary marketing literature on the new seniors market. It rhetorically links the clichés of the golden years and golden opportunity with the idea of money.

174

I will examine the effusive but contradictory discourse of this new improved marketing approach to aging. My interest is both imminent and immanent, for this aging body is my aging body, while the bodies previously ignored are the bodies of my grandparents.

MARKETING RESEARCH AND THE CONSUMER BODY

The study of consumption habits and our socialization into consumption is a long-term marketing strategy. The commodification of aging does not begin at 50: children are also a target and more telephone surveys ask to speak to the 'children of the house'.[7]

Since the 1950s, successful businesses have modified their strategies (general goals) and tactics (operational means by which a business implements these goals) from a sales approach to a marketing approach.[8] Marketing is not the same as sales or selling. Selling adapts the consumer's desires to the product, while marketing purports to adapt the product to the consumer. According to marketing guru Theodore Levitt, 'Marketing is preoccupied with the idea of satisfying *the needs* of the customer by means of *this product* and the whole cluster of things associated with creating, delivering and finally consuming it'.[9]

Marketing history has nurtured the following discourse on its own practice: marketing records ostensibly inherent desires, then creates new products (or repackages old ones) that ostensibly satisfy these desires. In doing so, there is a shift in level of abstraction. One does not sell a specific product, such as toothpaste, one sells oral hygiene. The product, toothpaste, is one potential profitable solution. One is not in the 'railroad' industry, one is in the transportation business; trains are only one way to move goods and services over distances.[10] More accurately, the shift from a production orientation to a marketing orientation is a shift in abstraction from thinking about the product as a material good with a specific use-value, to the idea of the product as only one possible way to provide a 'service', such as entertainment, or transportation. This service is then provided with an image or 'brand identity' adapted to the particular target markets that the manufacturer wants to reach.[11] Understanding these target markets is the object of contemporary marketing research.

It is in this sense that a 'Copernican revolution' in marketing took place after the Second World War when 'the consumer became the sun' around which contemporary marketing strategy was said to revolve.[12] Manufacturing's turn of the century concern with the sales of a product to a mass market, has given way to detailed studies of the lives and habits of consumers who are part of fragmented market segments.[13] While the tracking techniques and organization of data have been facilitated greatly because of the general availability of computers, in effect accelerating the entire process, this intense focus on the consumer is still the basis of modern marketing practice.[14] Within this rhetoric, as one marketer put it, 'not all consumers are created equal'. In modern marketing terms, a market is described as 'people or organizations with wants to satisfy, money to spend, and a willingness to spend it'.[15] This definition will come directly into effect with the over-50 market.

In other words mass marketing has been replaced by ever more sophisticated techniques of market segmentation in which consumer markets are identified and 'targeted'.[16] It is interesting to compare the two very visceral metaphors used to explain market segmentation. Visually, market segmentation most often is represented as a benign wedge of cake as opposed to a horizontal slice (market aggregation, otherwise known as sales differentiation based on the product) (see Figure 11.2). Linguistically, violent, militaristic metaphors are employed:

> Stated in another way, in market segmentation we enjoy a 'rifle' approach (separate programs, pinpointed targets) in our marketing activities. In contrast, market aggregation is a 'shotgun' approach (one program, broad target).[17]

According to the latest, most sophisticated doctrine in marketing, the new 'seniors' market is not a homogeneous body, but composed of many specialized sub-markets.

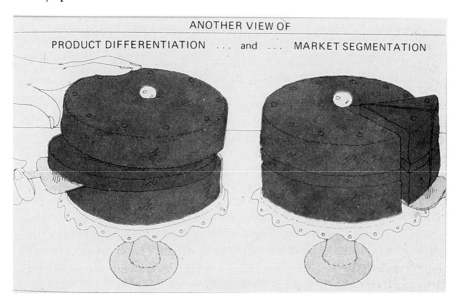

ANOTHER VIEW OF

PRODUCT DIFFERENTIATION ... and ... MARKET SEGMENTATION

Figure 11.2 Another view of product differentiation and market segmentation

FROM GLOOM TO BOOM:
THE NEW SENIORS MARKET

According to market research, approximately 95 per cent of the present broadcast media is targeted to the under-50 crowd, particularly the 25–49 age group.[18] Change is on the immediate horizon. By the year 2006 the over-50s are projected to be one-third of the Canadian population.[19] Because of this shifting demographic cohort, marketers are moving their attention rapidly to the new mature market. Marketers are becoming aware that the barrage of tools and theories they have, to analyse consumer behaviour, and influence purchasing patterns 'just aren't suited to plumbing the needs and desires of older consumers'. Because market research and communication techniques are geared to the young, 'Companies have got to study, study, study and listen, listen, listen'.[20]

It is worth comparing a sample of literature depicting senior consumers from the 1970s with the marketing literature of the 1980s. A conference on 'consumer attitudes, problems and needs of older consumers' was held in the mid-1970s but its focus was not exclusively marketing – it involved people from a variety of academic disciplines, such as urban studies, psychology, gerontology, and government organizations servicing the 'elderly'. The tenor of the conference and the book combines consumer advocacy with marketing concerns. In his preface to the volume, Fred Waddell comments on this disinterest in the elderly at this point in time:

> A computer search of every doctoral dissertation in the field of gerontology since the 1930's revealed only three such dissertations and these were no longer available. Other scholars have thoroughly searched marketing journals and literature on consumer behaviour and have reached the same conclusion.[21]

The marketing literature on aging that arises in the mid-1980s places the 'elderly' consumer at the centre of study, but there is an important shift in emphasis. The focus is not on how well to serve this group; the intention is much more aggressive: marketers want to know how to 'tap into', 'mine', 'plumb', 'capture' a lucrative market.

It is within this context that marketers now berate the myths we have about aging – myths that they have helped to create because of their past media strategies. Advertisers now state with extreme self-righteous indignation that the media previously depicted seniors as 'sexless, senile, crotchety, frail and unhappy'. In chorus, marketers admonish that seniors have been simplified as poor, ill, reclusive and insignificant.[22]

New sensitive marketing texts are out to shatter these stereotypes. Jeff Ostroff's book, for example, identifies 'The eight deadly misconceptions' about 'mature adults':

1 Mature adults are all the same;
2 Mature adults think of themselves as being 'old';
3 Older adults aren't an important consumer segment;
4 Mature adults won't try something new;
5 Older persons have impaired mental faculties;
6 Most older persons suffer from poor health;
7 Older adults keep to themselves;
8 Mature adults aren't physically active.[23]

While these *are* misconceptions one must ask to whom these mis-conceptions belong, where they were perpetuated, and how? Marketers don't connect their own past media practices which have catered to the 'baby boom market' to these attitudes towards aging and the aged, perceptions that they are now determined to overturn. This is not merely because they have suddenly been awakened to the elderly's concerns, but because the baby boom generation is aging, and the values and experiences of this cohort are markedly different from the values and experiences of their parents and grandparents. Theoretic-ally, the implication is this: within a given culture, age is not a static transhistorical identity category but one that is historically contingent.

Capitalism, in other words, has not acquired a social conscience. When the dictum is 'not all customers are created equal', concern is not enough. Consider the following statistics culled from marketing sources: in the United States, the over-50 market segment holds half of the discretionary income in the country: discretionary income is the money available for purchasing non-essential items. One-third of US households have such income.[24] In Canada the over-50 segment 'con-trols 80% of the country's personal wealth, 75% of all money in savings and trust institutions and spends 28% of all discretionary income'. In Quebec the over-60s number 1.5 million (22 per cent), and they reputedly 'have money, are active, watch their diet, have leisure time, and take care of their appearance, figure and health'. Golden agers represent the main buyers of many luxury products including deluxe cars, top brands of alcohol, trips to Europe and financial products.[25] Finally, to reiterate a previous point about initiating addictive con-sumption over a lifetime, the new generation of seniors tend to keep the buying habits of their youth: that is, the habits of a baby boom generation weaned on commodity culture and the mass media.[26]

According to a 1990 study conducted by the Ontario government, this market is accessible through the broadcast media, otherwise known as 'marketing channels'. The over-50s watch an average of 5.3 hours of television every day, listen to 3.8 hours of radio, and more than 60 per cent read the paper.[27] Their affinity for the mass media renders the baby-boom generation of North America seniors distinct from the pre-war generation of seniors.

Marketers point out that there are substantial distinctions within this over-50 market that must be acknowledged so that they can be hit with rifle-like precision to achieve the most efficacious effects. The mature market is divided according to more minute age segments, such as the 50–65 (prime lifers); 65–75 (recently retireds) and the 75+. They all have distinctive needs and spending patterns that can be divided according to an assumed shared identity based on age. Of these three sub-markets, the 50–65, or 'the prime lifers' are the most lucrative submarket segment. They spend the most money, approximately 5 per cent more than the national average. The 'recently retired' 64–75 year olds spend about 25 per cent less than the national average. While the 'prime lifers' are more likely to spend their discretionary income on luxury items. The older we get, the more likely we are to spend our income on basic 'maintenance' for the home and the body. According to marketing statistics, once one is over 75, poverty is more likely to be a problem. More than 20 per cent of those over 75 had incomes below or near the poverty line in 1986. This group, the 75+ market, spends the least of all household units – 56 per cent below the national American average.[28]

While marketers are developing consumption profiles, and the psycho-graphic categories to accompany them, this demographic data based on age is cross-referenced according to a number of possible variables such as ethnicity, region and sex. All marketers, regardless of their theoretical differences, acknowledge that the market is heterogeneous, rather than homogeneous. As one market study has shown, 'age is a strong correlate' of behaviour, but does not absolutely determine product preferences. As a result, marketing interest in specific sub-markets within these age cohorts varies. Chinese Canadians, for example, are a sub-market of intense marketing interest, but their spending habits and intergenera-tional 'patterns' are distinct. Atlantic Canada, with a perennially poor economy, probably doesn't contain such large numbers of the desirable aged. Statistically, women do not have as much money, but they occupy a pivotal role in terms of care giving, and therefore often control the buying of products that will be used by others.[29]

This whole process of documentation and strategic marketing to specific 'target markets' is an example of bio-power, to borrow a term from Michel Foucault, which brings life and its mechanisms 'into the realm of explicit calculations and made knowledge-power an agent of transformation of human life'.[30] Bio-power oscillates between 'two poles of development linked together by a whole intermediary cluster of relations'. This first pole, also associated with 'pastoral power', centres on the individual body – the different techniques developed for the 'care of the self' are part of this pole of the anatomo-politics of the body. The second pole of power focuses on the species body, such as large abstract groupings called populations: 'the body associated with the mechanics of life and serving as the basis of a biological process'.[31] These two poles are joined together in the form of concrete arrangements (*agencements concret*) that make up technologies of power in the nineteenth century.[32] However, Foucault's analysis is still pertinent today. Marketing research is one such contemporary social technology encompassing both poles of bio-power.

Because of this acknowledged heterogeneity, surveys are conducted which turn up data on how this age group perceives their health and age (rather than what age they actually are), their values, interests, concerns, how they spend their money and where they keep it. Habits are being watched, trends documented, strategies developed. Services, from facelifts, to fitness centres, to exclusive apartments, are popping up: the anxieties and concerns of the middle-aged baby boom generation are being adapted to the aging body. As Ostroff writes: 'Baby boomers won't age gracefully creating an enormous marketing industry centered on health and fitness'.[33] Marketers must manage a paradox. They must acknowledge the difference of age, 'tap into' our anxieties about its effects, yet paint a positive picture of aging.

THE PARADOXES OF MARKETING TO SENIORS

Let me return to the question of representation and 'images of aging' for a moment. Advertising is part of the smaller subset (promotions) of one of the famous four p's of marketing: place, promotions, price, product. The use of advertising images must be understood within the context of the marketing.[34]

To connect with 50+ consumers, advertisers realize that they need an entirely new visual and verbal vocabulary – 'imagery that captures the flavour and rhythm of their lives and reflects their needs and aspirations'. Now that business has recognized the power of this new group, marketing magazines are glowing with articles that are 'positive' towards seniors. Yet the use of 'positive' images to sell to this market is tricky. This paradox takes a number of forms.

First, as Ostroff notes, seniors are sceptical about overly-exuberant product claims because of their past experiences with advertising promising the world, and delivering nothing.[35] Second, marketers are divided on whether one should actually use older people to sell a product, even if the target audience are part of seniors market. Ostroff recommends that if one uses older people, use celebrities that seniors can identify with.[36] Researchers stress that people do not necessarily identify with their actual age cohort, but engage in what marketing 'futurist' Faith Popcorn calls 'down-aging'.[37] Because this generation of the elderly have identified so strongly with youth culture in the past they may not want to be segregated as a market in advertising.[38]

Marketers warn that using the elderly as spokespersons for some products may result in alienating a younger audience from the product. In other words, a change in attitudes towards the *elderly*, does not seem to indicate a shift in perception of the *process of aging* – while the elderly are desired as a consumer group, neither marketers, nor this same group of seniors, like aging. Advertising images that represent a target market, images intended to invoke an identification and therefore persuade consumers to buy, are only one part of any modern business strategy. In this instance it is seen as extremely risky.

Instead, modern marketers have a huge arsenal of weapons at their disposal.[39] Tactics are being developed to deal with the cynicism and complexity of this market segment. Here are some examples. Marketers warn that if you do advertise to this market segment, use a soft-sell approach. What is a soft-sell approach? Agencies advise that you may access your audience through non-profit seniors' organizations that seniors are familiar with and trust. Promote the quality of your product: seniors are interested in durability and quality rather than disposability. Harness the energy of the 50+ market in places other than in images. Enlist them to sell to each other: retired people constitute an important pool of reserve labour; they tend to be less expensive to employ, and these employees are more likely to understand the needs of older customers.[40] Even more, these older employees may provide valuable information for tapping into the needs of this growing grey consumer market. In other words, advertising and promotion cannot be separated from an analysis of marketing. There are other issues connected to this – for who are the elderly who are being targeted and thus serviced?

Keep in mind the definition of a market: people or organizations with wants, money to spend and the will to spend it:

> middle aged and older white males earn the most of all over 50. Women, especially those in minority groups, earn the least. In addition, while 12% of mature households have annual incomes in excess of $50,000 the remainder are divided about equally between those with incomes below $15,000 and those with incomes between $15,000 and $50,000.[41]

If my calculations are correct, 44 per cent of the population earns under $15,000, while the other 44 per cent has an annual income of $15,000 to $50,000. As the back pages inform us: 'Women, minorities, and those living alone characterize most of poverty's victims'. Many of the very poor are 'displaced homemakers', women who have lost the economic support of a spouse or a government programme.[42] In other words, education, health, and housing are related to class. As the text admits, 'the more income one has, the more likely one is to feel they are in excellent health'. Not only is this a 'feeling', but statistically, one probably suffers from few chronic illnesses, and is likely to live longer.[43] In and amongst these happy images of an aging population, 'negative' images – images of people whose health is poor in comparison to the national average – seem out of place.

Marketing doesn't address itself to the huge disparities of income distribution linked to race and gender in North America. When marketers talk about a seniors market they're talking about a small privileged sector of that age group with money to spend, a segment who have had the opportunity to build up assets and equity, savings and bonds.

FURTHER MARKETING LIMITATIONS

In marketing research, the aging body is regarded as a system, theorized in terms of local investment strategies and highly militarized in key areas of imagery and practice (I'm surprised that George Bush didn't declare a war on aging). As Donna Haraway writes of bodies in late industrial capitalism, 'the body ceases to be a stable spatial map of normalized functions and instead emerges as a highly mobile field of strategic differences. The biomedical-biotechnical body is a semiotic system, a complex meaning-producing field'.[44] In marketing terms, these strategic differences are carefully monitored and managed distinctions – not inherent differences – that can generate lucrative profits. As my marketing text puts it:

> A key to prosperity in surviving tomorrow's mature market will be knowing which chronic conditions are likely to affect older Americans and providing products/services that help them better manage these problems.[45]

The marketing 'system' forms an interconnected network that sets up ritualistic circuits of feedback in which the consumer is said to have ultimate control. Marketers believe that marketing is the ultimate form of democratic responsiveness. In the marketing confessional it is the subject who talks, and thus produces the signs to be interpreted and then translated into computerized data, who is ultimately subjectified and subjugated. The results of this data secure the self's consumer identity – these consumer bodies are then fragmented into ever more detailed problem areas for every conceivable part of the anatomy requiring ever more refined life-giving, health-inducing products. Although no studies of who responds to telephone marketing have been done, my own experience as a telemarketer suggests that the elderly are prime targets in this respect.

It is difficult to criticize advertisers on the basis of how they portray either people or products because there are more and more sophisticated means for monitoring audience responses to these images, and quite diverse marketing strategies that are not strictly image based. Images are tactical means in a much larger circuitry of image management connected to economic exchange. Advertisers have become very sensitive to public responses to their campaigns and work to pre-empt possible discontent with their representations. Marketing research is a strategy of deterrence in this respect. As one marketer puts it, 'advertising is "image management"'.[46] Yet, these techniques may make a marketing campaign more effective, although the results are never guaranteed: marketing deals in the realm of probability. It is for this reason that they must track such huge volumes of people and sustain this tracking over time.[47]

Marketing contends that it is about effective distribution. In effect, it is about effective distribution to markets: people with 'wants', a willingness to spend, and the money to spend on these needs. The homeless have a need, but they are not a market. I repeat: when marketers say there is no market, they do not mean that there are no people. They mean that there are not enough people with the money to spend and the willingness to spend it.[48] The distribution of services, and the economic inequality that this marketing approach depends upon does not simply result in some people having Winnebagos, luxury cruises, fur coats, or other kinds of ways to spend their money. It affects the distribution or development of some fundamental services, such as housing and health care.

There is money to be made from an aging, and suffering body. When marketers write:

> Marketers should monitor medical and national/state long-term care legislation very closely in the next few years. To a great extent it will foretell where some of the best mature market opportunities will be in the 21st century . . .[49]

. . . I worry. In fact, I am concerned about the affordable care for the elderly as a public service to which all are entitled. Contemporary side effects of this marketing mentality as it is applied to health care may mean that medical research and development devotes its research efforts to expensive treatments with long-term marketing potential rather than less expensive possibilities. An example is the ideological campaign recently waged against 'generic drugs' in Canada. To suit its agenda, marketing research conceives of target markets as isolated fragments. As people who engage with each other in a daily, integrated way, we need to read across these fragmented market segments and see what is in store for us, and what are our common problems. We need to push for an economy based on caring rather than aggressive individualism, an economy and politic where dependency is not simply a dirty word. The marketing answer to social problems is to build 'secure' spaces for the rich, walled fortresses that keep out these undesirable, negative social elements. The assumption that we live in a world that is separable into manageable market segments is not only unjust, but naïve. Racism, sexism, homophobia, poverty, and ageism in North America cannot be contained like marketing categories, nor can they be obliterated through marketing – at least marketing conducted with a profit-based agenda in mind.

Parenthetically, it is my guess that this emphasis on instilling identity that is limited to a consumer identity partially accounts for the growing conservative sentiment in North America. As one marketer notes gleefully, Canadians have become less 'conformist' and more 'modern', modern that is, in marketing terms. 'Their values are of the "me" generation; from the conformist to the individualistic; from the ascetic to the hedonistic'.[50] This is a sentiment and political practice based on the virtues of acquisition, personal wealth, and gratification at the expense of a shared sense of public welfare. While commodities can bring us pleasure, in this instance marketing doctrine confuses the servicing of a small minority with the public good. Increasingly, the Canadian government is using a business model to make decisions, turning to private marketing research firms to guide public affairs, and seeking advice from conservative lobby groups such as the Business Council on National Issues, located down the street from the House of Parliament in Ottawa.[51]

Alternative solutions, solutions not necessarily linked to a profitable product, to help seniors maintain their nutritional, housing, transportation, health, fitness and self-image needs are rarely addressed in this discourse. The point is to keep consumption expanding with age rather than contracting, as marketers are aware often happens. Many companies are eager to lend a marketing hand to the aged as long as the equation of happiness through consumption is kept intact.

There are examples, however, of seniors bucking this trend, engaging in consumer advocacy, demanding that their interests be taken into consideration in the development of advertising, public information campaigns, and the provision of services. One such group is the 'Wellness Group' based in the South Riverdale Community Health Centre in Toronto. Concerned that seniors are being blamed unfairly for the high cost of the medical care, this affinity group is working to change this misconception and identify ways to cut costs and improve services to seniors. In addition, the group addresses ways to make seniors aware that they have the right to question doctors and pharmacists, and gives them techniques to do this. They are promoting 'the wise use of medications', and alternative strategies to deal with the over-medication of seniors in our culture. In turn, they also discuss the desirability of generic brand drugs, and the undesirability of the user-fee system for doctors. Research findings and experience indicate that doctors spend more time with seniors answering questions if they are salaried rather than working on a fee-for-service basis. This 'Wellness Group' is an important reminder that other models for catering to the elderly are practical, economical in the long run, and possible.[52]

CONCLUSION

Successful Marketing to the 50+ Consumer, like so many of the most recent marketing discourses on aging, is devoted to dispelling traditional myths about the elderly. However, even if these stereotypes are not evident in the images, I can't help but feel that many prejudices that we have towards the process of aging are still being perpetuated in marketing journals.

What looks like a new attitude towards aging and a new market, is actually the same attitude to the same market – the baby boom generation. Within that market, the same people are being promised service as in the past. What has changed is that this awareness of their market potential has catalyzed a more aggressive pursuit of seniors. This is the key to the new aging consciousness that business has suddenly developed. Ironically, advertising and marketing are now having to deal with a set of prejudices that were installed throughout the 1960s, 1970s and 1980s. Marketing has depicted youth as the ultimate virtue, and aging as a horrible problem. It's not that older people haven't been around. It's just that the past generation of elderly people, who grew up with a 'depression mentality' had the wrong attitude toward getting and spending.

Marketing is about the exchange of money for profit. While we are all allowed to speak in the great marketing ritual, it is only certain people who are listened to, or serviced. In marketing to the elderly, 'Your opinion counts' – if you have the requisite money to spend.

NOTES

1 Michel Foucault, *The History of Sexuality, Volume 1: An Introduction*, trans. Robert Hurly, New York: Pantheon Books, 1978: 152.

2 Jeff Ostroff, *Successful Marketing to the 50+ Consumer: how to capture one of the biggest and fastest growing markets in America*, New Jersey: Prentice Hall, 1989: 269.

3 Michel Foucault, op. cit.: 152.

4 William J. Stanton, Montrose S. Sommers and James G. Barnes, *Fundamentals of Marketing*, 4th edn, Toronto: McGraw-Hill Ryerson Limited, 1985.

5 Some examples include: 'Grey can turn gold as firms see potential of new market', *Financial Post*, vol. 84, no. 1 (30 Dec. 1989/1 Jan, 1990): 25; 'A greying population presents golden marketing opportunities', *Marketing* (1 April 1985): 11; 'Golden opportunities: welcome to the new age of old age',

David Lees, *Canadian Business*, vol. 60, no. 5 (May 1987): 24, 26.

6 This is a sampling of headlines collected from the Social Science and Business Abstracts on CD ROM. The period covered is from 1982–November 1991. The citations, in order of appearance are as follows: *Financial Post Daily*, vol. 4, no. 31 (27 March 1991): 9, Jo Marney, *Marketing* vol. 95, no. 36 (3 September 1990): 17; *Marketing*, vol. 95, no. 12 (19 March 1990): 32; Ken Dychwald and Joe Flower, *Canadian Business Review*, vol. 12, no. 2 (Summer 1990): 59–60; *Vista*, vol. 2, no. 6 (September 1989): 72–7; *Financial Post Daily*, vol. 4, no. 100 (26 July 1991): 14; *Newsweek*, vol. 117, no. 13 (1 April 1991): 43.

7 See in particular, Jo Marney, 'Children: the powerful new consumers', *Marketing* (29 January 1990): 15, and 'Marketing to kids', *Marketing* (3 September 1990): 17. For a critical reading of this phenomenon see Stephen Kline, 'Limits to the imagination: marketing and children's culture', in Ian Angus and Sut Jhally (eds) *Cultural Politics in Contemporary America*, New York: Routledge, 1989.

8 Malcolm McDonald and John W. Leppard, *Marketing by Matrix: 100 practical ways to improve your strategic and tactical marketing*, Great Britain: Butterworth-Heinemann Ltd, 1992.

9 Theodore Levitt, 'Marketing myopia', in James G. Barnes and Montrose S. Sommers (eds) *Current Topics in Canadian Marketing*, Toronto: McGraw-Hill Ryerson Ltd, 1978: 39. (The italics are mine).

10 Levitt uses the railroads as an example in 'Marketing myopia', op. cit: 31.

11 Although his thinking on this issue is not about marketing, Baudrillard identifies the movement of the commodity as one from use-value, to exchange value, to its 'sign-value' in the contemporary era (*For a Critique of the Political Economy of the Sign*, trans. Charles Levin, St. Louis: Telos Press, 1981). It is also common for a product to have several brand identities tailored to different target markets. This is why magazine advertising is often preferable to television advertising – the readership is much more precise.

12 Robert Keith, 'The marketing revolution', in Ben M. Enis and Keith Cox, *Marketing Classics: A Selection of Influential Articles*, 4th edn, Toronto: Allen & Bacon Inc., 1981: 47.

13 Ibid. 46.

14 The idea that human beings are consumers was consolidated in this period by the discourse itself. There are parallels to be drawn here between this study of the 'seniors' market, and Kathy Myers' study of the teen market in *Understains: the Sense and Seduction of Advertising*, London: Comedia, 1986: 35.

15 Stanton, *et al.*, op. cit: 719.

16 Wendall Smith, 'Product differentiation and market segmentation as alternative market strategies', in Howard S. Thompson, *Great Writings in Marketing*, Plymouth: Commerce Press, 1976: 127.

17 *Ibid.*: 82

18 *Marketing* (5 March 1990).

19 Ibid.

20 Sandy Fife, 'Smashing age-old stereotypes', *Marketing* (15 February 1993): 1, 3.

21 Fred Waddell, *The Elderly Consumer*, Columbia, Maryland: The Human Ecology Center, Antioch College, 1976: iii.

22 *Marketing*, (11 December 1989).

23 Ostroff, op. cit.: 18.

24 *Ibid*: 314.

25 These statistics are taken from various issues of *Marketing*, issues that featured publicity for 'Today's seniors' (July 1989 and November 1989).

26 *Marketing* (19 March 1990).
27 *Marketing* (11 Dec. 1989).
28 These are American statistics (Ostroff, op.cit.: 323).
29 *Ibid.*: 26–7.
30 Foucault, op. cit.: 143.
31 *Ibid.*: 141.
32 *Ibid.*: 142.
33 *Ibid.*: 280.
34 See E. Jerome MacCarthy and Stanley Schapiro, *Essentials of Marketing*, 1st edn, Homewood, Illinois: Richard D. Irwin, 1983, for an explanation of the four p's, p. 37.
35 Ostroff, op. cit.: 222.
36 Ostroff, op. cit.: 216.
37 Faith Popcorn, *The Popcorn Report*, New York: HarperCollins, 1991: 56.
38 Alan J. Greco, 'Representation of the elderly in advertising: crisis or inconsequence?', in Charles D. Schewe and Ann L. Balzs (eds) *Marketing to an Aging Population: Selected Readings*, 2nd edn, United States: American Marketing Association, 1990: 231–8.
39 I specifically invoke a military metaphor here, because it is a part of the language of marketing. See Gerald Michelson, *Winning the Marketing War: a field manual for business leaders*, Cambridge, Mass.: Abt Books, 1987.
40 *Marketing* (9 March 1992).
41 Ostroff, op. cit.: 312.
42 *Ibid.*: 313.
43 *Ibid.*: 309. These observations on health and poverty were noted in some of the first studies done on elderly consumers. See Donald G. Fowles, 'Estimates of the size and characteristics of the older population in 1974 and projections to the year 2000', in Waddell, op. cit.: 29–41.
44 Donna Haraway, *Simeans Cyborg Women: The Invention of Nature*, London: Routledge, 1991: 211.
45 Stanton *et al.*, op. cit.: 270. For an explanation and critique of this marketing discourse on difference and distinction see Kim Sawchuk, '(Re)packaging Difference; Globalization and Culture', in Renee Baert, *Territories of Difference*, Banff, Walter Phillips Gallery, 1993: 112–134.
46 Thomas J. Reynolds and Jonathon Gutman, 'Advertising is image management', *Journal of Advertising Research* (Feb/March, 1984): 20–7.
47 For an explanation of tracking see Gordon Brown, 'Tracking studies and sales effects: A U.K. perspective', *Journal of Advertising Research* vol. 25, no. 1 (February/March 1985): 52–64.
48 Other researchers note that within the realm of consumption, huge disparities in pricing exist for the same articles and services designated for female and male markets. Charlotte Parsons, 'Women pay more for identical items', *The Globe and Mail-Toronto* (Tuesday, 3 August 1993): A1, A2.
49 Ostroff, op. cit.: 271.
50 *Marketing* (5 March 1990).
51 For more on the Business Council on National Issues, see Joyce Nelson's *The Sultans of Sleaze: Public Relations and the Media*, Toronto: BETWEEN THE LINES, 1989: 91.
52 Elsie Petch, *Wise Use Of Medications: A Health Promotion Approach To Community Programming For Safe Medication Use With And For Seniors*, Toronto: South Riverdale Community Health Centre, 1992.

12

CHAN IS MISSING: THE DEATH OF THE AGING ASIAN EYE

Norman K. Denzin

My topic is 'the looking, aging, Asian eye' as represented in the portrayals of the famous Hollywood Asian voyeurs, Charlie Chan, Mr Wong and Mr Moto.[1] These larger-than-life characters enact the cultural stereotype of the wise, aging Asian patriarch (Lau, 1991). American popular culture has historically associated age with wisdom, youth with irresponsibility, and childhood with innocence (see Fiedler, 1966: 271). The aging voyeur (for example, Charlie Chan, Art Carney in *The Late Show,* James Bond's superior, Le Carré's George Smiley, Ruth Gordon's Maude in *Harold and Maude*) is inevitably attached to, or obliged to work with a youthful voyeur who requires the age and wisdom of his (or her) superior to carry out the assignment in question. Thus are spaces constantly created in popular culture for the aging-looking eye able to disclose truths about life that youthful vision cannot reveal.

I seek here to unmask the cultural logics that structure the gazing eye of the aging, investigative voyeur, that figure who comes in multiple guises, including detective, sociologist, ethnographer, journalist and psychoanalyst (see Denzin, 1995, for a discussion of these other versions of the voyeur).

The voyeur's gaze has always been shaped by the structures of age, gender and race, for typically members of racial and ethnic minorities, children and women, are not allowed to gaze on majority male group members. The concept of a colour (see Blumer, 1965/1988: 208; Lyman, 1990b), gender (see Gamman, 1988), and age-gazing line (see Fiedler, 1966: 270–1) operates in this context, assigning to white and non-white males and females different gazing positions in the social order. The age-gazing line prohibits children from gazing on the sacred and taboo acts of adults. At the same time this line assigns to aging adults the power of truthful vision.

Here I focus on cinema's version of the gaze of the privileged, aging, minority male figure, the Asian detective, arguing that only certain members of racial and ethnic minorities are allowed to gaze on majority group members.[2] I examine the Charlie Chan series, contrasting this series with the experimental, 1982 film, *Chan Is Missing*,[3] a text which undoes the Asian stereotypes perpetuated by the Chan character. I will take one film from the Chan series (*Charlie Chan at the Opera* (1937))[4], which is representative of the entire series and is currently available for video rental.[5]

THE AGING ORIENTAL SLEUTH

While the Oriental sleuth was virtually ignored in silent film, he became a staple of the Hollywood screen with the third Chan movie, *Behind That Curtain* (1929) (Everson, 1972: 72–3; Hanke, 1989: xiii). Until the Chan figure, the concept of an Oriental hero was unthinkable. For the American audience the ultimate 'yellow peril' was the insidious, ageless Dr Fu Manchu, Sax Rohmer's Oriental master criminal (see Penzler, 1977: 43).[6] Indeed Asians were generally missing in early cinema, or if present, only as laundrymen, or lowly-paid workers (for example, *Chinese Laundry Scene*, 1894. See Musser, 1991: 43–4, 76, note 13).[7] However, Chan's third appearance opened the door for America's unique version of the Oriental sleuth. Over the next twenty years there would be more than sixty films starring Charlie Chan, Mr Moto and Mr Wong (forty-eight for Chan, eight for Moto, six for Wong).

To study this figure is to study ourselves, for through his persona are filtered all the arguments we as westerners give ourselves for looking and gazing upon others. We are the Asian voyeur. But today *Chan is Missing*,[8] and the warrant to look the way Charlie once looked is no longer automatically given.

A single, yet complicated thesis, drawing from Jameson (1990), Said (1979, 1989), Stam (1991), Bakhtin (1981, 1986), Shohat (1991), and Hall (1981) organizes my discussion. Modifying Edward Said (1979), I suggest that between the years 1929 and 1949 Hollywood aided in the containment of America's Asian-American population through the production of the more than sixty films featuring the Chan, Moto and Wong characters.[9] These middle-age and aging Oriental sleuths neutral-ized previous negative images of the Asian-American, offered to Asian-Americans (and Americans) a particular Americanized version of who they were and who they should be. In this, Hollywood operated as an 'Orientalizing' agency for the larger American culture. Hollywood cinema worked, that is, as an institutional apparatus which described, taught, and authorized a particular view of Asian culture, Asian men, women, and Asian family life. It created a system of discourse which constituted the 'Orient' and the Asian as 'imaginary others' who were simultaneously categorized, exteriorized, excluded and included within the western framework.[10]

These films contained a kernel of Utopian fantasy (see Jameson,

1990: 34; Shohat, 1991: 222). As such they may be seen as sites of ideological struggle for they projected a world where Americans and Asians could happily interact within a unified culture where the facts of bigotry, racism and discrimination were, if not absent, at least easily negotiable (see Desser, 1991a: 383). In this they operated as ethnic allegories which, even when 'narrating apparently private stories, managed to metaphorize the public sphere, where the micro-individual is doubled by the macro-nation and the personal, the political, the private and the historical, are inextricably linked' (Shohat, 1991: 234; see also Jameson, 1990: 32–3). Chan, Moto and Wong became positive stand-ins for the negative Asian other, and the 'yellow peril', even as their characters critiqued and made a parody of the ethnocentric, Eurocentric, racist stereotypes[11] which were ascribed to them (see also Shohat, 1991: 238). As kindly, aging patriarchal figures, they invoked the importance of the patriarchal family in American life. These figures marked a positive space for evil Asian culture, showing that a very American model of the family existed in this alien world.

These texts, and their heroes, however, were, in Bakhtin's terms (Stam, 1991: 253) complex discursive constructions. A polyphonic play of voices, from the ethnic margins and the centres of white society, interact in each film to produce characters who are not just unitary essences, but rather three-dimensional flesh-and-blood entities (see Stam, 1991: 253, 257–8). The characters cannot, that is, be read as flat stick figures. Charlie, Wong and Moto were always at the centre of 'conflicting and competing voices' (ibid.: 257); voices which constituted them as subjects within clashing racial and ethnic contradictions. At different moments within any of these films the heroes could be 'traversed by racist and antiracist discourse' (ibid.: 257). Each figure became a complex construction whose dialogical angle of vision on the American-Asian ethnic order was always at the very core of the 'American experience' (ibid.: 259). By being folded into the centre of crises produced by Americans, they were able to live racism from within, inside looking out, as they were outsiders brought into the inside.

On the surface Hollywood's Orientalist discourse distinguished the Oriental/Asian from the western/European figure, in terms of age, cultural and racial stereotyping (K. Lee, 1991: 1). The European/American was presented as the culturally known, familiar, comfortable other; the Asian as the unknown, dangerous, devious, sometimes childish dumb other. The European/American other was rational, virtuous, mature and normal; the Oriental was irrational, depraved, fallen, childlike, immature, a danger to society (K. Lee, 1991: 1; Said, 1979: 300). In these ways American cinema perpetuated its version of Orientalism, which, Said reminds us, is the 'corporate institution for dealing with the Orient . . . by making statements about it . . . ruling over it: in short Orientalism is a western style for dominating, re-structuring and having authority over the Orient' (Said, 1979: 3; see also Barthes, 1982; Kristeva, 1977; Doane, 1991: Ch. 9).

In the Chan, Moto and Wong movies, Hollywood offered the American audience a superficial, stereotyped image of the neutered, slant-eyed, greased-down hair, thin moustached (the Fu Manchu moustache), calm, implacable aging Oriental detective. This figure would work in the service of law and order, peace and justice. He would protect the world from sinister criminals, and take pleasure in solving crimes and catching criminals who alluded the dimwitted (childlike) police.

It is no accident that the Asian male would find acceptance in American culture as an aging voyeur and a sleuth, for there is a long tradition connecting Orientalism with voyeurism and at times scopophilia (see Doane, 1991: 180). His earlier image, after all, was as the sinister master criminal Dr Fu Manchu. It remained to capture this Oriental gaze and put it to western uses. As Foucault (1980: 155) implies, twentieth-century regimes of power and surveillance turned the observed into the observer, the deviant into the one who studies and controls deviants. Consequently, a major power strategy involved the state's recruitment of minority group members as surveillance agents. In the guise of these three male figures the master Oriental criminal was turned into a master sleuth, a person who could use his sinister qualities for positive purposes.

He was then invested with all of his culture's negative and positive characteristics. He carried the weight of being Asian upon his investigative shoulders, using his Oriental eyes as a way of being (and seeing) the truth that others could not see. He was forced to rely upon his wit and his age as vehicles for disarming cultural criticisms of his ethnic origins. While self-deprecating ('All my life I study to speak fine English words. Now I must strangle all such in my throat, lest suspicion rise up. Not a happy situation for me') his wit was always barbed, and passively aggressive ('Silence big sister of wisdom', 'Tongue often hang man quicker than rope') (Penzler, 1977: 47). Thus did he attack with words his western aggressors.

However, in its representation of the Oriental sleuth, Hollywood inverted the usual stereotyped picture of the Asian male. It gave this figure precisely those western/European/American traits which had been previously denied the Asian other. Chan, Moto and Wong were rational, virtuous, mature, normal men who were paired and pitted against irrational, depraved, childish, violent, immature westerners.[12] In this move the Asian male was simultaneously excluded from, and included inside a western-Orientalizing discourse which made him stranger and friend at the same time.

The comedy format of the Asian detective series facilitated this textual displacement, for these films must be read as comedy. In this they took their place in a long Hollywood history, for as Musser (1991: 43) argues, 'ethnic-based comedy has been a feature of American cinema from its beginnings until the present'. Ethnicity – being Asian – is presented in this series as a 'constraint and a construction from which characters and audiences can be at least temporarily liberated' (ibid. 1991: 43). Thus Charlie, Wong and Moto, in key moments in every film, are momentarily released from their Asian identities and turned into serious sleuths, often preceded by their movement into a disguise (for example, clown, shopkeeper, etc.). (The comedy basis of the Chan series is obvious, of course, given in the usual capers of Number One Son.) In the movements back and forth between serious detective film and comedy, the Asian detective films exaggerate ethnic stereotype through speech and dress patterns, and through dialogue directed to the Asian detective (for example, chop suey).

Through these comedic gestures the film-makers exercised a form of social control over the non-western figure, arguing that he should be made to accommodate to the central features of western culture. Thus these texts operated in an assimilationist manner, wiping out, in a single stroke, all of the distinctive, positive features of Oriental culture. Indeed, the fact that each Oriental detective was a master at disguise further reinforced the cultural message that the Oriental should be made to fit into American culture (see Musser, 1991: 55). This demand would be most evident in those situations where the detective would be forced to assume a 'false mask of politesse when waiting on the condescending and self-absorbed' westerner (ibid. 1991: 57).

Chan, Moto and Wong were never presented as a personal, or sexual threat to the white other. They became feminized, aging Asian men, even eunuchs (see Marchetti, 1991: 290, on the stereotype of the Asian male as sexual threat). Still, as Eugene Franklin Wong (1978) argues, and Marchetti (1991: 289) repeats, ethnicity is never neuter. Images of age, race, ethnicity and sexuality are always intertwined. Indeed racial and ethnic hierarchies are often maintained 'through fantasies which reinforce those differences through references to gender. Thus fantasies of threatening Asian men, aging patriarchs, emasculated eunuchs, alluring Asian "dragon ladies", and submissive female slaves all work to rationalize white, male domination' (ibid. 1991: 289). Sexually-passive Charlie, Mr Wong and Mr Moto reinforced the sexually-dominant position of the white males in the text. In these ways the series would foreground and then displace and repress ethnic identity and ethnic difference. Audiences could accept the Oriental detective as a familiar 'white' other, who was, at the same time different.

A double spectacular structure organized these texts. The centre of any given film in the series would typically unfold around, and be marked by moments of spectacle. There would be operatic perform-ances, vaudeville acts, the unveiling of new archaeological discoveries, carnival displays of dramatic violence, murders on stage, and so on. The ethnic, racial and age-linked hierarchy of selves would typically be realized through a 'spectacle of discovery' wherein Chan, Moto or Wong would ceremoniously unmask the murderer or villain. This would often occur in a group situation, where all of the suspects were brought together (sometimes in a locked room). The detective would create great anxiety by pointing out how each suspect could have been the murderer. (Typically the anxiety was sufficient to lead the 'real' murderer to confess.) Childish and feminine displays of out-of-control emotions were common in these scenes.

The spectacle of criminal discovery would occur within this larger specular (and spectacular) structure. It would allow for the 'contempla-tion of the racial and ethnic Other as an object, separated from and under the visual control of the viewer who was positioned with the camera, in power, as the eye of the dominant culture' (Marchetti, 1991: 287). In the moment of discovery Charlie, Wong or Moto would invariably be distanced from the westerners in the film, simultaneously object and subject of his own (and our) investigation. In this way the films would reinscribe racial and ethnic difference, and usually sexual and age-based differences as well. In his spectacular moment of dis-covery the Oriental detective became spectacle, and by implication his ethnicity became spectacle too.

Thus were the Asian detectives orientalized. Their ethnicity was ubiquitous, yet textually submerged, as they were given fixed, yet mutable ethnic identities. Never really pitted against the culturally-dominant group, they were always outsiders on the periphery who were brought into the cultural centre when a crisis appeared (see Shohat, 1991: 217 on the centre-periphery issue). Once they entered this inner, sacred space of the culturally-dominant group they performed their function with dispatch, humour and grace. Their ethnic identities were submerged and sutured into the dominant colonialist discourse which was itself turned into the discourse of crime, punishment and discovery. Through a dialectic of presence and absence (ibid.: 222), the Hollywood films on the Asian detective allowed this Asian other to be both present and absent at the same time. As he moved from disguise to disguise he became first you, and then me, and then someone else. In this way the investigative and comedic codes which contained these narratives undertook to speak for the marginalized Asian culture.

A superficial form of cultural integration was thereby produced. At one level these films simply inserted new heroes, 'drawn from the ranks of the subaltern, into old functional roles' (Stam, 1991: 263). The implication was clear. By playing the part of aging detective, or law enforcer, Chan, Wong and Moto had an Asian link to the American and international 'power structure' (ibid.). But of course this was ' quite out of keeping with the actual configuration of social power' (ibid.). The image of overlapping, conflicting de-centred, circles of ethnic identities was never considered (Shohat, 1991: 217). Such an image of the Asian-American identity would not appear until 1982 with Wayne Wang's *Chan is Missing.*

This is how the Asian detective movie series worked. It simultaneously contained and released the Asian eye to be just like you and me, while he was always different, foreign, strange and somewhat distant from our own experiences. Now *Charlie Chan at the Opera.*

CHARLIE CHAN AT THE OPERA

Lilli Rochelle, and Gravelle are famous opera singers who were married to one another. They have a daughter Kitty. Lilli has an affair with Enrico, also an opera singer. She and Enrico plot to kill Gravelle in a fire. Gravelle is trapped in the fire, loses his memory and is confined to an asylum. It is now thirteen years later. Now middle-aged, Gravelle's memory returns when he sees a picture of Lilli announcing her upcoming performance in *Carnival.* Gravelle escapes, vowing to kill the two of them. Charlie is brought in by Inspector Regan to help find Gravelle.[13] (William Demarest plays the part of Sergeant Kelly, an anti-Chinese policeman.) Lilli has since married Whitely, a wealthy and aging businessman. Enrico is married to Anita (also an opera singer). Enrico and Lilli have continued their affair. Lilli refuses to acknowledge her daughter Kitty. Anita hates Lilli for stealing her husband, and Whitely hates Enrico for stealing his wife. During the performance of *Faust* Gravelle (playing the part of Mephisto) knocks out Enrico and dons his costume. Immediately after the performance Lilli and Enrico are stabbed to death. There are four suspects: Gravelle, Phil, Kitty's boy friend, who is found with blood on his hands, Anita, and Whitely, who sent his wife a note (along with flowers) saying she would die that evening at the opera. In a spectacle of discovery (Gravelle and Anita re-enact their roles in the opera), Charlie eliminates every suspect, until he comes to Anita, who finally confesses. Gravelle is reunited with his daughter.

Reading the *Opera*

This is an investigative Oedipal tale with racist and anti-feminist overtones. It is a story of love, betrayal, vengeance and justice. Three strong women, Lilli, Anita and Kitty, paired with weak men,[14] structure the narrative. Two of the women, Lilli and Anita, are *femmes fatales*, *divas*, and suffer the fate of being such (see Doane, 1991: 2).[15] Lilli and Anita are the carriers of power, symptoms of 'male fears about feminism' (ibid.: 3). Each in her way embodies the threat of castration. Each is also the antithesis of the maternal, mothering figure (ibid.). Denying their reproductive functions, they are both carried and moved by out-of-control sexual desires.

The three women each want something the other has, or won't give up. Kitty wants her mother back. Lilli wants Anita's husband. Anita wants Lilli to give up her husband. Lilli dies because she betrayed her two husbands and rejected her daughter Kitty ('she was afraid a [grown] daughter would hurt her career'). Anita goes to prison because she did what a weak husband (Whitely) 'was not man enough to do anything about'. Their 'textual eradication involves a desperate reassertion of control on the part of the threatened male subject' (Doane, 1991: 2). At the anti-feminist level, the story is direct. Women-as-mothers (and wives) should not reject their daughters, and betray their husbands, nor should they attempt to get even. A woman's place is at home, caring for husband and daughter. Charlie functions as the arbiter of justice who also reunites a father with his daughter. He is the paternal figure, the law of patriarchy. The only male unafraid of and unmoved by the sexually-threatening figures of Lilli and Anita.

The *Opera* as a whodunit

The film's opening shots (thunder and lightning, the Gothic insane asylum) immediately locate it within the Gothic thriller, horror genre. Within minutes the thriller will be further defined as a murder mystery of the whodunit variety (although a murder has not yet occurred). Karloff's escape from the asylum (newspaper headlines: 'Madman eludes dragnet', 'Mad man in Los Angeles') sets the police on his trail, and brings Charlie in as the person who will find this maniac before he kills.

In classic fashion, the film has a geometric architecture: two murders, four suspects, four sets of clues, and four interrogations. In order: two dead bodies (Enrico, Anita); four suspects: (Phil, Whitely, Gravelle, Anita); four clues: blood on the hands of Phil, Whitely's fingerprints on the card to Anita, Gravelle's oiled knife with no blood stains, and the second, hidden knife, with blood on the handle, and Anita's second costume belt with blood stains. And four interrogations, wherein, following the hypo-deductive method, Charlie systematically eliminates each suspect, until he comes to Anita.

The film's geometric structure, including Charlie's use of the hypo-deductive method, serves to place reason and rationality on the side of

195

this particular aging Oriental eye. It underscores the text's commitment to the position that every event has a cause, every cause an effect, and every effect the cause of another effect (see Haycroft, 1972: 249; Todorov, 1977: 49). But like a pragmatist, Charlie always works from consequences back to causes.

EVERYDAY PRAGMATIC VOYEURISM AND THE WISDOM OF AGE

He could not do this if he were not an experienced investigative voyeur. Charlie's gaze carries the weight of experience and age. He moves slowly, with deliberation. His are not the secretive and hidden gazes of the criminal. His looks do not carry violent, sexual, or erotic overtones. His looks, done in the immediate presence of others, are focused always on small details (an unburned cigar in an ashtray, a note card in a wastebasket), overheard words, untoward gestures, footprints, smells and odours. Like Sherlock Holmes (Truzzi, 1976: 65), he deduces information from the traces left by human action. In this he is an aging voyeur of the visible, of the could-be-seen, but not noticed everyday world.

Charlie's method of inquiry is pragmatic, progressive, processual and transformative (on the pragmatic method see Farberman and Perinbanayagam, 1985: 8–9; Farberman, 1991: 480). The entire point of any one of Charlie's investigative activities is to produce an interpretive account of past action which squares with the facts. Facts are based on the consequences of actions.

Here is how this works in *Opera*. Charlie has all the suspects (except Gravelle) in the same room. Childlike, impulsive Sergeant Kelly has charged Charlie with threatening the life of Anita, 'Egg foo young! The guy who pulls rabbits out of the hat sends a woman out there to let a guy stick a knife in her. Well Chief, that about closes the case'. Wise Charlie contradicts him. 'Case still wide open, like swinging gate . . . will demonstrate with hypothesis'. He then lays the two knives side by side on a table. 'Proof most elemental. Fact in deduction . . . if Gravelle guilty, must have both knives on person before singing . . . Previous examination of costume disclose no tell tale blood stains. Madman not use Barelli's knife . . . Fact that Madame Barelli in wings during final singing final link in chain of evidence (camera shot of Anita). You are murderess (she jumps up) . . . you conceal knife on person after murder of husband'.

Charlie's pragmatic logic is impeccable. It squares with the facts. It is a logic and a method borne of experience, tested with the wisdom of age, and directly connected to Charlie's Oriental identity. He enacts the cultural belief that wise Asian men are able to to find the truth that escapes the investigative gaze of impulsive, childish westerners.

RACIAL OVERTONES

Consider the following lines, they are all spoken by the William Demarest character, Sergeant Kelly, or his immediate superior, Inspector Regan (Guy Usher). They reference the film's underlying racism. *Kelly*: 'You haven't called chop suey in on the case have you Chief?' *Regan*: 'You can learn a little politeness from the Chinese'. *Kelly*: I can pick him out, he's Chinese'. *Kelly*: 'He's (in reference to Charlie) hitting the pipe again'.

These lines occur in those pivotal investigative moments when Charlie's methods and techniques are contrasted to those employed by Sergeant Kelly. In each sequence Charlie's methods are shown to be superior to Kelly's. Kelly's racist lines are then paired with Charlie's epigrams usually spoken in pidgin English (Penzler, 1977: 44). These barbed exchanges between Charlie and Kelly serve four functions. They establish Charlie's superior investigative powers, while allowing him to speak his famous lines, which embody kernels of Chinese wisdom. These signature lines mark the film as a Charlie Chan movie. But most importantly they allow the racial subtext to be continually present. Even as Charlie rebuffs each of Kelly's charges, the charges, and their bigotry still stand. Thus the film is able to superficially transcend its own racism, as it depends on these racist lines to establish Charlie's superior skills. In these conversational exchanges the film simultaneously places Charlie inside and outside mainstream American culture. It aligns him with Asian stereotypes, while using these same stereotypes as a means of overcoming the stereotypes and their negative moral implications.

While Charlie Chan's mysteries changed from film to film (and within films), underneath each of these changes was a firm understanding. This tiny aging Asian male knew who he was, knew his place in society, and felt pride in his ability to always right a situation that had gone wrong. Of these things he was certain. All of this is undone in *Chan is Missing*.

CHAN IS MISSING

Several Chans are missing in this film. Mr Chan Hung cannot be found. Chan Hung is a middle-aged Taiwanese businessman who owes Joe, a humorous, soft-spoken, sweet-tempered middle-aged Chinese-American cabdriver, and his young Freddie Prinze-like, 'Americanized' nephew, Steve, $4,000. He has been missing for twenty-two days. (Joe and Steve decided to sublease a licence from an independent owner. Mr Chan

Hung was to deliver $4,000 to finalize the deal.) Charlie Chan and the Chan mystery series are missing, although the series is laughed at by Joe, who says, 'Those old films are a source of cheap laughs'. Charlie and Number One Son are not here, but their absence is several times noted, and their presence mocked. Laughingly, Joe and Steve, for example, introduce themselves to Mr Chan's daughter as Charlie Chan and Number One Son. In this film no clue leads anywhere and a mystery, in the conventional sense, is never solved. What's not here seems to have just as much meaning as what is here. Nothing means what it seems to mean.

But these easily identifiable absences are not what the film is about. Self, in its multiple Asian-American versions, and its empty centres are the topic at hand. Aging Asian bodies are everywhere present. The young, the old, and the middle-aged line the sidewalks of Wang's Chinatown. Everyone is looking, empty gazes. On the surface this is a 'whodunit', but more deeply it is a 'whoisit'. Its topic is epistemological. 'How do we know the self and its meanings' and are these meanings ever certain? The young have one answer (the future), the elderly another (the past), and the middle-aged are lost mid-way between the past and the future, groping through an uncertain present where nothing holds firm. And underneath it all Director Wayne Wang sends a chilling message: age does not bring wisdom, only greater uncertainty. *[Charlie] Chan* is missing (and maybe dead) and we have learned nothing since his absence.

The city is San Francisco. The setting Chinatown. The time now. The style is *cinéma vérité, film noir,* grainy screen, dark shadows, back-lit scenes, voice-over narration. Mosaic-like, *Chan Is Missing* is a collage of over-laid images, pictures, and close-up camera shots, many viewed through the front windshield of a cab, which glides through the streets of Chinatown, its window reflecting the scenes that pass by: stoop-shouldered, aged-Asian males and females shuffling along the sidewalk; young Asian-American children holding their parents' hands waiting for a bus; Kung-Fu warrior posters outside movie houses; pagoda roof tops in the distance; Chinese and Italian restaurants; smoked chickens hanging in café windows; signs in Chinese; a Christmas-decorated Buddha with tinsel and flashing lights; Chinese rock and roll ('Rock Around the Clock') and suspense music in the background, as a Pat Suzuki version of Rogers and Hammerstein's 'Grant Avenue' plays over the film's credits. A middle-aged voyeur's film from start to finish, the text is filled with shots of aging Joe gazing either directly into the camera, or slightly off-screen into the distance. His contemplative voyeurism yields nothing.

Joe and Steve set out to find the missing Chan. Steve wants to go to the police, but Joe resists. Their journey brings them in contact with four clues and over twelve persons who know, or knew Chan. Although he is never found, by the end of the film the $4,000 is delivered to Joe and Steve by Mr Chan's teenage daughter Jenny.

What is missing is the firm and steady, easily assimilated Chinese-American character embodied in the Chan films. Indeed the film offers a virtual dictionary of contemporary Asian-American identities: Chinese Richard Pryors; Chinese cooks who wear 'Samurai Night Fever' T-Shirts and sing 'Fry Me to the Moon'; FOBS (fresh off the boat); Kung-Fu warriors; China dolls; Chinese scholars with hot tubs and their Lo Fong girl friends; jade-faced rich old men; young Asian males with the Gentleman's Quarterly (GQ) look; two-faced schizophrenic Chinamen; Oakland Hill Wah; Ho Chi Minh look-alikes; young Asian males who eat US certified food, cows' ears and mushrooms from Des Moines, Iowa; People's Republic of China; Pro-Taiwan rich men; Asian males who sell Chinese-American apple pie; young Asian women who dress like American women; old Asian men and women who look like mainland peasants; young, streetwise, young Asian males wearing baseball caps.

These multiple images add up to one conclusion; there is no single Asian-American identity. The film's mystery seeks to unravel and find a solid core to this identity. The voyeur's project thus lies in the discovery that there is no Chan who can be missing, for every Chan (Asian-American) has an identity, even the three Chans, as Joe notes, who everyday appear on the missing person's list in the Police Department.

Middle-aged Joe summarizes this struggle to define self. To Steve, he states, 'It's hard enough for guys like me who've been here so long to find an identity. I can imagine Chan Hung's problem, somebody from China coming over here and trying to find himself'. Steve protests. 'That's a bunch of bullshit man! That identity shit. That's old news. Man that happened ten years ago'. Joe retorts, 'Its still going on'. Steve argues:

> Shit! I ran into this old friend from high school down town. We used to run together. He's all dressed up in his fuckin' GQ look with his Lo Fong girlfriend. He didn't want to talk to me man. He knew who I was. He's playing a game man. Fuck the identity shit. He knew what he was doin', I know what I'm doin'. I coulda kicked his fuckin' ass. Chinese all over this fuckin' city. Whatdaya mean about identity? They got their own identity. I got my identity!

Thus do youth and middle age clash.

This absence of a singular identity is itself political, for the Asian-American must take a stand on the American experience that is either Pro-Taiwan and assimilationist, or anti-American and pro-People's Republic of China. But this politicized identity is also mocked. For every character in the film has been deeply touched by the San Francisco version of the Asian-American experience, even the 83-year-old Asian male who murders his 79-year-old Asian neighbour over which flag should be carried in the Chinese New Year's Parade.

As Joe and Steve go looking for Chan, no two individuals describe him the same way. To his wife he is a man who never properly assimilated to the American way of life. To his daughter he is an honest and trustworthy man. Presco, the manager of the Manilla Senior Citizen's Center calls Mr Chan 'Hi Ho' and thinks he is an eccentric. George (who is marketing a version of Chinese apple pie), thinks Mr Chan is too Chinese. Amy thinks he is a hotheaded political activist. Frankie thinks he returned to the mainland. Mr Fong thinks Chan is a genius because he invented a Chinese word-processing system. Mr Lee says he is dimwitted, and an old man in Chan's hotel says Chan is a paranoid.

The film itself refuses a single identity. Reviewers called it a gumshoe thriller (Rickey, 1982), an original, eccentric, anthropological comedy (Gelmis, 1982), not a neatly-plotted Oriental mystery (Winston, 1982), a detective mystery that becomes a meditation on Chinese-American identity (Denby, 1982), a Chinatown mystery (Thomas, 1982), a dark comedy, a light melodrama, an existential mystery (Sterritt, 1982), a remake of *Citizen Kane* (Studlar, 1983: 115; Ansen, 1982), a film in the tradition of the French New Wave (Horton, 1982), a very Chinese mystery (Thomas, 1982), and a 'homely and funny cousin to *The Third Man*' (Denby, 1982). These descriptions point to the film's refusal to present a stereotypical picture of the Asian-American community. In its attempts to deconstruct and criticize previous images of the Asian-American subject, *Chan Is Missing* suggests that the Asian-Oriental other will no longer stand still and allow itself to be seen and understood through western eyes.

Chan is never found. This is a Chinese mystery, so says Joe. 'The murder article is missing. The photograph's not there. The other woman is not there. Nothing is what it seems to be'. Disclaiming his own identity, Joe states, 'I guess I'm not Chinese enough. I can't accept a mystery without a solution'. He returns to lines spoken earlier in the film by Presco. An old Chinese piano player who went crazy had reported that the only person who could fix him was the man who looked at him in the rain puddle on the ground. Presco tells Steve and Joe, 'Well, you guys lookin' for Mr. Chan, why don't you look in the puddle?' As these lines are spoken, the screen dissolves into a shot of glimmering water, ripples overlapping one another, to be replaced by a kaleidoscopic sequence of scenes which repeat the film's main narrative moments: the interviews with Presco, Mr Lee, Mr Fong, Mrs Chan, Amy, Henry, Frankie, George, Jenny, the old man.

Joe continues speaking. He is back in his cab. The windshield reflects street scenes.

> The problem with me is I believe what I see and hear. If I believe that with Mr Chan, I'll know nothing because everything is so contradictory. Here's a picture of Chan Hung (photo of a somewhat overweight Asian male, smiling, a second man in the shadows), then a shot from Chan's apartment where the missing picture once hung'.

With these lines Joe stops speaking. Pat Suzuki begins to sing 'Grant Avenue' and the screen once again fills with images from Chinatown (old men and women on the sidewalk, haggard, faded brick apartment buildings, torn curtains blowing through broken-out windows): 'They call it Grant Avenue, San Francisco, California, USA. Look for Chinatown. You travel there in a trolley, up you climb, dong-dong, you're in Hong Kong, having yourself a time'.

The viewer's ears are flooded with the sounds of these American Chinatown stereotypes, which are undercut by Wang's old men and women staring into the camera. Leaving these contradictory images in the viewer's field of vision, the film cuts to its credits.

Biting parody and pastiche, this film satirizes what it imitates and critiques, the 'neatly plotted oriental mystery' (Winston, 1982), the 'Charlie Chan Orientals' (Rickey, 1982). Its jumbled, collage and pastiche-like mosaic structure refuses to imitate the Chan mystery tradition which it draws upon. *Chan Is Missing*, with its absent protagonist, is like Welles's *Citizen Kane* (1941), Reed's *The Third Man* (1949), and an Antonioni philosophical puzzle (*Blow-Up, The Passenger*). The 'mystery evaporates in the face of the uncertainty of knowing anything for sure' (Denby, 1982: 72). Joe, like the investigative protagonists in *The Third Man* and *Citizen Kane*, is more interested in discovering who Chan *was* than in either getting his money back, or finding the real missing man. With *Citizen Kane*, the film is a story of contradiction. 'The riddle, not the solution is the point' (Gelmis, 1982: ll), the 'whodunit' dissolves into a 'whoisit' (Horton, 1982), a discourse on the mystery that lies behind every life and the faces people wear. This is not a TV mystery, Joe muses, for if it was 'an important clue would pop up at this time and clarify everything'. Yet much is revealed, for the many-sided Chan Hung becomes the perfect metaphor for the many-sided, complex Chinese-American community (Denby, 1982: 72).

It matters little if the plot reveals a murder, a gun, a missing photo and set of clothes that may or may not have been connected to Chan's disappearance. These absences and occurrences tell us, as Joe says to Steve, to 'use the negative to emphasize the positive', and to look into the puddle to find ourselves. What is absent is present, and what is present lacks no substance, and hence is absent.

As parody and spoof *Chan Is Missing* refuses the Utopian fantasies of the Orientalizing Chan series. Its multi-voiced (polyphonic) text isolates Chinatown from San Francisco's version of American society, and offers no assimilationist solution to the Asian-American experience. Indeed the film suggests that Chinatown has enough problems of its own. It does not need to be part of the larger society which demands conformity to America's version of the Asian other. Racism is right here, at home, with Asians who hurl racist epithets at one another (two-faced schizophrenic Chinaman, jade-faced rich old men, FOBS). No heroes or heroines here. No stars, no cultural models, for every model is a stereotype, and every stereotype itself a stereotype. Here in Chinatown there are no perfect western others who would stand as a measure of the Asian self. This self has become so thoroughly westernized, no otherness is any longer possible. That is why Chan Is Missing.

At the centre of the film are multiple images of overlapping, conflicting, decentred circles of ethnic Asian-American identities: Chinese Richard Pryors, Chinese cooks singing 'Fry Me to the Moon', GQ-dressed young Asian males, young women dressed like American teenagers, sad old Asian men and women. These multiple identities do not cohere into a single structure, for every Asian-American finds him or herself, only by looking into Presco's puddle of muddy water. And this self which is reflected back is always missing, always different for the next time I look I will look different. Its always a different puddle.

No successful sleuths, no masters of mystery, but a mystery is solved. In the film's odd, idiosyncratic way, it confronts its own spectacle of discovery. Three puzzles are solved. Joe discovers that you cannot be Chinese enough. You can no longer use the negative to emphasize the positive. And, you must believe more than what you can see or hear. If you only believe what you can see and hear then you are confined, like Charlie Chan's pragmatic voyeur, to a world of solid facts. In Joe's 'pure' Oriental-Chinese world there are no solid facts, only mysteries, puzzles and things that are not there. By not being Chinese enough, Joe recognizes the failure and poverty of the Charlie Chan orientalizing project. This project, which uses the negative to emphasize the positive, creates a world where Chinese men make American apple pies, and, as George argues, 'take the good things from our background, and the good things from this country to enhance our lives'. This produces Steve's world where that 'Identity shit becomes old news, something that happened ten years ago'.

That old news was not news to Rogers and Hammerstein. On their (and Ethel Merman's) Grant Avenue, San Francisco, USA you can still have yourself a time, sharkfin soup, China dolls, precious jade, and silk brocade. And so, the film, *Flower Drum Song* (1961), which contained Rogers and Hammerstein's song, is now critiqued in Wang's last gesture. There are no flower drum songs, wise Asian patriarchs, obedient sons and daughters and arranged marriages in his Chinatown, or on his Grant Avenue, San Francisco, California, USA.

Here at the end of the film, as viewers stare at the blank space on the wall where Chan Hung's picture once hung, they are told to accept a mystery without a solution. The old world that Charlie Chan inhabited no longer exists. Chan is not missing. Chan is Dead. And in that death dies the Oriental sleuth, the ever-present aging Oriental eye, always ready to solve a crime for the western other. Wang's message is clear. To the Americans in his audience he says, 'We have enough problems of our own. Stop asking us to help you solve your crimes. We did that for too long and look at where it got us'.

CHARLIE CHAN IS DEAD

Death, decay and aging are the recurring motifs of *Chan is Missing*. Charlie Chan is dead. His legacy is also dead. Aging voyeurs no longer find out certain truths about themselves, or others. Sidewalks are now lined by time-worn, bent-shouldered, peasant-looking, elderly Asian men and women. On their shoulders and in their eyes they bear witness to the poverty of Charlie Chan's project. There is no space for them in American culture. They search, but cannot find those certain identities Charlie enacted. In Wayne Wang's Chinatown there are no wise, sage, aging Asian patriarchs. No Number One Sons full of energy and optimism. Only slightly bored and jaded Joe, and his cynical side-kick Steve.

So the death of the aging, sage Asian investigative voyeur signals a turn too in American culture. If age no longer automatically brings wisdom, only death, then we have lost a valuable cultural myth. For with Chan's death comes our own, and if aging is no longer valued, then our world may soon look like Wang's Chinatown. But perhaps it already does.

NOTES

An earlier version of this manuscript was presented to the 1992 Annual Meeting of the Society for the Study of Symbolic Interaction, 22 August, Pittsburgh. I thank Patricia T. Clough, Andrea Fontana, Ruth Horowitz, Stanford Lyman, and an unidentified reviewer for their comments.

1 Here I focus only on the Chan series. Elsewhere (Denzin, 1995) I analyse the Mr Wong and Mr Moto Films.
2 The gaze and look of the female and the gay voyeur are examined in Denzin (1995, Ch. 4, 7, ll).

3 *Director*: Wayne Wang; *Screenplay*: Wayne Wang, Isaac Cronnin, Terrel Seltzer; *Cast*: Wood Moy (Jo), Marc Hayashi (Steve), Laureen Chew (Amy), Judy Mihei (lawy er), Peter Wang (Henry), Presco Tabios (Presco), Frankie Alarcon (Frankie), Ellen Yeung (Mrs Chan), George Woo (George), Emily Yamasaki (Jenny), Roy Chan (Mr Lee), Leong Pui Chee (Mr Fong); Wayne Wang Productions, 1981; New Yorker Films, 1989.

4 *Director*: H. Bruce Humbertstone; *Producer*: John Stone; *Screenplay*: Scott Darling and Charles S. Belden from a story by Bess Meredyth, based on the character Charlie Chan created by Earl Deer Biggers; Twentieth Century-Fox release; *Cast*: Warner Oland, Boris Karloff, Keye Luke, Charlotte Henry, Thomas Beck, Margaret Irving, Gregory Gaye, Nedda Harrigan, Frank Conroy, Guy Usher, William Demarest. Hanke (1989: 83) suggests that the film was an attempt to 'cash in on the then prevalent vogue of operatic subjects brought on by the brief popularity of Grace Moore and Lily Pons, not to mention *A Night at the Opera* with the Marx Brothers'.

5 According to Hanke (1989: 82–3) this is the Chan film most admired, even 'by people who are not fans of the series on the whole'.

6 Stanford Lyman (in correspondence) argues that Chan would emerge as the reverse mirror image of Fu Manchu. While each is possessed with uncanny oriental cunning, Charlie represents, at one level, the tamed Oriental spirit working in the service of the Occident, while Fu Manchu is the 'yellow peril' to the Occident. On another level, when compared to his sons, Charlie is the unassimilated Oriental, and his sons caricatures of assimilation. Lyman also suggests that Chan's sons are really social isolates, seeking to be recognized as full-fledged Americans, who also possess their father's Oriental skills.

7 Higashi (1991: 124) and Lyman (1990a: 154–9) present critical inter-pretations of the forms of institutional racism applied to Asians in the United States.

8 The title of Wayne Wang's 1982 film to be discussed below.

9 It is relevant, in this context, to examine the history of modern Chinese cinema during this time period, and to compare Hollywood's representa-tions of the Asian-other with those produced by Chinese film-makers. Chinese cinema during the 1929–49 time period was committed to a humanistic, social realism 'motivated by a concern for the plight of the Chinese people' (L. Lee, 1991: 8). Hsiung-Ping (1991), in an interesting comparison of the Hong Kong and Taiwanese film industries, observes that by the 1980s Hong Kong film-makers were committed to making films based on the American version of the violent, urban, macho male cop, skilled in kung fu and the martial arts. In contrast, Taiwanese film-makers were more committed to films reflecting a nostalgia for China's rural, pastoral past (see also Lau, 1991).

10 Springer (1991: 168) suggests that this system persists to the present day, in what she calls 'third-world investigation films' which merge the action-adventure genre (the Indiana Jones series) with the reporter-film genre (*The Year of Living Dangerously, The Killing Fields*). In such films the hero is surrounded 'with clichéd signifiers of the third world as mysterious, inscrutable, exotic, sensual, corrupt, and dangerous' (Springer, 1991: 168).

11 This is a version of what Stuart Hall (1981, 36–7) calls 'inferential racism'.

12 Of course in the Chan series Number One Son played the part of the immature, irrational, childish Asian; yet even this conduct was neutralized, by having Charlie act as the traditional-white-paternal father figure.

13 Charlie and Regan are presented as middle-aged men. Of the two, Charlie is less physically vigorous. His slow-paced, deliberate movements suggest a wisdom gained with age, while Regan's hurly-burly, rapid movements from scene to scene mark an excess of energy that does not produce useful knowledge about the case.

14 Lilli with Gravelle, the crazed maniac, Whitely, the ineffective upper-class male, and Enrico, the effete canary (so labelled by the Demarest character Sergeant Kelly); Anita with Enrico the betraying husband, manipulated by Lilli; Kitty with Phil, the traditional compliant, nurturing husband-to-be.

15 As *divas*, Lilli and Anita connect to nineteenth-century representations of the *femme fatale* who was associated with popular Orientalism (see Doane, 1991: 1). At this level the film joins two versions of Orientalism, female decadence and male voyeurism.

REFERENCES

Ansen, David (1982) 'Review of *Chan Is Missing*', *Newsweek* 21 June: 65.

Bakhtin, M. M. (1981) *The Dialogic Imagination*, Austin: University of Texas Press.

Bakhtin, M. M. (1986) *Speech Genre and Other Essays*, Austin: University of Texas Press.

Baran, Paul and Sweeze, Paul (1973) *Monopoly Capital*, London: Penguin.

Barthes, Roland (1982) *Empire of Signs*, New York: Hill & Wang.

Baudrillard, Jean (1983) *Simulations*, New York: Semiotext(e).

Blumer, Herbert (1965/1988) 'The future of the color line', in Stanford M. Lyman and Arthur J. Vidich, *Social Order and the Public Philosophy: An Analysis and Interpretation of the Work of Herbert Blumer*, Fayetteville: University of Arkansas Press, pp. 208–22 (originally published in J. C. McKinney and E. T. Thompson (eds) *The South in Continuity and Change*, Durham: Duke University Press, pp. 220–53.

Clough, Patricia Ticineto (1992) *The End(s) of Ethnography*, Newbury Park, CA: Sage.

de Lauretis, Terese (1987) *Technologies of Gender*, Bloomington: Indiana University Press.

Denby, David (1982) 'Review of *Chan Is Missing*', *New York*, 7 June: 72.

Denzin, Norman K. (1991) *Images of Postmodernism: Social Theory and Contemporary Cinema*, London: Sage.

Denzin, Norman K. (1992a) *Symbolic Interactionism and Cultural Studies*, New York and London: Basil Blackwell.

Denzin, Norman K. (1992b) 'The Conversation', *Symbolic Interaction*, 15: 135–49.

Denzin, Norman K. (1993a) 'The voyeur's desire', *Current Perspectives in Social Theory* 13: 139–58.

Denzin, Norman K. (1993b) 'Where Has Postmodernism Gone?', *Cultural Studies*, 7: 507–14.

Denzin, Norman K. (1995) *The Cinematic Society*, London: Sage.

Desser, David (1991a) 'The cinematic melting pot: ethnicity, Jews and psychoanalysis', in Lester D. Friedman (ed.) *Unspeakable Images: Ethnicity and the American Cinema*, Urbana: University of Illinois Press, pp. 378–403.

Desser, David (1991b) '"Charlie don't surf": race and culture in Vietnam films', in Michael Anderegg (ed.), *Inventing Vietnam: The War in Film and Television*, Philadelphia: Temple University Press, pp. 81–102.

Doane, Mary Anne (1991) *Femmes Fatales: Feminism, Film Theory, Psychoanalysis*, New York: Routledge.

Everson, William K. (1972) *The Detective In Film*, Secaucus, NJ: The Citadel Press.

Farberman, Harvey (1991) 'Symbolic interactionism and postmodernism: close encounter of a dubious kind', *Symbolic Interaction* 14: 471–88.

Farberman, Harvey and R. S. Perinbanayagam (1985) 'Introduction', in Harvey Farberman and R. S. Perinbanayagam (eds), *Studies in Symbolic Interaction: Supplement 1: Foundations of Interpretive Sociology: Original Essays in Symbolic Interaction*, Greenwich, CT: JAI Press, pp. 3–12.

Fiedler, Leslie A. (1966) *Love and Death in the American Novel*, rev. edn, New York: Stein & Day.

Foucault, Michel (1980) *Power/Knowledge*, New York: Pantheon

Gamman, Lorraine (1988) 'Watching the detectives: the enigma of the female gaze', in Lorraine Gamman and M. Marshment (eds), *The Female Gaze: Women as Viewers of Popular Culture*, London: The Women's Press, pp. 8–26.

Gelmis, Joseph (1982) 'Review of *Chan Is Missing*', *Newsday* 23 April (Part II): ll.

Goode, Greg (1982a) 'The oriental in mystery fiction, Part I', *The Armchair Detective* 15: 196–202;

Goode, Greg (1982b) 'The oriental in mystery fiction, Part II', *The Armchair Detective* 15: 306–13.

Goode, Greg (1983a) 'The oriental in mystery fiction, Part III', *The Armchair Detective* 16: 62–74.

Goode, Greg (1983b) 'The oriental in mystery fiction, Part IV', *The Armchair Detective* 16: 257–61.

Goode, Greg (1983c) 'The oriental in mystery fiction, Corrections', *The Armchair Detective* 16: 96, 218, 322.

Gramsci, Antonio (1934–35/1975) 'On the detective novel and detective novels', in *Quaderni del Carcere*, Turin: Einaudi, pp. 2128–30.

Hall, Stuart (1981) 'The whites of their eyes: racist ideologies and the media', in George Bridges and Rosalind Brunt (eds) *Silver Linings*, London: Laurence & Wishart, pp. 36–7.

Hall, Stuart (1992) 'Cultural studies and its theoretical legacies', in Lawrence Grossberg and Paul A. Trechler (eds), *Cultural Studies*, New York: Routledge, pp. 277–86.

Hanke, Ken (1989) *Charlie Chan at the Movies: History, Filmography, and Criticism*, Jefferson, North Carolina: McFarland.

Haycroft, Howard (1972) *Murder for Pleasure: The Life and Times of the Detective Story*, New York: Biblo and Tannen.

Higashi, Sumiko (1991) 'Ethnicity, class and gender in film: De Mille's *The Cheat*', in Lester D. Friedman (ed.) *Unspeakable Images: Ethnicity and the American Cinema*, Urbana: University of Illinois Press, pp. 112–39.

Horton, Arnold (1982) 'Review of *Chan Is Missing*', *Films In Review* December: 623.

Hsiung-Ping, Chiao (1991) 'The distinct Taiwanese and Hong Kong cinemas', in Chris Berry (ed.) *Perspectives On Chinese Cinema*, London: British Film Institute, pp. 155–65.

Jameson, Frederic (1990) *Signatures of the Visible*, New York: Routledge.

Jameson, Frederic (1991) *Postmodernism, or, The Cultural Logic of Late Capitalism*, Durham: Duke University Press.

Kristeva, Julia (1977) *About Chinese Women*, New York: Urizen.

Lau, Jenny Kwok Wah (1991) 'A cultural interpretation of the popular cinema of China and Hong Kong', in Chris Berry (ed.) *Perspectives On Chinese Cinema*, London: British Film Institute, pp. 166–74.

Lee, Keehyeung (1991) 'Orientalism in Japanese colonial discourse', unpublished manuscript, Department of Sociology, University of Illinois at Urbana-Champaign.

Lee, Leo Ou-Fan (1991) 'The tradition of modern Chinese cinema: some preliminary explorations and hypotheses', in Chris Berry (ed.) *Perspectives On Chinese Cinema*, London: British Film Institute, pp. 6–20.

Lyman, Stanford (1990a) *Civilization: Contents, Discontents, Malcontents and Other Essays in Social Theory*, Fayetteville: University of Arkansas Press.

Lyman, Stanford (1990b) 'Race, sex, and servitude: images of blacks in American cinema', *International Journal of Politics, Culture, and Society* 4: 49–77.

Marchetti, Gina (1991) 'Ethnicity, the cinema, and cultural studies', in Lester D. Friedman (ed.) *Unspeakable Images: Ethnicity and the American Cinema*, Urbana: University of Illinois Press, pp. 277–309.

Mayne, Judith (1988) *Private Novels, Public Films*, Athens, Georgia: University of Georgia Press.

Mayne, Judith (1990) *The Woman at the Keyhole: Feminism and Women's Cinema*, Bloomington: Indiana University Press.

Musser, Charles (1991) 'Ethnicity, role-playing and American film comedy: from Chinese laundry scene to Whoopee (1894–1930)', in Lester D. Friedman (ed.) *Unspeakable Images: Ethnicity and the American Cinema*, Urbana: University of Illinois Press, pp. 39–81.

Penzler, Otto (1977) *The Private Lives of Private Eyes, Spies, Crimefighters, & Other Good Guys*, New York: Grosset & Dunlap.

Pitts, Michael R. (1979) *Famous Movie Detectives*, Metuchen, NJ: Scarecrow Press.

Pitts, Michael R. (1990) *Famous Movie Detectives, Vol. II*, Metuchen, NJ: Scarecrow Press.

Rickey, Carrie (1982) 'Review of *Chan Is Missing*', *Village Voice* 27 April: 52.

Rubenstein, Leonard (1979) *The Great Spy Films*, Secaucus, NJ: Citadel Press.

Said, Edward (1979) *Orientalism*, New York: Vintage Books.

Said, Edward (1989) 'Representing the colonized: anthropology's interlocutors', *Critical Inquiry* 15: 205–25.

Sanders, William B. (1976) *The Sociologist as Detective*, 2nd edn, New York: Praeger.

Shohat, Elia (1991) 'Ethnicity-in-relations: toward a multicultural reading of American cinema', in Lester D. Friedman (ed.) *Unspeakable Images: Ethnicity and the American Cinema*, Urbana: University of Illinois Press, pp. 215–50.

Silverman, Kzaja (1992) *Male Subjectivity at the Margins*, New York: Routledge.

Springer, Claudia (1991) 'Comprehension and crisis: reporter films and the Third World', in Lester D. Friedman (ed.) *Unspeakable Images: Ethnicity and the American Cinema*, Urbana: University of Illinois Press, pp. 167–89.

Stam, Robert (1991) 'Bakhtin, polyphony, and ethnic/racial representation', in Lester D. Friedman (ed.) *Unspeakable Images: Ethnicity and the American Cinema*, Urbana: University of Illinois Press, pp. 251–76.

Sterritt, David (1982) 'Review of *Chan Is Missing*', *Christian Science Monitor* 1 July: 18.

Studlar, Gaylyn (1983) 'Review of *Chan Is Missing*', in Frank N. Magill (ed.) *Magill's Cinema Annual: A Survey of 1982 Films*, Englewood Cliffs, NJ: Salem Press, pp. 113–15.

Thomas, Kevin (1982) 'Review of *Chan is Missing*', *Los Angeles Times*, 13 August (Calendar section): 7.

Todorov, Tzvetan (1977) 'The typology of detective fiction', in T. Todorov, *The Poetics of Prose*, Ithaca: Cornell University Press, pp. 42–52.

Truzzi, Marcello (1976) 'Sherlock Holmes: applied social psychologist', in William B. Sanders (ed.) *The Sociologist as Detective*, 2nd edn, New York: Praeger, pp. 50–86.

Tuska, Jon (1978) *The Detective in Hollywood*, Westport, Conn.: Greenwood Press.

Tuska, Jon (1984) *Dark Cinema: American Film Noir in Cultural Perspective*, Westport, Conn.: Greenwood Press.

Vidich, Arthur and Lyman, Stanford M. (1985) *American Sociology*, New Haven: Yale University Press.

Vidich, Arthur and Lyman, Stanford M. (1988) *Social Order and the Public Philosophy*, Fayatteville.: University of Arkansas Press.

West, Cornel (1989) *The American Evasion of Philosophy*, Madison: University of Wisconsin Press.

Winston, Archer (1982) 'Review of *Chan Is Missing*', *New York Post*, 4 June: 44.

Wong, Eugene Franklin (1978) *On Visual Media Racism: Asians in American Motion Pictures*, New York: Arno Press.

Zaretsky, Eli (1976) *Capitalism, the Family and Personal Life*, New York: Harper & Row.

13

CREATING MEMORIES
Some images of aging in mass tourism
David Chaney

PART ONE

It is conventional to say that in the values of consumer culture youth is given a privileged status. Through a variety of modes of image and narrative we, as members of mass audiences, are encouraged to see being young as being strong, independent and sexy. It becomes a civic duty, indeed a moral responsibility, to undertake a number of remedies to prolong this stage of the life course (Hepworth and Featherstone, 1982). In contrast, therefore, aging is necessarily unattractive. It tends to be characterized by images that are the converse of strength, independence and sexiness. And yet there must be contradictions within marketing practices. While it might be easy to sell lifestyles on the back of youth, the facts that we do all more or less gracefully age, and that the elderly form an increasingly large proportion of the total population in late-modern societies, mean that the elderly are a large and potentially profitable market that will appreciate being approached positively. We can go further and say that our discourse of identity (the resources through which we find ways of giving ourselves social identity and points of reference on ways of living), must find some accommodation for the transitions of aging, particularly in the marketing of leisure.[1]

In this chapter I shall look at a small aspect of contemporary leisure – selling holidays for an exclusively elderly clientele. My instances will be drawn from marketing winter holidays to British customers. I am interested in this material because the authors of these brochures are, it seems to me, engaged in more than describing places and organizations that will create a nice holiday. They are also formulating ways in which people can understand themselves as members of an age-based social category. The brochures in part consist of images, but more generally constitute an image of the proper concerns of aging. They are in this sense a normative account of a collective identity. I have called the paper 'creating memories' because although the brochures are offering attractions to be looked forward to, these attractions are already cast within the ambit of an implied community that is as much concerned with how it has got where it has as where it might be going. More technically, I could say that memorable occasions are always reflexive enterprises, but that in the discourse of these holidays the reflexivity of memory is more self-consciously addressed.

The paper is therefore couched as an interplay between a specific version of images of aging and a more theoretical concern with understanding images and representations. While of course we can use collections of images as an archive of changing mores and conventions (Achenbaum, 1982; Covey, 1987), there is in such an analysis often an implied notion of ideology – that in the forms of representation we can see how meanings are generated and prescribed. Thus the term representation (or image) can encourage a comparative contrast between culture and reality. My approach here has a more active sense of culture as the play of representations. I argue that a literal view of images is inadequate and that it is more fruitful to see representations as embedded in cultural forms (Chaney, 1990). A cultural form does not just consist of a narrative and its means of inscription or performance but also encompasses the social occasion through which it is participated in by different audiences: 'I consider that the interpretation of television viewing, the study of the transactions which take place between institutions, programmes and audiences, is in certain important respects more akin to the study of talk than to the study of texts' (Sparks, 1992: 49, here discussing the social effects of the representation of criminality on television). I shall in this paper try a way of reading a particular body of material as more like a conversation between images and audience that is offering a way of understanding aging.

Aging is a process of cultural change in that the identity of those concerned changes interdependently with physical change (we have recognized for some years that becoming dead has the characteristics of a career and is at least as much a process of cultural transition as physical trauma). The status of adulthood is generally, if loosely, seen as achieved, the individual takes responsibility for accomplishments and defects, and the terms of identity are bound up with powers which inform a degree of autonomy. The process of aging in contrast involves a loss of autonomy (a process of disautonomy) in important respects (although see Kaufman, 1986). This is obviously not a uniform process and it is crucially affected by traditional structural factors such as class and wealth, gender and race. But after allowing for the greatest variety of circumstance, the commonality to aging is the idea of transition towards the ascription of age-related concerns (Bytheway et al., 1989; Dant, 1990).

As increasing numbers of the elderly either live with age-peers or alone rather than with a family of younger members, the process of aging for more of the cohort will be conducted in a community in which institutional structures for managing change will be particularly import- ant. It is not that the individuality of each person will disappear, but that their ability to impose that identity on social circumstance may be subordinate to more ascribed expectations (Hockey, 1989). We can use a concept of career to describe this type of processual change. As in an occupational career, the expectations of performers and significant others are less directed towards the accomplishment of a specific goal, than the management of performance as a competent and respected actor. The rewards of a metaphoric career such as aging are therefore those that derive from meeting normative expectations, rather than the gains of financial benefits (Goffman, 1968).

Giddens has suggested that the moments of transition in this career in late-modern culture are more likely to become something of an identity crisis. He argues that the rituals of transition between socio- biological stages have declined in significance, so that: 'In modern social conditions, . . . crises become more or less endemic, both on an individual and a collective level' (1991: 184). This idea suggests that the normative expectations of aging are continually being renegotiated. More precisely this means that the idealized (or normative) self as a personal role model, a ceremonial identity to which actors can orient themselves, may be experienced as imprecise, as lacking definition. In such circumstances it is likely that the institutional forms of aging will use a form of presentation that casts novelty within the reassurance of tradition. I will seek to show how the holidays I am dealing with are represented as traditional forms for novel experience.

The element of novelty comes from both changes in the career of aging and the development of new holiday opportunities. Winter holidays for mass audiences are a development of the consumer culture of this generation, for there are few traditions of age-based holidaying (for some examples of holidays for the elderly see Romsa and Blenman, 1989; see also Hendricks and Culter, 1990). In order to become institutionalized this form of leisure will require legitimation. Tradi- tions are forms of collective memory but they also provide a way of mediating personal experience and collective practice. For fairly obvious reasons, in previous generations the aging have been the guardians of, and authorities on, traditions. These have been usually articulated through the organization of family life. It is not so surprising that an innovation such as the development of forms of leisure outside family structures should seek to articulate the career of aging through the warrant of an invented tradition.

PART TWO

Although I have spoken of the problematic character of transitions in identity, the idea of taking a holiday is not in itself usually seen as being of major existential significance. The recurrent holiday is clearly an elaborately staged piece of social business in which distinctive social expectations operate for a limited period. Holidays, as other consumer choices, are usually planned to be consistent with other features of the lifestyle and to this extent it is important that they are seen to be appropriate. The holiday makes a claim upon a particular aspect of distinction through highly socially-differentiated ritualized repertoires of performance and presentation (Dann and Cohen, 1991).

The existence of secular or individualized (in the sense of personal choice rather than being undertaken individually) holidays can be seen to be a good criterion of the modernity of the organization of production. In order to modernize it was understood to be necessary, by the proponents of rational recreation, to strip away the ritual order of traditional society. The consequence has been that work, paid work, took on a central overwhelming significance in the organization of social meaning. The symbolic status of work, and the rewards of productive labour, are, however, never as complete as economic theorists would like. In the dramatization of modernity the symbolic space of popular culture has been one of the most important repertoires for the development of new languages of collective experience (Chaney, 1993). A central feature of this space has been a discourse of leisure emphasizing searches for meaning through personal choice and lifestyle (Rojek, 1993).

Leisure should be understood as the ways in which audiences are constituted for different forms of entertainment. Rather than inverting the organization of labour and collective creativity, themes of entertainment, relaxation and personal choice have been characterized as times 'away from' and 'free of' the obligations of work (Frey and Dickens, 1990; Haggard and Williams, 1992). Because leisure has typically been caught in a conceptual contrast with work, the leisure of those without 'work' has been neglected in social research (Deem, 1988). The standard examples are women who do not have paid work but 'only' domestic responsibilities, the long-term unemployed, children who play rather than have leisure and the retired (note for example that a recent text on the sociology of old age (Fennell et al., 1988) has no discussion of holidays, tourism or leisure). The standard assumption has been that an excess of free or unstructured time will create a variety of 'problems' culminating in the possibility of self-disintegration (although see Roche, 1990, for a theoretical account of more positive possibilities in the organization of time).

It is consistent with a contrast between leisure and work that the landscape of tourism, that is, the cultural terrain tourists are appropriating, is framed as a space 'out' of or away from work even if it contains, as it inevitably does, people working. (This was MacCannell's great insight, 1976, that in addition to those working to create leisure, any piece of work can be reframed as a prop for a tourist locale; and possibly be so sufficiently different that it can be claimed to be able to provide a 'transformation of the self' – see Bruner's, 1991, critique of this idea.) Urry's first characteristic of the social practices of tourism is then that: 'Tourism is a leisure activity which presupposes its opposite, namely regulated and organized work. It is one manifestation of how work and leisure are organized as separate and regulated spheres of social practice in "modern" societies' (1990: 2).

The logic of this approach would seem to be that the exceptional qualities of a holiday, as a time and place framed to some extent outside conventional social order, are harder to sustain if the obligations of work are not pressing. In practice of course, even for those whose age precludes full-time employment, there is never an absence of external obligations. Whether it is dealing with paramedical and welfare agencies, or the social obligations of family, friends and secondary associations, or the self-imposed constraints of looking after pets or the garden, or the necessities of shopping and domestic chores, there are innumerable commitments that structure the day to leave little time for 'relaxation'. (These heterogeneous demands can be seen as a more relaxed and fulfilling repertoire of ways of using time, as Roche, 1989, has argued.)

We are then faced with several innovations in relation to holiday-making by the aged in peer-exclusive enclaves. The first is the holidays themselves as new forms of leisure, particularly amongst those who have left full-time employment. Second, the fact that a much higher proportion of the age-cohort is able to afford to take such holidays. And third, that the stages (places) of a tourist industry can be adapted to the concerns of a more conservative hedonism. Combined, these innovations dramatize opportunities for those who are making the transition into being elderly to both sustain their identity and yet simultaneously be alerted to the expectations of a new form of community. This process of change through a denial of change is articulated through the presentation of holidays as reinforcements of normality. Holidays are not presented as Utopian contrasts but offer affirmations of identity which deny novelty through the invention of tradition.

When we turn to the brochures written to market holidays to those willing to see themselves as aging,[2] there are two main ways of reading these texts. First, as a set of instructions on how the places of this holiday landscape relate to everyday experience; and second, what the themes

213

are that characterize this cultural space. I will describe the second approach in the next section and concentrate on the first now.

The places of holidays for the aging are presented as less important as destinations and more as stages (that is, as sites for performance) for a distinctive social milieu. This is in part because these destinations will be extremely familiar to anyone with the least acquaintance with the package holiday industry over the last thirty years. And in part because there are only cursory references to the places beyond certain recurrent features. These features will include that it is warm and/or sunny without being uncomfortably hot, that it is colourful such as an emphasis upon flowers, and that it has a culture which is different but recognizably an inflection of 'our' own. Writing of the Costa del Sol in the Thomson brochure we are told: 'The climate during the winter months will remind you of the warmest English spring day. . . . Vibrant and ever colourful, this region evokes many romantic images' (p. 31).

I want to be able to show that in drawing the potential strangeness of the holiday place back into the landscape of home, it becomes easier to see the occasion of the holiday as a form of tradition. It does not matter that, as I have said, there is no tradition of winter-holidaying except for the very wealthy. The purpose of the invention of traditions is to institutionalize new social forms (Hobsbawm and Ranger, 1983). In this case the invention stresses both the legitimacy of this form of leisure for the audience, and the appropriateness of certain concerns as pleasurable activity. I shall argue that in the rhetoric of invented tradition a particular image of aging is being formulated.

The excursion is framed by the reflexive concerns of the participants – it is their sense of distinctiveness which governs their journey. The titles to the brochures pick up several aspects of the notion of a stage of life that has distinctive characteristics: Leisurely Days; Golden Times; Young at Heart; Golden Years; and Golden Circle. (I think the two metaphors here are the circle as an enclosing community, see below, and golden as the glow and comfortable, rather than scorching, warmth of a sunset. I also wonder if the recurrence of gold as a metaphoric resource is to evoke an honouring of seniority which is probably otherwise absent from their lives.)

Other ways in which the distinctiveness of their audience is unostentatiously acknowledged in the brochures are displayed through featured attractions of these holidays. For example, although the exact ability of these resorts to accommodate disabled visitors is glossed over (those concerned are told to enquire further), it is at least recognized as a common and legitimate concern. Their greater ability in this respect is one of the facilities that coach tour operators stress prominently. Second, these packages recognize that being single, although of course avoiding any mentioning of widowing, is normal rather than exceptional. One example of judicious phrasing comes from the Cosmos brochure: 'If you are planning to travel solo, Golden Times can save you money. We have negotiated special deals [so] . . . that you won't have to pay a single room supplement on certain dates' (p. 6); see also the use of photographs of same-sex couples illustrating dancing on these holidays.

More positively perhaps the significance of the ceremonialization of time in family imagery is recognized in recurrent offers of celebration: 'Whether it's your wedding anniversary, or your birthday or any other sort of celebration . . . we'll pull out all the stops to arrange a bouquet or bubbly to make it a truly memorable occasion!' (Airtours, p. 5). When one looks for further details readers might find it cheering to discover that honeymooners are equally as anticipated as celebrants of wedding anniversaries and birthdays. Another example of concern with special interests is the recurrent stress that is placed in the brochures on the fact that local hosts and hostesses are usually retired people: 'who [however] still enjoy life as much as ever' (Sunworld, p. 5).

In these protestations of similarity there is a clear suspicion that the new or different would be seen as threatening. The possibility can be suppressed through an incessant stress on commonality that can be taken for granted even while allowing for a difference: 'if you'd rather, you can go off in search of peace and quiet . . . and explore at your own leisurely pace. We don't want you to feel that we've organized every moment of your holiday' (Thomson, p. 6). I think it is a significant element in this presupposition of homogeneity that there is a complete absence of faces of ethnic minorities from images of holiday-makers, or indeed of any reference to the possibility of ethnic diversity amongst the visitors.

I want then to argue that for those who have passed from the obligations of paid employment the holiday comes to mean a different sort of reward. It is one of the ways in which the status of aging is inscribed in different forms of life. But the process of inscription is through a discourse which ignores difference and claims the warrant of tradition. The most striking characteristic of the discourse of places in these brochures is that the point of departure, the home of these travellers, is also their destination. The evocation of holidays is also a way of talking about the sorts of concerns that can be expected to dominate the culture of aging; and thus in this and a thousand other discursive forms a way in which this culture is learnt and understood.

PART THREE

I have suggested that the images of aging in these brochures are less a mirror or prescriptive model than a point of reference rather like overhearing someone talking about yourself. I shall argue in this section that a useful way of understanding the process in this case is to see that a particular version of citizenship and its accompanying rituals is being formulated. Representation in advertising works to dramatize a subject (whether it is a product, an idea or an identity), and create a relevance, however fleeting, between the subject and the anonymous members of an audience. The conventional complaint about advertising is that its promises are illusory but this is to mistake the character of the drama being performed. In the process of dramatization the consumer is not offered a vicarious space in the performance but a promise of association and of relevance. Advertising is therefore populist, it must seek to appeal to its audience, but it is also didactic in that it provides instructions for 'viewing' the subject. Michael Schudson has wittily described the idealizations of advertising as capitalist realism to point to an analogy with the socialist realism of countries that once had a different model of citizenship (1984: Ch. 7; see also Wernick, 1991).

Advertising in general articulates the several forms of social citizenship through a cryptic interplay of pictorial allusion and rhetorical address. The picturing, and it does not particularly matter if it is a single image or a short sequence of images, works through what Goffman has called a 'scene' as a method of organizing understanding (1976). Scenes are fleeting opportunities for viewing which are necessarily truncated and therefore comprehension is dependent upon broad interpretative categories and stylizations. The glimpses provided by the scenes of commercial realism have certain advantages over those of everyday experience in that they are: intentionally choreographed to be informative; the perspective from which the audience views is necessarily part of the information to be conveyed; and that which is seen in commercial staging is warrantably seen – there is no suspicion of voyeurism. The public pictures of advertising therefore invite an interpretative engagement: 'The point about an ad is what its composer means us to infer as to what is going on in the make-believe pictures seen, not what had actually been going on in the real doings that were pictured' (Goffman, 1976: 83).

The dramatization is persuasive, therefore, not by the degree to which it corresponds to some pre-photographic reality, but by the degree to which it is consistent with the interpretative frameworks that might be available in popular experience:

> I want to argue now that the job the advertiser has of dramatising the value of his product is not unlike the job a society has of infusing its social situations with ceremonial and ritual signs facilitating the orientation of participants to one another.
>
> (Goffman, 1976: 95)

216

Ceremony and ritual facilitate mutual orientation through the provision of selves that can be treated for the matters at hand as sufficient. In the ceremonies and rituals through which participants orient themselves with each other in the holiday settings being evoked, they are concerned with the provision of selves that can cope with the changing identities of aging. It is not so much then that holiday companies are forced to adapt to what they take to be public demand for certain sorts of holiday arrangements by the elderly, as that in these descriptions and even more in the holidays they represent (assuming as we must that the idealizations of representation gloss holiday practice through the provision of expectations), those who are aging learn how and what it is they are to be and become.

I shall point to three themes in the accounts of holiday-worlds and attempt to show how in relation to each a ritual self for the holidaymaker is being constituted. The first theme is a presupposition of insecurity which is linked to a pervasive emphasis upon the need for care. This theme is spelt out through a number of tropes which I can list as: convenience; authority; and security. In relation to the first, for example, for coach tour passengers there are a network of local collection points, from which individuals can be ferried to more central locations etc. These function to minimize the amount of journey for which the individual has to take personal responsibility: 'We try our utmost to ensure that our arrangements are as trouble-free as possible, as we understand that this is important for your own peace of mind' (Shearings, p. 3).

More generally than just the coach tour operators, the authors of all these brochures adopt an authoritative voice in relation to their readers. Not only are their fears recognized and given due weight, they can also be assuaged because they have been anticipated: 'We know that where you stay is one of the most important factors influencing the enjoyment of your holiday' (Wallace Arnold, Europe, p. 2); and it has to be said that: 'Official rating systems for hotels and apartments can be terribly confusing' (Thomson, p. 5). It is therefore very convenient that: 'It's now far simpler to choose the one that suits you best' (ibid.). This tone of authoritative paternalism, combined with a scope for personal choice where it is judged to be appropriate, persists in the descriptions of drivers, couriers and representatives, etc.

And finally under this heading the generalized anxieties assumed to be characteristic of the elderly are given prominence through a series of assurances on safety, experience, expertise, size of the operating company, guarantees and insurance. It is hard to précis the variety of assurances but the world of the aging is portrayed as being shot through with insecurity. Given the cavalier way in which operators actually treat their herds of customers these insecurities may well be justified, but they are not lessened by the reiteration of palliatives; rather given further substance and significance.

The second theme that characterizes the brochure literature is the positive emphasis that is given to communalism. It is assumed absolutely without qualification that the company of one's peers is an appropriate lifestyle. And that occasions of interaction are centrally concerned with entertainment which itself has a limited number of themes. The most obvious way in which this is presented is the emphasis upon certain hotels acting as clubs, for example: Hosted Hotels; Golden Club Hotels; Golden Circle Club Hotels; and Golden Years Hotel Clubs. There are many alternatives to these hotels but their echoes of holiday camp togetherness ring through all the holiday descriptions. There is also in the brochures a strong emphasis upon the desirability, as well as the financial advantages, of customers booking in groups.

It may well be that these echoes of earlier forms of holiday-making stem from the memories of a generational culture, except that a theme of clubiness is also caught up in quite different holidays for young adults. I suggest instead that an emphasis upon collective experience in holidays exemplifies a concern with managing transition. It is precisely the uncertainties of aging that make individuality peculiarly threatening. Loneliness is not just being left out but having no sense of a desirable autonomy. The clubs and groups of holidaying with one's peers provide a set of practical contingencies for a form, however provisional, of *gemeinschaft*. It is in this context that the universal provision of free afternoon tea and biscuits makes sense. This is a ceremony through which an uncomplicated self can be sustained. In its metaphoric echoes of neighbourliness and support in times of troubles, the hedonism of holiday-making is given a darker aura, and the need for mutual support in sustaining identity recognized.

When we turn to the activities that define the attractions of leisure, we find what I have called the lack of utopian contrast in these holidays more strongly emphasized. The activities offered are those of all the clubs and associations back home. I list them in no particular order: dancing; golf; bridge; tours; quizzes/competitions/bingo; library; walks; bowls; keep fit; and painting. There are obviously status discriminations in this medley but they speak collectively to a world that is shared in common rather than fissured by idiosyncrasy and difference. The idea that these are appropriate to the age-group is strengthened by noting that the ubiquitous provision of dancing is not necessarily for a generation of dancing enthusiasts: 'At the majority of our hotels we'll also be having regular tea dances. . . . This will be nothing too strenuous or too complicated . . . beginners to experienced dancers are welcome' (Thomson, p. 6).

The all-embracing communalism of the holiday is also underlined by

218

attempts to minimize social distance between tour operators and customers, and also by using a lot of actuality images of holiday-makers *in situ* in the brochures. A tone of common interest, us against them, is interwoven with that of authoritative paternalism I mentioned earlier. One example of an unusual use of the demotic to display a taken-for-granted common perspective is found in the Wallace Arnold *Autumn and Spring in Europe* brochure: 'We all expect higher and higher quality in everything we buy, whether products or services. Gone are the days of "making do", and this particularly applies to the accommodation we have on holiday' (p. 4). Another neat bit of social positioning comes from Cosmos: 'In days gone by, only the aristocracy could afford to escape the dreary cold of the British winter by wintering abroad. Today, you can follow suit' (p. 5).

The third and final theme characterizing these holiday worlds is a notion of ritualization. By this I mean that there is a reiterative form to the presentation of holidays which acts to frame the sort of occasion it will turn out to be. (In attributing significance to the aspects of ritualization I can detect in these accounts, I have been influenced by Jerrome's 1989a and 1989b analysis of the use of ritual in associations of the elderly as a way of grounding aspects of self-identity that may have been threatened by change.) I do not mean by reiterative form the rather trivial point that there is a standard rhetoric to marketing holidays, but a deeper sense of continuity and reiteration in features of social worlds that are remarked upon in brochures.

One example of what I mean is provided by the theme of repeat bookings. This is obviously something the companies would wish to encourage, as Thomson's FREE bonus trip repeat bookers earn by displaying last year's red guest card (although Lost Cards will not be replaced – in bold). More positively, several brochures direct their readers' attention to hotels which have been reportedly highly appreciated by previous visitors: 'Offering excellent service and a "home from home" atmosphere, many guests return to the hotels listed below, season after season' (Sun World, p. 5). And indeed this possibility is a fundamental premise so that: 'Golden Years is for people like *you* looking for memorable holidays with friendly people in winning winter destinations you will want to revisit again and again' (Airtours, p. 2).

The most striking aspect of ritualization comes, however, in the use of pictorial imagery. Pictures in holiday brochures are an established shorthand for the attractions of different places. Although there are photographs of models here, there are at least as many of 'real' people. In their awkward poses, unattractive clothes and a staginess characteristic of local journalism the people like you are meant to reassure and instruct. Frequently in groups larger than two and never alone, the holiday-makers' peers confront the reader through direct address. The models are slightly more attractive than those I shall call reals, trimmer and younger, but not very markedly so as it would be inconsistent to set up unattainable and off-putting idealizations. The reals are distinguished in their faulty posing by addressing the camera more directly and usually accompanied by some signifier of celebration such as toasting. When not toasting they are usually pointing out some remarkable feature of the environment to each other. The complement to toasting amongst the models is a repetitious touching of each other. Whether it is gripping a shoulder or holding the waist or another's hand there is a most un-English intimacy of address on display. I take this to be a faint and tasteful metaphor for sex for the over-sixties, but more powerfully a reassurance and ritualization of community. Isolation is the 'other' of this discourse.

The most striking feature of the photographs using models is the small corpus of models drawn upon. Not only do the same faces recur in different settings throughout one brochure, but they recur, and one couple in particular, across several brochures. One can think of several practical production reasons why this might be so, the most prominent being an economizing on production costs, but there is still a temptation to see this couple as stars for the snowy-haired. Rather than stress cheapness or idealization it is, however, more interesting to assume that the producers of these brochures will not necessarily want to treat their readers as cultural dopes. It may well be then that the semiotic function of this reiteration is precisely reiteration – difference both between holiday-makers and between places is minimized. It is consistent with this idea that there is never at any point in any brochure the slightest hint that leaving the country might involve meeting people who do not speak English. The foreign-ness of foreign places is inscribed here as a slightly more colourful and warmer version of home.

PART FOUR

It may be felt it is inappropriate to place too much stress on this particular illustrative resource. These representations of holidays are a particular type of marketing, and as such are a rather specialized extension of the package-tour holiday which has underlain the growth of mass international holiday-making amongst the British. There are of course many types of holiday, such as guided tours to the heritage sites of high cultural tradition, which through a combination of timing and cost are obviously aimed at a wealthy leisured élite largely amongst the 'young old'. The images of holidays I have tried to convey are more significant because they involve appropriating a site of conventional leisure, the tourist resort, for consumers that might, as we have noted, feel themselves excluded from a leisure culture. One way of doing this would be to rhetorically address them as though there was no difference, but instead in these images of aging difference is conveyed through a distinctive type of 'mirror' of collective life (Chaney, 1983).

As a tourist attraction it has become increasingly common to market some form of access to a site that carries some signifiers of a culture that has or is felt to be disappearing. This type of interest is often characterized as nostalgic, I think to distinguish its sentimentality from a more rigorous historical concern, and thus this variant of tourism is generally a nostalgia or heritage industry. There are several variants of heritage staging, often, of course, intensely bound up with nationalist rhetoric and the invention of traditions (Hewison, 1987). I do not want to suggest that heritage attractions are more popular with the elderly because they are closer to the period that is being enacted or represented, but rather that the themes of these little theatres parallel or replicate the characteristics of the holidays I have been describing.

I call the sites of heritage attractions little theatres because they require from their visitors, or audiences, a willing suspension of disbelief. In varying degree heritage places offer the possibility of some fragment of authentic experience. Whether it is a stately home or garden that we dutifully file round observing the directions on route and deportment, or a sanctioned historical site. Amongst the latter we can range from the almost real such as Shakespeare's Stratford or Bram Stoker's Whitby; to a purely fictional site such as Catherine Cookson Country on the south banks of the Tyne; or some form of themed experience such as the Jorvik Centre in York; or the representations of some aspects of working-class life from earlier in this century at the Beamish industrial museum in North-East England. In all these places the dramatic fiction seeks to minimize the cultural distance between then (there) and now.

The attractions of these places are not exclusively with older visitors, and neither are they popular just because older visitors prefer somewhere that is self-evidently 'interesting' rather than offering thrills or excitement or some other attraction. It is not, however, difficult to see underlying themes that are consonant with those of the holiday-worlds described. There is very strongly a theme of communalism, that there is some historical bridge between then and now. More generally, the ideology of heritage is to assert cultural continuity, to deny division in favour of difference or contrast. This easily works to reinforce values of security and mutuality in part because heritage sites are framed as exceptional windows within everyday experience. Visitors are rarely threatened by any sense of a rupture in cultural certainties, a reiteration of 'normality' through invented tradition that works through a variety of forms of ceremonialization: such as the route of the tour; the spectacular display of history; and the discourse of heritage in general.

221

In another paper I have taken over Lewis Mumford's notion of subtopia to capture the limited imaginings of an out-of-town shopping centre (Chaney, 1990). This sense of a topos which is less than idealized links the deceits of shopping malls with the securities of holidays for the elderly; and of course we know that older visitors particularly value the ways in which urban heterogeneity has been filtered and sanitized in shopping centres (see, for example, Graham *et al.*, 1991). The shopping centre or mall is a cultural form like holidays, and we can include here other related phenomena such as craft fairs or garden festivals, in which the audience is in important respects also the performing cast. In creating its own dramatic reality, what Urry has called a process: 'of the de-differentiation of leisure, tourism, shopping, culture, education, eating, and so on' (1990: 152), the shopping centre mimics metropolitan life to represent a Utopian alternative that is more realistically a spectacular evasion.

PART FIVE

In explicating the meaning of a particular set of images I have used the notion of citizenship at several points in this paper. I have done so because I believe that the image of being aged that is articulated in these representations of holidays involves a changing sense of civic status. In relation to advertising we can take from Strasser the idea that the cultural form of advertising acts to mediate between personal experience and the anonymity of mega-corporations (1989). In this sense advertising acts as a form of public sphere in which public discourse is endlessly malleable and reframeable (Wernick, 1991). Reading these brochures as advertising they can be seen to conform to this account, but I have been attempting to show that they are also providing a set of instructions on mediating between the individual and their cultural identity (what I have called their idealized self).

I borrowed the phrase capitalist realism in relation to advertising to summarize how advertising images combine naturalism with normative exhortations. In relation to the provision of holidays for the aging, the normative exhortation concerns the invention of tradition – new ceremonies and rituals with which to mark changing status and terms of identity; traditions which are subsequently re-enacted and reinforced through the telling of memories to friends and relatives. We have got used to the idea that the institutions of national society invented traditions with which to create a new language of citizenship. My extension of that idea is that in addition to corporate institutions, such as the legal and education systems, institutionalizations of identity have needed to be reformulated and inscribed in collective practices – some as humble as going on holiday and creating memories.

222

I have chosen to read certain accounts of holidays directed at the aged as images of both the sort of holiday concerned and of the moral career of aging. In conclusion, all I wish to do is summarize the relevance of this account for our understanding of images of social and cultural identities in advertising and other forms of exhortation. Images and representations function in common-sense discourse because they stand for, or function as, ways that can be taken for granted, practical, shorthand accounts of cultural phenomena. The phenomena do not, however, pre-exist the ways they are performed (except as normative expectations – recipes or scripts we could say). The play of performance in each instance is the ways in which a discourse, in this case that of aging, is formulated and enacted. It is only through the thick description of representations that the play of performance is rendered less self-evident.

NOTES

1 This paper is for Chris Rojek.
2 The brochures I am using are:
   Wallace Arnold Bee-Line Coach Holidays 1991–2
   Wallace Arnold Autumn and Spring in Europe 1991–2
   Airtours Golden Years Holidays '91–'92
   Cosmos Golden Times 1992–1993
   Shearings Continental 1991–1992
   Enterprise Leisurely Days 1992–1993
   Thomson Young at Heart Winter Sunshine Holidays 1991–2
   Sunworld Golden Circle Winter Holidays for the over 55s

REFERENCES

Achenbaum, A. (1982) *Images of Old Age in America, 1790 to the Present*, University of Michigan: Institute of Gerontology.

Bruner, E. M. (1991) 'Transformations of self in tourism', *Annals of Tourism Research* vol. 18(2).

Bytheway, W. R. *et al.* (eds) (1989) *Becoming and Being Old: Sociological Approaches to Later Life*, London: Sage.

Chaney, D. (1983) 'A symbolic mirror of ourselves', *Media, Culture and Society* vol. 5(2).

Chaney, D. (1990) 'Subtopia in Gateshead: the Metro Centre as cultural form', *Theory Culture and Society* vol.7(4).

Chaney, D. (1993) *Fictions of Collective Life: Public Drama in Late-modern Culture*, London: Routledge.

Covey, H. C. (1987) *Images of Older People in Western Art and Society*, New York: Praeger.

Dann G. and Cohen, E. (1991) 'Sociology and tourism', *Annals of Tourism Research* vol. 18(1).

Dant, T. (1990) 'Sociology of aging', *Ageing and Society* vol. 10(3).

Deem, R. (1988) *Work, Unemployment and Leisure*, London: Routledge.

Fennell, G. *et al.* (1988) *The Sociology of Old Age*, Milton Keynes: Open University Press.

Frey, J. and Dickens, D. (1990) 'Leisure as a primary institution', *Sociological Review* vol. 60(3).

Giddens, A. (1991) *Modernity and Self-Identity*, Cambridge: Polity Press.

Goffman, E. (1968) 'The moral career of the mental patient', in *Asylums*, London: Penguin.

Goffman, E. (1976) 'Gender advertisements', *Studies in the Anthropology of Visual Communication* vol. 3(2).

Graham, D. F. *et al.* (1991) 'Going to the Mall: a leisure activity of urban elderly people', *Canadian Journal on Aging* vol. 10(4).

Haggard, L. M. and Williams, D. R. (1992) 'Identity affirmation through leisure activities: leisure symbols of the self', *Journal of Leisure Research* vol. 24(1).

Hendricks, J. and Culter, S. J. (1990) 'Leisure and the structure of our life worlds', *Ageing and Society* vol. 10(1).

Hepworth, M. and Featherstone, M. (1982) *Surviving Middle Age* Oxford: Basil Blackwell.

Hewison, R. (1987) *The Heritage Industry*, London: Methuen.

Hobsbawm, E. and Ranger, T. (eds) (1983) *The Invention of Tradition*, Oxford: Basil Blackwell.

Hockey, J. (1989) 'Residential care and the maintenance of social identity', in M. Jefferys (ed.) *Growing Old in the Twentieth Century*, London: Routledge.

Jerrome, D. (1989a) 'Age relations in an English church', *Sociological Review* vol. 37(4).

Jerrome, D. (1989b) 'Virtue and vicissitude: the role of old people's clubs', in M. Jefferys (ed.) *Growing Old in the Twentieth Century*, London: Routledge.

Kaufman, S. R. (1986) *The Ageless Self: Sources of Meaning in Later Life*, Madison: University of Wisconsin Press.

MacCannell, D. (1976) *The Tourist*, London: Macmillan.

Roche, M. (1989) 'Lived time, leisure and retirement', in T. Winnifrith and C. Barrett (eds) *The Philosophy of Leisure*, London: Macmillan.

Roche, M. (1990) 'Time and unemployment', *Human Studies* vol. 13(1).

Rojek, C. (1993) *Ways of Escape*, London: Macmillan.

Romsa, G. and Blenman, M. (1989) 'Vacation patterns of the elderly German', *Annals of Tourism Research* vol. 16(1).

Schudson, M. (1984) *Advertising, The Uneasy Persuasion*, New York: Basic Books.

Sparks, R. (1992) *Television and the Drama of Crime: Moral Tales and the Place of Crime in Public Life*, Milton Keynes: Open University Press.

Strasser, S. (1989) *Satisfaction Guaranteed: The Making of the American Mass Market*, New York: Pantheon Books.

Urry, J. (1990) *The Tourist Gaze*, London: Sage.

Wernick, A. (1991) *Promotional Culture*, London: Sage.

Part V

THE BODY, AGING AND TECHNOLOGY

14

POST-BODIES, AGING AND VIRTUAL REALITY

Mike Featherstone

Print and radio tell; stage and film show; cyberspace embodies.
(Howard Rheingold, 1992: 192)

Essentially from a virtual reality perspective, the definition of the body is that part which you can move as fast as you can think.
(Jaron Lanier, quoted in Lanier and Biocca, 1992: 162)

When sense ratios change, men change.
(Marshall McLuhan [after Blake], 1962: 265)

INTRODUCTION

When we examine popular cultural representations of old age in contemporary western societies we tend to find two sets of images. In the first place there are the 'heroes of aging', those who adopt a positive attitude towards the aging process and seem to remain 'forever youthful' in their work habits, bodily posture, facial expressions and general demeanour. The second refers to those individuals who experience severe bodily decline through disabling illness to the extent that the outer body is seen as misrepresenting and imprisoning the inner self, something we have referred to as 'the mask of aging' (Featherstone and Hepworth, 1991a; 1995, forthcoming).

It can be argued that within consumer culture the first category is dominant and we are provided with a constant series of heroic images of active old people, many of them stars and celebrities. The second category provides glimpses of the hidden and more disagreeable aspects of the aging process, the voyeuristic fascination with the decrepit elderly represented as abominations of human nature. Such representations challenge our existing modes of classification and capacity to empathize with those whose bodies have so clearly betrayed them. These images of the elderly as subhuman or para-human beings comprise a suppressed minor strand within consumer culture; they form part of the repertoire of the pornography of old age.

But what of the future? Is this opposition fixed, or can it be transcended? What is the potential for progressive technological solutions to these problems? With regard to the first category, consumer culture already promotes solutions which draw upon medical and technical expertise in featuring active youthful elderly men and women engaged in diet, health fitness regimes, or undergoing cosmetic surgery and other longevity-inducing techniques and therapies (see Hepworth and Featherstone, 1982; Featherstone and Hepworth, 1982; Featherstone, 1991a, 1991b). These can be regarded as a continuation of the long-established tradition of interest in rejuvenation and longevity which has more recently managed to divest itself of many of the religious prohibitions (against vanity, hedonism, self-expression, self-love etc.) which denigrated the body in favour of the cultivation of the spirit (Gruman, 1966). From this perspective the malfunctioning body can be repaired and the ravages which time has wrought eliminated, or held at bay. Both the surface of the body and face (the outer body) can be refurbished, and its capacity to function smoothly in order to provide an enabling, and preferably effortless and painless, platform from which to engage in life's full range of activities (the inner body), repaired or enhanced. The various regimes and techniques of body maintenance coupled with increasingly sophisticated medical technology offer the prospect, for those who possess the necessary financial resources, of holding at bay the mask of aging and turning old age into an extended active phase of 'midlifestyle' (Featherstone and Hepworth, 1991b).

For those, however, who suffer disabling or degenerative illnesses in old age, for whom the body cannot be repaired, the metaphor of the mask of aging, or that of the body as a prison, can be more readily applied. One possible strategy here is to seek to escape the pain and discomfort of a body which no longer functions as an adequate base for interpersonal communication and self-expression, through leaving the body to venture into other worlds. Here we can think of the world of fantasy and day-dreams.[1] Yet for many people this does not represent a viable means of escape from the here-and-now embodiment of the everyday world. The degree of realism and capacity to suspend doubt, or the 'believability' of the experience may be relatively low.

A further possibility is vicarious escape through watching situations, interactions, people, places and dramas on television, film or videotape. Here it is possible to move over into the 'epoch' of this other world and suspend doubt. The drawback with this medium is that it relies solely on two of the human senses: seeing and hearing. It is also a non-interactive medium: one can switch on or off, fast-forward or rewind. There are, however, signs that this situation could be about to change through the development of new information technology. Strong claims are currently being made that virtual reality can offer highly realistic out-of-body experiences and the impression that one is able to move and interact with other beings in a parallel universe, with the potential to utilize the full range of human senses. This could be regarded as the actualization of Aldous Huxley's description of 'All-Super, Singing, Synthetic, Talking, Coloured, Stereoscopic Feely' in *Brave New World*. Yet for its advocates virtual reality promises much more. At a time of *fin-de-millennium* pessimism and the loss of the potency of visions of Utopian transcendence and hope in a better future (either religious-inspired, or the secular versions generated within modernity), virtual reality is seized on by some as something new and exciting which will open up new dimensions of human, or post-human existence.

Yet in all the dazzling descriptions of virtual reality that I have read there is no mention made of the elderly. This is strange, for it is well known that the elderly contains a high proportion of the disabled, as well as those who are dissatisfied with their physical appearance and have low self-esteem. Research on virtual reality clearly has some very important implications for our notions of embodiment, the structure and ordering of social encounters and out-of-body experiences. It therefore could well have significant implications for the creation of a new set of images of what it is to be old.

THE MODE OF INFORMATION AND DISEMBODIMENT

One of the developments frequently associated with the rise of modernity is a growth of abstract systems of knowledge which facilitate the compression of time-space and the integration of bigger populations and larger territorial units. In contrast to the dominance of face-to-face relationships amongst kin and locals within a bounded known world, it is generally assumed that modernity entails a proliferation of impersonal, secondary relationships as populations become integrated into larger units such as cities and nation-states. Such secondary relationships do, of course, involve face-to-face contact; but it can be argued that such contact between people whose knowledge of each other is limited and restricted to a segment of their everyday dealings and whose emotional investment in the relationship is similarly circumscribed, places a different emphasis upon the place and importance of the body.

On one level it can be suggested that the fact that many everyday encounters take place within a world of strangers in which fore-knowledge of others is necessarily partial and limited, means that a good deal of attention has to be given over to the problem of reading the other's appearance, demeanour and gestures for clues of actual status and intentions. In the nineteenth century advice books addressed the question of how to decipher the signs of potentially dangerous people and confidence tricksters in public situations, as well as how to comport oneself should an actual encounter become unavoidable. Parallel to this we also have the development of popular interest in physiognomy, in reading facial features, body shape and other surface features as indications of the character of the person (see Finkelstein, 1991).

In addition to this problem of reading appearance which became thematized and pronounced within the modern metropoles of the nineteenth century, we should also consider a further aspect of modern societies which runs in the opposite direction. This is the increasing capacity for interpersonal communication to become mediated by abstract systems. Indeed, for some, following in the footsteps of Weber's theory of rationalization, we live in an 'abstract society' (Zijderveld, 1971). One of the implications of the development of abstract symbol systems (for example, money) and the application of instrumental rational knowledge by the state and industrial organizations, has been the growth of forms of interaction which bypass direct face-to-face communication. It has become increasingly possible for money and other forms of data to flow to various parts of the world through the use of electronic media. Electronically mediated communication can be used to transmit a variety of different types of information, ranging from: highly-coded relatively unambiguous data (such as flows of money and financial market indices), to written or printed texts (requiring different degrees of interpretation in order to clarify context), to speech (apparently less ambiguous), to visual models (which can take the form of short-hand representations of complex symbolic information, such as models and maps), and photographic representations of human beings and their surrounding world (such representations in the form of photographs, film or television which are taken to provide a high degree of immediacy, an 'illusion of presence' and indexicality (see Falk, 1993)).

How does this relate to our discussion of the disempowerment which follows from a reduction of the symbolic capital of the body with the onset of old age, especially the visibility of the ravages which time has worked on the appearance of the body and face? In the first place it could be argued that by separating the speaking, or message-sending body from the listening, or message-receiving body in time and space and using electronic transfers of written information, the elderly person could benefit from the lack of co-presence and invisibility of his or her body. While some may be quick to condemn such abstract exchanges as depersonalizing, it can be argued that it enables the avoidance of being identified as an elderly person. In addition it provides a degree of control over the flow of the interchange in the response time and form taken to make a reply, something which can conceal impaired direct embodied communicative capacity (for example, cueing, response time, mishearing etc.). In effect in addressing a fax, letter, or electronic mail transfer into one's personal computer, the oft-cited usual range of stigmatizing social inequalities (gender, ethnicity, age, class etc.) while by no means eliminated, are not as immediately obvious as in the case of direct face-to-face encounters.

To take the example of the telephone. This is a medium which relies totally on the speaking/listening sensory dimension. The interaction takes place in simultaneous time between parties who are separated by spatial distance. Initially interactions were restricted to two parties, but increasingly technological developments have enabled the participation of a number of users in tele-conferencing. An associated example which has developed in recent years is computer bulletin board systems. Here a number of computers are linked together into a network using modems and telephone lines. Network members can leave written messages and engage in an electronic mail interchange (similar to an exchange of letters), or enact a quasi-conversation by using the computer simultaneously to reply immediately on receipt of each message. Alternatively users may post a message on a bulletin board open to any user of the network.

One interesting development in the usage of both the telephone and computer bulletin boards (BBSs) has been new forms of sexual encounters – dubbed as 'telesex', and 'cybersex', respectively (see King, 1992; Wiley, forthcoming). Telephone companies since the 1920s have used pre-recorded message services which users can dial (for example, the weather forecast). With deregulation in the 1980s 'dial-a-porn' services were set up within the United States and by the end of the 1980s over 40 per cent of all the 'dial-it' lines were telesex services (King, 1992: 3). There are three basic formats: direct recorded messages, live-talk encounters and bulletin board or party line services. The first two formats encourage sexual fantasies in which the disembodied female voice employs a range of characters, narratives and sounds to stimulate male masturbation. Needless to say the women (and men) who work in this industry are low paid and bear little physical relation to the fantasy characters they portray. One 'fantasy girl', Angelina, a grandmother in real life, comments:

> 'When they ask me what I look like, I tell them I'm five-four, 37c tits, 24 waist, 35 hips, and I have straight blond hair down to my ass,' she continues 'I'm actually not like that at all, I'm totally out of shape and have three kids'.
>
> (quoted in King, 1992: 10)

With regard to computer networks, a Californian one developed its own cybersex world, with members adopting anonymous call-signs (cf. CB handles) and detailing their preferences and availability. Then they can enter the 'nonplace' by booking a room in 'Hotel California' to engage in a range of rapid-keystroke heterosexual, bisexual, lesbian or gay sexual encounters with one or more partners. Paradoxically for some the disembodied sexual encounter is regarded as more real and meaningful and intimate than embodied sexuality. As one participant 'K.J. Jeep' remarked:

> I have found romance and an invitation to open myself to experiences of both love and life that some will never find. . . . given the opportunity to be jestful, serious, or just stone cold nuts. Through the intensity of such a communications system I have gotten to know the essence of people. . . . the people here for the most part remain faceless. There is no other choice than to leave the walls behind that people use for protection in a face-to-face, live social situation.
>
> (cited in Wiley, 1995: 158)

This sense that a deeper, better form of friendship and intimacy can be developed through the network is echoed by a further participant, 'JR':

> BBSing is the perfect tool for getting to know someone from the inside out. Such extraneous crap as looks, status, and money do not get in the way on-line – the only thing the person on the other end has to go by is what you type.
>
> (cited in Wiley, 1995: 159–60)

Yet while some may revel in the freedom emanating from loss of the face-to-face embodied encounters and the capacity to escape from the host of judgements about a person's habitus, status, capital and empowerment, there is always the danger of disclosure, or meeting the 'real' embodied person behind the text or voice. Stone (1992: 82ff) recounts the case of Julie, a totally disabled older woman, who could only push the keys of her computer with a headstick. She established close contact with a number of other women on the 'net', and offered them advice about their deepest troubles. After a number of years it was revealed that 'Julie' did not exist: in fact, she was a middle-aged male psychiatrist, who claims to have been mistaken for another woman the first time he logged in, and because he liked the intimacy, vulnerability, and depth he found in conversations between women, he decided to continue with the deception by elaborating the persona of a totally disabled single, older woman. The deception worked for years, until one of Julie's admirers determined to meet her, finally tracked her down. When the news hit the network some women were outraged. One said 'I felt raped. I felt that my deepest secrets had been violated' (Stone, 1992: 83). Julie was an early case of 'computer cross-dressing' which gives an indication of the new range of modes of interaction and identity explorations which are becoming possible through computer networks.

In summary, we can make a number of points. First, the capacity to develop new technology to facilitate modes of information exchange which enable communication to take place over distance, is increasing. Such modes as the telephone and Bulletin Board System (BBS) computer networks facilitate simultaneous interchanges based upon the voice and text which are disembodied modes of interaction. Second, disembodiment need not be regarded as a drawback, for some it is grasped as a benefit, as it facilitates anonymous interactions with strange others whom one has not met, or whom one would not seek to meet. Third, this facilitates the development of shared 'nonplace' worlds whereby simulated environments can be created in order to provide spaces for disembodied interactions which facilitate the expression of a range of playful or fantasy-based interactions. Fourth, rather than abstract technological modes of interchange being regarded as 'de-humanizing' in a negative sense through the loss of visibility, tactility and the alleged warmth of 'full-blooded' face-to-face encounters, they may open up new possibilities for intimacy and self-expression. Indeed for some, telesex or cybersex, and 'sex without a body', or 'hyperreal sex', are perceived as offering greater possibilities of fulfilment.[2] Fifth, this may lead to a series of experiences which are vivid, yet fragmented in the sense that they do not involve the whole body or self, in which the boundaries between reality and fantasy, body and technology, the organic and cybernetic, closeness and distance, intimacy and anonymity, primary and secondary relationships, become destabilized. Sixth, while the majority of people interested in disembodied interactions by telephone or computer network are the young, such interactions would seem to be ideally suited to the needs of the elderly faced with restricted mobility, impaired communicative competence and other 'bodily betrayals'. We will now turn to an examination of virtual reality with its potential to extend these developments into new dimensions.

VIRTUAL REALITY

Virtual reality represents the harnessing of computer and information technology to realize a long-held vision of humankind: the creation of a 'dream machine'.[3] It has often been stated that going to the cinema to watch a film involves entering a 'dream palace', in which we are encouraged to suspend disbelief and make the leap into an illusionary world. It can be argued that the history of the cinema is one in which the illusion of total immersion has been progressively sought. Cinerama and other forms of large screen or wrap-around cinema such as Imax, or the experiments with 3-D films in the 1950s, are examples of this search for technological developments which would provide a strong stereoscopic illusion of the depth of a scene and sense of immersion in 'reality'. Theme parks such as Disney World and Universal Studios also provide sophisticated versions of this film technology coupled with 'experience rides', such as *Star Wars, Body Invaders, Back to the Future*, in which the visual information is co-ordinated with surround sound and movement of the vehicle (rocking, tilting, juddering) (see Fjellman, 1992 for descriptions).

Virtual reality seeks to achieve a similar level of immersion and stereoscopic illusion of presence by sitting the operator in front of a wall screen, or wrap-around room screen, or by using head-mounted displays (HMDs) in which the operator has two tiny (spectacles-sized) television screens placed in front of his eyes which interleave left eye views with right eye views at a specific rate in order to simulate three-dimensional stereoscopic vision. Yet virtual reality is more than an upgraded version of cinerama or a theme park ride, as it achieves not only a greater sense of presence, but through the use of computer technology has developed an interface which facilitates 'interactivity', the capacity to direct one's gaze and movements so that one can explore and move around *inside* the illusory flow of images. It is this linkage between computer technology and movie-making which makes virtual reality possible.

The history of computer technology since the 1940s has been one in which the barriers between the computer and the user have pro-gressively been removed: in short computers have been increasingly made user-friendly through increasing the attention given to the human interface. As Rheingold (1992: 70) puts it, 'A virtual world is a computer that you operate with natural gestures, not by composing computer programs, but by walking around, looking around and using your hands'. In effect the keyboard, or the mouse directed at point and click icons ceases to be the interface with the computer; rather the computer is designed to respond to our body movements such as movements of the head, pointing, walking, speaking. Yet a crucial factor is that these actual bodily movements and signals appear to the operator to be taking place within a simulated world, the virtual world in which the operator seems to be 'in the movie'. While early virtual reality programmes possess a relatively low level of graphic resolution and definition, using wire-drawing or simplified cartoon-like objects, it is suggested that the capacity to produce 'realistic' filmic quality images and a sense of vividness and immersion will increase dramatically over the next decade.

Virtual reality, therefore is a system which provides a sense of being in an environment. This sense of presence which is achieved by means of a communications medium, has been referred to as *telepresence* to draw attention to the mediated perception of an environment. Telepresence depends upon two main dimensions: vividness and interactivity (Steuer, 1992). *Vividness* refers to the richness of the environment presented to the senses, which depends upon both the number of senses mobilized and their degree of resolution or 'believability'. Most traditional media rely on one or two senses only and lack the breadth and integration of sensory information which would produce a strong feeling of telepresence.[4] *Interactivity* refers to the extent to which operators can modify both the form and content of a mediated environment in real time. Virtual reality scores highly on both the speed, or response time, at which interactions can be achieved, as well as the range and the number of attributes which can be changed in a given environment.

From the technical point of view the sense of telepresence and degree of vividness and interactivity depends upon the sophistication of the array of *input* and *output* devices which are linked to the user's body (Biocca, 1992). Output devices which provide information to the user linked to the various senses include: head-mounted displays (visual); aural displays (three-dimensional spatial sound, such as hearing footsteps coming towards one and then receding away); tactile output through haptic displays which use electrotactile and vibrotactile devices (for example, to achieve the feel that one has a violin in one's hands and can experience the vibrations of bowing as it is played, or the sticky, viscous feeling of putting one's hands in treacle); proprioceptive devices, the feeling of force-feedback, that the world is capable of pushing back against you, that one has hit a hard surface which has resistance (exoskeletons, flight simulators and motion platforms are, for example, used in military and space research to simulate the experience of pressure, motion and force differentials of various environments such as the ocean depths or outer space); olfactory and oral displays – as these depend upon chemicals, little work has been done to date on simulating them in computer displays.

Input devices are necessary in order to feed back information to the computer which act as commands to change the constitution and structure of the virtual world, which are operated not through a keyboard, but through the development of systems which can read the user's own natural body movements, gestures and vocal commands. There is also the need to accurately represent the user's own body and range of motorskills, facial expressions and gestures in virtual space so that the full range of information normally conveyed through face-to-face interactions becomes practically recognizable and effectively understandable on the part of other simulated persons in virtual worlds. To facilitate this a number of complex tracking devices are necessary to, for example, monitor the position and direction of our gaze in order to recompute and reconfigure the virtual world in line with each new direction of vision (or hearing) in order to sustain the illusion of a complete world which appears to change dimensions with each turn of our bodies, or step forward. Exoskeletons and data gloves can be used which feed back digitalized information to the computer of the smallest movement of a limb, joint, or the flexing of a finger. In effect through the latter it is possible for a simulated finger which is constructed to be co-ordinated with, and have the feel of our real finger, to push a simulated button, or key on a virtual keyboard, in the virtual world which will bring into play operative systems in the virtual reality or everyday life. The developmental logic of the technology points towards the construction of full data suits which will feed back even the smallest body movement to the computer. Speech recognition systems are also being developed which recognize a range of verbal commands which are inputs to the computer, and also facilitate the development of full body simulations of human beings which are capable of talking to other simulated human beings in virtual environments.

In addition, a further important line of input device research is concerned with developing a realistic simulation of face-to-face communication, and therefore is focusing on the need to construct an accurate representation of a user's body and face, which is capable of conveying the normal range of information through facial gestures to facilitate interaction with simulations of other bodies in virtual space. Here a trade-off between input and output devices needs to be reached, for if the weighting is given to output devices, then the head-mounted display which conveys realistic impressions of the virtual world to the user should be given priority; whereas if input is prioritized then the visibility of the user's face for the filming and transmitting of facial expressions to produce a simulated three-dimensional model of the user for others to interact with inside the virtual space, becomes the key factor.

This excursus on the technological potential of virtual reality research input devices to convey the full range of embodied sensory information in simulated human encounters, as well as the potential of output devices to enable the user to receive the signals from other human beings, or when both are combined to experience, or construct a wide range of vivid alternative environments, is necessary if we are to understand the relationship between the body and virtual reality and potential implications for the aging body and future images of old age. A number of points can be made.

First, as Jaron Lanier has pointed out, in virtual reality it becomes difficult to define where the boundary of the body is (Lanier and Biocca, 1992: 162; see also Stone, 1992: 99ff). The body can effectively move as fast as the user can think, it can fly, walk, maintain a form near that of our normal body, or become something completely different such as another human being or animal, the body can merge with other bodies and exchange sense data in intimate situations instead of bodily fluids.

Even in the case of severe disability of the real body, it is possible for the user's virtual body to engage in mobility and sensory exploration. All it needs is for some limited sensory input into the computer, which can be taught to read a limited repertoire of bodily movements which can operate switches, conventions, keyboards in the virtual space, as well as enabling a range of movements and interactional possibilities for the virtual body. For example, cerebral palsied patients could use tongue-steered virtual reality. For those who suffer from near total paralysis of the body, technically it is possible for a camera to read small lip movements, or even eye movements, or tilts of the head, which once a set of conventions have been agreed can be digitally inputted into the computer via a camera to produce mobility and operative capacity for the user within a virtual world. There is also the capacity to artificially augment or extend the senses and develop cross-syntheses of the senses to help, for example, the deaf and the blind. In addition there is the potential for enhanced opportunities for those with physical and learning disabilities in 'virtual classrooms', or 'virtual rehabilitation centres' in which users operate specialist systems which use the poten-tial for freedom, movement and absorption of attention span, as well as the technical capacity for rapid input and output integration, of virtual worlds to design new learning techniques. There would seem to be a good deal of potential here to develop systems to deal with a wide range of disabilities, which of course are disproportionately concentrated in the elderly, such as strokes.[5]

With regard to disability it is important to emphasize that virtual reality's sole function need not be to provide a sense of escape from the 'body as prison', to generate an experience of freedom and mobility in sensorily exciting worlds, such as simulated mountain climbing. Rather it can have a much more prosaic function in its capacity to externalize and mobilize surrogate devices to carry out the full range of tasks which a fully operative normal body does in everyday life, through the manipulation of operative systems and recording of bodily movements which occur in the virtual world. In effect, virtual reality can be used as a command system with which to control the everyday environment. The user possesses a series of technological devices which act as a surrogate externalized functioning body, which he/she manipulates through operating a simulation of a free-moving body in virtual space through a very restricted and limited repertoire of sensory/bodily movements inputted from the disabled body. This would mean that for disabled people to operate their everyday environments, or escape into alternative worlds, they would have to spend a good part of their everyday lives in virtual reality. Indeed some commentators envisage the virtual reality user as akin to a scuba diver, who surfaces into the real world from time to time to refuel (to ingest and expel necessary bodily fluids) and then re-enters the virtual medium.

A second range of possibilities for the body relate to interaction with other human beings in virtual worlds. We have already mentioned virtual reality conferences in which an accurate three-dimensional simulation of the interactants' bodies relate to each other in a virtual room. Here one would expect that a series of conventions on body formatting, modes of presentation and respect of body space (whether flying around the room is permissible) would emerge in order for the interaction to proceed smoothly and cost-efficiently. Yet while there are strategic imperatives for business and organizational modes of communication, this need not be the case with other leisure virtual reality interactions. For example, one would assume that the businessman would seek some guarantee, equivalent to a fingerprint or DNA-print, that the virtual body of the person he interacts with is bona fide. At the same time there may well be all sorts of pressures to steal a march by upgrading or enhancing the beauty and expressive capacity of the virtual face and body (cf. here Steven Spielberg's use of a simulation of Albert Einstein's eyes for the gnomic sage Yoda in *The Empire Strikes Back*, to connote sensitivity, wisdom and intelligence). Likewise there might also be pressures to retain last year's simulation – or even one from the last decade. The pressures for such conventions and how they would be monitored and a body of law developed (does a deal conducted with an alternative body in virtual reality carry the legality as that between real persons?) and enforcement agencies instructed to deal with offenders, is an interesting subject for speculation.

With regard to leisure interactions, there exists a whole range of potential games involving different modes of interaction and the merging of bodies. One form which has attracted a good deal of interest is 'teledildonics' – dubbed 'sex with computers' by some sectors of the media (see Rheingold, 1992). This offers the potential for a massive upgrade of the Bulletin Boards System 'telesex' we discussed above. Yet like BBS sex, there may be equal latitude to play out a range of fantasy personas, with the additional potential to take on and 'inhabit' a range of different bodies for sexual encounters. Within the confines of the virtual world everyone can potentially look as, youthful, fit and beautiful as everyone else, provided they purchase or design the necessary simulation. It could be possible to wear a Sharon Stone body and have virtual sex with some anonymous other wearing a Richard Gere body. As in the BBS case of Julie discussed above, there would be potential latitude for 'computer cross-dressing', for men to wear women's bodies and vice versa. Here one might assume that users would enter the game deliberately suspending disbelief in appearances, and therefore insulated from the kind of sense of outrage over deception which occurred in the case of Julie. Yet this is by no means certain, and it is difficult to rule out the developments of emotional attachments and new forms of intimacy, which were some of the surprising developments from the BBS networks. For those who have bodies which do not match up to the cultural ideals, or are disabled or old, entering into a virtual reality 'teledildonic' network may offer a new range of opportunity structures, forms of intimacy and emotional attachments. Whether or not as Rheingold (1992: 352) remarks 'the physical comingling of genital sensations will come to be regarded as a less intimate act than sharing the data structures of your innermost self-representations', remains to be seen. There would therefore seem to be potential for greater tolerance of the possibilities of inhabiting, co-habiting (dwelling inside another's body), and merging (being co-wired in series with another's body in which senses are coupled together and a single body exists in the virtual world).

There is an argument, often associated with postmodernism, that we are currently about to enter a post-literate era as we move from a print culture whose dominant form was reading, into an image culture where information is conveyed through visual images such as film, television and video (Meyrowitz, 1985; Featherstone, 1991a). Virtual reality (VR) commentators take this a step further by suggesting that the VR medium is ideally suited for new forms of interpersonal communication which are more graphic and mimetic than spoken or written language, and potentially more economical. Jaron Lanier, for example, refers to this future computer-augmented metalanguage as 'post-symbolic communication', and argues that we will soon be able to communicate by exchanging images, sounds and dynamic models. In effect we will not write, but send a simulation, a miniature reality or virtual world, which the receiver will be able to enter, explore and understand.[6]

It is this potential for a range of new out-of-body experiences and the development of post-symbolic communication which has captured the imagination of a new generation of technophiliacs. The new cyberpunk literature has already been fed back into virtual reality design and theory: fiction and research are interacting and chasing each other in what some would see as a typically postmodern fashion. There is not the space here to refer to the growing literature on cyberspace which has been largely prompted by William Gibson's (1984) novel *Neuromancer* save to mention that Gibson depicts the corporate power struggles within a vast network of computer information which he calls the matrix. This 'cyberspace' is a vast three-dimensional system of data through which people can 'fly', or zoom in and out of, at almost instantaneous speed. Gibson's fiction gives us a world which has a massive range of para-bodies, meta-bodies and post-bodied forms: bodies are wired to computers, artificial intelligences assume human form, and those who move around at street level can purchase prosthetic aids to upgrade the human body and its sensorium.

CYBORGS, EXPERIENCE AND MEMORY

The fictional accounts of cyberspace provide a dystopian corrective to some of the more Utopian excesses of the advocates of virtual reality. With regard to the position of the elderly does this merely mean that we have come back to square one, to a world in which the possibilities of leaving behind a decrepit and betraying body as prison for the freedom of virtual reality is really a sham because new forms of power relationships and interdependencies will necessarily emerge? Will the contingencies of power games in the virtual world continue to reward those who have 'an edge', and penalize those whose bodies or post-bodied sensorium are deficient? Of course, the elderly will have increased possibilities of disguise, of adopting off-the-peg virtual bodies, or having their own body surfaces reinscribed and inner functions restructured and upgraded. Yet, it can be argued, the practical imperatives of recognition, of needing to make a judgement about the other, as to whether he/she/it is potentially dangerous, friendly or indifferent, is something all living entities need to do, whether in material everyday life or in a virtual world. The elderly will only be able to participate fully in the new virtual world, to the extent to which they possess the power resources to be able to purchase the technological upgrades necessary to achieve and maintain a competitive edge.

The alternative is to write off participation in the new emerging public world of the matrix, with all its dangers and excitement in favour of the potentially more controllable private world of leisure and fantasy. Here one could experience exhilarating directed-dreaming in which one summons up a world. It would even be technically possible to create beings with which one could interact in that world, who were granted a degree of autonomy. Or alternatively one may wish to preserve in that world simulations of one's friends, relatives or partners. Hence it may be possible for the elderly to relive and re-experience precious moments with simulations of former partners, and enjoy intimacy and shared sensory encounters – what the popular media would perhaps dub 'sex with dead people'. Where genuine interaction with others is concerned and the space becomes more public (or quasi- or para-public), the problems of risk and empowerment will emerge. For example, Jaron Lanier's discussion of the potential capacity to show our emotions by bodily transfiguration – turning into a red lobster when one wishes to express anger – may work, or be retained within certain contexts. Yet as in all types of communication it is to be expected that forms and conventions will emerge which provide the equivalents of everyday face-to-face cueing devices, turn-taking in conversations, body language etc. which are driven by the economizing imperative of being understood which, while operating most strongly in purposive work contexts, cannot be divorced entirely from apparently freer and more meandering, playful forms of sociability (cf. Simmel).

Yet it can be argued that the appeal of disembodied forms of experience, which are coupled into real risks and power games, may also appeal to the elderly. In *Neuromancer* we are given a sense that cyberspace is a place of rapture and erotic intensity (Heim, 1992). The loss of the capacity to re-enter this world, to remain confined in the 'body as prison', is a daunting threat for those who live for the exhilaration of cyberspace. This occurs in the book when the central character Case has his immune and nervous system tampered with and slowed down as a punishment for double-crossing a former employer:

> For Case, who'd lived for the bodiless exultation of cyberspace, it was the Fall. In the bars he'd frequented as a cowboy hotshot, the elite stance involved a certain relaxed contempt for the flesh. The body was meat. Case fell into the prison of his own flesh.
>
> (Gibson, 1984: 6)

What is the status of this experience and how do we evaluate it? For those who would view it from the perpective of a nostalgia for the real, the cyberspace experience would fall into the sector of intense, tactile, fragmented experiences which provide a series of shocks: the machine pleasures of speed, vertigo and immersion; something to contrast with 'genuine' experiences arrived at and articulated in collective situations, which reinforce the social bond and generate a sense of the sacred. Such experiences are held to feed the collective memory and generate lasting emotionally meaningful relations between people, which can be relived through rituals.

On the one side we can place Donna Haraway who argues for the liberatory potential of the new technology to alter the bodily infra-structure of human beings. Haraway celebrates the cyborg as a sign of hope for women to escape from the conceptual dualisms of culture/

nature and mind/body which help confine women to a rigid view of their gendered nature, and instead explore the ways to reinvent and reconfigure a host of new post-gendered possibilities. Hence her oft-quoted remark: 'I'd rather be a cyborg than a goddess' (Haraway, 1991). We could equally argue here that what Haraway has done for feminism in terms of reconceptualizing the relationship between women, techno-logy and the body, one could equally do for old age, through thinking through, in an equally radical manner, the potential for change.

On the other side we have figures such as Heidegger, whose opposi-tion to technology is well known and influential. For Heidegger (1978) such experiences as those we have described in virtual reality would be the opposite of 'dwelling': being able to build a meaningful relationship to the world. Walter Benjamin could be placed on either side, for at different places in his writings he actively supports the potential of the shocks and fragmentation of the new technologically-induced ex-periences, yet in other places he seeks to bemoan the shallowness of such truncated experiences (*Erlebnis*) and argue for the importance of experiences which have been grounded and sedimented into collective memory (*Erfahrung*) which provide continuity (see Benjamin, 1973). One could continue this argument, as many have done before and make a strong plea for the importance of a sense of place, tradition and continuity for the elderly, whose position in the life course necessarily means they will look backwards and need to have their past experiences validated to retain a sense of self-worth. But this argument holds if the elderly can only look back to remember the past and are not granted a future. The speculative technological developments we have spoken of certainly contain a range of possible future modes of bodied and disembodied experiences and empowerment for various groups of the elderly. Given this it is difficult to see why such experiences could not generate new forms of sociation, rituals, the sacred and liminoid repertoires (see Tomas, 1992; Heim, 1992). If this is the case, then virtual reality could not just be regarded as another distraction of the young, but as containing possibilities of extended hope and develop-ment, with all their associated excitement, risk and dangers.

NOTES

I would like to thank Roger Burrows, Mike Hepworth, Britt Robillard, Kevin Robins, Chris Rojek, Michael Schapiro, Ralph Schroeder, John Tulloch and Andy Wernick for numerous suggestions which were helpful in writing and revising this paper. Earlier versions of this paper were presented at the Second Images of Aging Conference, University of Geneva, Sierre, Switzerland, July 1993, the Department of Comparative Literature at the University of Hong Kong in November 1993, and The Center for the Body, Deakin University in February 1994.

242

1   See Schutz (1962) on the worlds of fantasy and day-dreams as separate 'finite provinces of meaning' which require a different natural attitude to that found in the paramount reality of everyday life. He also refers to the world of dreams (see also Halton, 1992). There is a considerable literature, much of it fictional, on the subject of dream-travel, in which trained subjects can consciously guide their movements around the world while in a dream-sleep. For fictional accounts see the Lobsang-Rampa autobiographical novels on Tibetan monks trained for adastral travel and Dennis Wheatley's novel *The Ka of Griffith Hillary*.

2   The term 'hyperreality' was developed by Baudrillard (1993) in his discussion of simulations (see also the discussions and use of the term by Rojek, 1993 and Gane, 1991).

3   The term 'virtual reality' was coined by Jaron Lanier (see Lanier and Biocca, 1992). For some who are strong on logical definitions the term, along with the related term 'artificial reality', has to be rejected because it is a contradiction in terms. For others the term 'cyberspace' is preferable, although there is a case for giving this term a more restricted meaning in terms of the vast three-dimensional graphic representation of data constellations, which William Gibson named 'the matrix', and which is featured in his cyberpunk novels. Gibson's work will be discussed in detail below.

4   Fictional accounts such as Huxley's description of the 'feelies', in *Brave New World*, or Ray Bradbury's description of a 'sentient room' in his short story 'The Veldt', and a fantasy machine in 'The Happiness Machine', provide depictions of the breadth, integration and resolution of sensory involvement in simulated environments.

5   The film *The Lawnmower Man* (director Brett Leonard, 1993), described as 'The UK's first virtual reality film', focuses on the way in which Joe Smith, 'a simple gardener', who is an educationally subnormal young man, is introduced to virtual reality learning systems and rapidly 'increases his brain power by 400%' with dramatic and spectacular consequences.

6   One potential implication here is the capacity to simulate environments in every country in the world, or indeed from past ages, which the virtual reality user can enter and explore. If such a system was perfected this would, it has been argued, mean the end of tourism and travel. For a humorous account of this future situation in the twenty-first century see Penley (1992).

REFERENCES

Baudrillard, Jean (1993) *Symbolic Exchange and Death*, London: Sage.

Benjamin, Walter (1973) *Charles Baudelaire*, London: New Left Books.

Biocca, Frank (1992) 'Virtual reality technology: a tutorial', *Journal of Communication* 42(4).

Falk, Pasi (1993) 'The representation of presence: outlining an anti-aesthetics of pornography', *Theory, Culture & Society* 10 (2).

Featherstone, Mike (1991a) *Consumer Culture and Postmodernism*, London: Sage.

Featherstone, Mike (1991b) 'The body in consumer culture', in M. Featherstone, M. Hepworth and Bryan S. Turner (eds) *The Body*, London: Sage.

Featherstone, Mike and Hepworth, Mike (1982) 'Ageing and inequality: consumer culture and the new middle age', in D. Robbins *et al.* (eds) *Rethinking Inequality*, Aldershot: Gower Press.

Featherstone, Mike and Hepworth, Mike (1991a) 'The mask of ageing', in M.

Featherstone, M. Hepworth and Bryan S. Turner (eds) *The Body*, London: Sage.

Featherstone, Mike and Hepworth, Mike (1991b) 'The midlifestyle of George and Lynne', in M. Featherstone, M. Hepworth and Bryan S. Turner (eds) *The Body*, London: Sage.

Featherstone, Mike and Hepworth, Mike (forthcoming) *The Mask of Ageing*, London: Sage (1995).

Finkelstein, Joanne (1991) *The Fashioned Self*, Oxford: Polity Press.

Fjellman, Steven (1992) *Vinyl Leaves: Walt Disney World and America*, Boulder: Westview Press.

Gane, Mike (1991) *Baudrillard: Critical and Fatal Theory*, London: Routledge.

Gibson, W. (1986) [1984] *Neuromancer*, New York: Fantasia Press.

Gruman, G.J. (1966) 'A history of ideas about the prolongation of life', Philadelphia: *American Philosophical Society Transactions* 56(9).

Halton, Eugene (1992) 'The reality of dreaming', *Theory, Culture & Society* 9(4).

Haraway, D. (1991) *Symians, Cyborgs and Women. The Reinvention of Nature*, London: Free Association Books.

Heidegger, Martin (1978) 'Building, dwelling, thinking', in D. F. Krell (ed.) *Basic Writings*, London: Routledge.

Heim, Martin (1992) 'The erotic ontology of cyberspace', in M. Benedikt (ed.) *Cyberspace: First Steps*, Cambridge, Mass.: MIT Press.

Hepworth, Mike and Featherstone, Mike (1982) *Surviving Middle Age*, Oxford: Blackwell.

King, Richard (1992) 'The siren scream of telesex: speech, seduction and simulation', mimeo.

Lanier, Jaron and Biocca, Frank (1992) 'An insider's view of the future of virtual reality', *Journal of Communication* 42(4).

McLuhan, Marshall (1962) *Guttenberg Galaxy: the Making of Typographical Man*, Toronto: Toronto University Press.

Meyrowitz, Joshua (1985) *No Sense of Place*, Oxford: Oxford University Press.

Penley, Christopher (1992) 'Future travel: anthropology and cultural distance in an age of virtual reality: or a past seen from a possible future', *Visual Anthropology Review* 8(1).

Rheingold, Howard (1992) *Virtual Reality*, New York: Simon & Schuster.

Rojek, C. (1993) *Ways of Escape*, London: Macmillan.

Schutz, Alfred (1962) 'On multiple realities', in *Collected Papers Volume 1*, The Hague: Nijhoff.

Steuer, Jonathan (1992) 'Defining virtual reality: dimensions determining telepresence', *Journal of Communication* 42(4).

Stone, A. R. (1992) 'Will the real body please stand up? Boundary stories about virtual cultures', in M. Benedikt (ed.) *Cyberspace: First Steps*, Cambridge, Mass.: MIT Press.

Tomas, David (1992) 'Old rituals for new space', in M. Benedikt (ed.) *Cyberspace: First Steps*, Cambridge, Mass.: MIT Press.

Wiley, J. (1995) 'Nobody's Doing It', *Body & Society* 1 (1).

Zijderveld, Anton (1971) *The Abstract Society*, Harmondsworth: Allen Lane.

15

AGING AND IDENTITY

Some reflections on the somatization of the self

Bryan S. Turner

INTRODUCTION

Although aging and 'the burden of dependency' continue to be issues which dominate the social-policy problems of the advanced industrial societies, the sociology of aging can be said to be in its infancy. An overview of textbooks and classics in sociology shows the paucity of genuine contributions to the study of aging in sociology. Although many introductions to sociology typically carry a chapter on population growth, very few sociologists have regarded the aging process as in any way central to sociology. Many classical introductions to sociology – Kingsley Davis, *Human Society* (1949), Ely Chinoy, *Society* (1961), Robert K. Merton *et al. Sociology Today* (1959), and W.F. Ogburn and Meyer F. Nimkoff, *Sociology* (1958) – have discussed aging briefly under ascriptive roles as a general aspect of social stratification. Similarly, although there have been important contributions to the study of generations by Karl Mannheim (1952) in 'The problem of generations' in 1928–9 and by S. N. Eisenstadt (1956) in *From Generation to Generation,* there are few comprehensive attempts to link the problem of generational changes with individual maturation. It is perhaps encouraging therefore that the most substantial statement of the core of (American) sociology, namely N. J. Smelser's *Handbook of Sociology* (1988), has a chapter on 'Sociology of age', but *The Social Science Encyclopedia* (Kuper and Kuper, 1985) contains two rather minimal and old-fashioned entries under 'Ageing – psychological aspects', 'Age organization' and 'Age-sex structure'. Finally, Michael Mann's *Student Encyclopedia of Sociology* (1983) has 'Age set. See rites of passage'.

I have attempted elsewhere (Turner, 1989) to speculate on the reasons which might explain the absence of a genuine and sustained interest in the aging process in sociology. The absence of a developed sociology (as opposed to social gerontology or psychology of aging) of aging is an effect of the absence of a sociology of the body; that is, in sociology we have few adequate paradigms for integrating research on the biological dimensions of life with the social and cultural features (Turner, 1984). There has been little serious attempt by sociologists to understand, comparatively and historically, the interaction between various forms of human embodiment, the physiological process of aging, and the socio-cultural definitions of aging. The consequence is that, at least until recently, the aging process as a social process has been handed over to gerontology, or to geriatric medicine, or to socio-biology, or aging appears in sociology as merely a secondary feature of social stratification. The dominant sociological paradigms of the aging process – the engagement and disengagement theories of aging – are in fact merely versions of the functionalist theory of social stratification as it was developed by Parsons (1942) and Davis and Moore (1945). Furthermore, as a general rule, sociologists have self-consciously steered away from the study of the biological bases of human action precisely because they wanted to establish the autonomy of 'the social' as a claim to an otherwise unoccupied terrain of science. This move is clearly the case in Emile Durkheim's outline of the field in *The Rules of Sociological Method*, (Durkheim, 1938) in 1895 or in Max Weber's definition of adequate sociological understanding in the logic of the cultural sciences (Weber, 1949). This sociological exclusion of the body can thus be seen as part of a Kantian legacy within the mainstream of German philosophy. It was, after all, Wilhelm Dilthey (1833–1911) the father of German hermeneutic sociology who observed that 'philosophy ends where the bodily dimension begins'. This idea that the embodiment of the social actor can be regarded as merely a 'condition of action' was finally enshrined in sociological wisdom as a consequence of Talcott Parsons's analysis of the problem of a positivistic approach to social action in *The Structure of Social Action* (1937).

There are some important exceptions to this general claim that classical sociology has ignored the body. There is a predominantly German tradition of philosophical anthropology which attempted to integrate the most recent findings of biological sciences with anthropology and sociology. The leading figures in this tradition were Max Scheler (1874–1928), Arnold Gehlen (1904–1975), and Helmuth Plessner (1892–1985). Their goal was to understand the basic biological structure of human nature (ontology) in relation to cultural and social requirements (sociology). Their influence was fundamental to the development of the sociology of knowledge in modern sociology, especially in Peter L. Berger and Thomas Luckmann's *The Social Construction of Reality* (1966). Although they did not write directly about aging, they were concerned with problems of biography, life-process, life-world and consciousness. One other exception is to be found in Norbert Elias's treatment of the civilizing process, which can be read as a historical study of the social management of human embodiment in so far as our 'natural' selves have to be civilized in order to make social life possible. Elias was also conscious of the absence of sociological studies of the experiences of aging and dying, an issue which he explored in *The Loneliness of the Dying* (1985). It is arguable that Elias would have been aware of the various aspects of the philosophical anthropology tradition, which was in any case linked to the whole intellectual world of *Lebensphilosophie*.

THE BODY IN PHILOSOPHICAL ANTHROPOLOGY

In *Medical Power and Social Knowledge* (Turner, 1987), I outlined three levels of analysis in medical sociology which could offer a systematic and coherent framework for the sociology of health and illness, namely, a phenomenology of individual illness experience, a sociology of the cultural categories of sickness at the social level, and finally a political economy of illness at the societal level of health-care systems. A similar framework might be valuable as a possible approach to the sociology of aging. In this particular discussion I want initially to amplify a phenomenological orientation to the experience of aging. The task here is to describe the varieties of our consciousness of the life-world as a first step towards other scientific procedures.

Phenomenological sociology can be seen as an attempt to describe the structure of the everyday world and the life-processes of individuals in such a life-world. The task of the medical sociologist guided by this phenomenological orientation, would include, indeed start with, an account of what it is like to be sick rather than merely to have an illness, or in this discussion of aging what it is like to be old.

We can get to the core of the issue by considering Arnold Gehlen's *Man, His Nature and Place in the World* (1988). The aim of Gehlen's anthropological inquiry was to establish some basic understanding of the special place of humans in the universe. The overt goal was to derive an 'elementary anthropology' from the trans-historical nature of human beings in order to secure a safe grounding for the social sciences. It is perhaps appropriate that Gehlen's first reference is to an idea of Nietzsche that man is 'an unfinished creature' or 'a not-yet determined animal' (*das noch nicht festgestellte Tier*). It is this quality of being unfinished that gives human beings this special place in the universe or, to use Gehlen's terminology, people are characterized by a 'world-openness'.

What does this world-openness (*Weltoffenheit)* mean? The essential idea is that human beings are not determined by specific drives or instincts to function in a specific or given environment. Human beings are open to the world, because they are not born with genetic structures which point them in the direction of a specific environmental habitus. In an expression which is now very familiar to us, human beings are forced to construct socially their own cultural environment which mediates between them and the natural habitat. Human beings are active beings, who are endlessly involved in building up their social environment. There are, in this sense, no 'natural men', because humans live in a cultural world. To replace these instincts, human societies build up institutions which over time acquire a solidity and facticity which masks their constructed character. There is a process which Gehlen called the crystallization of institutions. Hence, the importance of language is to facilitate this adaptation by storing up collective knowledge. This openness which gives human groups such enormous flexibility and adaptability is, however, bought at a cost, namely socialization.

The training of human beings, which particularly in infancy creates long periods of dependency, is lifelong. Following both Nietzsche and Freud, Gehlen argued that human beings have an excess of impulses which have to be constrained or inhibited in order to allow stable social life to evolve. The cost of civilization is the frustration of these drives and impulses. The undetermined animal thus requires education, self-discipline or morality, and social imprinting. The precarious nature of man's special place in nature means that human groups substituted 'culture' for instincts, but this also means that drives/motivation had to be stored up in disciplines, and this required consciousness, which in turn could not operate without memory. Accordingly, human beings are anticipatory beings directing their actions towards future contingencies, but also by the very fact of conscious memory they are necessarily aware of their own finitude, of the passing of time, and therefore inevitably and painfully aware of their own inexorable fate – their individual inescapable death. It is not surprising that all archaeological findings from human groups show evidence of the use of graves, funeral rituals and the religious disposal of the dead. These rituals are an essential feature of the ordering and regulation of what is necessarily a precarious and problematic environment, because humans are aware of its precarious nature. These ideas about the ontological rootedness of religion in human life were worked out in contemporary sociology with great insight by Peter Berger in *The Sacred Canopy* (1969). This very perfectly captures the essence of the philosophical anthropology of ritualized practices with respect to our unfinished natures, namely that we cover ourselves in a canopy to ward off chaos, disaster and death. We might summarize these notes by saying that human beings are historical creatures.

248

THE NOSTALGIC ANIMAL

It was Nietzsche who more than any other philosopher directed attention to the importance of time in the definition of human beings. Animals are happy, according to Nietzsche, because they live unhistorically. In human beings, pain, melancholy and boredom are consequences of our consciousness of time. Indeed we cannot escape from this awareness:

> He cannot learn to forget but always remains attached to the past: however far and fast he runs, the chains run with him ... And when death finally brings longed-for forgetfulness it also robs him of the present and of existence and impresses its seal on this knowledge: that existence is only an uninterrupted having been, a thing which lives by denying itself, consuming itself, and contradicting itself.
>
> (Nietzsche, 1980: 8–9)

We can say that, for Nietzsche, man is ontologically nostalgic, because memory is always a consciousness of aging and death. Our awareness of time is also an awareness of passing through time, but this consciousness must be connected with the very fact of our embodiment. The embodiment of human beings is necessarily of a limited duration because ultimately our bodies are not endlessly renewable. My continuity through time is a matter of my being embodied through time. My consciousness of this passing of non-renewable time means that human beings are ontologically nostalgic, because completed time has a security which by definition the future can never have. Alongside our biological world-openness, there exists an ontological quest for circumscribed space and secure time. It is for these reasons that Giddens (1991: 43–56) argues that human beings create everyday routines and rituals to provide a framework of ontological security.

While some philosophers have challenged what is called the tensed theory of time, it can be argued that most of these theories typically deal with the human being as a disembodied agent (Seddon, 1987). Our experience of time cannot be reduced simply to a set of cognitive problems about the grammatical character of verbs ('it was', 'it has been'). Although it is clearly the case that different languages have different grammatical forms of the tense of verbs and therefore it might be reasonable to argue that time varies according to language, our experience of our *own* time is phenomenologically bound up with being embodied. As Elias has noted, 'It is not easy to imagine that one's body, which is so fresh and often so full of pleasant feelings, could become sluggish, tired and clumsy' (Elias, 1985: 69). We are resistant to the thought that we might become old, and have difficulty consequently forming an empathy for the aged even when we are chronologically old. In fact we might say that we find difficulty empathizing with our own process of aging because we subjectively cling to an image of ourselves as unchangingly young. Goethe was thus perfectly correct to say that age takes us by surprise, because it is only as a consequence of some major event, such as the death of a close friend or a serious illness which we have suffered, that we are forced into an awareness of our own aging. In phenomenological terms, we might note that the inside of the body remains subjectively young or youthful while the outside body becomes both biologically and socially old. There is a necessary disjuncture between the inner self and the image of the body.

But what interests me about Elias's discussion of aging in *The Loneliness of the Dying* is that he talks about the process of aging precisely in terms of the physical transformation of his *own* body. The passage of time is experientially measured by the passing of *his* body. While this observation might appear blindingly obvious, we need to remind ourselves always of the centrality of our bodies to experience. This argument was central to Merleau-Ponty's phenomenology (1974) that perception always occurs from a particular point in time and space, namely from the perspective of a particular body. In short, we should not talk about memory without talking about body. For example, Simone de Beauvoir (1972) gives many illustrations of how fragile our memory of our past really is. In fact she says that as we move forwards, our past crumbles behind us, thereby apparently contradicting Nietzsche's assertion that we are chained to our past. In old age we may suffer the misfortune of senile dementia or cerebral atherosclerosis in which case much of our memory will disappear completely. I want, however, to insist on the importance of our embodiment in all of these processes, precisely because we might say that time is inscribed indelibly on our bodies. Although in western societies, which have a particular emphasis on the values of achievement and activism (Parsons, 1951), it may be difficult for elderly people to disengage from social roles, the body's finitude puts a limit on activism. While cosmetic surgery, diet and exercise may delay aging, there are no existing medical interventions which can prevent aging. My body is, so to speak, a walking memory. The inevitability of biological aging presents important difficulties for the popular view that aging is simply a social construct (Turner, 1992).

But why should I call this 'nostalgia'? Surely nostalgia refers to homesickness, to a yearning for place rather than time? One justification for its use is that we cannot in practice separate the experiences of the passing of time from the absence of places. I think this is what Kant had in mind in his *Anthropologie in pragmatischer Hinsicht* of 1798 when he argued that nostalgia was not a melancholy sentiment of place, but our longing for lost youth. In the terms of this argument here, we might say that nostalgia is the yearning for a particular body in its youthful habitus.

COLLECTIVE MEMORIES

The burden of my argument so far has been relatively simple. Sociology has neglected to analyse the experience of aging because it has failed to develop an adequate sociology of the body. This failure is particularly true of the tradition of interpretative sociology in Germany which inherited both a Kantian view of the centrality of mind as cognitive performance and a quasi-Christian legacy in which the life of the spirit (*Geist*) is the defining characteristic of what is truly human. To take one specific instance of this tendency, Artur Bogner, in what was in fact a compliment to Elias (1978/82), noted that '*The Civilizing Process*' has brought the bodily functions and expressions of human beings, the more 'animal' aspects of human social life, back on the horizon of modern sociologists (Bogner, 1986: 391). While voluntaristic action and will are generally social, the emotions, facial expressions, and the natural functions, in short the body, are features of our animality. By contrast, I want to argue that our embodiment is crucial, not only to our understanding of our most fundamental existential experiences such as birth and death, but also to an appreciation of basic processes such as memory and identity. Although this argument is fundamentally important, it is not as yet a particularly sociological observation.

In attempting to bring out the sociologically interesting aspects of aging and embodiment, I want to address three issues. First, time and memory have become more problematic in modern than in traditional societies. Thus, it is important to introduce a historical dimension to this argument. Second, it is important to keep in mind that our apparently individual memories are only possible in the social context of interaction. Finally, and in a way which is related to the idea of social memory, our individual aging takes place within a generational or cohort context. It may be the case that certain generations have collective memories which are radically different from other generations. In other words, memory is a feature of what Durkheim intended by the phrase 'conscience collective'.

In contemporary societies our individual memories are facilitated and also transformed by certain technological developments which have a direct mass effect. When we are interested in memory and the aging of bodies, we should also be interested in the technological possibilities for storing our personalized histories, namely, the development, for example, of photography, tape recorders, videos and computerized writing. The development of the idea of a life cycle which can be recorded presupposes the emergence of individualism, the construction of definite stages in a life-process, the expansion of life expectancy and the evolution of techniques for recording personal change over a long period. Although the idea of the individual has a long historical maturation in the west, a marked emphasis on the individual appears to develop in the late fifteenth and early sixteenth centuries (Abercrombie, Hill and Turner, 1986). Before this modern history of the individual, portrait paintings, which of necessity depicted the dominant social classes, were often more symbols of nobility, sovereignty or piety rather than attempts to capture the peculiarities of a particular person. There are of course many exceptions to this chronology, such as Leonardo da Vinci's many drawings of the heads of old men, including his self-portrait in old age from about 1513 (Popham, 1946). Representation of particular individuals in which the point of the study is to represent *that* person appear rather late in the history of western art. Velasquez's portrait of Pope Innocent X in 1650 is a good example, but Rembrandt's series of self-portraits into his old age are an almost unique record of the experience of aging. The point here is that the idea of an individualized experience of aging is part of the very history of western individualism. However, it is not until the discovery of photography and the development of cheap cameras for a mass market that a detailed personal memory becomes possible. As to the sociological meaning of photography, it is difficult to improve on Susan Sontag. First, the spread of photography is a fundamental feature of the democratization of mass society, but it also has the paradoxical effect of standardization. Second, the family photograph album becomes an essential basis of the collective memory of the (extended) family. Finally, the photograph is also about death:

> photographs actively promote nostalgia. Photography is an elegiac art, a twilight art. Most subjects photographed are, just by virtue of being photographed, touched with pathos . . . All photographs are memento mori.
>
> (Sontag, 1978: 15)

The development of the photograph has become an essential feature, therefore, not only of individual images of aging, but of collective, generational aging. We measure our personal aging, not simply by reference to the recorded transformation of our own image, but collectively by reference to our peers and our generation. The mass record of the history of our own generation – in newsclips, documentaries, films, archives, and photographs – becomes the basis of an institutionalization of our collective aging. This process permits the past – our past – to become richer or thicker, and perhaps as our collective future becomes more uncertain, problematic and dangerous, so our past can become more meaningful and nostalgic. British television series such as *The Last of the Summer Wine* or *All Things Bright and Beautiful* or *One Man and His Dog* present a picture of England as largely rural, secure and comfortable – a collective nostalgic portrait in which we can share the experience of a lost world.

The issue, from a sociological perspective, is that time is a social and collective experience. My memory of my past depends on a social network of shared experiences which are reinforced, changed or lost through the process of interaction with my own and other generations. The maintenance of these memories depends not only on having documentary evidence (through family albums, newspaper clippings and holiday slides), but more importantly on recalling this past in present conversations. An acceptable, verified and shared past emerges out of everyday interactions in which a shared past is constantly brought into the present by the question 'Do you remember when . . . ?' The problem with aging is that we run out of living participants who can meaningfully raise and answer such questions. Our past becomes literally a dead past, as a set of experiences which could be appropriately stored in a folk museum. To become old is, if there were such a verb, to be museumized. Theodor Adorno tells us:

> The German word 'museal' (museumlike) has unpleasant over-tones. It describes objects to which the observer no longer has a vital relationship and which are in the process of dying.
>
> (Adorno, 1981: 175)

Aging, in a society of rapid social change, means that the cultural artefacts of our particular generation rapidly become suitable as items of a museum. Even the protest generations of the 1960s and 1970s which celebrated youthfulness are now the subject of documentary films, nostalgic remakes and the investigations of social historians. The loneliness of aging involves the disappearance of co-participants for whom the items in the museum are not yet exhibits which we can observe with disinterest. We remember that the items in the folk museum were items we used 'in reality'. In Elias's study of aging 'loneliness' is a translation of '*einsamkeit*'. The English does not perhaps capture so well the notion that aging is a process whereby we become singular, separated into our oneness.

We have seen that the past can be approached sociologically in terms of the ongoing interactions of everyday life in which, for example, the aging body (the spread of grey hair, the decline of body mobility or the loss of skin tone) becomes the topic of comparisons ('You don't look a day over fifty!'). These social observations and interpersonal monitoring of the transformation of bodies is our best index of the passing of time. It is not simply that my body ages, but the bodies of my generational cohort age as well. Furthermore, this social aging process is now typically recorded by school photographs, marriage portraits, holiday snaps and so forth. Aging is a topic of detailed surveillance.

We may, however, also be able to think of aging in terms of age-cultures which have an autonomy of their own; in other words, we might be able to construct a Durkheimian model of collective aging in terms of a shared conscience collective. This project – a genuine sociology of the elementary structures of memory – was attempted by Maurice Halbachs (1877–1945) in *Les Cadres sociaux de la memoire* (1925) and *The Collective Memory* (1950). Halbachs argued that memory cannot be studied as a function of individual mental activity, because individuals remember within the context of their position in social groups. For Halbachs, memories were more than mere recollections; they are social reconstructions which involve a reshaping of the present by collective processes. Halbachs also developed a theory of nostalgia (Vromen, 1986) which had positive functions because it permitted individuals or groups to overcome the narrow boundaries of time. Nostalgia is also a yearning for continuity and familiarity. Nostalgia becomes focused on familiar places and buildings which allow us to establish some continuous contact with our own past. The speed of social change, especially where this change has involved massive urban reconstruction, in our epoch has often destroyed the landscape of our collective childhood. It may be yet again that the peculiar attraction of the nostalgia film is as a replacement for more vivid experiences of a lost youth.

Thus, these relations between body and self-image are historically not static, and therefore a sociology of aging would involve the historical analysis of the conditions under which the human body is represented. Although the issue has not been fully explored here, the changing relationship between self and society, especially with a growing emphasis on individualism in the west, is clearly important for the representation of the individual life course. These images and representations of the aging body need to be considered within a thoroughly sociologized view of collective memory. My aging takes place within the context of the cohort of people whom I regard as part of 'my generation' and thus in relationship to previous and coming generations. These generations develop a collective memory of themselves which, in a sense, is not allowed to grow old, with the result that individuals become labelled (now pejoratively) as 'a sixties person'. The actual bodies of cohorts are recognizably different from other generations. Various health movements in Germany and England in the 1920s and 1930s appear to produce a distinctive body which is recognizable by other members of such cohorts. We recognize ourselves (through our bodies) by the characteristic features of the bodies produced by the culture of specific generations. The pathways of aging are complicated, not just by occupation or gender, but by the specific histories of different generations in

254

their interaction with other generations. An individual experiences the process of aging in relationship to the maturation of their body, and also in relation to their collective generational body-image. These relationships between body, time and society can only be understood within a more general discussion of the issue of identity and modernity.

THE SOMATIZATION OF THE SELF

What I want to do in this section is to think about the implications of specific theories of detraditionalization and postmodernity for theories of the self and the body. Anthony Giddens (1992) claims that in conditions of high modernity we are all forced to choose a lifestyle embodying our tastes. I want to take that word 'embodying' both seriously and literally, because any discussion of the project of the self ought to include a discussion of the project of the body in the debate about detraditionalization and postmodernity.

By 'reflexive modernization' in the work of Ulrich Beck (1992) and Giddens, they are describing the idea of the self-monitoring personality, the idea of self-regulation and self-motivation. Second, they are depicting a culture, or a development, or a pattern of self-questioning, self-analysis, and self-reflexivity. Giddens has in mind, in particular, the idea of the emergence of the self as a project, that is, the notion that the self has a history with trajectories, with self-conscious lifestyles, with modes of operation and development: in this context therefore, the self is not to be taken for granted, not a fact of the person as it were. This idea of the self as a project is taking place in a society which is characterized by increasing complexity and systematic social reflexivity. Here again there may be a tension between the idea of self as a project, that is, a regulated attainment, and the idea of detraditionalization, postmodernization and the idea of the end of self-regulation. There may be a tension between the idea of having a unified or regulated self and the idea of having plural or multiple or exchangeable selves over time, the idea of the self as plastic, as a moveable feast. Detraditionalization presumably means that the self is pulled out of, or disembedded from, or taken away from its 'natural', traditional, cultural environment and that the self becomes a developmental project without a fixed framework. Therefore detraditionalization must imply some degree of the secularization of the self. We can view the self becoming the target of a series of secular practices, discourses, regimes and so forth, particularly of psychiatry, psychology, medicine and at a popular level of self-help manuals.

One criticism of the Beck-Giddens approach to the self and intimacy is that it has very little or nothing to say about the aging body, the image of the body and the tension between the inside/outside body and the reflexive self. What I am arguing is that any account of the detraditionalization of the self ought to take into account the idea of the detraditionalization of the body and that most modern critiques of Cartesian dualism have tried to develop the idea of an embodied self in order to break down the legacy of body/mind dualism. In contemporary sociology there have been a number of attempts to displace the idea of a cognitive dualism or a division between body and self. Sociologists like John O'Neill, Arthur Frank, Harvey Ferguson, Chris Shilling and others have attacked Cartesian dualism (Featherstone *et al.* 1991).

In contemporary societies, the body has become a site of regulative practices and as a consequence of these regulative practices the body has become a project. To put it in a wider historical framework, perhaps in western cultures the body has always been problematized by the cultural legacies of Christianity. The critique of the flesh and the denigration and denial of the body, which are the consequence of a radical Pauline theology, meant that in western civilization the body was problematic. In Christianity, therefore, you have the paradox that in Christian theology the body is a central topic in the resurrection of the dead and the idea of Christ's imminence but the legacy of Pauline theology was to separate the body off from the self, to treat the body as merely a vessel or vehicle for cognitive and spiritual activity. It is for this reason that sovereignty was expressed through the king's two bodies; the sovereign body is a spiritualized body, but the degenerative body is a secular human body. In Judaeo-Christian tradition, reflexivity about the body has been an inescapable cultural fact precisely because of the attempt to erase the body, as it were, from collective or social memory.

In my own work on the body (Turner 1984 and 1992), I have tried to focus, in particular, on the idea of diet as a way of talking about the body as regulated and produced, and I have tried to think about the body as the target of 'institutions of normative coercion, such as medicine and religion' (Turner, 1992). 'Diet' means regime or government, and in the idea of dieting we are already talking about a government of the body, or a regulation of our flesh. One of the main transitions from traditional to detraditional may be an inversion. In the traditional Christian teaching, one dieted the body in order to subordinate the flesh, in order to regulate and produce the soul, so that the idea is that the government of the body is the production of the soul. The government of the body is the production of the soul, and it is only by this regulation of bodies that the soul can emerge as some pure entity. In modern societies it is the other way round; we regulate the body in order to produce pleasure, we diet the body in order to enhance the surface of the body as a system of sexual symbolism. In modern societies, consumer culture has made the project of the body a general activity. The idea of the body beautiful has turned this traditional dieting practice in the opposite direction so that now we regulate the body in order to produce a fetishization of sexuality. We regulate the body in order to produce sexuality, not to deny it. The Protestant ethic is turned inside out and the body becomes a project alongside, or inextricably bound up with, the self as a project. To take one specific issue, in a culture in which the surface of the body is seen to be that which carries the signs of one's inner moral condition, aging is something which has to be denied. With aging, the outer body can be interpreted as a betrayal of the youthfulness of the inner body. I would like to put it in a slightly different way that aging intensifies the reflexivity which is forced upon us in a world in which we are all compelled to choose a lifestyle embodying tastes. The aging process is inevitably bound up with the reflexivity. With the aestheticization of everyday life the body becomes a project. The centrality of the gymnasium to modern culture and the importance of sport and fitness are further aspects of the body as project.

I would like finally to come to the topic of secularization and the body. Many of the discussions about the self as project presuppose a theory of the secularization of society. By contrast I propose that we live in a society in which problems about the body come to the centre of political debate, whether we are talking about transplants and the legal problems associated with them, or whether we are talking about gender and sexuality in gay and feminist politics, or whether we are talking about the genderization of issues. More importantly, and here I completely agree with Giddens, whether we are also describing a new understanding of the relationship between patriarchy, sexual politics and the pollution of the environment. The body could be argued to be at the centre of politics in modern society, and in the context of a debate about AIDS, HIV, technological possibilities of the body and the production of new bodies, perhaps we are living in a society in which we might plausibly argue that the body is our 'ultimate concern'. If we adopt a definition of religion from Paul Tillich as those things which ultimately concern us, then the body rather than being a target of secular practices is in fact a sacred issue in contemporary society. The embodiment of politics in a somatic society actually indicates not the secularization of culture, but in fact the presentation of the body as a project as that which is our ultimate concern.

CONCLUSION

In the last decade there have been interesting developments in the sociology of the body, the sociological study of the emotions and the interpretation of the self in modern societies. In this chapter I have attempted to integrate these three developments around a re-analysis of the aging process in relation to classical sociological theory. It is well known that age and aging have been neglected in traditional sociology. Indeed age only significantly appears in the traditional sociological approach to stratification. My argument in this chapter has been that the crucial sociological issue in the aging process is the contradictory relationship between the subjective sense of a inner youthfulness and an exterior process of biological aging. It is the disjuncture between these two which constitutes the core of personal tragedy. The outer body is available to collective observation and it is difficult for the individual therefore to avoid an exterior sense of the process of aging and generational change. I have therefore attempted to place the problem of nostalgia at the core of this contradiction between the inner self and outer body. This tension is the essential element of any phenomenological approach to the individual aging process.

Of course, sociology is essentially concerned with the social dimension of aging rather than the individual and the phenomenological condition of personal aging. However, these two issues, namely individual aging and collective generational change, are obviously interconnected. My social process of aging involves the collective disappearance of a generational cohort over time and space. My sense of personal nostalgia fits into the collective mythology of social memory for specific generational cohorts.

This approach to aging has to be placed within a macro analysis of modernization and postmodernity. For many writers the self in modern society has become a reflexive problem. For Beck and Giddens, the reflexive self is the central dimension of modernization and this approach to the self suggests that we are forced to choose various lifestyles and identities. However, the theory of reflexive modernization has yet to address the problem of aging, and therefore in this discussion I have suggested that necessarily any project of the self must be a project of the body. Within this context aging forces upon both individuals and groups a necessary reflexivity, because the self is subject to change, or at least there is an inherent tension between the inner reflexivity of the subjective self and the outer biological degeneration of the body. This type of modernization can finally be linked with the idea of emergence of a somatic society, that is, a society in which the problems of the body dominate the centre stage of political debate and political process. Within this somatic society the aging of generations and the aging of individuals becomes intensely problematic since the emphasis on activism and individualism must necessarily conflict with the inevitable biological decay of the individual self. This discussion therefore leads one to propose that reflexive aging must become much more central to sociological inquiry and sociological theory.

258

REFERENCES

Abercrombie, N., Hill, S. and Turner, B. S. (1986) *Sovereign Individuals of Capitalism*, London: Allen & Unwin.

Adorno, T. W. (1981) *Prisms*, Cambridge, Mass.: MIT Press.

Beauvoir, S. de (1972) *Old Age*, London: Weidenfeld & Nicolson.

Beck, U. (1992) *Risk Society*, London: Sage.

Berger, P. L. (1969) *The Sacred Canopy*, London: Faber & Faber.

Berger, P. L. and Luckmann, T. (1966) *The Social Construction of Reality*, London: Allen Lane.

Bogner, A. (1986) 'The structure of social processes: a commentary on the sociology of Norbert Elias', *Sociology* 20 (3): 387–411.

Bogner, A. (1987) 'Elias and the Frankfurt School', *Theory, Culture & Society* 4 (2–3).

Chinoy, E. (1961) *Society, an Introduction to Sociology*, New York: Random House.

Davis, K. (1949) *Human Society*, New York: Macmillan.

Davis, K. and Moore, W. E. (1945) 'Some principles of stratification', *American Sociological Review* 10: 242–9.

Durkheim, E. (1938) *The Rules of Sociological Method*, Chicago: University of Chicago Press.

Eisenstadt, S. N. (1956) *From Generation to Generation*, Glencoe, Ill.: Free Press.

Elias, N. (1978/82) *The Civilizing Process*, 2 vols. Oxford: Blackwell.

Elias, N. (1985) *The Loneliness of the Dying*, Oxford: Basil Blackwell.

Featherstone, M., Hepworth, M. and Turner, B. S. (eds) (1991) *The Body, Social Process and Cultural Theory*, London: Sage.

Gehlen, A. (1988) *Man, His Nature and Place in the World*, New York: Columbia University Press.

Giddens, A. (1991) *Modernity and Self-Identity: Self and Society in the Late Modern Age*, Cambridge: Polity Press.

Giddens, A. (1992) *The Transformation of Intimacy: Sexuality, Love and Eroticism in Modern Societies*, Cambridge: Polity Press.

Halbachs, M. (1925) *Les Cadres sociaux de la memoire*, Paris: Alcan.

Halbachs. M. (1950) *The Collective Memory*, New York: Harper.

Kant, I. (1798) *Anthropologie in pragmatischer Hinsicht*.

Kuper, A. and Kuper, J. (eds) (1985) *The Social Science Encyclopedia*, London: Routledge & Kegan Paul.

Mann, M. (ed) (1983) *Student Encyclopedia of Sociology*, London: Macmillan.

Mannheim, K. (1952) 'The problem of generations', *Essay on the Sociology of Knowledge*, London: Routledge & Kegan Paul.

Merleau-Ponty, M. (1974) *Phenomenology Language and Society*, London: Heinemann.

Merton, R. K., Broom, L. and Cottrell, L. S. (eds) (1959) *Sociology Today, Problems and Prospects*, New York: Harper Torchbooks.

Nietzsche, F. (1980) *On the Advantage and Disadvantage of History for Life*, Indianapolis: Hackett Publishing.

Ogburn, W. F. and Nimkoff, M. F. (1958) *Sociology*, Boston: Houghton Mifflin.

Parsons, T. (1937) *The Structure of Social Action*, New York: McGraw-Hill.

Parsons, T. (1942) 'Age and sex in the social structure of the United States', *American Sociological Review* 7: 604–16.

Parsons, T. (1951) *The Social System*, London: Routledge & Kegan Paul.

Popham, A. E. (1946) *The Drawings of Leonardo da Vinci*, London: The Reprint Society.

Seddon, K. (1987) *Time, a Philosophical Treatment*, London: Croom Helm.

Smelser, N. J. (ed.) (1988) *Handbook of Sociology*, Newbury Park: Sage.

Sontag, S. (1978) *On Photography*, London: Allen Lane.

Turner, B. S. (1984) *The Body and Society: Explorations in Social Theory*, Oxford: Basil Blackwell.

Turner, B. S. (1987) *Medical Power and Social Knowledge*, London: Sage.

Turner, B. S. (1989) 'Ageing, status politics and sociological theory', *British Journal of Sociology* 40(2): 588–606.

Turner, B. S. (1992) *Regulating Bodies: Essays in Medical Sociology*, London: Routledge.

Vromen, S. (1986) 'Maurice Halbachs and the concept of nostalgia', *Knowledge and Society, Studies in the Sociology of Culture Past and Present*, 6: 55–66.

Weber, M. (1949) *The Methodology of the Social Sciences*, New York: Free Press.

Part VI

DEATH

16

FROM GRIM REAPER TO CHEERY CONDOM

Images of Aging and Death in Australian AIDS Education Campaigns

John Tulloch

> Certainly the profound gerontophobia in our culture should be extirpated, and one of the ways to begin that process is to examine critically our representation of aging and to work to produce new ones.
>
> (Woodward, 1991: 193)

As Kathleen Woodward writes in *Aging and Its Discontents* (1991: 193–5), 'as the material conditions of aging are undergoing change, so too our culture is producing new representations of aging'. Much of this change, however, is encapsulated in the 'now for THE FUN YEARS' advertising of a 'vigorous silver-headed couple dressing in jogging outfits'. If Woodward is relieved that in these 'the body is not presented within the confining matrix of beauty and its opposite. It is, rather, health that is at stake', other commentators have pointed to the quite conventional marketing strategy – targeting the swelling ranks of the affluent elderly – that this apparent 'change' represents.

However, new representations of aging can appear in other contexts too. This article examines Australian Government HIV/AIDS TV commercials which prominently feature images of age, even while targeting 'youth'. I will concentrate particularly on two ads which mark the opening and closing stages of the late 1980s campaign. The first ('The Grim Reaper') took a ghostly bowling alley as its motif, with a horrific cowled figure of Death bowling a 'strike' in slo-mo. The pins are a variety of ordinary-looking Australians, falling one by one. The second ('Vox Pop Condom – Granny') has an interview format, with an unseen cheery media type quizzing people in the street (and beach) about their amused, matter-of-fact, positive etc. attitude to condoms. 'Granny' is the last interviewee.

Public health AIDS awareness campaigns world-wide have seldom shown aged people; in a review of ads from some thirty countries I came across only one other, a Danish ad where an older woman returns a young man's packet of condoms that he has left behind at the supermarket checkout. The humour is generated by the young man's embarrassment at being caught buying condoms contrasted with the unruffled 'wisdom' of the woman in making sure he has them. The Australian 'Vox Pop Condom – Granny' goes further in so far as the old 'granny', represented as especially lined and wrinkled, speaks positively, humorously and with evident pleasure about her *own* sexuality.

The aged, wrinkled female body is deeply embedded in western myth, generating a 'horror' image of aging that is in marked contrast to the 'FUN YEARS' one of recent times. As Arber and Ginn (1991: 36) note, 'Older women tend to be socially invisible'. But

> when they are portrayed in popular culture, the image is often a demeaning or a 'disgusting' one. In children's stories, where 'Good' and 'Bad' are most crudely identified, it is often old women who come to personify malevolence as 'old hags, evil crones, scary old witches and nasty biddies of all sorts'.

On the other hand, Featherstone and Hepworth point out that when old people are portrayed benignly, the best they can hope for is banal and stereotyped. 'The sanitised one-dimensional benign stereotypes "granny" and "grandpa" are good examples of the ageist trap' (1991: 382).

HORROR AND HUMOUR:
THE PRODUCTION CONTEXT

To understand what the Australian AIDS ads were 'trying to produce', it is important to understand the commercial discourses of production through which they were constructed. Representations of youth and aging in government health ads are produced by commercial advertising agencies, often the same ones which produce, for other clients, the images that 'retard, diminish or disguise the effects of aging' (Itzin, 1984: 77). In the case of health advertisements, however, generic understandings of both 'fun' and 'horror' also mediate the signifying process.

Andrew Wernick argues that advertising promotion 'is determinedly positive and upbeat. Within the field of polarities which make up the codes of culture, the product is identified with good not bad, comedy not tragedy, life not death' (Wernick, 1991: 42). Add this to Kathleen Woodward's point that in our culture 'Youth, represented by the youthful body, is good; old age, represented by the aging body, is bad' (Woodward, 1991: 7), and, of course, we have the scenario for any Coca-Cola ad. Yet, in health communication campaign advertisements, death and life, tragedy and humour are conventional polarities; and despite the fact that HIV/AIDS campaigns primarily target youth, old age and the aging body can in fact signify good. Thus in the Australian Department of Health and Community Services campaign the image of an old lady laughing openly and positively about her own (earlier) use of condoms, followed by the slogan 'Play it safe', was planned as a 'laid back' counter to the moralizing fear of 'Always use condoms. Always' of the first Australian TV AIDS ad, 'The Grim Reaper' (1987).

Discussing 'fear' and 'humour' in health campaigns, social marketers Kotler and Roberto ask:

> Are messages more effective when they appeal to emotion rather than to rational argument? Should an emotional appeal be negative or positive? . . . The most often used negative appeal is 'fear', and the many positive appeals feature people in normal life situations . . . Messages may be more effective in raising the visibility or salience of an idea or issue when they are surrounded by and project a mood or atmosphere, such as humour.
>
> (Kotler and Roberto, 1989: 197, 198)

Certainly if we examine the Australian government HIV/AIDS television ads, from the first 'Grim Reaper' ad in 1987 to the 'Vox Pop Condom' ads in 1990, they trace out this particular spectrum. In contrast to the fear-driven horror genre of 'The Grim Reaper', the 'Vox Pop Condom' ads are Kotler and Roberto's 'positive emotional' ads, featuring 'people in normal life situations', and adopting a tone that was 'positive', 'fun' 'light-hearted' and 'laid back'.

Typically, social marketing conventions about 'fear' and 'humour' in health campaigns have been embedded in psychologistic theories and KAB (knowledge/attitudes/behaviour) methodologies. The British Health Education Authority's document, 'Evaluation of the HEA Public Education Campaign, February-June, 1988' emphasizes, for instance, that

> we have concerned ourselves with the impact of the campaign, its apparent effects on knowledge, attitudes and behaviour . . . One of the cornerstones of HEA thinking on the current campaign was a concern for the complacency which seemed to have crept into the public consciousness of AIDS since the Government campaign of the previous year. At the same time we were anxious to avoid levels of fear which might set up cycles of defence avoidance to information and advice.
>
> (British Health Education Authority, 1988: 1, 7)

Similarly, the research and evaluation documents preceding the 1990 Australian campaign spoke of the initial need to break through 'youth's complacency and deflection barriers' (deemed to have risen again since the initial 'fear-inducing' success of 'The Grim Reaper' in 1987). Consequently the advice was to open the 1990 campaign with frightening ads that 'raised the level and tension and perceptions of personal risk'. But, as with the British HEA, the Australian Department of Community Services and Health (DCSH) documents were also concerned that a campaign which was *only* scary would hinder rather than enhance behaviour change. Consequently, the 'Vox Pop Condom – Granny' ad was designed to establish a casual and everyday feel, to create a 'comfort zone' that would facilitate behaviour change. The aim was to 'socialise the condom' – its purchase without embarrassment, its 'no big deal' spot in one's wallet or handbag, its regular use in sex, and its endorsement by parents and grandparents.

Both British and Australian pre-campaign research thus emphasized psychological rather than sociological understandings, emphasizing youth's 'self-protective barriers' and psychological 'deflective mechanisms', rather than socio-cultural matters like gender power in sexual negotiation (including the use of condoms) or class differences in attitudes to girls who carry condoms – or indeed, age differences in relation to cultural representation. Correlatively, there was a tendency to rely on 'hypodermic' theories of media 'effects' (with much emphasis on 'hard-edged advertising' that 'doesn't let them off the hook') rather than sociological theories of active subcultural readings and meanings (Crawford, Kippax and Tulloch, 1992).

In that light, it has become quite standard in Australia, both in academic writing and more widely, to criticize 'The Grim Reaper' campaign for scaring the wrong people and providing little useful information. Thus Turtle *et al.* note that 'The Grim Reaper's fear-raising image . . . produced a reaction that was off-target slightly, with a hugely increased interest among heterosexual persons in being tested for the presence of AIDS antibodies rather than in acquiring information about safer sexual practices' (1989: 375).

But this kind of analysis doesn't really tell us why 'The Grim Reaper' did have such an impact (even if 'off-target'), with Australians in their thousands having immediate blood tests. Nor does it explain why 'The Grim Reaper' is still being remembered as 'the most effective' AIDS information by the students I surveyed in 1990, 1992 and 1993–4 (in the latter case they would have only been about 10 years old when they saw the ad). Both in their staying power and behavioural effect, the 'Vox Pop Condom' ads also proved to be highly effective. They were designed to counter both the 'uncool' and 'promiscuous' image which research had indicated was still associated with condoms among young people. If these were, as the DCSH group research suggests, dominant views among young people in Australia before the 1990 campaign, they were much less so after it. My research (conducted with 892 16- to 17-year-old students in Sydney in 1990) into audience responses to 'Vox Pop Condom' indicated that after the campaign 95 per cent of the sample of 16- to 17-year-old students 'agreed with the message of the ad'; 91 per cent agreed that condoms 'aren't daggy' [grotty]; 69 per cent said they would carry condoms with them; 84 per cent agreed that 'it's OK for you to carry a condom – your friends won't think you're a sleaze bag'; and 78 per cent *disagreed* that 'you needn't use condoms with someone you have known a long time and trust'.

DYING AS A 'CRITICAL SITUATION'

There have been several major artistic studies of sick and aging people who, facing death, experience the trauma of colossal psychic upheaval – Tolstoy's *Death of Ivan Ilich*, Chekhov's *A Dreary Story*, Thomas Mann's *Death in Venice*, and on film Kurosawa's *Living* and Bergman's *Wild Strawberries* to name some of the best known. It is not surprising that artists concern themselves with old age and dying because death confronts the artist in a paradoxical way:

> On the one hand, as the most extreme of all marginal situations it threatens each individual and negates creativity itself . . . On the other hand, confrontation with death can strip away, lucidly and terrifyingly, the 'taken-for-granted' meanings of everyday life; a process which many artists also consider to be a central function of art.
>
> (Tulloch, 1977: 736)

In that sense, old age and dying can operate as a kind of metaphor whereby the artist explores reflexively his/her own identity *as* artist. Where someone is suddenly facing AIDS, however, that questioning of identity is very much more direct, though the quest for creativity may still be strong. Emmanuel Dreuilhe, for instance, considers the writing of his book, *Mortal Embrace*, as a moment of collectivity when

> we've reached the darkest hour, when the scope of this evil is all too evident, when researchers appear to be going around in circles, and when society seems ready to give in to the demons of selfishness and fear. It was in a similar situation, just after the collapse of the European continent, that Churchill sought to inspire hope in a demoralised nation.
>
> (Dreuilhe, 1988: 5)

Dreuilhe's creative account of his sickroom is similar to what Lukacs called the narrative of the 'socially uniform setting', often – like Thomas Mann's novel, *The Magic Mountain* – situated in the sanatorium or sick room. Lukacs writes,

267

one must remember that in *The Magic Mountain* . . . where a departure from normal everyday life is the basis of the novel, the confrontation with sickness, with the perspectives and reality of their own death tears only a fraction of those exiled to the sanatorium away from their external, accustomed way of life. Many will simply inwardly avoid such confrontations and, despite their changed conditions, endeavour to continue their old way of life unchanged and without taking stock of themselves anew.

(Lukacs, 1969: 45)

An alternative response, however, is for the sick person to evaluate more closely 'his existence and its meaning for himself and for his fellows . . ., and to make himself and others aware of it' (Lukacs, 1969: 44).

This latter role is Dreuilhe's who makes himself and others aware of the 'unreality of the non-AIDS universe of healthy people', leading him, as he puts it, to 'question their common sense and mistrust my own senses' (Dreuilhe, 1988: 6). Dreuilhe, and the characters in Chekhov, Bergman and Mann, are in what Anthony Giddens calls 'critical situations' which he defines as 'circumstances of radical disjuncture of an unpredictable kind that threaten or destroy the certitudes of institutionalised routines' (Giddens, 1984: 61). As Dreuilhe says, 'the futility of civilian life . . . is absurd when survival itself has become the main imperative' (Dreuilhe, 1988: 7).

Giddens, and also Bettelheim (1960) note that this imperative of survival can lead, in situations as disempowering as concentration camps, to, first of all, the attempt to maintain the old modes of conduct that Mann describes in the sanatorium; but then, later, to a renewed agency on the part of the prisoners, based on participation in the rituals of their own degradation. In contrast, Lukacs argues that writers like Solzhenitsyn, in his prison camp narrative, *One Day In The Life of Ivan Denisovich*, challenges exactly that feeling of 'senseless tasks, the lack of almost any time to oneself, the inability to plan ahead because of sudden changes in camp policy' (Bettelheim, 1960: 148) which Bettelheim found to be so destructive of identity. In this way, Lukacs believes, an artist like Solzhenitsyn can be discursive in the wider prison camp that was Stalinist society.

It is more in this *em*powering way, I think, that Dreuilhe sees himself as artist, that he questions, and is publicly discursive about, the absurdity of this 'common-sense' world of civilian life. For Lukacs, this questioning of common sense can be a creatively radical act, which urges the sick characters 'to achieve an awareness of and to master the crucial ideological and practical problems of their relationship to their own social existence' (Lukacs, 1969: 43). And it is this ideological awareness which is central to the movement of People Living With AIDS

(PLWA), their refusal of the disempowering 'tragic victim' role in media narratives about AIDS; and to Simon Watney's rejection of the 'common-sense' representation that the 'correct site of AIDS' is 'the hospital or the hospice, which join the prison as the just and proper latitude for the perverse' (Watney, 1987: 22). Unlike Bettelheim's fellow concentration camp prisoners, PLWAs have the possibility of being lifted – in their representation – out of this 'correct site' of treatment.

But the matter is still one of discourse and power; because, as Watney indicates, this 'common-sense' representation about the 'correct site of AIDS' has itself a number of very specific institutional sites: it 'is taking place on the "other side" of the lived experience of AIDS – amongst photographers, journalists, sub-editors and politicians', and in the discourses and professional practices around 'humour' and 'fear' of commercial advertising agencies, as we saw in the last section (Watney, 1987: 23). It is in these sites where the production of public discourse about AIDS takes place that, as Watney says, the person with AIDS is imprisoned 'within the demeaning category of the "victim", in which he or she is stripped of all power and control over the actual complex meaning and dignity of an individual's life' (Watney, 1987: 22).

As 'victim', as 'sign of mortality', the image of the PLWA is so often, as Watney insists, an '*admonitory* sign of the deadly danger of sex outside the confines of the family' (Watney, 1987: 22). In opposition to this 'morbid and essentially silent role' (ibid.: 23), Watney calls for an acceptance and celebration of 'the social, radical and sexual diversity of our species', for a recognition of 'Safer Sex as an enlargement of our lives, rather than a restriction' (ibid.: 24). With these two poles of response to 'critical situations' before us, of degrading, demeaning self-recognitions as 'prisoner' and 'victim' on one hand, and the complex meanings, dignity and enlargement of our lives on the other, it is well worth reconsidering the representations of HIV/AIDS in public health campaigns. To what extent are their pictures of young and older people 'an enlargement of our lives, rather than a restriction?' Certainly, the frightening claustrophobia of 'The Grim Reaper's horror-genre bowling alley is as closed and disempowering a space as any prison camp or hospital ward. But does the 'laid back' atmosphere of 'Vox Pop Condom – Granny' counter this representation? Does it promote not victims but 'safer sex as an enlargement of our lives'?

'GRIM REAPER' AND 'VOX POP CONDOM': CONTROL OR EMPOWERMENT?

We can begin by examining the moments of narrative closure of both the Australian HIV/AIDS ads discussed, 'The Grim Reaper' and 'Vox

Pop Condom – Granny'. Narrative theorists argue that the moment of narrative closure is a particularly important one in, as advertisers would say, grabbing an audience. 'The end of the narrative in fact not only completes the situation at the beginning of the tale, but *clarifies* it in the sense of explaining it in terms of a cultural law' (Tulloch, 1982: 191) – namely, 'The Grim Reaper's sombre and magisterial final voice-over 'Always use condoms. Always'. Narrative closure has two primary functions. First, it establishes the 'plenitude' of the tale, its cultural weight, certainty and sense of the 'good life', thus repairing the narrative 'lack' established earlier by the villain (in this case, the Reaper himself). Second, narrative closure supposedly secures and controls the knowledge of the viewer. As Sam Rohdie has argued, 'The knowledge that marks the narrative has, at this moment of plenitude, *become* the knowledge that marks the spectator . . . the spectator, secure[d], dominant. is now in a position to tell the whole story' (Rohdie, 1979: 86). Yet it seems clear that the closure of 'The Grim Reaper' did not leave its viewers 'dominant'; and this is because as well as the plenitudinous words, 'Always use condoms. Always', the ad also concluded with the horrifying image of age and death in the Reaper himself.

Here the signs of extreme old age as death itself are signs of decay (the skull) and dismemberment (the scythe). Together they represent, as Woodward has put it, the 'phantasm of the fragmenting body [that] is associated with old age and the death that decrepitude brings' (Woodward, 1991: 182). As Woodward says, beyond the conventional splitting of youth and age in our culture 'we find *subsplitting*: idealised images of old age constitute a polar opposite to those which express fear. But in the west our representations of old age reflect a dominant gerontophobia. Almost any text can confirm this' (Woodward, 1991: 7). The text that Woodward chooses as an example, Hawkes's *The Passion Artist* does indeed reflect a dominant gerontophobia which we see as well in 'The Grim Reaper'. Hawkes depicts a very old woman as 'crone':

> open mouth with its three amber-coloured teeth and the breath
> of a great age, small twisted ears that appeared to have been sewn
> to the sides of the skull with coarse thread, the skin that was tightly
> shrivelled to the bone . . . the ageless crafty spirit in a face that
> otherwise was only a small torn mask.
>
> (cited in Woodward, 1991: 7–8)

If, following Woodward, we put aside for the moment the gender differences carried by 'crone' and 'reaper' in order to focus on general representations of aging, we can certainly agree that these representations of old age as dismembered 'torn mask' convey 'horror and catastrophe' (Woodward, 1991: 8) rather than security. In other words, negative images associated with ageist 'subsplitting' coalesce here with social marketing conventions of horror in health campaigns.

Like Simon Watney, Kathleen Woodward's intention in *Aging and Its Discontents* is to seek representations which do not strip older people of 'power and control over the actual complex meaning and dignity of their lives'. Woodward asks 'Can we invent in our culture new meanings of old age . . . ? Can we associate not shock but other kinds of affect with growing old?' (Woodward, 1991: 70). Can we bridge that 'single binary' of youth with age that she sees as so central and so exploitative in our culture? Can we oppose to the aggressive 'look' of youthful desire the benevolent 'gaze' of older age?

If we turn now to the narrative closure of 'Vox Pop Condom – Granny', can we say that it is precisely this benevolent gaze from age to youth which is the plenitude, the cultural law, of this health story? Can we say, in Woodward's words, that the old lady's 'valuing of the young . . . is precisely not an *over*valuation. It is her security in herself that makes possible her benevolence' (Woodward, 1991: 87)? In important ways I think we can say 'yes'. Unlike the deep and permanent wrinkles of Hawkes's crone, 'granny', extraordinarily wrinkled herself, links age to youth via her confident pleasure in her own sexuality. Placed at the closure of the narrative, granny's 'benevolent gaze' is on youth, via memory of her own; and in this sense she does restore the 'sight lines between generations [that] have been broken' (Woodward, 1991: 89). Consequently, we might argue that this is one of the new representations of aging which allows us 'From the perspective of a healthy old age . . . to theorise the developments of strengths in old age rather than the ravages of regression' (ibid.: 88).

Critiquing 'youthfulness as masquerade' (in particular the visual disappearing act enabled by new anti-aging creams and cosmetic surgery), Woodward argues that the process of smoothing over and tightening up the skin by which 'the aging body is being remodelled so as to virtually eliminate it – to make it indistinguishable from a young or middle-aged body' (Woodward, 1991: 161), is hiding from the aged just as completely as the more conventional incarceration of old people in retirement communities. In an important sense, in this process of hiding, older people are participating, in Bettelheim's terms, in 'rituals of their own degradation'. In addition, as Featherstone and Hepworth argue, the ability to purchase and utilize new cellular therapy and cosmetic surgery expertise 'would be stronger in the most powerful and privileged groups who would use it to reinforce existing social inequalities and status distinctions' (Featherstone and Hepworth, 1990: 273).

In this situation, Woodward argues, it is 'not that traditional notions of aging are being accorded more currency (age as bringing wisdom . . .) or that aging is so much being redefined' (Woodward, 1991: 161),

271

but rather that age is banished from the chronology of wrinkles as surely as previously it was hidden in the confinement of the nursing home. Though these terminal places (terminal like Lukacs's prison camps and Watney's hospital wards) are apparently replaced by 'a democratic body, potentially available to everyone' (ibid.), the same exploitative binary of youth and age remains. 'For the most part the discourse is addressed to women. As an older woman, one's success is defined in terms of how closely one approaches the model of the younger woman. The deep structure of the look of mass culture is youth versus age' (ibid.: 159). As Susan Sontag has argued, this makes women deeply conservative. 'Women care for their bodies – against toughening, coarsening and fat. They *conserve* them' (Sontag, 1979: 80).

But in 'Vox Pop Condom – Granny', the older woman is not only brought out of the nursing home and on to the beach where young people 'look' sexually. She is also presented as deeply wrinkled while still speaking the desires of youth. Perhaps in this ad aging is being redefined (in Woodward's phrase, 'the pleasures of the body remain in force', ibid.: 196), while also parading the more traditional value that 'age brings wisdom'. Arguably, it is that combination of current day values (sexuality) and traditional ones (wisdom) which underpins the confidence of her 'benevolent gaze on youth'. Hendricks and Hendricks have argued that because of conventional stereotypes 'we do the elderly a great disservice by regarding them as just another problem rather than as a potential resource for resolving society's dilemmas' (Hendricks and Hendricks, 1986: 35). In this case, 'granny', in her complex combination of wrinkles, laughter and sexuality, is being drawn on to help resolve society's dilemmas.

However, there is an alternative way of examining the social meaning of 'Vox Pop Condom – Granny' in the context of the earlier 'Grim Reaper'. Woodward herself speaks of the 'panopticon of mass culture, the all-seeing television eye' (Woodward, 1991: 160), and from this more Foucauldian perspective we can think of government health campaigns in terms of medical control. In this context, how might we begin to understand the 'impact' of these two ads as vehicles for establishing behaviour change as social order?

If we look again at 'The Grim Reaper' and 'Vox Pop Condom' ads within this context, we can plausibly argue that 'The Grim Reaper' was so powerful in impact because it destroyed common-sense feelings of autonomy in ordinary daily routines – in this case, heterosex – by its construction of the AIDS virus's so called 'second wave'. It established in Giddens's term, a 'critical situation', shattering the routinization of accustomed daily life. As Giddens says, 'Ordinary day-to-day social life . . . involves an ontological security founded on an autonomy of bodily control within predictable routines and encounters' (Giddens, 1984:

64). But after 'The Grim Reaper' people suddenly encountered their bodies as potential enemies – hence the immediate rush to have tests to convince themselves that the enemy was not within. As Dreuilhe says,

> We have grown up in our bodies, they are our native lands . . . we have a natural affection for them, warts and all. My country has occasionally disappointed me, but like a Resistance fighter, I'll stop at nothing when it comes to throwing off the foreign viral yoke.
>
> (Dreuilhe, 1988: 8)

The narrative of 'invasion, metamorphosis and fusion', in which an external force enters the body and changes it irreversibly is, as Rosemary Jackson (1981) has pointed out, one of the key myths of the modern fantastic genre. This 'vampire' narrative has a powerful place in popular culture; and with the coming of AIDS and 'The Grim Reaper' this image of what Dreuilhe calls the 'foreign viral yoke . . . in our bodies' had an especially strong impact on the ontological security of masses of people's daily routines because science, our modern saviour, had no cure. The massive response – of rushing to science where it *could* help by observing and testing – is not altogether surprising.

One of the 'panopticon' functions of the media in these 'critical situations' where the certitudes of institutionalized routines are threatened is to reorganize routines, and establish new narratives of containment.

Examination of HIV/AIDS discourse on talk-back radio (Tulloch and Chapman, 1992) and women's magazines (Tulloch, 1992), for example, shows that the weakened figure of the 'scientific expert' is being popularly re-introduced. After the shock effect of 'The Grim Reaper', I would argue, the 'Vox Pop Condom' ads similarly served to re-establish conventional order and routine. But here it was 'the people' rather than scientific expertise which was the agent of safety. As we have seen, the main aim of 'Vox Pop Condom' was to 'normalize' the condom; and this was to be conveyed by the 'conversational, casual tone to the commercials which is in itself an important element in conveying that the subject of condoms is no big deal to talk about' (Health Advancement Campaign Unit, 1990: 35–6). There was to be 'a strong sense of realism conveyed through the honesty, sincerity and spontaneity of the people in the commercials' (ibid.: 35); and alternatively structured formats (for instance, with or without a visual interviewer) were carefully pre-tested to avoid what some audience groups saw as a 'staged execution' by 'actors rather than real people'.

But, of course, 'Vox Pop Condom – Granny' *was* a 'staged execution'; most notably in its careful reconstitution of the family that had been dismembered in 'The Grim Reaper'. A significant feature of the ad is

273

its use of people older than the target audience of young people – their off-stage mothers, and (most forcefully) the 'granny' (as the producers of the ad and many students called her). This family nomination ('granny') is itself significant; since arguably the ad was not in fact a progressive promo for the sexuality of the aged, but rather a careful restoration of sexuality to the confining supervisory 'wisdom' of the family. If, as Watney argues, 'We have to establish Safer Sex as an enlargement of our lives, rather than a restriction', then to what extent was the representation of 'the sexual diversity of our species' (Watney, 1987: 24) enlarged by this ad? To what extent, for instance, *are* the aged presented as sexually-active beings (as has begun to happen in Australian soap operas, like *G.P.*).

At first sight textual analysis of 'Vox Pop Condom' points to a negative conclusion. The intention was to soft sell the acceptability and widespread use of condoms. Thus the *mise-en-scène* was 'everywhere in daily life' (the beach, the street, shopping malls, parties, the pub), the narrative was repetitive rather than sequentially driven, the body language was humorous (the embarrassed girl, the Italian boy), the lighting was 'natural' rather than oppressively dark, the sound was 'real' (without music overlay), and the voice-over (where it occurred) was that of a conventional 'vox pop' interviewer (with the added humorous inflection of Australian comedian Andrew Denton). In addition, the editing was based on contiguous cuts (that is, verbal/visual contiguity from 'most guys now carry them around in their wallets anyway' to the visual of the Italian boy producing his wallet; verbal/verbal contiguity from 'my mum's going to be watching' to 'my mum's found a few in the wash'; and verbal/natural sound contiguity, from 'they can make me laugh a lot' to the actual laughter of the embarrassed girl in the street). This editing style constructed a casually organized but coherent world where the young are comfortably and light-heartedly in control of their fate, where mums are 'glad' to find their son's condoms, and even grans used them for pleasure.

Despite its apparent formlessness, then, 'Vox Pop Condom' was carefully constructed to reconstruct the *cycle of generations* within the family – the sense, in Giddens's phrase, of a long *durée* which re-establishes certitude, a sense of human control and agency, and hence 'ontological security'. In this sense it quite specifically addressed the particular 'critical situation' opened by 'The Grim Reaper', reconstituting a sphere of control and self-esteem within the family institution – hence its impact and considerable popularity. The image of aging was used here quite consciously at the end of the ad (the DCSH document spoke of the need for 'a beginning, a middle and an end' so that the viewer was presented with the familiar format of advertising messages) for a conservative resolution. Far from this being Watney's enlargement of our lives via a representation of age and sexual diversity, in this context it seems a restriction, confining 'gran's' sexuality (her use of condoms) safely to the past.

However, such a conclusion is based on narrative and textual analysis alone. Audience theorists have rightly criticized a textual approach which privileges 'preferred' textual readings over the responses of actual audiences. David Morley, for instance argues that 'the equation of "preferred reading" and "narrative closure" (or hierarchy of discourse) always runs the risk of reducing a . . . text to the mere vehicle of a banal substantive proposition which can then be labelled as "ideological"' (Morley, 1981: 6).

I must confess that my initial, 'ideological', reading of 'Vox Pop Condom – Granny' (in terms of its ageism) was indeed what I was predicting most of the young target audience would produce from the text. However, I followed up my earlier textual analysis of these ads with an audience study which indicated that to some extent my reading of 'Vox Pop Condom – Granny' was a property of the analyst (though as we will see, not entirely so).

The audience study was conducted in April 1992 on a small-scale audience sample, about 100 year 11, 16- to 17-year-old state school students in Sydney. Students were shown the 'Vox Pop Condom' ad, asked to write three to four sentences of 'what it was about', and then to fill in a short questionnaire. Questions included (in order) 'Which person in this condom ad did you like best? Say why.'; 'Which person did you like least? Say why.'; 'Was it a good idea having the old lady in the ad? Say why.'.

'Most liked' character among males (both working and middle-class) was the 'ethnic' boy who showed his wallet. Of those who responded, 39 per cent of the males named him as 'most liked' character; but this was closely followed in second place by the older lady (36 per cent). Among girls (both working-class and middle-class) the bronzed life-saver (a symptom of 'youth's desire to be looked at') was 'most liked' (43 per cent), again followed in second place by the older lady. But overall (male + female responses) though, the older lady was 'most liked' (36 per cent) followed by the 'ethnic' boy and the life-saver (34 per cent).

Asked whether the older lady was a 'good idea' in the ad, 87 per cent said 'yes' (82 per cent boys, 91 per cent girls). The 'Yes – Why' responses were post-coded into five categories; the two most significant of which were:

(i) 'Shows old people have sex too, so all generations have to use condoms' (41 per cent of total student sample);
(ii) 'Shows that condoms have been around for a while, weren't invented yesterday' (22 per cent).

We were able to be quite precise in post-coding 'sex now' and 'sex in the past' responses of students in relation to the older lady. Responses like 'As it showed that all people of all ages use and should use condoms', 'It shows that you're never too old', 'Because people think that when you get older you don't have sex', or 'All ages have sex not just young people' seem quite clearly to be accepting that older people have sex *now* and need to use condoms too in the face of AIDS. In contrast, responses like 'It shows that she used condoms too and that they've been around for a long time' seem clearly to be situating the older lady's sex life in the past, in *her* youth (we conservatively post-coded *all* past tense responses, as in 'It shows that she used condoms too', in the 'sex in the past' category).

I found the results surprising. Though I did find what Woodward calls the 'cold and murderous fury' (Woodward, 1991: 103) of young people's 'disgusted' responses to the sexuality of older people (as in the comments, 'No one would have sex with her/she made me sick'), these responses were relatively rare. The majority of students read the older lady in 'Vox Pop Condom – Granny' in terms of her *present* sexuality, and they read her favourably in that light. Even those students who nominated the old lady as 'least-liked' character (21 per cent), often still admitted it was a 'good idea' having her in the ad. One middle-class boy disliked her, for instance, for the following reason: 'Not the sort of thing you would expect from the older generation – how would you feel if it was your own grandmother?' But he said, despite this that it was good to have her in the ad 'because it does show that condoms are accepted across all generations'. In this particular case, the ideological closure of the family seems to be struggling with the boy's own, more open values and sexual experiences. This boy, for instance, believed that both boys and girls should take responsibility to provide condoms, and when asked 'If you have sex, do you always use condoms?' replied 'No – not all sex calls for condoms, e.g. oral sex'.

CONCLUSION

I have hardly begun to unpack the specific cultural (class, gender and ethnic) issues here. What I have wanted to do is begin to discuss issues of aging and death in the Australian AIDS ads outside the psychologistic framework in which they are so often contained in health authority documents, as well as in much academic research. I have also wanted to suggest – using fairly broad brush strokes at this stage – why 'The Grim Reaper' and 'Vox Pop Condom – Granny' had such an impact in Australia. The passage from Grim Reaper to Cheery Condom was, I have argued, a major media event in which a 'critical situation' was articulated and 'ontological insecurity' was first established (in the absence of the familiar myth of science) and then expunged (in the presence of the long *durée* of the family).

In that process, young people (and older) were initially imprisoned as helpless victims, and later empowered in terms of their own sexuality. Young people have rejected in large numbers the new prison house of old morality that many journalists were constructing for them in 1986/7, when 'The Grim Reaper' appeared (exemplified by headlines like 'Matrimony is Back in Fashion – Here Comes the New Morality' and 'Disease Fear Heralds the Cautious 1980s'). Government campaigns have aided that empowerment by emphasizing the 'normality' of condoms, a message which young people in Australia are clearly responding to. Also, my recent survey suggests that the majority of young people are reading representations of older people's sexuality as 'good', 'open', 'truthful' and 'frank' rather than 'sick'. Recent soap operas in Australia, like *G.P.*, which emphasize the importance and normality of old people's sexuality, may have helped in this regard. In this important sense our public institutions are working to produce new representations of aging. Arber and Ginn note that:

> In western societies the advantages of aging which women could look forward to in (some) traditional societies have been lost. Older people are devalued because they are seen as having reduced capacity for production in the formal economy (reflecting the priorities of industrialism) and women are devalued when deemed past fulfilling sexual, reproductive and domestic servicing roles (reflecting the priorities of men).
>
> (Arber and Ginn, 1991: 48)

The argument of this article is that things are changing in both these areas. The priorities of capital now include the aging audience as an important target for advertising; and older people are beginning to be displayed in positive sexual terms. But I am also suggesting that this is an ambiguous progress. As regards the 'empowerment' thesis, two specific notes of caution are in order:

1 The sexuality of older people in 'Vox Pop Condom' is embedded within the reconstitution of the *family* as agent in relation to sexuality and HIV/AIDS. Andrew Wernick argues that 'Through the activities of lobby groups, regulatory bodies and intra-industry voluntary codes, the middle-of-the-road character of imagistic advertising, its inherent disinclination to offend any sizable sector of its potential audience/market, had been politically institutionalized' (Wernick, 1991: 46); and I think that 'Condom Vox Pop – Granny' is a very good example of this. The DCSH and its advertisers were always extremely concerned not to offend parents, who were seen as a potentially powerful

lobby group. Parents – together with the so-called 'cultures' of intravenous drug users and young heterosexuals – were always included in the pre-testing research for HIV/AIDS ads; and 'Vox Pop Condom – Granny' was conceived as a compromise, as Wernick would say, constituted at a perceived point of overlap. In this sense 'Vox Pop Condom – Granny' only re-represents the relationship between older women and power in a limited way. By reconstituting her place within the family cycle, 'Vox Pop Condom – Granny' removes the 'dangerous' threat of the powerful older woman.

2 The 'normalizing' of condoms also naturalizes the notion that 'safe sex' = penetrative sex. As Crawford and Kippax argue 'there is no suggestion in the television campaign material that non-penetrative sex is a possible form of "safe-sex" (Crawford, Kippax and Tulloch, 1992: 69); and this in itself, they argue, implicitly supports quasi-scientific rationales that 'Men have the urge to pursue and penetrate and women recognising this biological necessity yield and submit' (ibid.: 68). Within *that* discourse, where the 'taken-for-granted nature of heterosex makes it very difficult to negotiate issues of "safe" sex' *beyond* the condom (ibid.), any empowerment of sexual practice in the sense Watney means (of celebrating 'the social, radical and sexual diversity of our species'), seems limited indeed – whether the focus is on the young or on older people. In the last instance, the overall emphasis of the advertisement is on what Woodward calls the gendered, competitive and aggressive 'look' of youthful desire rather than on the negotiative, socially bonding and benevolent 'gaze' of older age with which it ends.

REFERENCES

Arber, S. and Ginn, J. (1991) *Gender and Later Life. A Sociological Analysis of Resources and Constraints*, London: Sage.

Bettelheim, B. (1960) *The Informed Heart*, Glencoe: Free Press.

British Health Education Authority (1988) 'Evaluation of the HEA Public Education Campaign', February – June.

Crawford, J, Kippax, S. and Tulloch, J. (1992) *Evaluating the National AIDS Education Campaigns*, Canberra: Department of Community Services and Health.

Dreuilhe, E. (1988) *Mortal Embrace*, Toronto: Hill & Wang.

Featherstone, M. and Hepworth, M. (1990) 'Images of aging', in J. Bond and P. Coleman (eds) *Ageing in Society. An Introduction to Social Gerontology*, London: Sage, pp. 250–75.

Featherstone, M. and Hepworth, M. (1991) 'The mask of aging and the postmodern life course', in M. Featherstone, M. Hepworth and B. S. Turner (eds) *The Body: Social Process and Cultural Theory*, London: Sage, pp. 371–89.

Giddens, A. (1984) *The Constitution of Society*, Cambridge: Polity Press.

Health Advancement Campaign Unit (1990) '1990 AIDS campaign – creative development research', Canberra: Australian Department of Community Services and Health.

Hendricks, J. and Hendricks, C. D. (1986) *Aging in Mass Society. Myth and Realities*, Boston: Little, Brown.

Itzin, C. (1984) 'The double jeopardy of ageism and sexism: media images of women', in D. B. Bromley (ed.) *Gerontology: Social and Behavioural Perspectives*, London: Croom Helm, pp. 170–84.

Jackson, R. (1981) *Fantasy: The Literature of Subversion*, London: Methuen.

Kotler, P. and Roberto, R. (1989) *Social Marketing: Strategies for Changing Public Behavior*, New York: Free Press.

Lukacs, G. (1969) *Solzhenitsyn*, London: Merlin.

Morley, D. (1981) 'The "Nationwide Audience" – a critical postscript', *Screen Education*, 39: 3–14.

Rohdie, S. (1979) 'The reality of the text: a segment of Roma, Citta Aperta', (unpublished Ph D thesis, La Trobe University).

Sontag, S. (1979) 'The double standard of aging', in V. Carver and P. Liddiard (eds) *An Aging Population: A Reader and Sourcebook*, New York, Holmes and Meier, pp. 72–80.

Tulloch, J. (1977) 'Conventions of dying: structural contrasts in Chekhov and Bergman', in J. Tulloch (ed.) *Conflict and Control in the Cinema. A Reader in Film and Society*, Melbourne: Macmillan.

Tulloch, J. (1982) *Australian Cinema: Industry, Narrative and Meaning*, Sydney: Allen & Unwin.

Tulloch, J. (1992) 'Discoursing AIDS and sexuality: popular media, magazines and young audiences', *Social Semiotics*.

Tulloch, J. and Chapman, S. (1992) 'Experts in crisis: the framing of radio debate about the risk of AIDS to heterosexuals', *Discourse and Society* 3 (4): 437–67.

Turtle, A. M. *et al.* (1989) 'AIDS-related beliefs and behaviours of Australian university students', *Medical Journal of Australia* 151: 371–6.

Watney, S. (1987) 'Photography and AIDS', *Ten* 8 (26): 14–29.

Wernick, A. (1991) *Promotional Culture. Advertising, Ideology and Symbolic Expression*, London: Sage.

Woodward, K. (1991) *Aging and Its Discontents. Freud and Other Fictions*, Bloomington: University of Indiana.

17

SELLING FUNERALS, IMAGING DEATH

Andrew Wernick

And death once dead there's no more dying then.
(William Shakespeare: Sonnet cv)

DEATH DENIAL AND THE AMERICAN COMPROMISE

If dying has been medicalized, death, or at least the disposal of the dead and the ceremonials which surround this process, has been commodified. In North America there are about 30,000 commercial funeral homes, cemeteries and crematoria plus a host of companies for the manufacture of everything from caskets, vaults, urns and monuments to hearses, casket lifts and embalming fluid.[1] Funerals, costing around $7,000 for the normal package, are usually pre-financed, which further brings into play a range of banks, insurance, legal and trust companies. Taken together, this network of enterprises constitutes what its managers call 'the death-care industry'. The immaterial terms in which funeral and cemetery directors describe their function ('We sell service not merchandise') are not wholly false. Physical disposition and the materials necessary serve as the vehicle for a luxuriant sign production; in which role the industry has subordinated the churches that once presided over all the rituals of the life course, and has itself come to exercise a virtual monopoly over the organized symbology of death.

A peculiarity of the death-care industry is that its products and services are not eagerly sought. The very topic of death is troublesome, particularly in a technologically-driven civilization wherein its occurrence at all has come to seem gratuitous and obscene. Philippe Ariès (1981) documents the rise of death denial as a revolution in western 'mentalities'. Its specifically modern character was pinpointed, according to him, by an argument advanced by Chardouillet in the 1870s. Chardouillet's book, *Les Cimetières: Sont Ils Des Foyers D'Infection?*, fiercely attacked a hygiene-rationalized plan by the municipal council of Paris to move the city's cemeteries to a distant site at Méry-sur-Oise. 'Let them admit,' he wrote, 'if they do not have the courage to endure it, that the spectacle of death is distressing; that in a world of happy industrialism, no one has time for the dead' (Ariès 1981: 544).

Industrialism has no doubt been less happy in actuality than in the promotional images it has given itself, particularly in the effusions of consumer advertising that have come to pervade its culture. There, at least, the repressive effects of death denial have been evident. And what applies narrowly to the Good Life imagery of ads applies as well to the wider context in which they are delivered. In so far as the media, through which the signs of death, as of everything else, must circulate, have become subordinated to a selling function, its distressing shadow, as of negativity in general, must be neutralized or even expunged.

The repression is notable in outlets like consumer magazines for 'the mature' which especially target those whose lives are beginning to be affected by the shortness of human time. In such monthlies as *Modern Maturity* (US), *Discovery* (Canada), and *Choice* (UK) there are no obituaries, no columns on existentially preparing for death, and a persistent identification of happy old age with leisure activities and staying young. The 'positive images of aging' which liberal social workers counterpose to ageist prejudice, and which advertisers deploy to organize the pre- and post-retirement market, conjure positivity out of not being old at all. Extending the cult of youth to the elderly avoids the unpleasant aspects of infirmity and disease. It also displaces attention from the enormous loss of status and position which the elderly experience in a society where acquired knowledge becomes rapidly redundant, and accumulated experience guarantees neither social function nor prestige.

The marketing of funerals and related services is constrained, then, to be discreet. Even in the ultra-commercial United States there is little direct media advertising, and scarcely any in the kind of lifestyle magazines already mentioned.[2] Caskets, urns, and other paraphernalia are not for immediate public sale, but distributed (and showcased) through funeral homes and commercial cemeteries. The primary advertising vehicles for the death-care industry are, indeed, funeral homes and cemeteries themselves. Just by being there they promote. The park-type cemeteries introduced in the United States at the beginning of the century are pleasant, life affirming green spaces that welcome visitors. Some, like LA's Forest Lawn, set out to be tourist attractions with weddings, concerts and other special events. For funeral homes, normally a grieving family's first port of call, physical design has also been important. Tastefully set in residential neighbourhoods, however, their primary promotional strategy has been the build-up of a locally respected name over generations of family ownership, reinforced by 'repeat business' from the procession of mourners passing through.

As these examples suggest, the indirectness of funeral promotion has been supplemented by a euphemistic transformation of what funerals connote. Since the establishment of the National Funeral Directors Association in the 1880s the services of the 'the dismal trade' have been progressively refashioned to be as feel-good as circumstances will allow. In a funeral form whose basic ingredients have changed little since then, the disruptive expression of grief in public places has been obviated by the circumscribed sites and prettified conditions in which its ceremonials occur. In flower-bedecked viewing room and chapel, before and even during the service, the embalmed corpse is dressed, cosmetically made up, and displayed as if in good health and only resting. Funerals, as the trade cliché has it, are 'for the living'. They provide 'grief therapy', and some establishments even offer 'aftercare' in addition to 'the perpetual care' of remains (or 'cremains') reposing in the vaults and mausoleums of the cemetery.

The 'dying of death' noted with alarm by a reviewer in 1899[3] was in no simple sense caused by the rise of commercialism. As James Farfell (1980) has shown, besides the earlier removal of cemeteries from cities, it can be independently traced in nineteenth century theological trends: the excision of hell from the eschatology of after-life, and the transposition of that eschatology on to the manifest destiny of a society that embraced progress as the route to heaven on earth. But the promotional uses to which this secularizing shift was put in pasting a happy, or at any rate restorative, face on the services sold by the funeral business should equally not be overlooked.

Of course, if a this-worldly and present-minded exclusion of death from the public domain were the only cultural impulse at work there would be no spontaneous market for the elaborate and expensive arrangements sold by the death-care industry at all. From the outset of modernity, however, the desire to exclude the dead as a pollutant reminder of the vacuousness of the industrial show was counterbalanced by the rise of a contrary impulse to memorialize the deceased in a veritable cult of the dead. The French Positivists who joined forces with the Catholic Church to oppose removal of the Parisian cemeteries (Ariès 1981: 541–7) were emphatic about the need for such veneration. Society was an immortal organism which included the dead as well as the living and the unborn. The fetishism of the tomb was a religious duty, vital to the moral integration of industrial society. These lofty social engineering sentiments found their political echo in the shrines and statuary built throughout the west for the state, military, business and artistic heroes of the classical bourgeois age. They coincided as well with the 'cult of remembrance' that Walter Benjamin noted was associated with the early mass reception of photography, and that democratized portrait painting as a way to perpetuate the memory of past family members.

The persistence well into this century of the sentimentalized 'death of the other' which, Ariès (1981: 409–75) tells us, assimilated the monumentalizing aspect of early industrial attitudes to death to a romantic sensibility, has provided the funeral business with its principal opportunities for profit and growth. Simple Puritan burial has been replaced by an elaborate array of memorializing steps, each of which, from pre-funeral viewing to the cemetery's perpetual cave, provides the occasion for lucrative commodity sale. The genius of the American funeral business, however, is not only to have developed a source of profit that perpetuates the memorializing impulse on which it feeds. It is to have done so while simultaneously catering for the opposite wish to put death and the dead out of mind.

The commercial mediation of this cultural contradiction is precisely what accounts for the funerary complex which Jessica Mitford (1963) described as 'the American way of death'. Hence, burial grounds as huge but beautiful parks, with markers flush with the grass so that the eye of the visitor is not distracted by morbid signs. Hence, too, the pervasive rhetoric of grief therapy, which rationalizes and shapes the memorial vocabulary as a controlled abreaction scientifically designed to get the grieving over their grief so that normal life can resume. Hence, finally, that most extraordinary invention of post-Civil War American funeral practice: embalming.[4] Since embalming is for display, and display means caskets and other paraphernalia, its central place in the economy of funeral homes is evident. More interesting is the ambiguity of what it signifies. Temporarily preserving and beautifying the corpse for visitation prior to the funeral simulates physical immortality as an iconic sign of enduring personal presence. But in providing the bereaved with a 'memory picture' it also fixes an image of the deceased, in pleasant repose, as both happy in death and irrevocably gone.

DISTURBING THE CASKET

This, however, is only a first approximation. In the period since the 1960s when modern North American funerary culture began to come under sustained critical fire, a number of trends have emerged which suggest that the compromise just outlined is neither as fixed nor as stable as had earlier seemed.

The most obvious new factor is the one associated with the rise of anti-industry criticism itself. Trade papers still recall with pain the frontal attack launched on the American funeral business by Jessica Mitford. It was the first of several, with critics from outside the industry like Ruth Mulvey Harmer, in *The High Cost of Dying* (1963), joining with renegade voices from within, like the anonymous Canadian author ('Coriolis', 1967) of *Death, Here Is Thy Sting*.[5] The titles give the flavour: funeral directors and cemetery owners as greedy fleecers of the dead and grieving, pushing empty but expensive rituals (and merchandise) on those most helpless to resist. In this we see the confluence of two streams: on the one side, populist consumerism in the style of Ralph Nader (is embalmment a rip-off?); on the other, a utilitarian scepticism about symbolic displays, tinged with Protestant iconoclasm, behind whose dignified matter of factness can also be discerned an impulse to keep the disruptions of 'untamed' death at bay.[6] If the American way of death equals the disguised negation of death denial, then this counter movement is the negation of that negation. But in an equally confused way, first, because it fails to see its own continuity with the death-denying razzmatazz it excoriates; second, because it condenses a traditional humanist aversion to symbols and rituals, especially as linked to organized religion, with a more contemporary – even neo-traditional – distaste for their stylized simulacra.

In the public at large, the most extreme expression of this counter-movement has been in the revived growth of Memorial Societies. These non-profit co-operatives, offering no frills disposition, would be an industry nightmare if they achieved market power. However, lacking promotional resources and media access, and perhaps because of the very severity of their rationalism, they have remained marginal. More significant have been three more limited shifts in funeral demand. Each has been commercially accommodated. Yet, taken together, they represent a profound stirring of the industry's client base, which has sharpened considerably the cultural tensions that beset what it does.

First is the growing demand for cremation. In the UK it is already the manner of disposition of choice, and in the western United States is rapidly approaching that status. For the US as a whole the proportion of cremations reached 19 per cent by 1992 from virtually zero in 1960 (Canadian figures are double this), and the current increase of 1 per cent per year is expected to continue for the indefinite future.[7] Besides waning belief in the Final Resurrection of the Body and land-scarcity (evidently a factor in the UK), the correlation which industry data show between cremation choice and higher education strongly implies that it is motivated by the same complex of no-nonsense secular rationalism as Memorial Societies appeal to. In the western imaginary, no more complete way can be conceived of expelling the dead from the circle of the living than by burning their remains.

At first, the implicit rejection of not only cemeteries (and their costs), but also of the embalming/casket system, panicked funeral homes into discouraging clients from making this choice altogether. In the past twenty years, though, wise adaptations have been made so that cremation is offered as a simple variant on the standard model. Either way, buried or burnt, casket and 'memory picture' are strongly advised, and the overall charge is roughly the same. In place of vaults, families are encouraged to store the ashes in a memorial urn, and, for the full treatment, to store the latter in a columbarium or mausoleum niche. For grievers who wish to scatter, special urns for that purpose can also be bought.

As the case of cremation indicates, the wish of the deceased for a simple disposal can be compromised by the more elaborate funeral and memorial arrangements made by survivors. It is here that we see a second major change in the post-1960s funeral market. The dominant responsibility of survivors (normally family) for funeral arrangement has been eroded by a dramatic increase in the proportion of funerals which are pre-arranged and/or prepaid by those whose passage they are designed to mark.

What the industry calls 'pre-need' sales were pioneered in the early decades of this century by cemetery interests. The pitch was to invest in a grave-site (and any other services leading up to it) at an inflation-proof, discounted price. The aim was to bypass the funeral directors whose immediate relation with the bereaved ensured them first crack at available funds. More recently, other factors, including consumer awareness (promoted and turned into lobbying power by the American Association for Retired Persons) and the attenuation of family ties, have provided a real basis of growing demand. Funeral directors have naturally been defensive. Those arranging their own funerals are more liable than grievers to do so on the cheap. But as with cremation, market pressures have proved ineluctable. Pre-need funeral sales in North America are currently about 20 per cent of the total, and growing at more than 1 per cent a year.[8] As a result, pre-arrangement and prepaying schemes, offered by specialized companies as well as by funeral homes themselves, are now part of the regularly publicized fare.

Strip-mining the future can evidently outweigh the benefits of acceler-ated cash flow. But leaving aside economic risks to the industry, the shift in clientele from those dealing with the death of others to those planning for their own has profound implications for the way death itself is culturally defined. Most fundamentally, it reintroduces into social discourse the dying subject. That is, the living individual in so far as their inner and outer conduct is actively oriented towards the present and future of the process in which they pass from the world. Of course, the contemporary 'dying subject' is quite different from earlier versions of that figure. It bears little relation, for example, to the penitential Christian, reviewing past deeds at the hour of death (or earlier) for signs that salvation, or at least not too long in purgatory, lies ahead. Still further is it from the classical 'art of dying' which Montaigne and others reintroduced during the Renaissance as a wise guide to life. Here, more narrowly, the subject who is interpellated as the one who is always already about-to-die, is the economic consumer of a service. Or rather, of a number of related services, including life insurance, estate management and living wills, to which funeral arrangement has been added as perhaps the most baffling, and symbolically charged, of a lengthening list.

A particular puzzle for living arrangers of their own funerals is what to do about those (highly expensive) aspects of the ceremonial process which the industry promotes as psychologically beneficial for the bereaved. The memorials plied by the cemetery or crematorium, not to mention the 'memory picture', are poor surrogates, not only for physical immortality, but even for the symbolic immortality they unconvincingly mime. On the other hand, meditating on what is now taken to be the therapeutic function of 'memorialization' only emphasizes the sad truth: that the funeral industry's cult of the dead merely simulates what its nineteenth century champions had taken it to be; that in the mobile and fragmentary spaces of contemporary culture the collective memory has virtually dissolved; and – celebrityhood aside – that any real power individuals might once have had to institute themselves beyond the grave, whether as vital members of an organic community or in the heroic mode of bourgeois individualism, is irremediably on the wane.

All this presents special difficulties for the competitive promotion of pre-need sales. What such promotion tends to stress, then, is not so much the advantages to self of prepaying and pre-arranging, as to those on whom the responsibility would otherwise fall. In North America, the historical strength of the funeral director lobby in curbing the promotional activities of the cemeteries, plus continuing funeral home reluctance to beat their own pre-arrangement drum, has kept the rhetorical possibilities in check. A glimpse of what these might be, however, is provided by a series of ads that recently appeared in the UK. They were placed in *Choice* magazine ('For The Good Times Ahead') by Dignity in Destiny, a pre-needs consortium co-sponsored by Hodgson Holdings, Kenyon International and the giant British charity Help the Aged.[9]

'Why did Ann pre-arrange?', asks one such ad in the June 1990 issue. The answer is a true life vignette:

A windy night in the Pennine village of Delph; a sprightly pensioner celebrates her birthday. The patrons of the Green Ash restaurant would be surprised to learn that this active, practical Yorkshire lady has recently pre-arranged her own funeral! . . . She purchased her Dignity in Destiny pre-arranged funeral plan because she believes in 'putting her house in order'. Her Dignity in Destiny plan gives her 'peace of mind and security, takes away all the worries about funeral costs, and removes from her family the burden of funeral arrangements'.

Besides its patronizing folksiness and reference to perpetual youth, the pitch is notable in its final altruistic appeal. Pre-arrangement is for the sake of family, an emblem for whose solidarity it can be taken to stand. Illustrating the text is a photograph. In a green and sunny meadow, edged with trees, a three-generational family are happily, and co-operatively, at play: Mum and Dad mock-straining at opposite ends of a rope, two kids (one of each) in the middle, and Grandma and Grandpa smiling down on the scene. The picture belies, though, what is further reported about 80-year-old Ann herself. Not only is she a widow, but there is no mention of children, siblings, nephews or nieces. In family terms she is alone. Presumably her situation, selected for reader appeal, accords with much of pre-needs demand, particularly on its down-market side. If Ann does not organize her own funeral ('put her house in order'), who else will?

The growing need, on a wide social scale, to arrange for one's own disposal signifies a radical step in the detachment of the individual from communal life. In a society where interpersonal association is shrinking to a network of age peers, the extended family has become a nostalgic icon. Given gender differences in mortality, particularly among the less affluent, the number of solitary older women like Anne is on the rise. The *Choice* ad completely erases this. Its reassuring portrait of the extended family as a sign of generational continuity is a mendacious alibi for the commercial service its dissolution makes necessary. Here, in other words, the promotional acknowledgement of the self's mortality is achieved at the price of denying the death of the social; at the price, that is, of denying the loss of significance which befalls individual death when it becomes a purely individual matter. A third shift in the funerals market has more generally concerned the provenance and vintage of the symbolism dispensed. From a number of directions the pressure has been for diversification, and the opening up of wider consumer choice.

One aspect of this is the growing individuation of funeral style. A chanteuse departs to the strains of her favourite tune: a hunter's ashes are shot to oblivion over his most treasured marsh. Such personal touches, associated in part with the trend to pre-arrangement, may reflect the express wishes of the (pre-)deceased (a bizarre instance of which is the videotaped final farewell).[10] At the same time, like the older practice of including memory books and personal articles in the casket display, they may also be introduced by grieving family and friends. In this and other respects the ritual wishes of survivors, too, are being more clearly asserted. Privately-organized events like receptions, parties and wakes have become customary, whether to supplement or even as substitutes for 'regular' funerals.

Pressure to expand the range of funeral and memorial symbolism has also arisen at the ethno-religious level. The roll-out-the-crucifix (or menorah) mix-and-match of the owner-operated funeral home was always able to cope at least with that measure of ceremonial flexibility demanded by the multi denominationalism of the continent's British and European settlers. Contemporary multiculturalism, though, strains beyond the limits of that model, including the design limits of the standard funeral chapel. In the case of Jewish, Chinese. and African-American funerals, community-specific demand already provided the basis for specialized businesses, and similar developments in Moslem and aboriginal communities have followed.

As with personalization, menu enrichment and targeted provision by death-care providers have been able to accommodate the shift to diversity while drawing its autonomizing sting. At the level of funeral symbolics, however, these developments have also introduced strains. The traditional, that is, sentimentally Victorian, blended-Christian iconography described by Mitford has lost its unquestioned conventional hold. Pretend-preserving the dead in a mock-Christian Heaven rendered as sweetly tranquil Nature was already dead as metaphorics by mid-century. The rise of individual and collective identity concerns has rendered it, for many, offensively dead a generation further on. Overall, the symbolic system that had loosely unified funeral homes and cemeteries as a system has both ceased to be hegemonic and (for all the ubiquity of caskets and flowers) has fractured as anything approaching a coherent totality.

A further pointer to coming symbological disorder is that the cultural marginality which burst on to the stage in the 1960s is again making its presence felt. The greying of that generation brings its lingering counterculture, variously anti-corporate, ironic, and mellowed by the nostrums and neospiritualism of the New Age, into contact with the ritual (and other) exigencies of death. A curiosity item in the August 1992 issue of *The Canadian Funeral News* indicates the potential gulf between these exigencies and what most casket, cemetery and funeral companies still sell. The article is about Ghia Gallery, 'a showroom of death' in San Francisco

> where the terminally ill can plan, and accessorise, their own funerals. Coffins and urns of every description (King Tut, Joe Cool, arts-and-craft, polka dotted, plain) are available at cut-rate prices, together with free information about burial and cremation costs at area mortuaries.

At once self-consciously anti-commercial and assimilable to petty capitalism, the boutique is a small but spectacular example of the movement towards personalized pre-arrangement. What gives the example its edge, however, is that 40 per cent of Ghia's clientele are suffering from AIDS.

288

On both the mortuary and grief-counselling side, the industry has certainly geared up to handle AIDS deaths. In so far as AIDS-related funerals are a particular preoccupation for the newly-emergent gay community, they also become subject to intra-industry market specialization. However, the great symbolic charge of the AIDS metaphor, together with the highly-politicized and activist milieu associated with the disease, evince funerary gestures, like the great AIDS Quilt, which exceed the bounds of what can be commodified, even in Ghia Gallery form. Still more significant is the symbolic status of the HIV-positive themselves. Moves to quarantine them have echoed nineteenth century moves to expel cemeteries. But though stigma and discrimination persist, exclusion, at least medical and legal, has been prevented. In the news media, if not yet for all in everyday life, persons with AIDS have become a familiar and normalized category. After more than a century of determined death denial, then, the living dead are visibly back among us, a *memento mori* that refuses to be neutralized or denied.

DEATH CARE AND CAPITAL

At the same time as the symbolic services rendered by the death-care industry have been buffeted by shifts in consumer demand, and partly for that reason, the economic structure of the industry has itself begun to change. Exacerbated by the speculative boom of the 1980s and the deep recession that followed, increased regulation, a relatively stalled death rate, the rise of pre-arrangement, and growing labour costs have intensified competition and exposed over-capacity, particularly among funeral homes. The result has been a rapid round of capital concentration.

It has taken a variety of forms. Funeral homes, like cemeteries before them, have seen the rise of acquisitively active chains. More radically, the long-standing separation of funeral homes and cemeteries has been eroded by mergers and take-overs, as well as by the building of new funeral homes on cemetery and crematorium grounds, combining the character of chains and combinations. Finally, a small number of industry-wide giants have emerged, publicly listed, with professional management teams, and with a rapidly-growing ownership stake and market share. The two biggest are Service Corporation International, formed in 1962, and the Loewen Group, established in the mid-1980s. According to stockholder reports,[11] SCI, with book assets of $2.6 billion and revenues of $770 million, owns 674 funeral homes and 167 cemeteries. The Loewen Group has 472 funeral homes, 38 cemeteries and 18 crematoria, but is expanding at a faster rate. Economies of scale and the organizational capacity to deliver a larger and more targeted range of services yield competitive advantages that can only accelerate the trend. The family-owned and operated enterprise, which is long gone from the cemetery business, as well as from all the intermediary suppliers of funeral-related goods, is ceasing to be the dominant form for funeral homes too.

At first sight, with specialization of ancillary service, regional clusters, rationalization of hours etc., it is only backstage that things have changed. A taken-over funeral home conducts exactly the same business with its clients as before. For the large chains, indeed, it is a matter of policy that all the signs of continuity be preserved. As the SCI Report puts it:

> Funeral homes and cemeteries acquired by SCI are among the finest in their cities of operation. SCI capitalises on the history and goodwill associated with these firms by retaining their original names and, when possible, retaining the services of original family members.

Takeover language is eschewed in a lexicon that stresses 'partners', 'sharing', and 'joining the team'. Nevertheless, and however managerially devolved, corporate ownership and organization changes the valency of funeral home symbolism even when this nominally stays the same.

The funeral home had always been designed to evoke the family home whose parlour its own 'viewing room' replaced. But in that replacement, the link between the two, which transferred from dwelling to business connotations of social rootedness, moral rectitude, and inter-generational continuity, was not entirely reduced to myth. It was socially sustained through actual family ownership and the 'tradition of service' for which that could immediately be made to stand. With a takeover that reduces the old family owner to the status, at most, of a franchise manager, this appearance can scarcely be saved. Those who own no longer manage; and the former, if not the latter, are no longer well-implanted pillars of the community they serve. The same goes double for the new facilities corporately built (for example, on cemeteries) to look like up-to-date but still classically stylized reminders of the old. With capital concentration, then, the funeral home itself is becoming a dead metaphor, a purely staged appearance, detached from its nominal referent to float self-interestedly in the promotional circulation of signs.

It should be emphasized that the relation, here, between capital and the demise of the family firm has not been simply that of aggressor to victim. In addition to rising costs and regulations, and the vagaries of the business cycle, independent funeral homes have come to face a real problem of succession. Personnel turnover at the base of the industry has been disturbingly high for more than a decade. Sons and daughters have been increasingly disinclined to follow their parents into the funeral home trade. This has created a niche for the growth of 'succession companies', called just that, which offer help to ailing companies, not least in arranging a dignified and orderly plan through which to wind up their temporal affairs. It is exactly in these terms that the Loewen Group presents its own acquisition strategy:

> Our purpose, as a company, is to provide a corporate vehicle which facilitates the orderly succession of funeral homes from one generation to the next, in the interests of the principals and the communities they serve. We call this quality succession planning.
>
> (Report to the Shareholders, 20 May 1993)

What the big chains offer, in effect, is pre-arranged funerals and estate planning for economically dying elders of the death care-industry itself. The continuity between the discourse that surrounds this and the selling of literal funerals is striking. In both cases death denial ('quality succession') is combined with pseudo-memorialization (the branch name stays the same). And at both levels what the similarity of euphemism highlights is not only the force of the analogy, but the almost parodic relation they both bear with what Marx considered the morbid logic of capital itself: dead labour expanding itself through surplus extracted in the business of disposing of the dead.

FUNERALS TODAY

Two summary reflections suggest themselves. The first is that the compromise between death denial and (pseudo-)memorial, which has been economically as well as symbolically essential to the North American death-care industry throughout its history, has begun to unravel. The weak point in the system was always the second term, memorialization, whose weakened force was already evident in the functionalist hype of grief therapy. The trend to arrangement has cut at the root by undercutting sales pressure for memorialization at the point of funeral purchase. While this extension of the death-care market has, at least in the theatre of consumption, brought the dying subject back on to the stage, it has strengthened the denied force of death denial by increasing the demand for simple disposal. Against a backdrop of individual and ethno-cultural customizing, the power of traditional (that is 1880–1980) funeral symbolism has been further eroded, finally, by corporate rationalization. As funeral homes become assimilated into wider enterprises, the seemingly rooted agency that mediated death care to funeral arrangers turns into a simulacrum of the copy it was. Its hollowness as such cuts commercially-administered memorial practices off from their remaining 'personal' guarantee.

Optimists might see in this approaching death of the American way of death signs of a revitalizing reversal. For example: in tendencies towards spontaneous rituals, or towards the formation of non-denying attitudes which fully accept and confront the evanescence of life. Pessimists will remind us, however, that the collapsed meaning of memorialization removes the solace of surviving in memory, and plunges the disenchanted subject deeper into the nihilist abyss.

The second point is more methodological. It is just to note that examining the symbolic place of bio-individual death in our culture is complicated by the intersection of this with a parallel set of attestations concerning the death of the social. The 'dying of death' is evidently part of the latter. At the same time, the metaphorics surrounding the death of the social (not to mention, of History, God and the Subject) have literal funerals as their immediate source. At both levels – compare Park Lawn with 'living museums' or period movies – we find a similar mechanism for coping with death and its denial: a simulated remembrance which similarly conceals a failure, indeed the failure of all current communication, to transmit instituted meanings through time. What those rooted in an older, and in fantasy redeemed, culture may find extraordinary is the apparent absence of melancholy which accompanies this state of affairs.

NOTES

1 Here and throughout this essay I have relied on data supplied in the following trade papers: *The Canadian Funeral News, The American Funeral Director, The Canadian Funeral Director* and *Morticians of the South West.* Help given by the Nesbitt Funeral Home and Chapel in Peterborough, Ontario, in obtaining these is gratefully acknowledged.
2 I owe to Marvin Chen the information that *Maturity,* distributed by the Bank of Montreal, has .just ended its editorial ban on funeral advertising. At the time of writing, though, no such promotion had appeared.
3 Farfell (1980) cites an article of that title which appeared in the September 1899 issue of *Review of Reviews.* The author's name is not given.
4 For the introduction of embalming into American funeral practice following the Civil War (where it was used as a three-day preservative for bodies sent back to parents by train) see Farfell (1980: 157–69). Corpse-viewing has an older history in some chiefly Catholic parts of Europe, from which it spread into the New World. However, Farfell does not trace this influence.
5 Dedicated to 'a father who trod a rough path that his son's might be smoother', the preface of this exposé roundly declares that 'the funeral director's freedom to charge outrageous prices and implement dubious sales gimmicks must be curbed'.
6 Death, for Ariès (1981: 297–30), became 'untamed' in Enlightenment Europe, as the terrorizing flipside of this-worldly optimism. 'Tame death', culturally dominant in Europe for more than a millennium, had incorporated dying, with clearly marked public stages, into the familiar fabric of the everyday.

7 Figures taken from *The American Funeral Director,* October 1992: 72–82 and November 1992: 44.

8 Figures taken from *The American Funeral Director,* May 1992: 38–44.

9 *Choice* has a sister publication, *Yours,* a tabloid geared for the older and poorer. Just as *Choice* is associated with the Pre-Retirement Association (whose organ it initially was), it so happens that *Yours* involves collaboration with Help the Aged. Needless to say, *Yours* is equally full of ads for Dignity in Destiny. Both magazines are published by the European publishing combine, EMAP.

10 This was long anticipated. Among the ten uses Edison listed for his phonograph in 1890 was 'The "Family Record", a registry of sayings, reminiscences, etc., by members of a family, in their own voices: and of the last words of the dying'. The full list is cited in Attali (1985: 93).

11 Service Corporation International 1992 Annual Report, and Loewen Group Inc. Common Threads 1992 Annual Report. I thank Tony Hyde for providing me with these.

REFERENCES

Ariès, Philippe (1981) *The Hour of Our Death,* New York: Alfred A Knopf.

Attali, Jacques (1985) *Noise: The Political Economy of Music,* Minneapolis: University of Minnesota Press.

'Coriolis' (1967) *Death, Here Is Thy Sting,* Toronto/Montreal: McClelland & Stewart.

Farfell, James (1980) *Inventing the American Way of Death, 1830–1920,* Philadelphia: Temple University Press.

Harmer, Ruth Mulvey (1963) *The High Cost of Dying,* London: Collier Macmillan.

Mitford, Jessica (1963) *The American Way of Death,* New York: Simon and Schuster.

INDEX

Abegglen, J. C. 52
Abelin, E. A. 85
Achenbaum, A. 5
adolescence 122–3; *see also* youth
Adorno, Theodor 253
adulthood 128–30, 138
advertising: Australian HIV/AIDS
  263–7, 269–76; capitalist realism
  10, 216, 222; images 19;
  representation 26, 180–2, 183,
  216; scenes 216–17; soft-sell 181
affect 79–82
ageism 4–9, 30, 88
aging: cultural factors 24–5, 48–51,
  121, 141, 210; death 10–13, 267,
  270, 280; dependency 7, 56,
  135–8, 144–5, 248; gender factors
  8, 23, 98; historical views 63,
  69–70, 126; images 20, 29–32,
  49–51; life stages 23, 26–7,
  121–30, 132, 174; physical
  symptoms 12, 31, 56, 66–7, 120,
  181–2, 228, 255–6, 258;
  psychological factors 119, 146–7,
  196–7, 211, 218, 253, 255–8; and
  representation 20, 125, 180–2,
  209, 227, 264; sexuality 145–6,
  264, 274; social status 1–2, 24,
  30–1, 100–2, 121, 139, 173, 211,
  222, 231, 254, 263; *see also* mask of
  aging; positive aging
AIDS 13, 104, 267, 268–9, 289
anthropology, philosophical 246,
  247–8
Arber, S. 264, 277
Ariès, Philippe 3, 122, 131, 138,
  280–1, 282, 283
Asian-Americans 189, 191, 197–203

Australia, HIV/AIDS TV
  commercials 263–7, 269–76
autobiography 104

Bacon, Francis 63–5, 71 (n5)
Bailey, Thomas 66–7
Bauman, Z. 62
Beard, George 120
Beck, Ulrich 255
Benjamin, Jessica 81, 82, 92 (n2)
Benjamin, Walter 242, 282
Bennett, J. W. 51
Berger, Peter L. 246, 248
Bettelheim, B. 268
Between the Acts (Porter and Weeks)
  104, 105
Biggs, Simon 109–10
bio-power 179
Birren, J. E. 20
body: childish 142–6;
  detraditionalization 255–7;
  identity 141, 255–7; metonymic
  relationships 143–4; philosophical
  anthropology 246, 247–8; physical
  breakdown 106–7; postmodern
  10–13, 255–7; as prison 237–8;
  reflexivity 256–7; sexuality 256–7;
  as signifier 140–2; and sociology
  245–7; symbolic capital 230–1; as
  walking memory 250
Bogner, Artur 251
Bowlby, John 81
Bradotti, Rosi 94 (n16)
bulletin board system 231, 232–3

Canada, elderly 177, 179, 184
Carlisle, Sir Anthony 66, 71 (n7)
Cartesian dualism 256

ceremonialization 215, 217
Chan, Charlie 11, 188–92, 194–7, 203
Chan is Missing 197–203
Charlie Chan at the Opera 194–7
childhood: cultural differences 143;
    ideology and physical body 142–6;
    images 139–40; labour and
    education laws 132, 138; and old
    age 135–6; socially constructed
    122, 138–9; victimization 139–40
children's drawings 158–68; analysis
    155–67; psychological influence
    149–54; research 154–7;
    sociological perspective 153–4
Chodorow, Nancy 89–90
Choice 31, 33–4, 40–3, 45
Chopra, D. 61
civilizing process 246–7, 248, 251
Cixous, Hélène 81
clothing, age-related 34, 37
Cole, Thomas 26–7
Cole, Thomas R. 30–1, 46, 72 (n13)
collective memory 11–13, 19, 211,
    214–15, 251–5
collectivity 251, 254, 267
comedy, ethnic-based 192
communalism 218, 221
communications: bulletin board
    systems 231, 232–3; electronic
    230–1; e-mail 231; sexual
    encounters 231–2, 238–9;
    telephone 231
condoms 266–7, 278
Confucian philosophy 50, 53, 144–5
conscience collective 251, 254
consumer advocacy 184
consumer markets 173
consumerism 7, 9–10, 102, 110, 174,
    184, 227, 281
Copper, Baba 89
Cornaro, Luigi 63–4, 71 (n3)
cremation 284–5
cross-dressing 233, 239
cultural differences: aging 24–5,
    48–51, 121, 141, 210; childhood
    143; children's drawings of
    grandparents 153, 159–65;
    dependency 56, 137–8, 144–5;
    funerals 288; gerontology 30;
    representation 210, 227;
    stereotyping 188–94, 197
cyberspace 239–40
cyborgs 240–2

Davies, D. 69
death 10–13, 267, 270, 280
death denial 12–13, 280–3
death-care industry 280, 283–91
de Beauvoir, Simone 2, 87–8, 91, 250
demographic changes 97–8, 122,
    177, 179
dependency: cultural differences 56,
    137–8, 144–5; infantilization
    136–7, 144, 145; old age and
    childhood 135; and resistance
    146; second childhood 7, 111,
    135, 137–9, 146–7; socialization
    248
Descartes, René 256
detraditionalization, of body 255–7
difference, and identity 85–6
Dilthey, Wilhelm 246
disability 214, 237–8
disembodiment 229–33
disempowerment 5, 269
disengagement 100, 112, 246
diversity, in elderly 21, 22–5, 85–6
Dore, R. 51
down-aging 72 (n14), 180
drawings, children's: *see* children's
    drawings
Dreuilhe, Emmanuel 267, 268, 273
Durkheim, Émile 246, 251
dying person, social discourse 285–7

elderly people: consumer advocacy
    184; diversity 21, 22–5, 85–6;
    frailty 7, 141; income/opportunity
    44; as marketing opportunity
    9–10, 32–3, 209; metaphorically
    transformed 137, 141–2; negative
    image 227; old–old 22, 44, 146;
    physical needs/personalities 144;
    sexuality 145–6; in social order
    123–4; suicide 50; television
    viewing 25–6; virtual reality 229,
    240–2; young–old 31, 44, 110
Elderly People in Modern Society
    (Tinker) 30
electronic mail 231
Elias, Norbert 246–7, 249–50, 253
embodiment 249, 251
Emerson, R. E. 19
emotions and psychoanalysis 80,
    81–2, 92
empowerment 271, 277
engagement 246

Enlightenment 6, 62–3
Ennew, J. 139
epistemophilia 93 (n7)
Erikson, Erik 121
ethnicity 192, 197
experience, and memory 240–2

family: age configuration 119, 127–8,
  131; changes 130–1; in children's
  drawings 153–4; and economic life
  126–7, 129; and households 129;
  Japanese 53–6; nuclear 82–3, 89
fantasy, out-of-body 228, 243 (n1)
fatherhood 103
Featherstone, M. 264
feminism, ageist 88
films, images of aging: *Chan is
  Missing* 197–203; Charlie Chan
  188–92, 194–7, 203; older men
  110; *On Golden Pond* 110; spectacle
  of discovery 192–3
Firestone, S. 139
Foucault, Michel 173, 179–80
frailty 7, 141
Freud: affect 80; aging women 86–7;
  'Disturbance of memory' 80–1;
  'Femininity' 83–4; gender 83
Fu Manchu 191
funerals 281–2; individuated 287;
  multiculturism 288; pre-need sales
  285–7; present-day 291–2;
  showroom of death 288

Garvey, A. 146
gaze: benevolent 271, 272; and social
  order 188; voyeur 188; and
  wisdom 196–7
Gehlen, Arnold 246, 247–8
gender: aging 8, 22–3, 98; Freud 83;
  identity 90; imaging 99; and
  sexuality 87
generations: continuity 82–5, 90,
  274; and identity 86; otherness 94
  (n16); power 88–9, 102; studies
  245
gerontocracy 144–5
gerontology 67, 125; cultural values
  30; positive outlook 70; social 31;
  studies 1–2, 20, 61–2
gerontophobia 263
Gibson, William 240
Giddens, Anthony 211, 255, 268, 272
Ginn, J. 264, 277

Goethe, J. W. von 250
Goffman, Erving 131, 211, 216
government health advertisements,
  HIV/AIDS 263–7, 269–76
grandfatherhood 102, 112, 159–65
grandmothers 88–9, 158–65
grandparents in children's drawings
  158–68; activities 166; as
  caregivers 168; cultural
  specificities 159–65; gender
  differentiation 159, 162, 168;
  typology 167–8
Green, André 80
grief therapy 282, 283
'Grim Reaper' ad 265, 269–78
Grossberg, L. 82, 92 (n4)

Halbachs, Maurice 254
Hall, G. Stanley 119–20, 122
Haraway, Donna 182, 241–2
Harvey, William 65
health care, and market 183–4
Heidegger, Martin 1, 242
Hendricks, C. D. 272
Hendricks, J. 272
Hepworth, M. 264
heritage industry 221
hierarchy 51–2, 53–6, 139
Hirsch, Marianne 88
HIV/AIDS commercials 263–7,
  269–76
holiday brochures 209–10, 216–20
holidays for elderly 10, 209–10, 211;
  age-peer grouping 213–14;
  communalism 218, 221;
  destinations 214; disabled visitors
  214; as marketing 220–1;
  ritualization 217, 219–20; single
  visitors 214–15
Holt, J. 139, 142
homosexuality 104–5
hooks, bell 91–2

identity: bodily condition 141;
  collective 209–10; as consumer
  173; and difference 85–6; ethnic
  192; gender 90; generations 86;
  politicized 199–200; and
  ritualization 219–20; sexuality 87;
  spoiled 131
image 3–4; advertising 19; aging 20,
  29–32, 49–51; childhood 139–40;
  gender 99; negative 6, 182, 189,

191, 197, 209; postmodern 10–13; and representation 19
Images of Old Age in America (Achenbaum and Kusnerz) 5, 20–7
individualism 138, 218
industrialization 7, 100, 138
infantilization 136–7, 144, 145
information modes 229–33
Irigaray, Luce 84, 93 (n8)
Ishino, I. 51
Itzin, C. 98

Jackson, David 105–7
Japan: aging 7–8, 48–51; benevolence (*on*) 56–7, 58 (n3); family ideology (*kô*) 53–6; hierarchy 51–2, 53–6; Meiji government 53, 54; modernization 48; *obasute* 50; *okina* 56–7; paternalism 48–9, 51–3; patriarchy 53–4, 55
Jardine, Alice 88–9
Jenkins, Henry 67, 68
Johns, Jasper 27
Jones, S. 52

Kant, Immanuel 250–1
kô ideology 53–6
Krampen, Martin 153
Kristeva, Julia 83
Kusnerz, Peg 25

labour force 100, 138
Lanier, Jaron 227, 239, 241
leisure 212–13, 218–19
Leonardo da Vinci 86–7, 94 (n13), 252
life expectancy 25, 174
life stages 23, 26–7; consumerism 174; discovery of 121–5; discontinuities 125–30; segregation 132
life-prolonging medicines 64–5
life-span 61, 64–5, 69, 71 (n7)
longevity 6–7, 61, 62–9, 228
Lorand, Arnold 67
Luckmann, Thomas 246
Lukacs, G. 267–8
Luquet, Georges-Henri 150–1

MacDonald, Barbara 89
MacDonald, S. 139
McLuhan, Marshall 227

magazines for elderly 31, 33–45, 111, 281
market segmentation 176
marketing: age sectors 9–10; health care 183–4; holidays 220–1; social conventions 265; stereotyping 177–8, 185; targets 175–6, 179; by telephone 182
marketing research 173–6, 177–80
marriage 129
Masciarotte, G.-J. 93 (n7)
mask of aging 7, 227, 228
mature market: *see* seniors market
maturity 56–7, 119–20, 173
media, imaging older men 107–11
Memorial Societies 284
memory: body as 250; collective 11–13, 19, 211, 214–15, 251–5; and experience 240–2; as social reconstructions 254; through photography 252
men: aging 8–9, 22, 23–4, 97, 99–100, 109; autobiography 104; consumerism 102; experience 103–9; fatherhood 103; grandfatherhood 102, 112, 159–65; media imaging 107–11; physical breakdown 106–7; power 100–7; retirement 100–1, 102; sexuality 104; social construction 22, 23–4, 99, 103
metaphors, root 138–9
Metchnikoff, Elie 67
metonymic relationships 143–4
middle age 102, 109–10, 123, 199
Mitford, Jessica 283
modernization 48, 53, 229; reflexive 255–7, 258
Moi, Toril 93 (n7)
mood 82
motherhood 83–4, 89, 91
Moto, Mr 188, 190, 191, 192

Nascher, I. L. 120
Neuromancer (Gibson) 240, 241
Nietzsche, F. 247, 249
nostalgia 92, 221, 249, 250–4, 258
Nuttall, R. 153–4

obasute (abandoning granny) 50
050 32
okina (old man) 56–7
old age: *see* aging

Oldie, The 111
On Golden Pond (Rydell) 110
on (benefit) 56–7, 58 (n3)
Orientalism, and the imaginary
    other 189–90
Ostroff, Jeff 72 (n14), 173, 177–8,
    180
Other 189–90, 193
out-of-body experiences 228, 239–40

parody 201–2
Parr, Thomas 65, 66, 67, 68
paternalism 48–9, 51–3, 54
patriarchy, Asian 53–4, 55, 188,
    189–90, 195
pensions 44, 97, 100–1
personality, self-monitoring 255–6
Phillipson, C. 98
philosophical anthropology 246,
    247–8
photography 24, 252, 254, 282
physical breakdown 106–7
physiognomy 230
Pitskhelauri, G. Z. 69
Plessner, Helmuth 246
Porter, Kevin 104–5
positive aging 29–33; consumer
    choice 10, 40, 281; cultural
    representations 227; death denial
    13; groups 6; as myth 72 (n13)
post-literacy 239
postmodernism: body 10–13, 255–7;
    post-literacy 239; survival 62;
    timelessness 69–70
poverty 101, 181
Pre-Retirement Association 38
Pre-Retirement Choice 37–8
product differentiation 176
psychoanalysis: affect 79–82;
    emotions 80, 81–2, 92; mood 82

Quetelet, Adolphe 68–9, 72 (n11)

racism 197
realism, capitalist 10, 216, 222
reflexive modernization 255–7, 258
regeneration 146–7
rejuvenation 228
Rembrandt 252
representation of aging 20, 180–2,
    209, 227; advertising 26, 180–2,
    183, 216; cultural factors 210, 227;
    empowerment 271, 277; images

19; literary/artistic 2–3
retirement 33, 34, 37, 40, 100–1,
    124
Retirement Choice 33–43, 44
Rheingold, Howard 227
Roberts, D. 54
Rohdie, Sam 270

Said, Edward 190
Sankar, A. 145
Scheler, Max 246
second childhood 7, 111, 135, 137–9,
    146–7
self, somatized 255–7
senescence 7, 119, 120
seniors market 177–80; limitations
    182–5; magazines 33–45, 111, 281;
    paradoxes 180–2
sexual encounters, communication
    systems 231–2, 238–9
sexuality: aging 145–6, 264, 274;
    body 256–7; and ethnicity 192;
    femininity 91; gender 87; identity
    87; older men 104
siblings 92–3 (n7), 128
Silverman, Kaja 86, 93–4 (n12)
Sinclair, Sir John 66
slavery 24
Smith, Dr John 65
social action 246
social age 121–2, 253–4
social constructionism 22–4, 30–1,
    99, 103, 122, 138–9, 248
social security 124
sociology: of aging 245; and body
    245–7; children's drawings 153–4;
    hermeneutic 246, 251; medical
    247; phenomenological 247
Solzhenitsyn, A. I. 268
Sontag, Susan 252, 272
Stalk, G. 52
stereotyping: aging 125, 264; cultural
    188–94, 197; ethnic 192, 197; in
    marketing 177–8, 185; media
    109–10; negative 132; and parody
    202; second childhood 137–8
stigmatizing 2, 7–8, 231
suicide, amongst elderly 50
survival 268

target markets 175–6, 179
tele-conferencing 231
telephone 182, 231

Tholome, E. 151
Thoms, William J. 67–8
time: ceremonialized 215; social and collective 253; structures of 212–13; tensed theory 249–50
timelessness 69–70
Tinker, A. 30
tomb, fetishized 282
tourism 213
Tulloch, J. 267
Turner, B. S. 245, 247
Turner, V. 138–9

Uhlenberg, Peter 127–8
Unmasking Masculinity (Jackson) 105–7
USA: aging 120–1, 124–5, 126; Asian-Americans 189, 191, 197–203; childhood 122; elderly 50

virtual reality 11–12, 229, 233–40, 243 (n3)
Vos, G. A. de 51–2
'Vox Pop Condom' ad 265, 269–78

voyeurism 188, 191, 196–7, 227

Waddell, F. 177
Walking After Midnight 105
Watney, Simon 269
Weber, Max 246
Weeks, Jeffrey 104–5
Wellness Group 184
Wernick, Andrew 264, 277
women: aging 8, 9, 22, 23–4, 86–7; as carers 138; grandmotherhood 88–9, 158–65; motherhood 83–4, 89, 91; older 86, 90–2, 264, 272; retirement 101
Wong, Mr 188, 190, 191, 192
Woodward, Kathleen 263, 264, 270–1
work and status 212

Yamaori, T. 57
youth: and age 264–5; cult 7, 209; and middle age 199; *see also* adolescence

Zealy, J. T. 24